Stana Neradić

# OBSERVATIONS

# IN HUSBANDRY

EDWARD LISLE ESQ.

# OBSERVATIONS
## IN
# HUSBANDRY.

## By EDWARD LISLE, Esq;

### LATE OF

### CRUX-EASTON, in HAMPSHIRE.

*Satis mirari non possim, quod animi sibi quisque formatorem præcepto-remque virtutis è cœtu sapientium arcessat; sola res rustica, quæ sine dubitatione proxima & quasi consanguinea sapientiæ est, tam discentibus egeat quam magistris. Adhuc enim scholas rhetorum, & geometrarum, musicorumque, vel, quod magis mirandum est, contemptissimorum vitio-rum officinas, gulosius condiendi cibos, & luxuriosius fercula struendi, capitumque & capillorum concinnatores non solum esse audivi, sed & ipse vidi: agricolationis neque doctores qui se profiterentur, neque discipulos cognovi. Cum etiam, si prædictarum artium civitas egeret, tamen, sicut apud priscos, florere posset respublica; nam sine ludicris artibus, atque etiam sine causidicis olim satis felices fuere futuræque sunt urbes; at sine agricultoribus nec consistere mortales, nec ali posse manifestum est.*

COLUMELLA, lib. I.

## THE SECOND EDITION,

## IN TWO VOLUMES,

## VOL. I.

### LONDON:

Printed by J. HUGHS, near Lincoln's-Inn-Fields:

For C. HITCH and L. HAWES, J. RIVINGTON and J. FLETCHER, in Pater-noster-row; W. SANDBY, in Fleet-street; J. RIVINGTON, in St. Paul's Church-yard; and R. and J. DODSLEY, in Pall-Mall.

M DCC LVII.

1757

Complete set - ISBN 0 576 53185 5
This volume - ISBN 0 576 53210 X

Republished in 1970 by Gregg International Publishers Limited
Westmead, Farnborough, Hants., England.

Printed in Offset by Kingprint Limited
Teddington, Middx., England.

# ADVERTISEMENT.

AS I think myſelf obliged to make ſome apology for the uncommon form in which the following obſervations are offered to the public, I ' beg leave to detain the reader a few moments, in giving him a ſhort account of my father's deſign in making and collecting them, with the method he purſued in it, and the reaſons that induced me to print them in the manner they now appear.

To enter into a detail of the author's life and character would, in my opinion, be no ways neceſſary to this work, nor could I perhaps ſay many things I know of him, without drawing ſome imputation of vanity on myſelf. It may be ſufficient therefore to take notice, that he ſettled at Crux-Eaſton in Hampſhire, as far as I can collect, about the 27th year of his age, and in 1693, or 4, where he immediately de-

termined

termined to make the study of agriculture one of the chief amusements of his life.

In pursuance of this resolution, not only at the place, and in the neighbourhood where he lived, but in his journies, either to Dorsetshire, where he had concerns, or to Leicestershire, in visits to his father-in-law, Sir Ambrose Phillipps of Garenton, or to his own estates in Wiltshire and the Isle of Wight, and to other parts of the kingdom, he made it his business to search out the most reputable farmers, and get the best informations he could, in all the branches of husbandry that were known and practised in those countries. His constant method was to note down the opinions and advices he thought might be useful to him, and afterwards to add occasional remarks on them from his own experience. For many years, I believe, he had no other drift, in employing himself after this manner, than merely his own information and improvement; but about the year 1713, he seems to have entered into a design of making his observations public; for I find he had begun an index, and had thrown

thrown together some thoughts, as an essay towards an introduction, dated at that
period. Though his other studies however,
which were chiefly in divinity, in which
he hath left a very long and laborious
work ; his frequent attendance on the
business of his neighbours in the capacity
of justice of the peace, and the care of a
numerous family (for he had no less than
twenty children, of whom seventeen sur-
vived him) hindered him from pursuing
this his intention, yet they did not interrupt his first design, but he continued
writing down his inquiries and experiments
to the time of his death, which happened
in the year 1722.

As these observations therefore were left
in such disorder, as to require no small
pains and application to regulate and digest
them, and as all his sons, except the eldest,
were bred to professions, and those very
foreign to that of agriculture, and had neither leisure nor inclination for an undertaking of this nature, they would, in all
probability, have been entirely suppressed,
had not I accidentally communicated them

to

to some farmers of my acquaintance, as likewise to some gentlemen, who amuse themselves in husbandry, who were all of opinion they might be of use to the profession, and encouraged me to collect them under their several heads, and put them into the order in which they are here published.

Some of his readers will smile, no doubt, to see the names of many of our English farmers mingled together with those of the ancient Romans, Varro, Cato, Pliny, Columella, and Palladius, and with those also of our own writers, Lord Verulam, Evelyn, Ray, Grew, Boyle, and Mortimer ; but, had I thrown them out, I must have given an entire new form to the whole, and when I had done all this, the reader, in my judgment, would have owed me no thanks for my pains : it would have robbed the work of an agreeable simplicity, and made it appear less genuine. I was inclined therefore to print it as I found it, and was pleased to find this inclination seconded by the advice of many of my friends.

For

For the ftile, I think, I need make no apology; for what correctnefs can be expected
in obfervations haftily penned down, and
thofe oftentimes from the mouths of common farmers ? In a book intended for the
inftruction of hufbandmen ornaments would
be mifplaced : it is fufficient if the lan-
guage be intelligible; nor is it at all my
wifh, that the author fhould be efteemed
a fine writer, but a ufeful obferver.

The reader muft not expect a compleat
body of hufbandry in thefe papers. Some
things are but flightly touched on, as hops
and rye, and fome others not mentioned at
all, as hemp, flax, &c. and many ufeful
obfervations might perhaps be added, even
in thofe matters that are treated on at
large, and in which the author was moft
converfant; for fuch is the extent and variety of the fubject, that, according to his
remark in the introduction, it is never to
be exhaufted. Every day produces new
inventions and improvements in agriculture, but perfection is unattainable; and,
I believe, there is no farmer, of whatfoever induftry, age, judgment, and expe-

A 4                          rience,

rience, that is not often deceived, and that will not acknowledge himself deficient in many particulars relating to his profession.

Nor is the knowledge of husbandry to be acquired by reading without practice. Books may give valuable hints to those who have judgment to make use of them, but, to learn the first rudiments of this art, it is necessary to serve an apprenticeship to it as to other trades. Many, and indeed the chief part, of these observations therefore are not calculated for the instruction of mere novices, but to assist those, who are already practitioners; to shew them the opinions of others in doubtful and disputed cases, the rules laid down by the ancient and modern writers, and the usages of distant counties in this kingdom; to encourage them in making trials; to caution them against many errors; and oftentimes save them much labour and expence, by communicating experiments already made to their hands.

As Mr. Lisle however began his collection at a time when he was but young in the

the bufinefs, and that purely for his own information, there are fome rules in it, without doubt, that experienced farmers will have no need of, and fome perhaps that may be thought of too little import- ance to enter into a work of this kind ; but however common and unneceffary they appear to fome, they may be new and ufe- ful to others. Whatever imperfections there are of this nature, I muft fubmit to take them on myfelf, and freely acknowledge, I know not how to feparate the chaff from the corn. I intreat the reader's favour therefore, that, whatever fuch faults he finds, he would impute them to my igno- rance in this art or fcience, and not to the author, who died without revifing, or put- ting his obfervations into any form, and who probably would have made them bet- ter worth the public view, had it pleafed God to have continued the bleffing of his life to his family.--Such as they are, they are all copied from his manufcript, not fcraped to- gether from other books for the fake of gain, and would never have feen the light, had I not thought they would be of bene- fit to my countrymen ; and, that I may

be

## x ADVERTISEMENT.

be the more readily believed, I aſſure them, except a few copies to preſent to my friends, I reap no kind of profit from the publication.

Burclere, Hants ;
  Sept. 1, 1756.

### THOMAS LISLE.

THE

# THE
# AUTHOR's
# INTRODUCTION.

## M DCC XIII.

IT may be looked on, in my opinion, as one of the chief misfortunes of this age, that we have not such honourable conceptions of a country life, as might engage our gentlemen of the greatest abilities in parts and learning, to live upon and direct the management of their estates. It is what I have in my most serious reflections often lamented, not only as a considerable disadvantage to themselves, but a great loss to the public. Among the Greeks the knowledge and estimation of agriculture was at the greatest height in their best times; among the Romans their senators ploughed; and the great examples they gave of virtue and industry laid the foundation of all their after-greatness; but as agriculture decreased in their esteem, luxury took place, and soon put a period to their power.—I would recommend it to our English gentlemen to consider how much this may be our case at present; to look round them, and see how many fine estates are daily mortgaged or sold, and how many ancient and noble families destroyed by this pernicious and almost epidemic turn to idleness and extravagance. The yeomanry of England, who in former times were the

flower

flower of our militia, and the boaft of our nation, have always continued to be of great confequence and ufe to us, and a very neceffary link in the chain of government, as having an immediate connection with the gentleman on the one fide, and the labourer on the other. Being diftributed among the feveral parifhes, and fitted for various offices, under the ecclefiaftical and civil jurifdiction, as of churchwardens, overfeers, headboroughs, and the like, which will not hereafter be fo worthily filled, they carried a refpect with them, and were of efpecial fervice in keeping the meaner people to their duty ; add too, that, being men of fubftance, they were of wonderful advantage to the neighbourhood they dwelt in, by employing the poor, by affording them comfort and affiftance in their ficknefs or misfortunes, in advifing them in their family concerns, and in compofing differences among them ; and alfo to the commonwealth in general, in keeping up a fpirit of liberty in the country withour licentioufnefs, in withftanding corruption and oppreffion, in maintaining the laws, and in afferting the privileges of a free people. Thefe too however have caught the infection, and will be mimicking the manners of their betters : it is a melancholy truth, but I fpeak it knowingly ; I fee old reputable families in my neighbourhood every day falling away to nothing, and may take upon me to prophefy, pafs but a few years, this race of veterans will be loft in the kingdom. Nor can the gentry, with like management, be long able to furvive them ; they muft one way or other return to their original, the plough ; if they will not do it by choice, and for their own advantage, they will hereafter be neceffitated

fitated to do it for the advantage of others; for we seem to be forming ourselves apace after the French model, here and there a great man, the reft all vaffals and flaves. As this threatens to be the cafe, I fhould think it no fmall happinefs, and myfelf no inconfiderable patriot, if I could contribute any thing towards raifing the reputation of hufbandry among the gentlemen of this kingdom. It is an undertaking, I acknowledge, that affords but little profpect of fuccefs; for fo far are we now from efteeming it either honourable or gainful, that we will not fuffer it to be ranked among the liberal arts, and that we look on it as the high road for a gentleman to be undone; nay, it is become fo decried, and out of fafhion, that the writing on the fubject feems to render me accountable for an apology. I am fatisfied notwithftanding, if gentlemen would ufe fuch proper methods to attain a fkill in this, as they muft do to be mafters of any other art or fcience, they would foon find an entertainment in it not unworthy the moft exalted genius. It was the method of life that our Creator firft defigned us, and that to a farther end than our temporal good alone. Other worldly bufinefs carries our minds off from God, whereas in this we draw nearer to him, not only as the country life gives the greater opportunity vacare Deo, but as the bufinefs of hufbandry is of that nature, as muft often raife in us good reflections, and turn our thoughts towards him. Every feafon, and every change of weather in the feafon, awakens in us the confideration of his providence, and a more than common fenfe of our dependence on his bleffing, from the perpetual occafions we have of obferving and reflecting how he gives us our daily bread.

A man

A man cannot be bufied in the offices of hufbandry (they confift of fo great variety) but many things will come under his obfervation, from which divine, moral, and philofophical conclufions are fo natural and obvious, that, if he will avoid making them, he muft fhut his eyes againft the light of the fun. It is a great miftake therefore in thofe gentlemen, who confider hufbandry as too narrow and mean a bufinefs for a perfon of parts and education to employ himfelf in. Can they propofe a nobler entertainment for the mind of man than he would find in the inquiries he muft make into all the powers and operations of nature wherein hufbandry is concerned? The fubject is fo vaft it can never be exhaufted; could he live, and fpend ages in agriculture, he might ftill go on in his fearches, and ftill make frefh difcoveries, that would excite afrefh his admiration of the riches of God's wifdom. Add too, that fcene of nature, which the country lays before us, has I know not what charms to calm a man's paffions, and fo to compofe his mind, and fix his thoughts, that his foul feems to be got clear of the world; and the farther his education enables him to carry his inquiries, the higher are his reflections raifed. In the fields methinks God is walking, and, it is to be hoped, when he finds man fo virtuoufly employed, in the way of his own defignation and appointment, he may be pleafed fo to vifit him with his grace, as to give more light and warmth to the good thoughts at that time in his mind, and to fix a deep impreffion of them on his heart.

If we confider hufbandry in regard to our temporal good, provided it be carried on with induftry and judgment, it is a fure way to improve our fortunes,

and

and indeed the only way the landed gentleman can take ; it were to be wifhed therefore they would exhort their children early, particularly their eldeft fons, to think of it with emulation, and to enter into it as a fchool of profit and education ; whereas it is rather looked on as a purgatory for the difobedient, a fcene of punifhment, to which a fon, who anfwers not his father's expectation, is to be abandoned ; or a condition of life of which none would make choice, but fuch whom fortune has not in other refpects favoured. If the country-gentlemen therefore frequently confift of perfons, who are either rufticated by their parents in anger, or who, making a virtue of neceffity, fettle on their eftates with averfion or indifference, it is no wonder the comedians exhibit them on our ftage in fo defpicable and ridiculous a figure ; but this is the fault of the perfons, and not of the art. Were they properly initiated in the ftudy of agriculture, and purfued it as they ought, it would be fo far from excluding them from ufeful knowledge, and bringing them into contempt, that I may venture to affert, they would find it the beft fchool of education, and the fitteft to prepare them for the fervice of their country in the two houfes of parliament of Great Britain.

It is not only an employment, whereby the health and conftitution is eftablifhed, which is very neceffary for the attendance on, and the difcharge of that great duty, but the bufinefs of hufbandry, if they will not mifpend their precious opportunities, brings them acquainted with the condition and myftery of all forts of inland trades, inafmuch as, for the moft part, they depend on, and have rela-

tion

tion to the plough, or produce of the land, and their interests are mutually interwoven with the husbandman's; nor can a discouragement fall on husbandry, either by bad seasons, or an ill timed act of parliament, but the meanest artisan, the merchant, and even the sovereign on the throne must feel it. Thus we see it is a vast field of science the husbandman is exercised in, and undoubtedly it must be a very great advantage to him, and give him weight in either of those assemblies, by furnishing him with solid arguments, and enabling him to deliver his opinion clearly and confidently on what he thoroughly understands and knows. It is a general observation, that they speak best, and are best heard, who are more of an active than bookish life; the infirmities of the latter leading them oftener to adorn themselves than the subject, and to take a compass, to shew rather what they have read than what is only pertinent to the debate : men of business are concise in words, and choice in matter; men of small experience and great reading voluminious in both kinds.

Again, it is surely no small recommendation to husbandry, that it is productive of long life and health. The nerves and all the solids of the farmers and labourers bodies are much stronger than those of gentlemen, who live an idle and unactive life, their fluids much purer and unmixed ; their bones consolidate easily ; their strained ligatures return soon, and with small help to their tones ; their blood circulates better, and opens the channels of the vessels in bruised places of its own accord, sooner than in a gentleman by the assistance of oils and plaisters; and ordinary medicines work more successfully on

their

their difeafes than the moft fovereign fpecifics on perfons of higher quality. As they are lefs paffive therefore in their conftitutions, they often arrive at their fulnefs of years, which citizens, and gentlemen who are not exercifed in country employments, feldom reach.

From what has been here obferved of the ftrength and athletic condition of the countryman's body, it is eafy to conceive how a greater fhare of health fhould be his portion ; and here I take upon me to affirm, that I have made myfelf acquainted with the difeafes of the farmers and labourers in my neighbourhood, and have hardly found one who is fubject to either gout, ftone, or cholic, or indeed to any chronical diftemper ; nor do they lie under that common infirmity of the gentry, arifing from ill habits of body and mind, called vapours, which is fuch a drawback from life, as to ballance it's value, and render it little preferable to death: Their fenfes alfo feldom fail ; but they enjoy a comfortable ufe of them throughout their old age. Their appetites to their food are much keener, and they receive much more nourifhment from it than the idle part of mankind would do from the fame in quality and quantity, or indeed from the richeft foops and fauces ; for their bowels are faithful ftewards of what they are entrufted with ; they ftrain it to the laft drop, and fling away nothing to wafte. I have obferved in their death-bed ficknefs they have kept a found memory and underftanding, within a few minutes of their laft extremity ; for their nerves, having not been vitiated in their tones by debauches, are ftrong; and the juices of their bodies not being depraved by vifcid, grumous, and inflamed materials,

rials, the difeafed matter is not fo fiery as to affect
them with fuch fad delirious fymptoms as the
fevers of the gentry are commonly attended with.

The hufbandman's death's blow is generally from
a great cold, to catch which he probably took a
method fufficient to have killed the ftrongeft animal.
For the moft part I have found it proceeded from
imprudence, in ftanding ftill without his cloaths, or
drinking a great quantity of fmall beer, when in a
violent fweat, by which the cold has ftruck fo deep
as to coagulate the blood and juices, and deaden the
tones of all the folids; fo that the difficulty has been
to fet the wheels again in motion, and to open ob-
ftructions by giving a fpring and hurry to the blood.
But even in this his laft and dying ftate, as I faid,
his complaints are few, in comparifon to what I have
feen thofe of higher condition labour under; and
his brain is not difturbed like theirs in the common
malignant cafes; and this is no fmall advantage and
comfort to our hufbandman, who is hereby enabled
to fettle thofe worldly affairs he had before neglected, to recommend himfelf to the divine mercy, and,
like a patriarch, to beftow his dying bleffing on his
children. Before I leave this article, concerniug
health, let me in particular recommend the confideration of it to men of letters. I make no great
queftion, if they would plough one day, that is,
bufy themfelves as hufbandmen ufually do, and
ftudy the other, they would improve the ftate of
learning far beyond what they now do or can. My
meaning is, they would probably live longer, enjoy
much greater health, and more active fpirits; whereas the ftudious inquirers after knowledge, for the
moft part, bring early decay on themfelves, for want
of

of free ufe of air and exercife, and relaxations of the mind; and, tho' moderate in other refpects, yet through the common irregularities incident to bookifh people, by the time they arrive to a little more than the middle age of man, they are under complicated diftempers, of an irreparable and broken conftitution, and the remaining part of their lives is fpent in nurfing their infirmities, and pur-fuing knowledge in a fickly and ungrateful manner.

But, among all the advantages arifing to a gentleman from the employments of a country life, the principal is that of doing good, of which no one, in a private ftation, has greater opportunities. If he applies himfelf to the variety of country bufinefs as he ought, he will not only give bread to a great number of indigent and induftrious people, but his actions alfo are on the ftage; his light is not buried under a bufhel. The characters of thofe who live in a great city, where they have few tranfactions with their neighbours in the fame ftreet, are loft by their difperfed dealings, at diftant places, and among people unknown to each other; an excellent perfon therefore cannot in this fituation be propofed for a public example, to attract the veneration of his neighbourhood. His fecret admirers are ftrangers to one another, and to the inhabitants near him, and perhaps know but fingle inftances of fuch a gentleman's worth; whereas it is the uniformity that gives the great luftre to his actions, and renders them moft amiable. With the gentleman, who is engaged in country affairs, it is far different. He muft unavoidably concern himfelf with the families of the farmers and labourers round about him, and

with

with the tradefmen of the neighbouring towns and villages; and, if he be of fhining virtues, I cannot conceive but he muft be a great blefling to the parifhes within the knowledge of him. By his frequent dealing with, and employing the inhabitants, he will of courfe have fome cognifance of their lives and converfations, and having an opportunity of knowing them, may encourage them as they feem beft to deferve from God and man. They too, in their return, even the loweft labourers, from frequent and intimate views, will conceive a noble idea of their mafter, which will be heightened by their concurrent teftimony when they meet together : by his actions and fentiments they will quadrate their own ; and, if he be of a piece, and uniform through all the parts of a good and prudent life, he is miftaken much, if he thinks the benefit of his virtues confined to himfelf only : he is obferved and imitated by this ordinary fort of people, and it is they too, for the chief part, that will fix the character he muft bear. The difcourfe on their mafter is the fauce to their bread and cheefe, when two or three at breakfaft or dinner-time fit under a hedge ; nay, their work by the tafk alfo fhall loiter, but fome remark they will make on the conduct of one gentleman or other ; and we cannot be ignorant that every perfon of this ftation in the country has acted a part, either good or bad, fufficient to occafion a general talk in the neighbourhood ; his fpeech and behaviour in all his dealings are reported again, tho' but one witnefs prefent, and how juft or how difagreeable his fentiments or actions were, in any cafe that happened, is canvafs'd amongft them, and judgment is paffed on his wifdom, virtue, and

religion ;

religion; and the labourer's wife muſt hear the tale over again when the huſband comes home. In a word, there is no action ſo minute in a gentleman but it is worth the gazing on ; and, though it be of a nature indifferent, yet the manner of doing it may carry an unaffected beauty and grace with it, which if it does, be aſſured, theſe country people will ſee a great way into it, and ſecretly revere the perſon according to his merits. Nor is this all, for the reſpect they bear him ſhall influence their thoughts, cruſh their evil imaginations, left he, if they proceed to action, ſhould have the knowledge of it; ſo that a country gentleman, eſpecially if in commiſſion of the peace, ſhall, in this ſtation, do a world of more good in preventing evil by his exam-ple, than by puniſhing it. If, in the courſe of country buſineſs, he determines differences without humour and peeviſhneſs, ſhews à diſpleaſure without anger or ſwearing, ſets a mark of diſtinction ac-cording to juſtice and equity, the common people are ſenſible enough of the right judgment : he ſows wiſdom and goodneſs in their hearts, and the in-creaſe may certainly be expected amongſt them.

I have but one word more to add to the advan-tages of huſbandry already enumerated, which is, that of all profeſſions there is none more innocent or more pleaſant. The buſineſs of it goes on, in a known and certain courſe, from ſeaſon to ſeaſon, from year to year ; the gains from it are moſt ſatiſ-factory to a ſcrupulous conſcience, becauſe our goods are ſold in an open market, are ſet up together with thoſe of our neighbours, and of the ſame kind and ſpecies, whereby the ignorant may make the better compariſon of their worth ; we do not grow

rich

rich by jobbing, or by buying or selling again, the profit of which too often consists in outwitting and preying on one another; but our advantages arise from the gifts of our beneficent mother, the earth, whose gratitude generally requites the tiller's care, and by whose increase we hurt nobody; our dependence, next to God's blessing, is on our own industry and skill, and, tho' the season disappoints us sometimes, yet that disappointment is neither so often, so great, nor so fatal as the disappointments of those in other professions, whose trust and dependence is more on man. What miserable calamities fall out from the necessary trust in trade one citizen must give to another, and to his customers, whereas the farmer sells for ready money: he may thrive also without supplanting his brother, which the courtier can rarely do.——Certainly that person must live a pleasant life, whose death every one desires to die; and there are very few, of any art or employ, but who propose to themselves, if they are able, a country retirement, with at least some little of husbandry, in the last stage of their lives. If so, tho' other occupations may be in themselves innocent, yet this almost universal desire in men to quit them before they die, looks as if they found it difficult to discharge their consciences in them: they must be sensible, they can make no great figure as husbandmen, but there is some delight even in negative virtue, in being awake, and doing no ill.

To conclude; as I have had some taste and relish of these pleasures, I am desirous to propagate the sense of them as universally as I can, and it would greatly add to my own satisfaction to have partakers with me in the enjoyment of it.

OBSER-

# OBSERVATIONS
## IN
# HUSBANDRY.

---

### ARABLE LAND.

§. 1. PALLADIUS has laid down the following rule, by which we may make a judgment of of the good or bad quality of land [a]. Dig a ditch, or hole in the ground; and if, on casting in the earth again, there is too much to be contained in the place it came from, this shews it to be a rich soil; if the hole would have taken a greater quantity, it is a mark of a poor soil; but, if it just holds it, the soil is of a middling quality.

Of the quality of land, and how to judge of it.

It is an indication of a good soil, says Pliny, if the crows and other birds flock eagerly to the new-turned-up earth, and follow close on the plough-man's heels [b]. I doubt not indeed but the sorts of

---

[a] Pinguem terram sic agnoscis, scrobe effossâ et repletâ si superaverit terra, pinguis est; si defuerit, exilis; si convenerit æquata, mediocris est. Pallad. fol. 51.

[b] Est indicatio bonæ terræ, si recentem exquirunt improbæ alites vomerem comitantes, corvique aratoris vestigia ipsa rodentes. Plin. lib. 17. ch. 5.

beetles,

beetles, which lay their maggots in the ground in autumn, and are to be produced in spring (such as the rook-worms) are so wise as to lay them in rich ground, that they may be the better nourished, as other insects do also choose the tenderest plants to lay their brood on. Worm-earths also abound most in the richest land.

If you observe any ground to bear a light crop of corn, and at the same time to be grassy, it is to be presumed the ground, thus running to, and bearing grass, would have born corn also, if it had been well managed, and that such ground is in good heart; but, if ground bears little corn, and no grass, it is very suspicious that such ground is poor.

Mr. Evelyn observes, there are diverse indications, by which we may know good mold or earth, as, among others, an infallible one is it's disposition to melt, and crumble into small morsels, not turn to mud and mortar upon the descent of gentle showers, how hard soever it seemed before, and if in stirring it rise rather in granules than massy clods. As the kind of it's natural plant is, says he, you may prognosticate for what tillage, layer, or other use the ground is proper; thyme, strawberries, and betony direct to wood; and Sir Francis Bacon takes notice, as have others also, that camomile (I suppose he means mayweed) shews a land is disposed to corn, burnet to pasture, mallows to roots; but moss, rushes, wild tansy, sedge, flags, fern, yarrow, and where plants appear withered and blasted, shrubby and curled, (which are the effects of immoderate wet, heat, and cold interchangeably) these are natural auguries of a cursed soil. —— When there is any vein of ground that breaks up iron mold, no corn will grow there.

§. 2.

§. 2. ᶜ The ancient writers agree, that a deep and moiſt ſoil, and Palladius adds a chalky alſo, is moſt ſuitable to wheat, and a light dry ſoil to barley, which will be killed, they ſay, if ſown in wet muddy ground ; (and ſo indeed barley might very well be in their countries, where it was ſowed in November) that wet ground agrees beſt with peas and beans, which, if committed to a dry ſoil, will periſh in the earth, or, if they are not abſolutely killed, will come up in a ſickly ſtarved condition ; that the reſt of the leguminous kind will bear a dry ſoil, but thrive moſt in a wet one : of all theſe however I ſhall treat under their ſeveral diſtinct heads.

§. 3. Mr. Evelyn does not reckon loam among *Of loam.* the clays, though it ſeems to be but a ſucculent kind of argilla, imparting a natural ligament to the earth, where you mix it, eſpecially the more friable, and is therefore of all others the moſt excellent mean between extremes ; faſtening and uniting that which is too looſe and ſtony, cooling that which is hot, and gently entertaining the moiſture.

§. 4. I ſee plainly by the temper of a field this *Of ſtrong* year (1706) (ſown with barley on wheaten fallows) *clay lands.* which is mixt land, and alſo by the temper of my clay-lands, (ſown after a whole fortnight of dry and hot weather, at the latter end of March, and three weeks cold drying windy weather following in April) that lands of the vales of England, or ſtrong

ᶜ Spiſſa, et cretoſa, et humida terra bene far et triticum nutrit, hordeum agro ſoluto delectatur, et ſicco ; nam in lutoſo ſparſum moritur. Pallad. lib. 1. fol. 53. Hordeum in terra non humida ſed valde arida potius ſerere oportet, frumentum vero in lutoſa et humida terra ſeminandum eſt ; in tali enim magis augeſcit : fabus autem et piſum in lutoſa ſerere convenit ; in arida enim conciduntur priuſquam enaſcuntur, et pereunt ; quæ vero non conciduntur degeneres fiunt : reliqua legumina ſuſtinent quidem in arida terra ſationem, verum meliora etiam ipſa fiunt et generoſiora in irrigua ſeminata. Leontius in Geoponicis, fol. 43.

clay-

clay-lands, such as they are forced to ridge round, cannot but be moist enough to bring up the corn, even in the driest summers.

At Oxford (anno 1708) in discourse with Mr. Bobart about the best methods to tame harsh, churlish, obstinate clay, he said, by experience he had found the best way was to fling it up in ridges in the winter, and after the first frost, when it thaws and molders, to fling and temper amongst it ashes or chalk, or whatsoever you have to qualify it; for the time being nickt, wherein you can catch the clayey corpuscles under the greatest disunion and separation, is the time for keeping them so, by mixing these other lighter bodies amongst them, which will the longest prevent them from their re-union: this I think to be good advice.

§. 5. If some sorts of stiff and binding land be sown dry, and a sharp scudd of rain falls before the earth has time to settle, it is observed that the crust of such land will bake, so that the corn cannot come through, to the great damage of a crop; this evil happens not, if after such a scudd of rain cool cloudy weather ensue, and not hot sun-shiny; for then the earth will not lie so hollow as to be baked. The best way I think to prevent this, when one has such land to deal with, is, to roll it immediately after sowing, which fastens the earth together, whereby the sun has not that power of piercing into it, and consequently not of baking it.

§. 6. I have a field that is very apt to bind, if rain comes on soon after it is sowed with spring-corn, and a hot gloom on it, so that the corn cannot come through; therefore I advise that such ground, a stiff clay, be sowed, as often as conveniently may be, with winter-corn, such as wheat and vetches; for though wet comes then, the sun is not strong enough at that time of the year to scorch the ground up and to bind it; and it is observed

served that this ground has been always lucky for vetches, which I suppose is for the reason above.

§. 7. "A land that eateth up the inhabitants Of white "thereof," Numb. xiii. 32. may very properly be land. applied to some of our chalky hill-country land, which, in return for ploughing and all charges, brings the farmer out of pocket.

Some of my neighbouring farmers coming to see me, one of them asked me if I intended to sow a certain field with wheat this year (1707); I said, yes. He replied, he thought it would not bear twice ploughing, being white land, and having lain still but two summers; and, said he, for one earth it had better lie still three years. I asked him why; he seemed to be at a loss about a reason; I told him, I thought the reason of what he said depended on the firmness and fatness of the ground; for, said I, if white land that is lay, is loose at top, and not very close and well settled, then it is too early to sow it on one earth, because the bottom that is turned down will be loose, and consequently will not hold rain well enough, but it will run through too soon. Said he, you say well; but my reason is, because this field is apt to have redweed; and if such land with us is ploughed up under three years, and sowed to one earth, we observe it runs much to weed. If that holds, said I, the reason must be, because the seed of the redweed being turned under the earth, where there is not a fastness it grows through, whereas, where the land is fast, it is choak'd; but this field seeming to me a fast and well-settled white ground, the reason will not hold in either case.

Note, it is common with farmers to say, that generally their whitish land, unless a very barren mortar-earth, produces as good wheat and barley, and fuller bodied, than their clay-land and stronger earth : but I doubt the reason of it is, because the
lighter

lighter whiter earth needs not more tillage than
they give it, and is not much damaged with unsea-
sonable ploughing; whereas the clay-land is seldom
ploughed enough by them, and that often unseasonably, by which it much suffers.

**Of black spungy land.**

§. 8. About the middle of a field near me, there
runs a vein of black, coary, spungy, and yet dry
earth, of the colour of Bagshot-heath, only dry;
in this land the farmer never had good corn in his
life-time, but here and there a tuft; therefore he
never more sows it. In Woodcot-down there is
such a piece of land abutting to this field; the farmer burn-bak'd it, notwithstanding I told him he
would have no corn; and he had none.----Note,
in these sort of grounds the rook-worms are bred;
and where rook-worms breed argues a rotten loose
earth, but not always fit for corn, notwithstanding
my former remark on the sagacity of those insects;
this black land to many strangers would promise
more than any other land on the farm.

**Of red, sandy land.**

§. 9, A red, sandy, ferny ground, not worth
twelve-pence per acre, should be managed thus:
the sword of the ground is not to be killed under
two or three crops, if you winter-fallow for summer corn; and such ground will be so beggar'd as
to bring but pitiful grasses after two or three crops,
which crops also are likely to be very mean; therefore I propose that such ground should be Midsum-
mer-fallowed to rot the roots of the grass, and
stirred in the winter, and ploughed and sowed with
black oats and rye-grass early in the spring, and
sowed very thick, so as to bind the ground by such
means; this ground will be in good heart to bear
the rye-grass, and hold it a year or two, or longer;
then this ground is to be ploughed up, and managed again in the same manner; for such ground
will pay best to be laid down to grass.

§. 10.

§. 10. Some of my grounds are subject to blight, *Of land* for which reason I would never plough such a *subject to* ground to white oats or barley, though never so *blights.* good ; for barley and white oats must be sown later than other corn, and consequently will not have so much time to be settled in the ground, for which reason such a ground will be more subject to blight; black oats therefore, and wheat, I hold the properest grains for such ground, and do believe in such ground the black oats should be dragged in.

I sowed barley the second and third days of May, anno 1703 ; I had a great burthen of rath-ripe barley, but thin and blighted for the most part; for indeed clay-land is so slow in forwarding corn, especially if it lies to the north, and has a hedge-row to the south to shade it, and a wet summer to boot, as there was this year, that 'tis not to be expected it can carry a full-bodied corn ; therefore such ground ought to be sowed earlier. I observed on the north side of the hedge-row, where the head-land was, the corn seemed riper than any in the field, but very thin of flower, which I take to be, because it had so little sun, that nature could not carry it on to it's perfection, consequently, having done it's utmost, the corn soon withered and grew dry.

Our white land at Crux-Easton, though poor, is said to bear the best bodied corn, which I am satisfied, according to the common way of management, it does in wet or dripping summers ; but, if the summer proves very dry, as this year (1704) was, I find the barley, especially before it begins to ripen, shrinks and runs to a brown colour, and blights, the ground not being able to nourish it any longer ; when the clay-land shall better support it's barley, and produce a fuller and finer rin'd grain : the leaves on trees in white land in such years shall soon decay and turn yellow.

2 The

The reason why those grounds which hang from the horizon to the east are most subject to mildew, and to blasting, may be (as I judge) from the sun drawing these vapours towards it, just as a great fire in a room draws the air towards it; so the sun having set these in motion, but not having strength enough to draw them into the middle region, to form them into a cloud, doth yet draw them till he is below our horizon; then these dews tend to the earth from whence they were taken, and in their motion to the west do fall on that ground which hangs eastward, at right angles; therefore offensive to them most. Cook, fo. 8.——This seems to hold in corn land also.

**Of side-lands.** §. 11. The side-lands in the hill country are always the poorest, because the good grete, or mold, is washed down by rain.

**Of head-lands.** I was observing the great difference between the lower head-land of my wheat and the other parts, the head-land being much the best wheat: this must be occasioned by the horses much treading on the turns, whereby the head-land was laid so close, that it kept in the moisture better than the lighter parts, which soon burnt up.

I observe the head-lands of all corn are first out in ear, not only on account of their being generally better in heart, but because, lying under the hedge, the corn lies warmer.

**Of light moldering land.** §. 12. Light land is said to be the best and kindliest land for corn, whilst it will hold it, and that may be for three years; but strong clay-land, though it will bring the less crops, will hold it longest, and endure ploughing possibly for six or seven years.

We have in the hill-country of Hampshire a light moldering ground, especially on the side-lands, which the countrymen think not fit to plough up for a wheaten crop till it has laid still five or six

years,

years, and got a fword, but will then plough it to a
barley and wheaten crop : the very life of thefe
grounds, when fowed, confifts in holding the feed
faft together, which girt it cannot have, being moldering, without a fword ; therefore they are out
who will fow it beyond a wheaten crop (which is
fowed on one earth) the ground after a wheaten
crop being too loofe ; I hold it beft therefore
to lay it down upon the wheaten crop, fowing
rye-grafs with it, which will not only grow up
with the wheat, and keep the top of the ground
firm againft moldering in fummer and winter,
but by the ftrength of the fold on the wheat will
give good burthens of grafs till to be ploughed to
wheat again.——The beft hufbandry for all light
barren ground feems to be, to fow it to rye-grafs,
and fo to plough it up to corn once in four or five
years, and fow it again on the firft crop to rye-grafs.
Such ground is to be valued only on account of it's
grafs, but, if fowed to hop-clover, it will not at
every two years end be ftrong enough to carry
corn.

§. 13. [d] Cato, in the fituation of a farm, advifes Situation
his countrymen to choofe a fouthern afpect ; of fo of a farm.
great confequence was the nearer neighbourhood of
the fun even in thofe hot countries, and therefore
not to be defpifed in thefe colder ; for it is plain to
me, that the corpufcular bodies of the fun injected
not only into our bodies, but into all vegetables by
it's heat, are in their influences prodigioufly more
powerful towards fructifying all forts of plants, than
any other manner of heat, or other rich manures
whatfoever ; for foot, nitre, afhes, blood, artificial
falts, or other mangonifms and compofitions Glau-

---

[d] Cato fcripfit, optimum agrum effe, qui fub radice montis
fitus fit, et fpectet ad meridianam cœli partem. Varro, fol.
1.—In meridiem fpectet. Cato, fol. 1.

ber has made, though they may perform wonders
in our cold countries, yet cannot produce above a
fifth part of the increase the earth shall do, without
these arts, in those countries nearer the sun, as
Africa, and the West-Indies. And the heat of the
sun is, I doubt not, so corporeal a body, as to have
fixed in the earth of those countries it's minutest
particles so far, that, if we were to bring from
thence a bushel or two of their earth, it would for
some time do wonders in our cold country, till the
treasures, the sun had by it's activity injected, were
exhausted; and according to the above notion is
the great benefit of summer-fallowing to be accounted for: the often turning the earth in the summer
grinds it into small mellow parts, each of which receives those subtle luminous emanations of the sun
in a more abundant manner, when it's parts are so
loosened by the plough and spade. And I doubt
not but in the hot climes, in their rainy or wintry
seasons, by reason of the richness of the soil, made
so by the corpuscles of the sun so plentifully injected, that the trees strike roots much deeper than
with us, and that corn does so also, though possibly
the straw may not exceed the length of ours, because
the sun checks it's growth, and confirms the fibres
and stalks of the leaves too fast.

A field of mine has a hedge-row to the south-
west, on a rising ground; this hedge-row keeps off
the sun from it a great part of the day; it is a very
good clay piece of land, through which the whole
flock of sheep pass as often as they move from one
ground to the other; the corn here runs much
into halm, to shew the land is good, but produces
a very thin grain: and the same proportion does a
farm hold with this land, which lies shelving from
the sun to the north; for the same reason all head-
lands fenced from the sun must be treated accordingly, and sweetened, not with dung, but chalk,
ashes,

aſhes, &c. and ſuch land is to be concluded always
four : for the ſame reaſon ſuch lands are eaſily over-
ploughed.

I have in the former obſervation taken notice of
the ſun's checking the growth of ſtraw, and con-
firming the fibres and leaves too faſt, which is the
reaſon I have aſſigned, why the ſtraw may not in
hot countries exceed the length of ours : this however may perhaps be no hindrance to the increaſe
of the grain ; for from what I have remarked of
this field, and alſo from other obſervations, I am
inclined to think Dr. Woodward's hypotheſis not
improbable.—The vegetative particles of the earth,
which are particularly adapted for nouriſhing the
ſeed of a plant, may poſſibly conſiſt of a much more
ſubtilized body than the other particles of earth,
that nouriſh the ſtraw, leaves, &c. and this body
may require longer time to be ſo rarified, concocted, and digeſted, probably by the ſun and air working on it, that by ſuch means it may be aſſimilated ;
for dung laid on very barren ground does not, by
experience, conſiſt of abundance of theſe refined
particles, and may therefore produce abundance of
ſtraw, in our cold climate, but not of corn.——If
this be the caſe, it ſeems probable alſo, that in every
plant, among the innumerable tubes, which paſs
thro' the ſtalk (ſuppoſing of wheat) to the ear, ſome
peculiar tubes or fibres may be appointed by the
All-wiſe Creator, which run from the root upwards
to the ſummit, and are much finer and ſtraiter than
the other tubes of the plant, for receiving and con-
veying to the ſeed the ſimilar and ſeminal parts and
juices ; conſequently, where earth does not abound
in theſe parts, poverty ariſeth in the increaſe, tho'
the earth may abound in the more groſs vegetative
parts, allotted for nouriſhing the ſtalk. From
hence it may be, that after one crop of peas you may
have the next crop of peas full in halm or ſtraw,

but never in kids ; from hence we find, that often
ſtirring the earth, ſubtilizing it's parts, and turning
it up to the air and ſun, is exceedingly conducive to
the multiplying of grain, tho' the length of ſtraw
may not be much increaſed by it : this may probably give a reaſon why aſhes, ſoot, &c. may have
ſuch copious vegetative paiticles in them, as to
force ſo ſtrongly the growth of plants ; for the fire
having ſeparated and looſed the heterogeneous
parts, which clogged each other, the vegetative
particles are thereby enab!ed to be more active, and,
being reduced into their minuter corpuſcles, do aſ-
cend in greater numbers up the tubes of plants.
Nor is it to be objected, that by fire theſe vegetative particles ſhould be deſtroyed, ſeeing they are
ſuppoſed to be ſolids.   The proper alimental juices
being thus prepared by nature, and the different
tubes being fitted to receive them, vegetation appears to be performed in plants no otherwiſe than
by the riſing of juices up the tubes by the heat of
the ſun, in the ſame order and manner as the diſſimi-
lar juices and ſpirits riſe in an alembic ; the orifices
of the tubes, conducting either to the ſtraw or ſeed,
being fitted to receive the juices appropriated to
either [e].  This order is however ſometimes inter-
rupted,

* The common opinion, maintained by Mr. Evelyn and
others, is, that every plant exhauſts it's own proper nutriment,
leaving that which is appropriated to the other plants quiet
and undiſturbed.   Dr. Woodward not only ſubſcribes to this
notion, but adds, That there are very many and different ingredients to go to the compoſition of the ſame individual plant ;
of which ingredients every part of the plant has one allotted to
it for it's ſeparate and peculiar uſe.   Our author, though he
Of change  aſſerts nothing, yet, in this ſuppoſition, that the ſtraw and ſeed
of ſpecies.  may be nouriſhed by different kinds of juices, received at different orifices, and conveyed from the root upwards by different
tubes, ſeems not to diſſent from Dr. Woodward's opinion.   The
doctor reaſons from the vaſt variety of taſtes, ſmells, colours,
forms, and ſolidneſs, that it is impoſſible one homogeneous
matter

rupted, by reason that the atoms of heterogeneous
juices will sometimes shoot themselves up in different angular stirias from what are adapted to the
orifices of the tubes ; whereas in an alembic, where
the passage of rising is free, the apothecary can call
for the order he knows his spirits will rise in.

What

matter of the same substance, constitution, magnitude, figure, and
gravity, should make up all this variety ; and concludes, that
there want not good indications, that every kind of vegetable
requires a peculiar and specific matter for it's formation and
nourishment ; Yea, saith he, each part of the same vegetable
doth so. The former part of this conclusion is assigned by the
doctor as the cause of the necessity of frequently changing the
species of vegetables. But Mr. Tull, in his 14th chapter of
Horse-hoeing husbandry, treats the doctor's arguments with
great contempt, and in contradiction to them advances the
three following propositions,

1. *That plants of the most different nature feed on the same sort
of food* ;

2. *That there is no plant but what must rob any other plant
within it's reach* ;

3. *That a soil which is proper for one sort of vegetables once,*
is, IN RESPECT TO THE SORT OF FOOD IT GIVES, *proper to
it always* ;

And concludes, that if any one of the propositions are true,
there is no need to change the species of vegetables from one
year to another, IN RESPECT TO THE DIFFERENT FOOD THE
SAME SOIL IS, THOUGH FALSLY, SUPPOSED TO YIELD.

In support of these propositions he argues, that, if in this
series of crops each sort were so just as to take only such particles as are particularly proper to it, letting all the rest alone
to the other sorts to which they belonged, then it would be
equal to them all which of the sorts were sown first or last. But
let the wheat be sown after the barley, peas, and oats, instead
of being sown before them, and then it would evidently appear,
by the starved crop of wheat, either that some or all of those
other grains had violated this natural probity, or else that nature has given to vegetables no such law of meum and tuum.
Again, if all plants did not feed on the same sort of food, they
could not rob one another, as they are allowed to do ; a charlock could not rob a turnip, and starve it more than several turnips can do, unless the charlock did take from it the same particles which would nourish a turnip, and unless the charlock

C 2

did

What thefe alimental juices confift of, it is not eafy
to fay : Sir John Floyer, in his Touchftone of
Medicines, is of opinion, that plants only fpread
their roots in the common earth, but draw their
nutriment from the rain water, impregnated with
the fulphureous acid of the air ; but Dr. Woodward

did devour a greater quantity of that nourifhment than feveral
turnips could take. Flax, oats, and poppy, could not burn or
wafte the foil, and make it lefs able to produce fucceeding crops
of different fpecies, unlefs they did exhauft the fame particles
which would have nourifhed plants of different fpecies ; for, let
the quantity of particles thefe burners take be never fo great,
the following crops would not mifs them, or fuffer any damage
by the want or lofs of them, were they not the fame particles,
which would have nourifhed thofe crops, if the burners had left
them behind, quiet and undifturbed. Neither could weeds be
any prejudice to corn, if they did draw off thofe particles only
that fuit the bodies of weeds ; but conftant experience fhews,
that all forts of weeds, more or lefs, diminifh the crop of corn.
Thefe are his principal arguments, and as a confirmation of the
fact, that plants of the moft different nature feed on the fame
fort of food, he produces this experiment. At the proper feafon, tap a birch-tree in the body or boughs, and you may have
thence a large quantity of clear liquor, very little altered from
water ; and you may fee, that every other fpecies of plants,
that will grow in water, will receive this, live and grow in it as
well as in common water. Having thus given his objections
to Dr. Woodward's hypothefis, concerning the caufe of the neceffity of frequently changing the fpecies of plants, he proceeds
to propofe his own. One true caufe of a crop's failing, faith
he, is want of a quantity of food to maintain the quantity of vegetables which the food fhould nourifh. When the quantity of
food is fufficient for another fpecies (that requires lefs) but not
for that which laft grew, to grow again the next year, then
that other is beneficial to be planted after it ; for the conftitution of plants are different ; fome require more food than
others, and fome are of a ftronger make, and better able to penetrate the earth, and forage for themfelves. Therefore oats
may fucceed a crop of wheat on ftrong land, with once ploughing, when barley will not, becaufe barley is not fo well able to
penetrate, as oats, or beans, or peas are. Long tap-rooted
plants will not fucceed immediately after thofe of their own or
any other fpecies of long tap roots, fo well as after horizontal-
rooted

ward by many experiments has confuted this, and
the like opinions delivered by other authors, and
fufficiently proved, that the watery part imbibed, and
running up the tubes, is only the vehicle to a certain vegetable terreftrial matter, which gives nourifhment and increafe to plants. Thefe minute,

rooted plants; but horizontal will fucceed thofe tap-roots as
well or better than they will fucceed horizontal; for the food
at a greater depth has already been exhaufted by the one, and
chiefly that which lies nearer the furface by the other. The
reader muft obferve here, that thefe caufes, to which Mr. Tull
imputes the neceffity of changing the fpecies of plants, are caufes
only in the common way of hufbandry; for by his new method
of conftant tillage, he tells us, he prevents their effects. For
example, wheat is not, in the common way, (efpecially on any
ftrong foil) to be fown immediately after wheat; for the firft
wheat ftanding almoft a year on the ground, by which the
ground muft grow harder, and wheat feed-time being foon after harveft in England, there is not fpace of time to till the land,
after having been thus exhaufted, fo much as a fecond crop of
wheat requires; but wheat, in his new method, may be fown
immediately after wheat; for by keeping the ground in conftent
tillage he procures a fufficient quantity of food for his plants,
and ftrengthens their conftitutions: if ground therefore be managed according to the rules prefcribed in his book, he afferts,
there is no neceffity of ever changing the fpecies. I think it
may be objected to this affertion of Mr. Tull's, that it is not
only the farmer but the gardener alfo who complains, that
his ground is grown tired of fuch and fuch a plant; and finds
himfelf under a neceffity of changing it for another fpecies; and
yet in his hands the hough and the fpade are in conftant ufe,
and he is perpetually manuring, turning, and pulverizing his
ground; and, if what Mr. Lifle has taken notice of be fact,
that after one crop of peas you may have the next crop of peas
full in halm or ftraw, but never in kids, it feems to follow that
the feed and the ftraw require different juices for their nourifhment. See article Peas, title, Land fowed to peas will not
bear peas well again for fix years, §. 12. alfo §. 11. Upon
the whole however, which of thefe two gentlemen is in the
right, or whether either of them is fo, I muft leave to the de-
termination of thofe who have bufied themfelves in thefe inquiries.

☞ Of the order in which the fpecies fhould be changed, fee
the author's remarks at the end of the article Sowing.

C 3                                                atomical.

atomical, imperceptible bodies arife up thro' thefe watery tubes with wonderful fwiftnefs, according to the rules of levity aud gravity, by how much their atomical parts are lighter than the water, or have a figure ferviceable to that fpeed; and the water thrufting ftill forwards at the extremity, thefe minute parts are forced to the fide of the tube or pipe, and every minute part helps to the increafing and lengthening it.

## MANURE and MANURING.

§. 1. MR. Evelyn has given us an account of the various manures, either experienced by himfelf, or in ufe in his time, or of which he had conceived a good opinion; of thefe I fhall prefent the reader with the following abftract. Amongft his compofts, he fays, cold and dry winters, with ftore of fnow, is one which I reckon equal to the richeft manures, being impregnated, as they are, with celeftial nitre. fo. 312.

'Tis falts, which entice roots to affect the upper, and faline furface of the earth, upon which the nitrous rains and dews defcend, and are the caufe that fome plants the moft racy, and more charged with juice than any other, fuch as the vine, thrive fo well amongft rocks and pumices, and in whatever maintains this vital pickle. fo. 312.

'Tis falt which makes all covered and long fhaded earths abound in fertility, ib. — Obferve therefore, how under corn and hay-reeks corn grows; but yet it feems in meads, grafs comes not up well under hay-reeks, becaufe poffibly the ground may be too rich, or falt, for perennial grafs, tho' not for annual corn.

Salt fown in gravel-walks (as I have experienced it) for a time burns the earth, fo that nothing will grow

grow upon it ; but when the rains have once di-
luted it, it springs up more wantonly than ever ;
for which I have left it off. fo. 314.

He has a wonderful opinion of nitre. fo. 315.——
But, for ought I find, he is strangely confounded
about the principles of vegetation, what they are.

§. 2. Woad and hemp are said to destroy the Woad and
vegetable virtue where they grow. fo. 316. hemp.

§. 3. He is against the use of human dung, un- Human
less it be well ventilated and aired, notwithstanding dung.
Columella. fo. 317.

§. 4. Aquatick fowls dung is too fiery, and Dung of
therefore not to be laid on ground, till the volatile water fowl.
salts have their mordicant and piercing spirits qualified. ib.

§. 5. If gravel be wet and cold, lime is prefera- Manures
ble. fo. 304. for diffe-
rent soils.

§. 6 Arenous and sandy earths want ligature; Gravel.
and besides, consisting of sharp and asperous angles, Sand.
wound and gall, curl and dwarf our plants, without
extraordinary help to render the passages more slippery and easy ; therefore relenting chalks, with cal-
cinations of turf, are profitable fo. 305.

§. 7. Sand, being of an open and loose contex-
ture, is apt to put forth a forward spring, as more
easily admitting the solar rays, but it does not continue ; this is an infirmity which may be remedied
with loam, which unites it closer. ib.

§. 8. With a hungry, or weeping, or cold sort of Cold clay.
clay, lime is not to be mixt, which being slack'd is
raw and cold fo. 307.——To these laxatives are
best, such as drift sand, small gritty gravel, saw-
dust with marl, or chalk, and continual turning it
with the spade and plough. fo. 307.

Chalk is healing, and therefore proper for clay,
cold, and spewing grounds.

§. 9. Scouring of pond, or ditch-earth, is a most Pond mud.
excellent manure for light land. fo 309.

§. 10.

Swine's-
dung.

Horse-
dung.

§. 10. Lands that are hot and burning allay with swine's-dung, or neats-dung. fo. 309.

§. 11. Horse-dung, the least pinguid and fat of any, taken as it falls, being the most fiery, excites to sudden fermentation above any; wherefore 'tis then fit only for the hot-bed: but for fields it had need be well rotten, left it bring a couch, and pernicious weeds; the seeds of hay and other plants of which the horses eat, come oftentimes entire from them: such vegetables do commonly spring up from the soil of cattle, of which they chiefly eat, as long knot-grass from horse-dung; short, clean, and sweet pasture, from the dung of sheep and cows; the sonchus or sow-thistle from swine. fo. 317.

Neats-
dung.

§. 12. Neats-dung universally of all others is most harmless, and the most useful; excellent to mix with sandy and hot grounds, lean, or dry. fo. 318.

Sheep's-
dung.

§. 13. Sheep's-dung is of a middle temper between cows-dung and pigeons-dung; profitable in cold grounds. fo. 318.

Pigeons-
dung.

§. 14. Pigeons-dung and that of poultry is full of volatile salts, hot and fiery, and therefore most applicable to the coldest ground. Be this observed as a constant rule, that the hotter composts be early and thinly spread, and contrary the colder. fo. 318.—Very efficacious is this dung to keep frost out of the earth. ib.—As the effect of this dung is sudden, so it lasts not long, and therefore must be the oftener renewed. fo. 319.

Blood.

§. 15. Blood is excellent with any soil where fruit is planted; and, as to it's improvements of cornland, he tells you a strange story of the battle in Badnam fields in Devonshire. fo. 319.

After the battle of Badnam fields in Devonshire, says he, where Lord Hopton had a signal victory, the blood of the slain did so fertilize the ground, that most of the wheat stalks bore 2, 3, 4,

yea

yea to 7, and some to 14 ears ; a thing almost incredible, but assuredly reported by diverse eye-witnesses. fo. 319—I have given my opinion of this and the like tales under the article, Corn in general—see—Of many ears on one stalk.—He adds, that the blood and flesh of animals is much more powerful for the enriching of land than their dung and excrements, and is computed at twenty times the advantage, and to the same advance above this is hair and calcined bones ; and so the dung of pigeons and poultry feeding on corn does as much exceed that of beasts, which feed on gross vegetables, and one load of seed contains as much virtue as ten load of dung.

§. 16. Wood-ashes are fit for wet ground : in Wood-ashes. the East-Indies, burning trees to ashes is the only improvement, of which they strew not above a bushel to an acre ; it likewise kills the worms ; but in ground that is subject to over-heat and chap much, ashes and burning composts do but increase the fever, and therefore contrary remedies should be sought, such as neats and swine's-dung ; but not so, when lands are naturally or accidentally cold. fo. 320.

§. 17. He disapproves of laying dung in heaps Dung should not lay exposed to the sun and air. in the field, exposed to the sun, rain, and drying winds, whereby all the spirit and strength is carried away ; and pretends to put us in a better method of managing our dunghills.——Let the bottom or sides of a pit, says he, be about four feet deep, paved so with small chalk or clay at the bottom, that it may hold water like a cistern ; direct your channels and gutters about your house and stables to it. The pit must be under covert, so that the down-right rains at least may not fall into it. Lay a bed of dung in it a foot thick, on that a bed of fine mold, on that another bed of cyder-mere, rotton

fruit,

fruit, and garden offal, on this a couch of pigeons
and poultry-dung, with more litter, and beds of all
other variety of foil ; upon all this caft water plentifully from time to time : as for frefh dung, fuch
as fheep make when folded, 'tis good to cover it
with mold as foon as poffible from the fun. fo.
326.

§. 18. He accounts the warmth of the woolly
fleeces of fheep an improvement to land as well as
their dung. fo. 308 ; and the very breath and
treading of cattle, and their warm bodies, is comfortable, and marvelloufly cherifhing. ib.——Thus
far Mr. Evelyn.——There is no great matter to be
collected from the ancient writers on hufbandy in

**Manures used by the an-cients.** respect to this article of Manuring. Pliny prefers
cow-dung to horfe-dung ; and, if the cows, or cat-
tle that chew the cud, feed on as good meat as
horfes, without doubt the dung, by reafon of fuch
chewing, will be the finer. [f] Columella gives a
like reafon for preferring affes dung to that of any
other beaft ; becaufe, fays he, the afs is a long time
in grinding his meat, by which means it is more
thoroughly digefted, and fit to be laid on the ground
immediately, as foon as made. Hogs dung he
efteems the worft of all.——[h] Varro and Pamphilus
agree, that the dung of geefe, and all aquatick
fowls, is of a bad kind ; but the latter of thefe
affigns a different caufe for it from that given by
our Englifh writer : he attributes it only to it's too

[f] Inter fimos bovum præfertur antequam jumentorum. Plin.
lib. 17. c. 9.

[g] Inter pecudum ftercus optimum exiftimatur quod afinus fa-
cit, quandoquidem id animal lentiffimè mandit, ideòque fa-
cilius conquoquit, et benè confectum aque idoneum protinus arvo
fimum reddit. Deterrimum ex omnibus fuillum habetur. Columella, lib 2. c. 14.

[h] Malum eft ftercus anferum, et aquaticarum volucrum, propter humiditatem. Pamphilus in Geoponicis, fol. 5.

great

great humidity, whereas Mr. Evelyn reports it to
of a fiery quality.—— Columella joins with [k] Varro
in giviug great commendations to pigeons-dung,
beyond that of all other birds, on account of it's
fermenting heat, and in advising to sow it on the
ground before the corn is harrowed-in ; but, if this
is not to be procured, he directs us to make use of
goats-dung in it's stead. [l] Pliny recommends earth
that is salt, as preventive of, or destructive to insects ; and this may be one of the great advantages
from lime, soot, pigeons-dung, and often tilling
the ground : [m] It is agreed on, says he, by every
one, that there is no manure more profitable than
lupines, ploughed into the ground before they
have kidded.

§. 19. The maintenance corn must depend on, ~Dung, its~
is the innate digested salts of the earth, and well ~insuffi-~
concocted juices, which are not to be obtained by ~poor land.~
the præcocious way, the same year the land is
dunged ; dunging is but a weak support for very
poor land to depend on ; 'tis a good sauce to the
noble juices, which are before in the land, to
heighten them : but if you think dung alone a sufficient nourishment, where the land is before poor,
you will find, that in such case the corn will run out

[i] Antequam sarrias, more seminantis, ex aviariis pulverem
stercoris per segetem sparge ; si et is non erit, caprinum manu
jacere, atque ita terram sarculis permiscere, ea res lætas segetes
reddit.　Columella, lib. 2. fol. 108.

[k] Stercus optimum est volucrum, præter palustrium et nan-
tium ; de hisce præstare columbinum, quod sit calidissimum, et
fermentare possit terram : id ut semen aspergi in agro oportere.
Varro, lib. 1. sect. 43.

[l] Salsæ terræ multo melius creduntur, tutiora a vitiis innas-
centium animalium.

[m] Inter omnes constat nihil esse utilius lupini segete, prius-
quam siliquetur, aratro vel bidentibus versa. Plin. lib. 17. c. 9.

☞ Mr. Miller remarks, that in Italy, to this day, they cut
down the narrow-leaved tall blue lupines, when in flower, and
plough them into their ground as manure.

to a ftraw, and the grain to a thin body with little flour; and that very poor land fhall be as little able to bear good dunging, as a poor man, whofe blood is poor, much ftrong drink: the very quintefcence in earth, which improves grain, feems to depend very much on the air, fun, and rains, incorporated with the enrth, which feem principally to give birth and life to vegetables; for the receiving of which principles the dung has not had time, which is newly depofited on the earth: how much is to be attributed to thefe principles is eafy to be feen, if Mr. Ray, Grew, and Malpigius be confulted.

**Dung of cattle good in proportion to the goodnefs of their food.**

§. 20. In difcourfe with farmer Sartain of Broughton in Wilts, and other farmers, I was fayihg, that the tails and the improvement of the dung of cattle was anfwerable to the food they feed on, and gave feveral inftances of it; to which farmer Sartain replied, They were fenfible alfo, that, when they foddered with the beft meadow-hay, it made their grounds quite another thing in goodnefs, than when they foddered with a coarfer hay. —— Farmer Stephens of Pomeroy affented to this, and added, that the fheep flate in the common of Pomeroy was of fo rowety or roweny, wet, and poor a grafs, that the tails of the fheep that feed on it would do land no good: to confirm his report, he led me to a good healthy ground, which he had fowed to wheat, and which he had folded with thefe fheep, fo rich in appearance, that no ground could be feen for the trundles, and yet by the corn there was no fign of the good effects it had on the land; and the trundles, if you broke them, were as coarfe as rabbet-dung. This makes therefore for the improvements by grafs-feeds in poor lands, forafmuch as the fheep gain not thereby a good belly-full only, but alfo their dung has greater virtue.

**Of dunging poor land next a hedge.**

§. 21. If you divide the poorer part of a ground from the better, leave two or three lugg in depth

of

of the poorer ground within the hedge of the better ground ; because the cattle love to creep to the hedge-side, and will improve that poorer part by their dunging on it.

§. 22. That part of my barley, which had been dunged with horse-dung the year before for wheat, was twice as good as that part, which the same year was dunged with cow-dung, though that part dunged with cow-dung was rather the better land.

*Horse-dung preferable to cow-dung.*

§. 23. Horse-dung being laid on wheat-land just before it is sowed, and then ploughed in, and sowed on one earth, (which is often done in the hill-country, where the land is light) is apt through the fire of the dung to run out the corn faster than the digestion of the stalk can be made ; and so the parts being loose and hollow in the texture, when the winter comes, the cold pierces it so, that it withers and dies ; whereas dung should either, on such land, be laid and spread a month before the ground is ploughed and sowed, or else should be ploughed in a fortnight before the ground is sowed.

*Horse-dung when to lay it on.*

§. 24. Lord Shaftsbury complained to me, that he did not find feeding his grounds with cows improved them. I told his lordship the reason I believed was, because his cows were milch cows, not fatting beasts ; for the dung of milch cattle cannot improve lands like the dung of fatting beasts, the milking them solliciting the fat and nourishment of the creature to follow the current of the milk, whereby the dung is much the poorer ; and why weather-fold is worse than ewe-fold, I conceive to be, because the nourishment of the weather goes into his growth.

*Dung of fatting beasts preferable to that of milch cows.*

§. 25. I asked a Wiltshire man what the tails of a hundred sheep might be worth, if one was to hire them. He said, that sometimes he had known sheep to be let out, and they have had 12 d. per night for lending a hundred sheep to fold, which is looked

*Of hiring sheep for their dung.*

looked on of as good a value as a good load of pot-dung. Note, in Leiceſterſhire one may have the fold of 200 for 12 d. per night.

Ewes dung preferable to that of weathers.

§. 26. Mr Davers of Cauſum in Wiltſhire aſſures me, that notable countrymen have told him, that in dividing the ewes from the weathers, in folding in the ſame ground, they have had much the better corn where they have folded the ewes. Mr. Davers thought it was from the lambs, becauſe their dung muſt be richer from the milk they ſucked from the ewes. I have given my ſentiments on this point in a former obſervation ; but quære whether the ſoil of all gelt creatures, is not leſs generous and rich than that of others. I told Mr. Davers, that I had been aſſured, if cattle had poor mean hay given them, the ſoil of them would do the ground little ſervice, to which he aſſented ; and he ſaid further, that horſes dung when they were at graſs rather impoveriſhed than bettered the land, whereas what came out of the ſtable was otherwiſe.

Time of carrying out ſome ſorts of manure. Malt-duſt mixed with pigeons-dung.

§. 27. Carry out horſe-piſs, cows-piſs, hogs-piſs, when they are frozen and in ice.

Many huſbandmen fling layers of malt-duſt into the pigeon-houſes, and, when it is well covered, fling another layer, and ſow it mixed thus together on their grounds, and find, they ſay, great advantage in it. I have not as yet had experience of it, but have heard it greatly commended, and believe it to be a good way.

Cautions in uſing pigeon and poultry-dung.

§. 28. Sharrock ſays, fo. 91. For cold land, pigeon and poultry-dung [n] is very uſeful, which

[n] Mr. Miller ſays, the dung of pigeons, hens, and geeſe, are great improvers of meadow or corn-land ; the firſt of theſe being the beſt ſuperficial improvement that can be laid on meadow or corn-land : but, before it is uſed, it ought to have lain abroad out of the dove-houſe ſome time, that the air may have a little ſweetened it, and mollified the fiery heat that is in this dung.

**abound**

abound in volatile falt; thefe are only fowed by the hand, for fear of burning the corn in the chitting of the grain.—— I have obferved where thefe dungs have been over-plentifully laid, that the place bore no corn at all, whereas in other places, where it was moderately strewed, the crop was exceeding great; the fame effect there is in urine and foot, from the very eager fpirit, and volatile falt, and therefore the fame caution is to be had in their ufe : horfe-dung, if not rotten, lying thick will do the fame.

§. 29. Mr. Putching of Leicefterfhire fays, they commonly fow two quarters of pigeons-dung on an acre (which is fixteen bufhels) and their method of fowing it is, to fow it after the corn, and before the corn is harrowed in.: in meadows he fuppofes eight bufhels on an acre is enough.

*Quantity of pigeons-dung on an acre.*

§. 30. It may be judged that pigeons-dung is better than poultry-dung, from Mr. Evelyn's view of them by a microfcope ; for he fays, that pigeons-dung is conftituted of a ftiff glutinous matter, eafily reducible to a duft, of a grey colour, with fome hufky atoms after dilution ; but the dung of poultry was fo full of gravelly fmall ftones and fand, that there appeared no other fubftance, fave a very fmall portion both of white and blackifh vifcous matter, twifted up together, of all other the moft fætid and ill-fmelling. Evelyn, fo. 295.

*Pigeons-dung preferable to poultry-dung.*

§. 31. Sir Ambrofe Phillipps fells his pigeons-dung for 4 d. per bufhel, which is 2 s. 8 d. per quarter; one Gimfon bought it, and laid it on light fandy land, and, it proving a hot fummer, he thought it did his barley rather harm than good. Mr. Putching is very fond of this dung, and buys it for 2 s. 6 d. per quarter, and fows two quarters, and fometimes three on an acre, which he thinks is beft : he fows it after his barley is in the ground,

*Pigeons-dung, price and manner of fowing it.*

before

before harrowing, and harrows in both together: he alfo fows it in the fame manner on his wheat-land, and in cafe a wet and cold fpring comes upon his barley, fo that he is like to have little in his fur-rows, he flings about a fack on an acre, between the furrows, and finds it to ftrengthen and comfort the cold land fo, that he has as good corn there as on the ridges : he bad me but try, and I fhould have as good an opinion of it as he had.   Mr. Clerk of Ditchly told me afterwards, that Sir Ambrofe fow-ed commonly five quarters on an acre.

**To ma-nage pigeons-dung.**

§. 32.  The gentlemen mentioned in the preced-ing obfervation agreed, that the beft way to manage pigeons-dung in a dove-houfe, was often to lay a layer of ftraw upon it ; but then it will be amaffed to fo great a bulk, that it muft often be removed to fome place, where it may lie from the power of the weather.

**Soot and pigeons-dung.**

§. 33.  Sharrock tells us, fo. 134. Soot and pigeons-dung abound much in volatile falt; and I have this year (1703) on a cold and moift clay, feen excellent advantage on the grafs thereby, it being only ftrewed thin on the grafs before fpring ; but of the two foot was the beft.

**Soot to kill mofs.**

§. 34.  Cook fays, fo. 19.  Soot is good to kill mofs ; it's heat kills the roots, for they lie on the top of the earth.

**Soot to lay on green wheat.**

§. 35.  I find in Leicefterfhire many do fling foot on their green wheat in February, fo as to blacken the land with it ; therefore I need not fear burning my wheat with it, at that time at Eafton.  The foot from the fea-coal is efteemed the beft.

**Coal afhes good for St. Foin.**

§. 36.  A notable farmer told me, that he had tried all ways of managing French-grafs, by dung, and fold, &c. and had found coal-afhes the only, or beft improvement. —— Qu. therefore why not beak-land burnt ; and why may not thefe be the
beft

beſt improvements, becauſe they will not create and encourage a rowety or roweny graſs to ariſe, to choak the French-graſs, as Mr. Methuen had ob-ſerved dung to do.

It ſeems to me, that aſhes may be propereſt to French-graſs, inaſmuch as they kill the natural graſs, from the ſame reaſon as the ſalt of brine does, or urine thrown on gravel-walks ; and aſhes have a ſtrong ſalt in them ; yet this ſalt is beneficial to the roots of the French-graſs, becauſe it has a tap-root, which runs deep, and the ſalt of the aſhes is very well qualified before it ſinks down to the roots of the French graſs. *Id. the reaſon.*

§. 37. J. Mortimer, Eſq; F. R. S. fo. 380. reckons rotten wood of hedges and coppices to be a great improver of the ſoil where it drops, and inſtances the earth where faggot-piles have been uſed to ſtand. *Rotten wood.*

§. 38. Quinteny ſays, the dung of leaves thoroughly rotten, is hardly fit for any thing but to be thrown over new-ſown beds, to hinder the rains, or waterings, from beating too much on the ſurface, and ſo hinder the ſeeds from riſing ; —— and no doubt 'tis the ſame with corn. Part 1. fo. 5. *Rotten leaves.*

§. 39. Martin of the Weſtern iſles ſays, the manuring with ſea-ware is an univerſal huſbandry throughout thoſe iſlands, fo. 53. &c. In the iſle of Altig, he reports, that, by manuring healthy ground with ſea-ware, many ſtalks had five ears growing on them ; fo. 140; and in the iſle of Skie, by an improvement of marle, 35 fold increaſe was had, and many ſtalks carried five ears of barley ; and he aſſures us this account was given him by the then poſſeſſor of the land ; fo. 132. ° But I have in another place given my opinion, that theſe ſuperfætations are not probable. *Sea ware and marle.*

° Vid. Corn in general.

§. 40. King of Ilſley in Berkſhire ſays, that the malt-duſt ſowed on barley-land did very little good laſt ſummer (anno 1699) by reaſon of the drought; for, no rain falling from ſowing-time till the ſeed was come up, the ſtrength of the duſt was not waſhed into the land.

He ſaid, it was common in thoſe parts of Berkſhire, to lay malt-duſt on wheat land, and to fling it on. at the ſame time they ſow the wheat, and harrow it in together, and a very good improvement it was; but, ſaid he withal, I have heard huſbandmen argue that point, and hold, that malt-duſt is better for ſummer-corn than for wheat, and they give this reaſon for it; the winter corn lies a whole year in the ground, and the malt-duſt will have ſpent it's ſtrength by the time the winter is over, and not hold up the corn in heart all the ſummer; they ſow with the wheat two quarters of malt-duſt to an acre, which makes four quarters of corn-meaſure.

Farmer Ratty aſſured me, that malt-duſt went beyond dung on clay-land; for 'tis on ſuch land, not on light land, that he has had the experience of it: and that farmer Hawkins knows this very well, tho' he does not care others ſhould, leſt the price ſhould grow dearer: he ſays, he lays twenty ſacks on an acre, of the ordinary four-buſhel ſacks, which he buys at Whitchurch at 1 s. per ſack. He ſows on his wheat ground, not dung'd nor folded, about February, and he ſays the wheat will ſurpaſs the dunged-wheat, and the ground will produce a good barley-crop afterwards, tho' ſuppoſed to the contrary.

Mr. Thomſon of Loughborough aſſures me, that malt-duſt laid on cold graſs-grounds makes a great improvement: he ſays, he lays after the rate of four quarters on an acre, on ſuch ground, but 'twould be better to lay ſix or ſeven. Note, five quarters on an acre is a peck on a lugg-ſquare; 7½

quarters

quarters is a peck and an half. It seems it would be agreeable on our cold clay-meadows.

I have observed of dungs, and lime, and strong beer, that they afford no spirits, or vegetable salts, till they have passed a fermentation by fire, whereby their spirits or salts are raised and secreted; so I look on the same observation to hold good in malt and barley; ground barley being of little profit to land if laid on it; whereas ground-malt laid on land, (tho' 'twould be madness to do it) as we may judge by the malt-dust, would yield a great produce.

Mr. Clerk says, he uses the kiln-dust of the malt himself, viz. that dust which comes through the hair-cloth, which he looks on to be better than the other: he laid (he said) ten quarters upon an acre, both on his grass-ground and barley, about January or February. I asked him if it would not be apt to burn the ground, not being laid on earlier; he said, one shower of rain he thought wash'd the heat out of it. As to the largest tail-dust of the malt, he sold it for 4 d. per bushel, to people to feed pigs with.

§. 43. In discourse with King on the subject of Woollen rags. woollen rags, he assured me of strange effects from them, which improve to four or five crops. He said they migh tbe bought at London for 2s. or 2s. and 6 d. per hundred weight, 112 lb. to the hundred; old people might be hired to cut them on a block, which would cost about 6 d. per hundred. Lay of these chopt small, to an inch or two square; sow them by scattering them out of the seed-lip at the second ploughing or earth, about the latter end of July: being thus covered, they will grow finnowy or moldy by seed-time *.

§. 44. It

* Beside the manures spoken of by our author, there are two others much commended by Mr. Miller, which are rotten tanners bark, and rotten vegetables.---Oak bark, says he, after the tanners have

D 2          used

§. 44. It is a common and well approved of method in hufbandry, at Litchfield in Hampfhire, and the neighbourhood thereof, to carry out long dung, and lay it on lay-ground, that is light and whitifh, and to let the worms draw it in, being laid early ; then to plough it up and fow it on one earth ; but it muft not be ftrong land, becaufe that can't be fowed on one earth.

*Worms good for drawing long dung into the ground.*

§. 45. It is a frequent practice in the hill-country to pot-dung land, run to grafs and to a fword, in July, and to plough in the dung, and fow it on one earth with wheat, the latter end of Auguft, or a week in September ; and true it is, that though the ground be graffy and fwordy, as it will be in our hill-country by two years lying to grafs, and tho' the fpring be very dry, as alfo the fummer, yet in April and May,

*Dung, time of laying it on.*

ufed it for tanning of leather, when laid in a heap, and rotted, is an excellent manure, efpecially for ftiff cold land ; in which one load of this manure will improve the ground more, and laft longer, than two loads of the richeft dungs. It is better for cold ftrong land than for light hot ground, becaufe it is of a warm nature, and will loofen and feparate the earth : fo that where this manure has been ufed three or four times, it hath made the land very loofe, which before was ftrong, and not eafy to be wrought. When this manure is laid on grafs, it fhould be done foon after Michaelmas, that the winter rains may wafh it into the ground ; for, if it is laid on in the fpring, it will burn the grafs, and, inftead of improving it, will greatly injure it for that feafon. Where it is ufed for corn land, it fhould be fpread on the furface before the laft ploughing, that it may be turned down for the fibres of the corn to reach it in the fpring , for, if it lies too near the furface, it will forward the growth of corn in winter ; but in the fpring, when the nourifhment is chiefly wanted to encourage the ftems, it will be nearly confumed, and the corn will receive little advantage from it.—Rotten vegetables of moft forts alfo greatly enrich land ; fo that, where other manure is fcarce, thefe may be ufed with great fuccefs. The weeds of ponds, lakes, or ditches, being dragged out before they feed, and laid in heaps to rot, will make excellent manure, as will moft other forts of weeds. But wherever any of thefe are employed, they fhould be cut down as foon as they begin to flower ;
for,

May, when the sun gets strength, and warms the ground, the spirits of the dung will be drawn out of the ground upwards, as will plainly appear by the good deep colour of the wheat, and the thickness and thriving condition of it: however 'tis plain by several experiments I have made this way, that the mellower and looser the ground is, you thus manage, the better the spirits of the dung will be drawn upwards, through the earth, to the roots of the corn, as has appeared to me, both by the thickness and colour; therefore the husbanding land this way, which is run to a matted sword, ought, as much as can be, to be avoided. Corn thus husbanded will thrive very little during the winter, nor until warm weather comes: from hence it may seem, that to carry out dung on such land the beginning of June, and plough it in whilst the sun is hot, and has a good

for, if they are suffered to stand until their seeds are ripe, the land will be stored with weeds, which cannot be destroyed in two or three years; nay, some kinds of weeds, if they are permitted to stand so long as to form their seed, will perfect them after they are cut down, which may be equally prejudicial to the land: therefore the surest method is to cut them down just as they begin to flower; at which time most sorts of vegetables are in their greatest vigour, being then stronger, and fuller of juice, than when their seeds are farther advanced; so that at that time they abound most with salts, and therefore are more proper for the intended purpose. In rotting these vegetables it will be proper to mix some earth, mud, or any other such like substance with them, to prevent their taking fire in their fermentation; which they are very subject to, where they are laid in large heaps, without any other mixture to prevent it; and it will be proper to cover the heaps over with earth, mud, or dung, to detain the salts; otherwise many of the finer particles will evaporate in fermenting. When these vegetables are thoroughly rotted, they will form a solid mass, which will cut like butter, and be very full of oil, which will greatly enrich the land. —— He commends likewise sea-sand, shells, and corals, especially for a strong loam, inclining to clay; but adds, as these bodies are hard, the improvement is not the first or second year, because they require time to pulverize them, before their salts can mix with the earth to impregnate it.

D 3

feafon to hold fo, is better hufbandry than to defer it
till Auguft ; for the fun will exhale upwards the
fpirit of the dung.   In poor ground it feems proper
to me to fummer-fallow it,  (if lay-ground run to
grafs) and ftir it in the winter, in order to fow it at
fpring with oats or barley and French-grafs, in order
to feed the French-grafs with cows during the fummer, after the roots are well eftablifhed ;  and fuch
feeding will not kill the French-grafs in fuch poor
ground ;  for there can be no danger of fuch exuberancy of fap, that the root fhould fall under a plethory :  in autumn it may be fed a little with fheep
without prejudice.

From the above obfervation, how the dung
plough'd in under furrow is drawn up to the roots
of the corn by the ftrength of the fun, may be ex-
plained, in the fame manner, how grafs in the hotteft fummers comes to have moft goodnefs and fpirit,
as is experimentally proved by deer, fheep, and
other cattle thriving by it (tho' plenty of rain does
moft contribute to increafe of growth) the effluvia
which lie deep, being fo exhaled to the roots.

Mr. Biffy and Mr. Slade being with me, when in
the month of July or Auguft I was carrying out my
dung to lay on land that was fwordy, in order to
fpread it, and turn it under furrow, they did not approve of that hufbandry ;  Mr. Slade faid, he found
it a much better way to carry it out in the fpring,
i. e. about May, to lay on ground not apt to run to
grafs, and let it be wafh'd in, which will mellow the
ground, and hollow it ;  and then turn it in at Mid-
fummer, and fow it on one earth.  Mr. Biffy faid, he
found it always the beft way, if dung was free from
weeds, and fhort, fuch as ox-dung and horfe-dung
that would fpit, to carry it out on the ground
plough'd up to fow on one earth, a little before you
fow it, and drag it in : he faid, he always found the
beft corn by fuch hufbandry, and would have per-
fuaded me to try it.                          §. 46. It

§. 46. It seems to me, that the grounds near the house ought to have the dung, in regard of the cheapness of carriage, and in regard that three loads of corn may be carried in from thence, instead of one from a farther distance; and if such grounds consequently by rich crops of grass-seeds maintain a treble stock, what matter is it whether the grounds at a distance have the dung at the first hand or second, I mean by the tails of sheep? Besides, the richer the grounds near to your backside are, the more they will answer in the produce of grass, and in being of more general conveniency, as in maintaining lambs at lambing-time, in fatting * hogs by broad-clover, in maintaining horses and mares with food, in bringing good goar-vetches, in the easy carting of a good burthen of grass-seed hay; and, if not folding, other methods may be used in manuring grounds at a distance, such as ploughing in goar-vetches, liming, rags, sowing to French-grass, watering, &c.—The farmers however argue from experience, that we must sometimes change our manure from the fold to pot-dung, and not always fold on the same land.

*To lay pot-dung near home.*

*\* Hog, or young sheep.*

§. 47. They who are curious in selling seed-corn, will not allow a load of corn or dung at harvest to come through their wheat-fallow.

§. 48. If dung lies near the corn-carting, and not carried out before harvest, so many sorts of corn will be littered in it, which will not have time to rot, that you must expect a crop foul with trumpery.

*Dung should not lie near the corn-carting.*

§. 49. I hold it much the better way, if earth be carried out as a soil to land, not to spread the earth on the land till the last earth be given for the corn, and then to spread it, and harrow it in with the corn with new harrow tinings or drags; hereby the earth will not be buried.

*Mold, to lay it on.*

§. 50. One of my labourers was going to turn the dung for me into heaps in the foddering barton;

*Of turning dung.*

he

he afked me, if he fhould ftir it all ; he faid, 'twas beft to turn it all, and not lay the mixen he flung up on the top of the reft ; for though 'twas fomething more charge, yet 'twould rot the better. Farmer Elton coming by, told me, I did well in it, for 'twas much the better way.

§. 51. If ftraw, not half dung, be carried out into the fields, and laid in heaps, and after rains turned, it will become dung in good time.

Mr. Raymond of Puck-Shipton in Wiltfhire vifiting me, I told him, I intended to dig my farmyard into holes, whereabouts the kine foddered, that in thofe holes I might let the wet into my dung, that it might rot the better. He immediately difapproved much of it, and faid, that way the dung would never rot; for ftraw was like weed, and other things, which lying always wet would never rot; but that which would make ftraw rot was to let it lie often wet and often dry ; therefore, faid he, we always covet as dry a farm-yard as we can get, for the rains will wet the ftraw often enough ; or, if it chance to be a very long dry feafon, you may wet it by throwing water on it.— I have fince found by experience, that, if dung lies always wet, it will not heat well, nor rot, and that it waftes itfelf and it's ftrength by the wet ; therefore no better hufbandry than to fling it into a heap.

1701 was a mighty corn-year, and a year which ran much to halm ; fo that the beafts could not eat up their ftraw, but it lay in the barton not half dung ; I propofed carrying out the ftraw or longifh dung, and laying it on my wheaten lay ; a layer of ftraw, and a layer of wet and rottenifh dung, thinking the wet and tolerably digefted dung might rot the ftraw ; but John Stephens of Afhmonfworth, and farmer Crofs faid, the long ftraw had better lie in the barton to take fome rains, and then being

*Straw, to manage it for dung.*

3        well

well wetted, and carried forth, it might by the
wheat-feed-time be dung, but, according to the way
I proposed, by that time it would produce nothing
but finnowy or moldy straw.

§. 52. Columella advises to keep dung in a heap *Age of*
till it is a year old, and no longer ; for after that *dung.*
age, says he, it loses it's strength.

That new dung on cold land will run corn into
straw, and make a great shew of corn, I doubt not ;
but I do believe, the dung of one year old will produce the fuller bodied corn.—Using dung however
of only a year old, to dung a wheaten crop, seems
to be the occasion of the great produce of weeds in
our corn-land in England.

§. 53. For three or four years they were very *Time and*
fond at Husborne in Hampshire of laying their *manner of*
dung on the land, and spreading it after the corn *laying on*
was sown and harrowed ; but they grew weary of *dung.*
it ; for their land was pretty light of itself, and the
worms working up for the dung made it too light.

I was going from Holt through Tilshade to Salisbury ; Tilshade is on the downs ; I observed the
village was carrying out long dung, which being in
or about October (as I thought an improper season)
it invited me to ask the reason. They told me, it
was to lay on their ground sowed to vetches, and
that they did not sow their vetches till the middle
or latter end of October, when their wheat-land was
sowed. Quære farther of this husbandry ; for it
seems to me, where land is sowed late, it must be
good husbandry, and bring the vetches forward,
and warm, and comfort them, especially where
land is light and weak, as it is generally about Tilshade, being a fine barley land.

Farmer Elton advised me always, when I carried my dung out into the ground, to spread it immediately ; it will, said he, make the ground kirnel and fallow better, whereas to leave it in the heaps
will

will rather hurt the corn, and make it lodge and
grow up rank.——— But, said Oliver afterwards,
when I was talking to him of it, we often lay it in
heaps on the ground; and in such case, when we
carry it on the land, we dig away from the mixen
the earth underneath about half a foot.

I was observing to farmer Biggs, that farmer
Bond of Highclear flung no dung, in the spurning
or spreading it, into the furrows, but carried a spit
all along from the heap, and spread it near to the
brink of the furrows, and so spurned to it. John
Biggs said, he never saw it done, but that doubtless 'twas a very good way; for to fling dung into
the furrows was to double dung them, by reason
that on each side the furrow a furrow was veered in
on the furrow——— [p] Prudent husbandmen, says Columella, choose to lay their dung on the upper
ground rather than on the lower (or to dung the
ridges rather than the furrows) because the rains
will wash down the richer particles.

Quære, if ploughing in dung at stirring time
may not be best, because of making the weeds grow,
which are ploughed in at sowing the wheat.

Columella advises to plough in dung as soon as
it is spread, that it's strength may not be exhausted
by the power of the sun, and that the ground may
be mellowed and enriched by thus lying mixed with
it; therefore, adds he, you ought not to spread
more dung than you can plough in a day [q].

[p] Prudentes agricolæ etiam in aratis collem magis quam val-
lem stercorant, quia pluviæ semper omnem pinguiorem materi-
am in ima deducunt. Columella, lib. 2. ch. 18.

[q] Disjectum protinus fimum inarari, et obrui convenit, ne so-
lis habitu vires amittat, et ut permista humus prædicto alimen-
to pinguescat; itaque, cum in agro disponentur acervi stercoris,
non debet major modus eorum dissipari, quam quem bubulci
eodem die possint obruere. Columella, lib. 8. fo. 100.

Method

## Method of MANURING different Lands.

§. 54. Dunged land, in a wet year, bears the worst corn, especially if it be low stiff land; for dung then holdeth the moisture, and the ground being then wet withal, commonly doth produce a great many weeds, which can digest the spirit of the earth and water better than the corn can, because they grow much quicker. Cook, fo. 31. *Of dunged land in a wet year.*

§. 55. Ground hard ploughed is apt to run to weeds, and dunging it, or folding on it early, will make it more subject so to do; for that will promote and forward the natural produce of the ground. *Of dunging land that is hard ploughed.*

§. 56. When we go on the improvements of land by dung, fold, or other manures, it ought first to be considered, what return we expect of profit; upon which consideration, I think, the gentleman, who undertakes the management of his own land, ought first to apply his manures in improvements to his clay-arable and mixt-arable; because the same expence shall double the value of such lands, and thereby render an acre of 10 s. per ann. to be worth 20 s. ——Whereas the same expence on poor white land, or poor sandy land, &c. of perhaps no more than 1 s. per acre, though it augments the value of the acre four times, is an improvement but of 4 s. per acre per ann. and then the improvements on such poor lands are not so lasting. 'Tis true however, there is one sort of manure always to be applied to white, sandy, or poor light lands from the first entrance into husbandry, which is your marles and strong earths, from whencesoever they are removed. From hence it may be inferred, that those do not best, who, when they build farm-houses, choose the situation on the most barren parts; for, if their grounds be healthy, and not worth above *The best ground ought to be most and principally improved.*

10 s.

10 s. per acre per ann. 'tis more profitable to have the situation of a farm there.

Land that is worth 5 s. per acre, and land that is worth 10 s. per acre, and land that will bear two quarters per acre, and land that will bear four quarters per acre, do differ vastly in proportion of value; for, whereas the land that is worth 10 s. per acre is only double the value of that which is worth 5, the land that will bear four quarters may very well be worth ten times the value of the land that will bear but two quarters; because the price of seeding, dunging, folding, sowing, ploughing, weeding, mowing or reaping, &c. of the four quarters per acre barley is no more than of the two quarters per acre barley.

**Wet ground to be dunged more than dry.**

§. 57. Palladius tells us, that a wet soil requires more dung than a dry one [r].

**Of suiting your dung to your soil.**

§. 58. Monsieur de Quinteny's observation, a-bridged by London and Wise, fo. 29, is as follows, viz. Since the great defects of earth are too much moisture, coldness, and heaviness, as also lightness, and an inclination to parching, so amongst dungs some are fat and cooling, as the dung of oxen and cows; others hot and light, as sheep, horses, and pigeons-dung: and whereas the remedy must have virtues contrary to the distemper it is to cure; therefore hot and dry dungs must be used in cold, moist, heavy earths, and open and loose dung, in lean, dry, light earths, to make them fatter and closer.

**Dung on sandy ground, how to be laid on.**

§. 59. If you lay dung on a sandy or rocky ground, where it will be weeping away, the oftener, and less at a time you lay, so much the better; for if one lay treble the quantity, it will as soon pass through as a less quantity.

---

[r] Ager aquosus plus stercoris quærit, siccus minus. Pallad. lib. 1. sect. 6.

§. 60. It

§. 60. It seems to me, that he who sows whitish land to wheat, and dungs it, ought to dung it early in the year, and plough it in, that so the earth may have time to drink it up; for, if white land be dunged late, being of a dry nature, the wheat will have little goodnefs from it: I experienced this to my coft.

Time of dunging whitish land.

§. 61. I had been to view a neighbouring farmer's black, moorish earth, which was truly of the nature of black heath: I asked him, what manure he found beft for such land; he answered me, to fling pigeons-dung or malt-duft upon the surface of it; nay, said he, if I dung it, I fling dung upon it after 'tis sowed. And truly I think this the beft way to manage such land; for hereby the dung will be kept longeft in the ground, which is too apt to run downwards, and to be loft in ploughing it in, and to wafh away; and if such ground was never sowed but one crop at a time, and laid down to grafs, and the goodnefs of the surface turned in, for a second crop, it would I believe be beft; and if it was refrefhed again by a sprinkling of pigeons-dung, whilft the crop is growing, it would not be amifs.

Manure for black, moorish land.

§. 62. The wet spewy clays about Holt in Wiltshire, (of which sort, as well as in other places, there are abundance) are observed by moft experienced persons in husbandry not to answer the defigns of those who pretend to improve by dung; the reason of which I fully observed this spring (anno 1707); for being here (at Holt) in the month of March, when the wind was very busy, every lugg square of the ground cleft many thousand ways, so that there was not a piece of earth to be seen, on which one might set the sole of one's foot, but it had large gapings in it. The same also it suffers in the heat of summer; from whence it is plain, that though these lands are of a strong clay, which generally pay

Cause why wet spewy clays are not improved by dunging.

for

for their manure the beſt, yet being in this caſe too obſtinate, and clung ſo that they could not eaſily dry, without ſplitting juſt like green boards, the moiſture of all manures muſt needs be waſhed down, when rains come, through many hiatus's, which in a moſt hungry manner ſeem to gape for the vital ſubſtance of the earth ; and ſo the ſoil is immediately carried down below the roots of all vegetables.

**Whether to lay dung on the lay-land or fallows.** §. 63. Diſcourſing with ſeveral farmers about the beſt way to lay dung on the ground, whether on the lay-land or fallows, they ſeemed in general to agree, that the beſt huſbandry was to lay it on the wheat-fallows, and then to ſtir it lightly in, if the land be ſtrong clay-ground ; for it if be laid on the lay, and then ploughed in, it will be apt to break up ſo deep, and thereby the dung be ſo covered, that it will hardly turn up in the other ſtirrings afterwards.

**When to dung meadows.** §. 64. I found by experience this year (1701) that the earlier dung, or eſpecially pond-mud, and coal-aſhes, are laid on the meads, ſo that they may be waſhed in, the better the graſs may be mowed.

**Benefit of dunging them.** §. 65. To dung meadows and make them very rich in our hill-country, is excellent huſbandry, not only for the greater quantity of hay they produce, but becauſe thereby they yield a good bite of graſs at lambing-time, which is to be valued according to the occaſion, and with which we cannot be ſupplied for money ; the aftermaſs alſo, which is much the greater for it, leſſens the conſumption of corn by horſes, and makes a halt cow fat, with neither of which one can be ſupplied but at unreaſonable rates.

**When to dung them.** §. 66. In March this year (1706) I folded at lambing-time part of a mead, and fed the whole mead that year ; but both cows and horſes neglected that part that had been folded, and ſuffered it to grow up to great rankneſs ; whereas the other part of the mead, eſpecially the ſideling piece, which had

aſhes

aſhes laid on it in the winter, they eat very bare; by which I do infer, all ſorts of dung ought to be laid on in October, that the heat of them may be waſted by ſpring, and not taint the juices of the graſs, and that aſhes make the ſweeter graſs.

§. 67. I had farmer Biggs, Bachelour, and Crap, three excellent farmers, with me.—In our diſcourſe about the improvement of meadows, they all allowed of the bringing ſtraw thereon in the winter, for the worms to draw it in, to be very exceeding good huſbandry; and farmer Bachelour ſaid, he knew of nothing better than old thatch ſo drawn in upon meadows. *Straw, lay it on the meadows in winter.*

§. 68. I believe that fine mortar-earth or mixed mold, which is excellent good for barley, carries the finer barley for being dung'd; for the dung mends the deficiency of ſuch ground, which is inclinable to be too poor; but I do believe, on coarſe clay-land, whereon the barley runs naturally coarſe, dung rather makes it the coarſer; for the infirmity of ſuch ground is to be too rank, and coarſe, and is ſtill coarſer for the dung. *Dung for barleyland.*

§. 69. They never dung oats nor barley in Hants. In the hill country oats do well without dung, and barley has the ſtrength of the dung ſufficiently after the wheaten crop. *Oats and barley not dunged in the hill-country.*

§. 70. I was telling an experienced farmer, that I had ploughed down the linchet of a certain acre; and that my bailiff foretold me, I ſhould have the pooreſt wheat on that linchet; which I wondered at, in regard of the richneſs of the ground; his reaſon was, that the harrows would draw down all the good * grete on the half lugg-lands-breadth below. The farmer ſaid, 'twas very true, that in about three years ploughing 'twould be ſo, but not in one year, as he knew by experience; therefore the brows of the linchets are to be well dunged. *Of dunging linchets.* *Mold.*

This

This argues, to dung a linchet you must lay the heaps above it.

*Of dung-ing rye-grass.*

§. 71. Though I approve not of dunging French-grass, nor clover, for reasons given in another place, yet it is proper to dung rye-grass; for thereby the roots of it will tillow and mat the more on the ground, and will consequently occasion the greater destruction and suppression of the couch-grass.

## Of CHALK and chalking LANDS.

§. 72. Pliny tells of the custom of the Britons to chalk their lands to great improvement, which, he says, lasted their lives. lib. 17. c. 8.

*Different opinions about chalking.*

§. 73. It is said in general, that chalking is better for the father than the son; however, others agree, it is as good an improvement for twenty years as dung; and that the clay-land has been always the better for it.

*Chalk not to be ploughed in deep.*

§. 74. Farmer Farthing, farmer Wey, and divers others of the Isle of Wight, all agreed, that chalk should not be ploughed in too deep, but kept above ground as long as possible; for it would be apt enough of itself to sink down and be buried; on which farmer Farthing took occasion to say, that Col. Heming, in moring and grubbing up wood, had to his knowledge found whole beds of chalk, an half spit thick, half a yard or near a yard deep in the ground, which, without doubt, was nothing else but the chalk laid in the ground before it was made coppice; for the chalk was of that nature, that it would sink downwards till it became a bed of chalk: to this they all agreed, but seemed to talk of it, as if it sunk in whole bits and pieces; but I told them, the truth of the case could be no other than this; the rain washed continually the chalk off by a white water, the sediment of which, when it came to

the

the clay, there settled, and became a vein or bed of chalk, and then settled into a solid body: but in that solid body it did never sink, for that was impossible: chalk, however, by being ploughed in, without giving it time to waste, may perhaps be turned down and buried too deep, and being laid at the bottom of the furrow may not be ploughed up again.

§. 75. Chalk is not an improver to land in the same way as dung, which gives virtue to the land, and improves it by a fat, salt, nitrous quality, and by communicating to it the very principles of vegetation ; but chalk is rather an improver to land, as it is a great sweetener to sour land, but more especially as it opens the pores and particles of the land, and enables it to give up all it's strength, even till it is a caput mortuum ; so that chalk is not like dung, rich in it's own nature, but only mellows the land, so as to loosen the parts, thereby enabling every particle of it to communicate it's vegetative principle ; for which reason, it is true, that land abused by over-ploughing after chalking, or ploughed as long as it would carry corn, will be laid down to grass in a poorer condition than land can be when only dunged ; for it is almost impossible to draw out the goodness of such land, inasmuch as without chalk 'tis impossible to loosen it's parts, and unlock every clot, to let it's virtue fly out ; so that, properly speaking, chalk is rather a midwife to deliver the land of it's fruitfulness, than what gives the fruitful principles of vegetation to it.

§. 76. Chalk is commonly the greatest improvement of those lands that lie farthest from it ; because the lands that lie near it, partake and have too much of the nature of the chalk in them : they commonly lay twelve or fourteen loads of chalk upon an acre, where they lay it single, which will upon some lands cause extraordinary crops of corn for

*marginal notes:*
How chalk improves land.

Chalk improves most the land that lies farthest from it.

fourteen or fifteen years together; and, where 'tis laid on grafs-grounds, it will not fo much increafe the bulk of it, as it will make the grafs fweet, fo as to caufe cattle to fat fpeedily, and cows to give thick milk. J. Mortimer, Efq; F. R S. fo. 70.

In the Ifle of Wight they fometimes lay twenty-five waggon loads of chalk on an acre ; their chalk is of a fat foapy kind, and they call it marle. The farmers in the hundreds of Effex bring their chalk as far as from Gravefend, but lay not fo much on an acre by half as thofe in the Ifle of Wight.

Chalk, when to be laid on the ground.

§. 77. If chalk be dug out of the pit, and lie a fummer before it be fcattered, it will be fo hardened and dryed, that it will not eafily flat or diffolve ; therefore it fhould be dug at the beginning of winter, and laid on the ground forthwith ; it cannot however be fo well carried in winter, the days being fhort, and, being more fat and clammy at that feafon, you cannot load it fo faft as in fummer.

Chalk, an improvement to hot land.

§. 78. Mr. Worlidge in his art of gardening, fo. 13, fays, that you may deal with chalky-land as with clay-land, tho' in a moderate way ; for chalky land is naturally cold, and therefore requires warm applications ; · it is alfo fad, and will the better bear with light compofts, which is the reafon that chalk is fo great an improver of light, hot, and dry grounds, efpecially having fuffered a calcination.

Chalk finks thro' clay, and vice verfa.

§. 79. If chalk be laid on clay, it will in time be loft, and the ground again return to it's clay ; and if clay be laid on chalk, in time the clay will be loft, and the ground return again to it's chalky fubftance. Many people think the land, on which the other is laid for a manure, being predominant, converts the manure into it's own foil ; but I conceive in both cafes the chalk and clay is filtrated through the land on which 'tis laid by time, and, being foluble by rains into fmall corpufcles, is wafhed through the land on which 'tis laid ; for neither of

these

thefe manures is able to unite in it's fineft corpufcles with the corpufcles of the land on which it is
laid, fo as to make fo ftrict an union and texture
with it as the land doth with it's felf, and is therefore liable to be born downwards with rains, till no
fign of it be left.

§. 80. I was arguing with Dr. Heron how bene- Chalk on
ficial it was to chalk meadows, even in the hill- meadows.
country : he affured me, that fome of the notable
hufbandmen of Woodhay in Hampfhire had told
him, 'twas a common practice with tenants, three or
four years before they left their farms, to chalk their
meadows ; whereby 'tis true they would for three or
four years fling out a great crop of grafs, but then
they would be much the worfe for it ever after ; and
this feems to carry fome reafon with it ; for the
chalk fo mellows and opens the pores of the meadow,
that it enables the land to exhauft it's ftrength in all
parts : for chalk does not carry fo much fatnefs as
dung does to the land 'tis laid on ; but it difpofes
the land to bear fuch crops by it's fweetnefs, and
well difpofing of, and correcting an ill quality the
land had before : but ftill I fee not that this is any
objection to chalking of meadows, provided, whilft
by virtue of the chalk they are bearing fuch burthens, you fee they be refrefh'd with dung.

Though chalk laid on meadows enables them to Id. and on
give a great crop for three or four years, and will pafture.
then impoverifh them, yet I take it to hold quite
contrary in pafture ; for the grafs being thereby fo
much fweetened and increafed, keeps conftantly fo
much the more ftock, by which it is maintained always in the fame vigor.

§. 81. I do fuppofe that chalk laid on fandy, or Chalk good
wood-feary ground laid up for pafture, may wafh for fandy
and fink in, and fill up the interftices, and thereby and clay
confolidate and mend the texture of fuch ground, the reafon.
and fweeten it, as it is a great alkali ; and tho' by

E 2 time

time most of the chalk may be washed downwards so that the ground may lose the virtue, yet I do suppose the strength of the ground may still continue much the better, by reason that such manure having made the sword of the grass come thicker and sweeter, the good pasturage on both accounts enlarges the quantity, and betters the quality of dung the cattle leave on it, which in return maintains a better coat and surface to the ground : and as chalk fills up the vacuities of sandy, or wood-seary ground, so on the contrary, it insinuates it's particles into obstinate clayey and strong land, and divides it, by making in a manner a scissure, thereby hollowing and mellowing it ; so the two contrary extreams are cured by chalk.

**Chalk improves hop-clover and rye-grass.**

§. 82. Chalk laid on hop-clover and rye-grass is a mighty sweetener, and improver of those grasses, being laid upon it after harvest, at the beginning of winter, or whensoever one can best tend it ; it will quickly shew the benefit, especially if the ground be of a sour clay, and apt to run to coarse grass.

## Of LIME and liming LANDS.

§. 83. All sorts of flints will make an extraordinary lime, but they are hard to burn except in a reverberatory kiln, because they are apt ro run to glass.  Mortimer, fo. 70.

**Of a limekiln and burning lime in Leicestershire.**

§. 84. December 9th 1699, I went to Gracedieu, and discours'd with the person who rents the lime-kilns of Sir Ambrose Phillipps; and, two or three of his workmen being present, I with them took the measures of the kilns, which was $2\frac{1}{2}$ yards high from the very bottom to the top, one yard length-wise in the bottom, and two feet wide : they told me, that I must take care not to widen it too much at top, not exceeding two yards, by reason

of

of the greater confumption of coals; for the more gradual the widening is, the better : there was a layer of bricks run within-fide of the kiln, a-crofs, between the two vent-holes where they draw out the lime, for the better fupport of the lime from tumbling down too foon. They burnt with culm, or coal-flack, which they accounted as well, or better than the other coal, and cofts but 1 s. per load, whereas the fine coal would coft 6 s.——The kiln had five air-holes, two on each fide of the bottom, and two on each fide of the top, and one in the middle, of about a brick thicknefs wide ; the ftone is very hard, and they faid, three quarters of coal would only burn feven or eight quarters of lime ; the larger the kiln the more profitable. There was a ftone that laid the length of the kiln to keep up the walls from falling : the wall of the kiln againft the bank was but the thicknefs of a brick, but the oppofite fide a brick length in thicknefs. This kiln would burn twelve quarters of lime in twenty-four hours.

Farmer Farthing, (of the Ifle of Wight) when I view'd his lime-kiln, told me, I muft not fet up a kiln to burn above eighty quarters at a time; he burns but fixty ; that the kiln muft be made to belly like a ftone-mug, that the flame may be beat down by the narrownefs of the top, and check'd from flying out too faft. The kiln will be two days and two nights burning. The chalk muft be arch'd over the fire like an oven, and carefully laid, left it tumble in.—In his kiln, to burn fixty quarters he ufed to confume two hundred furze-faggots; but now, as a great improvement in the price of liming, he ufes peat in heating the kiln, and furze-faggots afterwards, and can heat his kiln with two thoufand of peat, and burn it off to lime with five hundred furze-faggots. Of their country peat, he fays, one may bring a thoufand in a waggon. Note, the defign of the peat (being a flack fire) is only to dry the

*Id. in the Ifle of Wight.*

the marle or chalk by degrees, in order for the furze-faggots to burn it off to lime; for if the fire be not flack and gentle, the chalk or marle drying too faft will fly, and the arch with the chalk fall down; therefore when they ufed all furze-faggots, and no peat, he ufed not to put the furzes at firft into the oven of the kiln, becaufe the fire would then be too fierce, but only put the ends lighted to the mouth of the oven, and flack'd the fire as he faw occafion, by it's beginning to fly, which was a great trouble, aad made a great wafte of the furzes, whereas the peat is all put into the oven. When the kiln is fit for the furzes to be lighted, one may try by feeing whether the marle or chalk will bear their blazing without flying, and, when the furzes are fet on fire, one may know when the lime is thoroughly made by the flame iffuing out at top; for the flame will break out of the kiln for three or four hours red; but when the topmoft chalk is lime (and then of courfe the undermoft is fo) the flame will be pale, like the flame of a candle. He thinks what I make lime of, being chalk, and not a chalky marle, as theirs is, may be perfected with lefs fuel than theirs, which is of a moift nature.—As foon as ever it is burnt he carries it out, and, when it is flack'd, fpreads it. It muft be carried out, though never fo wet, otherwife it will give with wet weather, and run together to a plaifter, that it cannot be dug up without great difficulty with mattocks; this muft be done, though it is very troublefome to remove it in wet weather; for it will burn the mens hands, and blifter them. He lays a bufhel and half on a lugg-fquare, which is about thirty quarters on an acre. It muft be fpread the firft ftill day, as foon as flacked, and very carefully, for in the true fpread-ing of it is a great advantage, and ftirr'd fhallow in. —Two men muft attend the burning, who have each 12 d. per day, and 12 d. per-night, and victuals.

the

the man who lays the chalk in has 2 s. 6 d. for doing
it.—Quære, If bean-stalks well dry'd may not make
a fire as good as furze.—I was afterwards telling
Mr. Thomas Beach in Wilts, that I thought the
way of burning lime with peat not practicable with
them, because they made it of a hard stone, which
the peat could not work on : but he said, he was of
another opinion ; for in the north, he knew very
well, they burnt the iron-oar, and melted it with
peat ; therefore he was sure, 'twould be a fire strong
enough to burn the lime-stone.—Four or five hundred faggots less will burn a kiln, where the chalk
is dry ; therefore it is of consequence to have your
chalk dug a week before, that it may dry.

§. 85. Morris, my tenant in the Isle of Wight, *Lime to be plough'd in as soon as slatted.*
and brick-burner, who came to burn lime for me,
assures me, that in the island they have tried all sorts
of ways of burning lime, and using it ; and that by
experience they have found it the better way, when
they have covered the heaps of lime with earth, to
plough it in, and spurn or spread it immediately as
soon as it is slatted fit for spurning, rather than to
let it lie long covered with the earth in heaps ; and
that the best way of all, they have found, is, not
to carry it out into the field till the third earth that
they plough for sowing their wheat, and then on the
first slatting they have spurned it ; and, tho' the
ploughing-in in such case has burnt the hair off their
horses heels, yet it has not hurt the wheat, but
they have then had the best wheat. — Note, I do
judge the letting the lime lie in heaps, mixt with
heaps of earth, for a long time, in Somersetshire,
&c. is because the fallows will not work fine
enough without being long exposed to the sun, and,
if so, the lime would not be well dispersed, to the
great disadvantage of the ground ; but, in lands
working mellow, I am of Morris's opinion.

§. 86. I burnt a kiln of lime to a greater degree than ordinary, so that the bricks were all glazed, and in making and wetting up the lime I particularly observed the water, as soon as flung on, to boil and dance more than ordinary, and the lime to heave more, and in bulk the mortar (tho' the content of lime in bushels was the same) was much bigger: I observed it to the masons, who seemed much pleased with the goodness of the lime. —— On which one of the labourers observed, that the case of lime was the same as of bread-corn; for as the drier the wheat is, the flour of such corn takes up the more water, and plimbs the more, and makes more bread in bulk, both lighter and hollower, (whereas the flour of cold damp wheat heaves not with the water, drinks little water, and makes heavy bread) so my lime, being higher burnt, took more water, plimb'd into a greater bulk, and would be mellower and lighter under the trowel; and so all the masons agreed.

§. 87. When I told a gentleman, used to lime-burning in Wiltshire, that in the Isle of Wight they used to burn off a kiln of eighty quarters of lime at a time, he wondered at it; saying, how could they be assured to get it out before rain came, for I, that burn but a little, am forced to get a cover to keep out the rain, lest the lime when made should by rain fall into a plaister.

§. 88. Slack-lime cannot be so beneficially laid on land as stone-lime; because a greater virtue must be attributed to the stone-lime for it's burning quality after it is laid on.

Lime not
so good for
meadow
and pas-
ture as for
arable.

§. 89. Lime being laid on meadows or pastures slacks and cools by slow degrees, so as not to undergo such a heat and fermentation, as when it is covered with the hillocks of earth flung up in arable; therefore it cannot be of that great advantage to pasture.

§. 60. Worlidge

§. 90. Worlidge says, fo. 242. A mixture of lime is very good in most grounds ; but the salt of limes extracted by water, and your ground watered therewith, is much to be preferred : it hath also this singular property, that it makes the worms soon leave the place so watered.

*Salt of lime extracted by water commended.*

§. 91. In Wiltshire they lay twenty-four or thirty quarters of lime on an acre, as the ground is.——— But at Winterhays, and thereabouts in Dorsetshire, they never lay above twenty hogsheads on an acre, every hogshead is four bushels.———The lighter the land is the more lime it will require, the stronger the less.

*Quantity of lime on an acre.*

§. 92. In Leicestershire they sow or scatter the lime on wheat-land when they sow the wheat, but on barley-land the last earth save one ; and so plough it in, lest, if they should sow it with the barley in the spring, it might burn it. They lay five quarters on an acre of each, according to the measure as it comes from the kiln, for after it is slack'd those five quarters will near make ten.

*When to scatter lime on wheat and barley, and what quantity.*

§. 93. Liming of land being to bind it, it seems to me, land should not be limed late in the year, no more than building should go on then ; because, the land being then cold and moist, and but a weak sun to consolidate it, the end of liming is lost ; for if it consolidate not at first liming, it will not afterwards.

*Time of liming land.*

§. 94. Farmer Wey and others say, in the Isle of Wight they have a practice (which is the easiest way, in case a bushel of lime be laid in a lugg-square) when a bushel of lime is laid down, and the cart going, to tie a piece of leather to the spoke, and when that goes just round, it measures a lugg ; for the compass of a cart wheel is a lugg, that is $16\frac{1}{2}$ feet : and, if you would lay it in a lugg and half, you may manage it accordingly.

*Of scattering lime.*

§ 95 Mr.

§. 95. Mr. Taunton of Dorſetſhire, in form of a bill for work, gave me the following account of the method and prices of liming ; (the prices I think extravagant) viz. For covering an acre of lime, 1 s. 8 d.— Covering is when the lime is firſt laid on the land, it may be a peck in a place, and ſo covered over with earth.—For turning an acre of lime, 2 s. 6 d.— Turning is mixing the earth and lime together.— For ſpurning an acre of lime, 2 s. 8 d.— Spurning is throwing it abroad on the earth juſt before ſowed.—For hacking an acre of lime, 1 s. 6 d.— Hacking is breaking the clots abroad after 'tis ſown.— For ſhoveling the furrows of an acre of lime, 8 d. — Shoveling is the cleanſing the furrows, and throwing it on the land.— 9 s. per acre.

§. 96. I aſk'd Mr. Clerk about the method of liming about Loughborough ; he ſaid, they laid on their grounds they laid up to graſs forty buſhels per acre about the beginning of October, and on their arable lands the ſame meaſure ; their way is, as the cart goes along the ground, to fling it over with

ſhovels, and to ſpread it thin. It ſeems it has been very hurtful to their graſs-ground in rotting their ſheep in wet years; for it has proved the graſs ſo faſt, as to rot the ſheep.—— I ſuppoſed the lands were ſubject to rot before, or elſe the lime would not have ſubjected them to it ; but Mr. Clerk ſaid, no, that the lands were high up-land downy grounds, never ſubject to the rot before ; and that many men in that country had proved it to their ſad experience ; and, ſince they had found it, their way was to remove ſuch ſheep in a wet ſummer out of ſuch grounds, and put others in. Note, the lime in this country is ſtrong : Mr. Cheſtlin is of the ſame opinion.

Mr. Cheſtlin of Leiceſterſhire ſays, he pays but 12 d. per quarter for his ſtone-lime, and fetches it two miles ; he lays fifty buſhels on an acre, becauſe his is colder moiſter land than his neighbours.—

He

He fays, as it binds fandy ground, fo it mellows and
flats cold and clay-land. He can with a dung-pot
and two men fhovel it on about an acre and half
per day. He fays, he has had a fill-horfe's black
coat burnt red with it; if it be wet weather when
they fpread it out of the dung-pots, they cover their
horfes with old hammock-cloths, and yet it will
burn them very much. —— Mr. Bowly fays, he never lays above forty bufhels on an acre, but that
forty when flack'd will be near eighty; if it lies out
in the weather any little time, to have the dews or a
fhower of rain, it will flack of itfelf, but if they fetch
it and lay it on their grounds directly, then they
flack it with water ——— He thinks lime fhews not
it's full ftrength and power till the third crop. One
may over-lime; for where the lime is laid in heaps
in the field before fpreading or fpurning it, there
will feldom grow any corn for a year or two. — He
fays, they generally fow the lime on the ground, and
then the wheat, and then turn it in under furrow:
but in fowing it with barley, they generally fow it
the laft earth fave one, and turn it in, and then
give the laft earth for fowing the barley; but, if
they fow with a wheaten crop, and then lay down to
grafs, they fow the wheat on the ploughed land,
and harrow it in, and then fow the lime, and harrow it in, in order to lay it down fmooth to grafs;
for if they fhould harrow the lime in firft, and fow
their wheat, they would not in the fecond harrowing it be able to bury it, the ground would be fo fine.

§. 97. A very underftanding hufbandman of
Shropfhire coming to me at Sir Ambrofe Phillipps's,
I afked him, whether his was as deep a country as
Leicefterfhire: he faid, it was. I afked him, if
they ufed liming; he faid, they did, and on enquiry
I found the method in all refpects agreed with the
Leicefterfhire manner, faving that they laid dung
and lime together, viz. about twenty load of dung,

Method of
liming in
Shropfhire.

and

and but twenty bushels of lime on an acre. In the wheaten crop they ploughed in the dung the last fallow before sowing, and before the sowing the wheat sowed lime. — They fetched the lime fourteen miles on horses backs, because in their deep country the carts could not so well go : it was a stone-lime, not a chalk. He said, it cost at the kiln 3 d. per bushel, therefore with the carriage it must be very dear.

**Of over-ploughing after liming.** §. 98. I deliver it as a rule to all husbandmen to be cautious of liming ground, and then ploughing out the heart of it. I limed some years ago in Wiltshire seven acres for an experiment, and laid down one acre to it's own natural grass in two years time, the grass of which is to this day worth 40 s. an acre. The third year I laid down another acre, which is to this day worth 30 s. per acre. The rest I ploughed five or six years farther, which is not worth fifteen groats per acre. The like experience I have had in burn-beaking ground.

**Of harrowing the ground fine before liming.** §. 99. Farmer Farthing, farmer Wey, and F. Loving of the Isle of Wight, told me, that if, after I fallowed, before I plough'd my lime in, I dragg'd or harrow'd the ground fine, the lime would mix much the better with the earth, and it would answer that charge very well.

**Lime good for sandy ground.** §. 100. If we try the experiment, we shall soon find it very visible, that lime agrees with sandy ground by it's binding quality ; and the like observation may be taken from the mortar commonly made of these two ingredients [s]

Of

[s] Of liming from Mr. Du Hamel, a French author. Vol. 3. edit. 1754. p. 48. to 57.

Lime is used chiefly on fresh broke up lands ; after having plough'd them up not very deep, they lay on the lime in the manner following.

They carry on the lime as it comes from the kiln ; and lay about one hundred pound weight in a heap on every square perch ; so that the heaps lie at a perch distance one from another,

## Of BURN-BEAKING.

§. 101. Worlidge, fo. 234, says—In the burn-beaking of land the rustic observes, that over-burning the turf is injurious, and that a more moderate burning makes the ground more fertile. The reason is plain ; for in the burning any vegetable, a gentle,

ther ; then they raise the earth all round the heaps in form of so many basins ; the earth that forms the sides of these basins should be a foot thick ; and lastly, they cover the heaps, half a foot thick, with earth, in form of a dome. The lime slacks under this covering of earth, and is reduced to powder ; but then it increases in bulk, and cracks the covering of earth ; if you do not carefully stop these cracks, the rain will insinuate itself, and reduce the lime into a paste which will not mix well with the earth, or make a sort of mortar, which will not answer the end proposed. The farmers therefore are very careful to examine the heaps from time to time and stop the cracks : some only press the top of the heaps with the back of a shovel ; but this practice is subject to an inconvenience, for if the lime is in a paste within the heap, by this means you beat it so together that it will not easily mix with the earth ; wherefore it is better to stop the chinks by throwing some fresh earth over the heap.

When the lime is thoroughly slack'd, and reduced to powder, they cut the heaps with a shovel, and mix the lime as well as possible with the earth that covered it, and then having thrown it up in heaps again, leave it exposed to the air for six weeks or two months ; for then the rain will do no harm.

About the month of June they spread this mixture of lime and earth upon the land ; but not all over as may happen ; on the contrary they take it up by shovelfulls, and distribute it in little heaps at equal distances on each perch of land ; they observe that these little heaps promote vegetation more than if it was spread uniformly all over the field, and they don't mind leaving little intervals unlimed between each shovelfull. Afterwards they plough the field, for the last time, very deep : then towards the end of June they sow buck-wheat, and cover it with the harrow, and if any heaps remain break them with a hoe.

Buck-wheat occupies the land about one hundred days ; so that this grain sown about the end of June is gathered about the end of September.

When the stalks and roots of this plant are dead and dried, they plough it up, and immediately sow wheat and cover it with the harrow.

About

gentle, easy, and smothering fire doth not waste the volatile nitrous spirit so much as a quick fire would do, and causeth more of it to fix and remain behind.

§. 102. Where much long moss grows thick, tho' the ground be never so sandy in it's nature, yet the ground underneath must be of a most cold and sour nature by being kept from the sun, and the wet more sogging in it than if it had been solid earth upon it ; for nothing retains water longer than such a spungy body, nor breaks the rays of the sun more from penetrating. Therefore such ground ought to be burn-beak'd, or the moss harrowed up before seeding, and burnt in heaps, but rather burn-beak'd to destroy the seeds.

§. 103. Quære, in burn-beak'd ground what weeds or plants appear the first year, because according-
ing

*Of burn-beaking mossy ground.*

About the month of July or August, after the wheat crop, they plough as soon as possible ; they plough for the last time in February or March in order to sow oats, or in April for barley, but in this case they stir the land two or three times to make it fine.

They harrow in all these different grains, and when they are come up they pass a roller over the oats, and if there remain any clods in the barley they break them with a hoe.

The next February or March they sow grey peas or vetches.

After the harvest of these pulse, they give one or two ploughings to prepare the land for wheat the ensuing autumn.

The year after they sow oats mixt with clover, and then lay it down to pasture for three or four years.

In some new broke up lands they sow no buck-wheat, but let it lie fallow from the month of March when it was first broken up, till October, when they sow it with wheat ; making use of the intermediate time to give it several ploughings ; these lands by this means being much finer, they use little more than three fourths of the quantity of lime above prescribed, and generally have a better crop than when they begin with buck-wheat.

Some farmers think a perch too great a distance for the convenience of spreading the lime; therefore they make the heaps less, and increase the number in proportion. Being persuaded that lime is most efficacious when near the surface, they first plough it in, and then give it a second ploughing before they sow, by which means the lime lies chiefly near their face.

Others lay the lime in a ridge from one end of the field to the other ; this disposition is the least trouble to spread.

ing to Mr. Bobart of the physic garden at Oxford, their seeds are destroyed ; only some few may be supposed to have lain deeper than the fire went into the earth [t].

## PLOUGH and CART-TACKLE.

§. 1. MR. Baily (who had many times set his Of differ-own hand to the plough, and got ent kinds of 200 l. per annum, from a small beginning by it) and ploughs. I were talking about the different varieties of ploughs

[t] The following is an extract from Mr. Du Hamel's account of burn-beaking in France, which I have here inserted, hoping it might be of use to the reader.

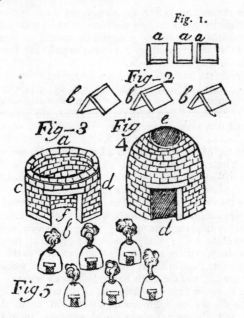

*Fig.* 1.

## Of BURN-BEAKING.

With regard to lands which are ploughed up but once in eight Page 75— or ten years, it is the custom to burn them, to the end that the　83. fire

ploughs in different countries, and I asked him, wherein he thought a two-wheel plough had the advantage of a foot plough, or a plough without wheels. He said, he knew of no other use of a two-wheel plough, but that the ploughman could keep it more steady in stony-lands, so that every jolt should

---

fire may divide the particles of the earth, and that it may be fertilised by the ashes of the roots and leaves. This is the method of the operation.

They raise the surface with a hoe or crooked pickax, the iron of which is very broad and thin, cutting each turf as regular as possible in the form (a. a. a. fig. 1.) about eight or ten inches square, and two or three inches thick.

As soon as these turfs are cut, they employ women to pile them one against another, with the grass side inward in the manner (b. b. b. fig. 2.)

When the weather is fine, the air will dry them in a couple of days, sufficiently for making the furnaces and burning them; but, if it should prove rainy, you must be careful to turn the turfs, for they must be well dry'd, before you make the furnaces, of which we are going to speak.

In forming the furnaces, they begin by raising a sort of cilindric tower (a. b.) of * *one foot* diameter (c. d. fig. 3.) as the walls of this little tower are made of the turfs, their size determines the thickness; but in building them they always lay the grass downwards, and they make a door on the windward side, of a foot wide.

On the top of this door they lay a large piece of wood, which serves as a lintel. Then they fill all the inside with small dry wood mixt with straw; and finish the furnace by making a vault of the same turfs, like the top of an oven.

Before the vault is entirely finished, they light the wood that fills the furnace; then they quickly shut the door (d.) with turfs, and finish by stopping the opening (e. fig 4.) which was left at the top of the vault; taking care to lay turfs on all the places where the smoke comes out too plentifully, exactly as the charcoal-makers do; for without that precaution, the wood will consume too fast, and the earth be not sufficiently burnt.

If you cover the furnaces with earth, all the crevices being too closely stop'd, the fire will be extinguished; but, as you use only turfs, and always put the grass downwards, there is air enough to keep the fire burning.

* This must be a mistake, I suppose three or four feet may be a convenient size, as may be judged from the figure.

When

should not fling it out of it's work; for it stands to reason that the wheels cannot be so easily jostled off, as the plough might be without wheels : for the outward wheel goes in a seam, and is kept in by the whole land; for the same reason, in hill-country-lands, where one ploughs along the side of a hill, any jolt would be apt to lift a plough without wheels out of it's furrow towards the declivious ground. — I asked him, wherein he conceived the advantage of a plough

When all the furnaces are made, the field seems covered with little hay-cocks ranged in quincunx's (fig. 5.) but you must watch the furnaces till the earth is red hot; to stop with turfs any cracks that may happen ; to repair such as may be in danger of falling, and to light again such as may be extinguished. When the earth seems all on fire they want no further care ; even rain itself, tho' before much to be feared, will not hinder their being sufficiently burnt; so you have nothing more to do but to let them go out of themselves.

At the end of twenty-four or twenty-eight hours, when the fire is extinct, all the heaps are reduced to powder, except some of the tops which will remain not sufficiently burnt, they not being enough exposed to the action of the fire ; and 'tis for this reason that we advise not to make the furnaces too big, because, the walls being proportionably thick, the turfs on the outside will not be done enough, when the inside is over-done ; for if you burn them like bricks it will not be fit for vegetation. Besides, in making large furnaces you will have too far to carry the turfs. You might even make them less ; but that would consume too much wood : thus you will find it necessary to conform pretty near to the proportions we have prescribed.

When the furnaces are cooled, they wait till it rains, and then spread the burnt earth as even as possible, leaving none on the spots where the furnaces stood, which nevertheless will produce finer grain than the rest of the field, for which reason they leave only such turfs as are not burnt enough on those spots.

They immediately plough it very lightly, to begin to mix the burnt earth with the surface; but they go deeper in the following ploughings.

If you can give the first ploughing in June, and rain follows, it is possible to reap some advantage from the land immediately, by sowing turnips, radishes or millet ; which will not prevent your sowing wheat or rye the autumn following.

Nevertheless it is better to lose the advantage of such a first crop, that you may have the whole time to prepare the land well for the reception of wheat.

a plough with one wheel to confift: he faid, in the fame points as the former; he knew of no other reafon for ufing them.

Of profciffion.

§. 2. In the Ifle of Harries, &c. the way of tillage is commonly by ploughing, and fometimes by digging; the ordinary plough is drawn by four horfes; and they have a little plough there commonly called a riftle, i. e. a thing that cleaves, the coulter of which is in form of a fickle: it is drawn fometimes by one, and fometimes by two horfes, according as the ground is: the defign of this plough is to draw a deep line in the ground, to make it more eafy for the great plough to follow, which otherwife would be much retarded by the ftrong roots of bent lying deep in the ground, that are cut by the little plough: the little plough is ufed alfo to facilitate digging as well as ploughing. Martin, fo. 34. ―― This was alfo a common method ufed amongft the Romans, where the foil would allow of it. But it feems not practicable in ftony and flinty lands, but without doubt in deep lands is good hufbandry, and enables the ploughman to turn up the fallow in an exact and beautiful manner: I wonder thefe bar-
barous

---

Some choofe to fow rye rather than wheat, becaufe the firft production being very vigorous, wheat is more apt to be laid than rye.

Some do not fpread the burnt earth till juft before the laft ploughing for wheat; they content themfelves with ploughing well between the furnaces, which they take care to fet exactly in a line, in order to leave a free paffage for the plough. But this is a bad method; for, fince wheat is always apt to be laid the firft year after burning, it is better to fpread the burnt earth early before it lofes part of it's heat, and for the convenience of well preparing the land; for it is very material that the burnt earth fhould be perfectly well mixt with the foil.

It muft be owned that this method of burning is very expenfive, becaufe the labour muft be performed by men, and that it confumes a great deal of wood; but it is very advantageous, for after this fingle operation, the land is better prepared than it would be by many ploughings.

See

barous iflanders fhould have it in ufe, and not we in
in England [a]. [b] The Romans in rich ground, that
was apt to detain the wet, ufed this cutting plough,
or what they called profciffion, in fpring, after the
weeds were all come up, and before the feeds were
ripened.

§. 3. I find in Leicefterfhire they ufe Danifh
iron in all plough-tackle and horfe-fhoes, except
the coulters and the plough-fhares, which are Englifh iron. They hold the Danifh iron to be more
durable, and tougher than the Englifh iron, which
they cannot work fo well, as being much brittler,
and wearing fafter : they can in Leicefterfhire afford
the Danifh as cheap as the Englifh iron.—I afked
the Loughborough fmith, if Danifh iron would
make wheel-tire, he faid care muft be taken that
the fmith puts not in iron rank with fteel, for
then 'twill break prefently; but by breaking a bar
before 'tis ufed the fmith will know it.

*Of the forts of iron ufed in plough-ing-tackle.*

§. 4. It is much the intereft of a gentleman to
agree with the fmith for his plough-irons by the
great; for it is impoffible fuch a perfon fhould
watch his fervants, fo as to fee that they fent to the
fmith fuch fhares and coulters only, as were worn
out, or to take an account how often; whereas fervants are apt before there is occafion, or the irons
are worn out, confulting their own and their horfes
eafe, to fend them to the fmith, who fets down the
fame price as if the irons had been quite worn out :
fo that if fervants and fmith be left to themfelves,
irons fhall come again no better than they were
when they were fent.

*Agree with the fmith by the great.*

[a] See Pliny fo. 291, 294.—Pallad. fo. 94 to 98.—Varro,
book 1ft, fo. 37. Of profciffion.

[b] Pingues campi, qui diutius continent aquam, profcindendi
funt anni tempore jam incalefcente, cum omnes herbas ediderint,
neque adhuc earum femina maturuerint. Columella, lib. 2. fo.
99.—Of feveral new invented ploughs and their conftruction,
fee Mr. Tull's book of horfe-hoeing hufbandry.

§. 5. The

On keep-
ing the
irons in
order.

§. 5. The better order you keep your irons in, the easier it is to the man that holds the sull, and the easier to the horses that plough : the longer the point of your share is, the more steady does it go, and carries an evener furrow.

Of keeping
a spare
coulter and
share.

§. 6. I take care to have a spare coulter and share always by me, which is in readiness, whilst the worn-out one might be sent to the smith to be new pointed ; and this I do, because I expect the smith himself, and not his man, should have the pointing of it ; for I depend on him for the well hardening it, which could not be, if I sent the worn-out one over-night to have it the next morning ; I must then take who could be found, either master or man. Add also, that such coulter will be much the harder for lying by two or three days before used.

Old iron
bands on
new wheels
ill husban-
dry.

§. 7. To put old iron bands on new wheels is very ill husbandry, for the wood must necessarily wear out presently, the iron not being broad enough to save it.

Of mak-
ing the
bands to
wheels.

§. 8. An old Nottingham smith told me, it was much the durablest way to turn up the edges of the bands to wheels, which adds to the thickness of the edgings, and is the main security to the bands ; for in the edgings they wear away first ; but, for their own interest, wheel-wrights will pretend there is no advantage in it ; yet where the edgings are not turn-ed up, in the using the edges shall be worn away, and the fillies so worn, that the spokes shall be ready to start out of their sockets, when the timber in other respects shall be very sound. The smith said, the making them so was a penny in a stone diffe-rence to him.

Split ash
good to
make fil-
lies.

§. 9. Note, for fillies, ash that will split is with us thought fittest, and much the strongest; but the arms of an ash-tree are commonly put in, if they be not too frowe, and they must be saw'd, and the bo-dy of an ash likewise if it be knotty ; because that
will

will not split ; yet, becaufe fuch fillies are faw'd crofs the grain, they are not like to be durable.

§. 10. Farmer Farthing, Wey, and Loving of the Ifle of Wight, all affure me, that elm fillies are beft for wheels, efpecially in deep ways, where the waggon fways, and only fuch they ufe in the Ifle of Wight : for they will not crack with the nails being drove into them, as the afhen will ; but we at Crux-Eafton, &c. ufe only afhen ones ; but I fuppofe the reafon is, becaufe elm grows not in the hill-country, and I the rather think fo, becaufe below the hill, where elm grows, they all ufe elm fillies. *Elm good for fillies.*

§. 11. If the farmers boarded their waggons in Hampfhire, as they do in Hertfordfhire, the price of the boards would be gained in one harveft by faving the droppings of the corn. *Of boarding waggons.*

§. 12. It is found by experience, that tying the fide-boards to the raths of the waggon with leather thongs greafed, is much better and more lafting than nailing them, becaufe the heads of the nails are continually breaking out by the fhaking of the waggon, &c. *Of tying on the fide-boards of waggons.*

§. 13. It is a vaft damage waggons receive in winter by lying abroad : when they are wet the froft cracks the wood. *Of houfing waggons.*

§. 14. Every body grows weary of chequer-harnefs ; for tho' it looks pretty at firft, yet it foon flies to pieces : chequer-harnefs is that which is work'd up with thongs. —— The cheapeft way is to work up the harnefs at ones own houfe ; the harnefs-maker has but 1 s. per day and diet, you finding the ftuff ; in fuch cafe you muft provide three or four bull-hides two or three years before, and put them out to dreffing to the collar-maker ; the dreffing commonly cofts as much as the hide is worth, be it bigger or lefs ; when hides hold a pretty good price, a fmall bull's hide is worth 12 s. and it is common for the currier to drefs one half for the other ; when thefe hides are drefs'd they'll take no harm *Of harnefs, and the cheapeft way of making it.*

F 3

harm for four or five years if kept dry, as suppose laid on the ground under the beds that lie on it; tho' it is said that is rather too dry. —— A bull's hide should never be used by the shoe-maker, nor a cow's hide by the collar-maker, there being a statute that provides in that case, tho' not strictly observed.— A careful and good farmer in my neighbourhood keeps bull-hides always by him, and uses them on all occasions about his harness in mending it, unless for sewing-thongs, and there must be white leather, but otherwise the bull-hide is always best. —— The common price for a horse-hide undrest is 5 s. and the dressing 5 s. If the eyes of the plough-traces are lined with leather, (which is good husbandry, to save them from fretting out) such lining costs no more than hempen traces.

The halters and cruppers and back-bands should be made of bull-hide, the belly-bands of heifer-hide, double-lined with horse-hide; the fill-hangs of horse-hide, the rigg-rope of white leather, that, is horse-hide; the pipes of the back and the collars of the belly of bull-hide. If the leather be not well tawed, that is, dress'd thoroughly with allum and salt, it will have a raw black seam run throughout, which, when it grows dry, will be hard and horny, and crack in bending; whereas, what is dress'd kindly, is like buff, soft, and one may blow thro' it. Few harness-makers, that are white tawers, understand how to dress their hides, but have them of the glovers or felmongers, and such can less answer for their goods. Such leather as is white tawed, is never tann'd: of my set of harness only the pipes and collars pass'd through the tanner's hands. With good usage they may last a dozen years, and wet weather will not damage them, if well drest, and made according to the above directions; but great care must be taken not to hang them against a plaister wall in the winter, that being the likeliest way to rot and spoil them.

§. 15. The

§. 15. The smith, carpenter, wheel-wright and har-ness-maker, may be said to be the landlords of those gentlemen who keep much husbandry in their hands.

# P L O U G H I N G.

§. 1.    THE ancient writers on husbandry lay a Of pulve-very great stress on making the ground ration. fine by frequent ploughings. [a] It is adviseable, says Pliny, in strong land, such as we generally have in Italy, to plough five earths, but in Tuscany nine earths ; [b] and Virgil, adds he, is supposed to have prescribed four earths, or two summer and two winter ploughings, by the rule he lays down in his first Georgic.

> Illa seges demum votis respondet avari
> Agricolæ, bis quæ solem, bis frigora sensit.

[c] It was the constant maxim indeed among the Roman farmers, that they could not give their ground too much tillage : and, if a field required harrowing after the seed was sown, it was a sign, with them, that such field had not been sufficiently ploughed. Land, say their authors, especially if it be of a rich nature, and that is apt to hold water, ought to be turned up so often, and reduced to so fine a powder, that the track of the plough-share may

---

[a] Spissius solum, sicut plerumque in Italia, quinto sulco melius seri est, in Tuscis verò nono. Plin.

[b] Quarto seri sulco Virgilius existimatur voluisse, cum dixit optimam esse segetem, quæ bis solem, bis frigora sensisset. Plin.

[c] Malè aratur arvum, quod satis frugibus occandum est ; id demum rectè subactum erit, ubi non intelligetur utro vomer ierit. —Pingues campi, qui diutius continent aquam tam frequentibus densisque sulcis arandi sunt, ut vix dignoscatur in utram partem vomer actus sit ; quandoquidem sic omnes radices herbarum perruptæ necantur : sed et compluribus iterationibus sic resolvatur vervactum in pulverem, ut vel nullam, vel exiguam deside-ret occationem, cum seminaverimus ; nam veteres Romani dixe-runt malè subactum agrum, qui satis frugibus occandus sit. Co-lumel. lib. 2. fol. 99.

hardly

hardly be diftinguifhable in it ; for by this methcd
the roots of all weeds will be torn in pieces, and
deftroyed.

Among the moderns Mr. Ray affigns feveral reafons for making land fine ᵈ and mellow before it is
fown. It is beneficial, fays he, that the nitrous particles of the air, which chiefly promote vegetation,
may infinuate themfelves more freely and in greater
quantity thro' the cracks and interftices of the land,
and there be precipitated and adhere to it ; perhaps
the rain water alfo may be of ufe in diffolving thofe
falts, which they carry with them into the pores of
plants. Befides, the water finks more eafily thro'
light loofe earth, fo that the roots are in lefs danger
of being fuffocated by too much moifture, or of being corrupted and killed by too much cold ; and
there is this farther advantage in it, that by letting
the air more plentifully into the air-veffels of the
roots, it gives them a freer refpiration, which we
have already fhewn is not lefs neceffary to plants
than animals.—Mr. Evelyn explodes thofe, who
fancy the turning and ploughing land frequently in
the winter, before it is employed for a crop, caufes
it to exhale, and fpend the virtue it fhould retain,
there being in truth no compoft or lætation com-
parable to this continual motion : it evaporates the
malignant halitus and impurities of the imprifoned
air, laxing the parts, and giving eafy deliverance to
it's offspring. Thefe feminal falts and rudiments,
wherever

Tum ut particulæ aeris nitrofæ, quibus præcipuè vegetatio
promovetur, in terreni interftitia liberius et copiofius fe infinuan-
tes ibidem præcipitentur, et terreno adhærefcant : quin et aquæ
pluviæ fortaffe ad falium folutionem conducunt, quos fecum unà
in radicum poros convehunt : præterea in terra laxa et foluta
aquæ promptius fubfidunt, adeoque nec humore nimio radices
fuffocant, nec frigore corrumpunt : præterea terra laxá et foluta
ad hoc conducit, ut aer copiofior radicum tracheas fubeat, ad
refpirationis ufum, quam plantis non minus neceffariam effe quam
animalibus oftendimus. Ray, fol. 33.

wherever latent, are free to move and exert their virtue, when these chains and weights, which fetter and depress them, are taken off. He ascribes more benefit to often opening, stirring, and ventilating the earth, than to dunging.

But if to pulverize and grind the ground was the only end of ploughing, without any regard to the taking in the corporeal emanations of the sun, a frosty winter fallow would chasten the earth, and make it as fryable as a summer one: but the difference is vastly great; for the sun improves the earth more than dung does. — As fire in lime, or burn-beaking, raises and fixes the salts, so does the sun, which is a fire; therefore the more you let the sun into the ground by ploughing, the greater the benefit.

In Asia and the hot countries their corn does not burn up, but is able to come out of the ground, which in England it would not do, if we had their hot weather. This seems to be owing to the mighty fineness to which their ground is reducible by the plough, they having such dry seasons for fallowings and stirrings, whereby their ground falls much closer than ours, and does not gape by the heat, but, by reason of it's mellow parts, drinks in abundance of the dews, which our land, less fryable, does not, and which dews, in great probability, fall more with them than with us.

§. 2. ᵉ The method among the ancients of plough-ing from one tilt to another is laid down by Colu-mella

The order of fallow-ing among the an-cients.

ᵉ Uliginosi campi proscindi debent post idus mensis Aprilis; quo tempore cum arati fuerint, diebus interpositis, circa solstitium, quòd est nono vel octavo calendarum Juliarum, iteratos esse oportebit: ac deinde circa Septembris calendas tertiatos: sed quandocunque arabitur, observabimus, ne lutosus ager tractetur, neve exiguis nimbis semimadidus, quam terram rustici variam, cariosamque appellant; ea est cum post longas siccitates levis pluvia superiorem partem glebarum madefacit, inferiorum
non

mella as follows : Lands that are inclined to be
moist ought to be first broken up from about the
middle to the latter end of April, and, after this
first ploughing, to lie still towards the latter end of
June, or about the time of the summer solstice,
when they are to be ploughed a second time, and
about the beginning of September they are to receive
their third ploughing : but it is better to omit either or all these ploughings, than to turn up the
ground, when it is wet and in mortar, or even when
the upper part of it, after a long dry season, has
been wetted by sudden small showers, which have
not sunk deep into it; for, if you plough up the
ground when in a wet and dawby condition, there
will be no meddling with it again for the whole
year, but it must lie useless ; and, if you plough it
up when the surface only has been thus wetted, it
will be barren for three years afterwards. The best
season for ploughing is, when the ground is in a
moderate temperament, neither very wet, nor very
dry; for by too much moisture, as I said before, it
will cling together, and be like mortar, and, after a
long drought, tho' a little moistened at top, the
plough-share will either not be able to penetrate it,
and be continually thrown off by the hardness of
the earth, or, if it should penetrate it, it will not

non attingit ; nam quando limosa versantur arva, toto anno de-
sinunt posse tractari, nec sunt habilia sementi, aut occationi, aut
iationi : at rursus quæ varia subacta sunt, continuo triennio steri-
litate afficiuntur, mediam igitur temperamentum maxime sequa-
mur in arandis agris, ut neque succo careant, nec abundant uli-
gine ; quippe nimius humor, ut dixi, limosos, lutososque reddit,
at qui siccitatibus aruerunt, expediri probe non possunt, nam vel
respuitur duritiâ soli dens aratri, vel siquâ parte penetravit, non
minute diffindit humum, sed vastos cespites convellit, quibus ob-
jacentibus impeditum arvum minus recte possit iterari : quo
evenit ut in iteratione quoque scamna fiant. Accedit huc, quod
omnis humus quamvis lætissima, tamen inferiorem partem je-
juniorem habet. Columella, lib. 2. fol. 99.

make

make it fine, but turn it up in large clods, which will be a continual hindrance to you at it's next ploughing, and at laft be left unbroken and in lumps on the field. Add to this, that even in rich foils, the part that lies deepeft is always the moft barren.

§. 3. One great reafon of a fummer-fallowing's enriching all ground feems to me to be, becaufe the fteams and vapours of the earth, which lie beneath the turf and furrow ploughed up, are, in the fummer-time, conftantly exhaling upwards, which being ftopp'd and retarded by the furrow, and lodged in the caverns, are, after evaporation of the watery parts, by the fire of the fun, digefted into fixed falts; for the continuation of the channels or pores of perfpiration being broken by the furrow turned down, the effluviums are ftopped, and fix, as againft a cieling of a vault. *Summer-fallowing, caufe of the benefit of it.*

I fummer-fallowed the one half of a field in May and June for wheat; the other half I ploughed in September for winter vetches: the winter after I could obferve the half fowed to vetches very much over-run with geranium columbinum, but the wheaten part had not the tenth part of that weed, notwithftanding it's having been dunged for wheat. So much is owing to a fummer-fallow, which deftroys the weeds before feeding-time, whereas in the vetch ground the weeds had feeded before it was ploughed. That winter vetches prepare the earth for a barley-crop next year, is very much to be imputed to the fummer-fallow fuch ground may be fuppofed to have received the year the vetches were fown in it; and the dominion the vetches get over weeds the following fummer, by killing them, lays open the bare earth to the fun the fecond fummer alfo, which in a manner anfwers to two fummerfallows.

It.

It seems to me no small regard ought to be had to keep cold clay-ground from running out of tilt, in respect that when it is so, the natural grass so matts it, and it is so clung with the roots thereof, that the sun cannot easily penetrate, to cherish and ferment the juices into vegetable salts ; whereas, if you keep your ground knot-fine by summer-fallows, and clover-grass, which gets dominion over the natural grass, and plough it up before it runs to a sword, the ground will be loose and open, and easily penetrable by the sun, rain, and air, whereby it will be capable of being impregnated much more with those salts.

**Not to summer-fallow when wet.** §. 4. On sound experience I am thoroughly confirmed, that no land, especially clayey, ought to be summer-fallowed, when it is the least heavy by wet, in order to prepare it for spring-corn the spring following ; for, tho' the ground may work mellow enough, as to the temper of the earth, having the summer's sun to shine on it, yet, being ploughed wet or heavy, the grass will grow so as to clod it together, and so matt the earth, that it will plough too rough in the spring to sow spring-corn at once ploughing.——It is the same, in case strong land or sworded land be winter-fallowed wet, or stiff, and heavy, in order to prepare it for stirring the next summer for a wheaten crop ; it will turn up monstrous stiff and rough : in both cases you give away your first labour.

## Of FALLOWING.

I summer-fallowed a field when one part was burning-dry, the other part very dry also, but yet moister than the former ; at Michaelmass that part which had been ploughed burning-dry had ten times more weeds come up in it than the other ; from whence I infer, that the dryer you fallow still

the

the better to deſtroy the weeds.— Again, I fallowed part of a field burning-dry in July, immediately
on which came a very hard rain, which made the
furrows, though ploughed dry, fall flat and hard, in
which at Michaelmaſs very few weeds, comparative-
ly of what might have been expected, if ſuch rain
had not fallen, were come up ; for the ground was
thereby faſtened before the ſeeds could chitt.

§. 5. The huſbandry of cold, wet, ſtrong clay-
land in Wiltſhire is to turn it up as early as one can
in the ſpring for a wheaten fallow; if the ground
be ſo dry and ſtarky, that eight oxen and an horſe
muſt be put to the plough, ſo much the better ; on
this fallow (that is, on this one earth) they ſow
their wheat and drag it in, and have much better
corn than if they gave their wheaten land three
earths.— I think this huſbandry founded on very
good reaſon ; for ſuch land, being ploughed up
in ſo hot weather and ſo dry, becomes mellow and
perfect duſty ; the earth being hard underneath, it
will caſt off the rains into the hollowneſs between
the furrows, and will lie dry all the winter ; whereas, if ſuch wet clay-land had been hollowed with
two or three earths, it had lain ſogging in the wet,
and drunk it up like a ſpunge, and the chill would
have killed the corn ; nor would it have fallen
mellower under the harrow than the grete as above
would do under the drag ; and the common ſaying
of the farmers in Hants, that they ſee not but white
land brings as good corn as clay-land, ſeems to
make good, that they often manage clay-land in
Hampſhire ill in their ploughing.

§. 6. I am very ſenſible on experience, that you
ought not to let ground you intend to ſummer-fallow for wheat run too far to a head of graſs, ſo that
the ſheep ſhall refuſe to keep it ſhort or bare ; for
if the graſs comes to that pitch, you will not be
able to make the ſheep eat it, but a great deal of it

*On ſummer fallowing early in cold ſtrong land.*

*Caution againſt letting the graſs grow too long on land to be ſummer-fallowed.*

will

will run to bents ; and when you summer-fallow, the furrows will not cover and turn over the ends of the grass, but it will lie out at the seams, and so being not covered from the air will keep growing, and the roots will consequently live, and matt, and plough up very rough when it is thwarted, tho' the ground was summer-fallowed never so dry.

Manner of
fallowing
in Leicef-
-terfhire.

§. 7. In their common fields in Leicestershire they give five tilts for their barley, and four for their wheat, five for their oats, and one for their peas and beans ; their first fallowing for barley is about March, as soon as seed-time will give them leave ; the second the latter end of May, or in June, as hay-making-time will give them leave ; the third in July or August, as harvesting will permit ; the fourth the latter end of October, or sooner, as the wheat season will allow ; the last earth is when they sow, at the latter end of February or beginning of March : they say, if they did not make these many tilts the weeds would come up so fast, and feed, that they would be quite destroyed with weeds. The tilts for wheat commence, as for barley, about March, and so they hold on according to their leisure till they sow, which is about Michaelmass, and within three weeks after.—From hence it may be observed, that the deep land of the north can never want rain at seed-time, or soon after, for their fourth earth being taken about September, or October, the winter passing over it, and the earth being four months stale when they come to sow it, it must needs turn up so moist, as both to bring up the corn and to support it against the drought of any summer.

My servant was observing to me, that in Leicestershire they cared not how deep they went with their furrow, when they summer-fallowed, which, considering how subject they were to weeds, he look-ed on as a great fault ; for, said he, if they went

† 　　　　　　　　shallow,

shallow, the sun would have power to scorch up the weeds and their seeds in a shallow furrow, as soon as it moldered after the first rain; whereas when they turn up so deep a furrow, the seeds and the roots of weeds are buried and kept moist, and cool, and lie quiet, and not being influenced from the sun and air to germinate and chitt, and thereby to be malted, they are secured in a safe repository, in order for vegetation, when the earth is again ploughed up for wheat.

## Of the DURABLENESS of some SEEDS.

§. 8. It is manifest a great many seeds will endure many years buried in the ground, and yet never rot nor perish, but rise up again in their plants, when the ground by tillage is made a fit matrix for them : but, forasmuch as I can observe, these seeds are the smallest of seeds, such as poppy, charlock, and mustard-seed ; for peas, beans, and other corn-grain, and acorns, and the like, will perish soon, being buried in the ground ; the reason of which seems to be, because these small seeds consist of more oily or bitter juices, which preserve them from moisture, and, in the next place, they consist of such small fibres or vessels, that it is impossible, when they lie half a foot, or a foot deep in the earth, for the power of the sun so to rarify the juices into such particles, as to penetrate those minute tubes, on which all vegetation depends : whereas, when by tillage they have a light bed of earth, those seeds, which are turned up on the surface, lie in the warmth of the sun, where the particles of the earth are made very active and fine to pass their tubes. Thus those larger seeds abovementioned, whose juices are less oily, and their tubes more open, are easily penetrated by the heavy and gross juices, which lie a foot deep in the earth, but not

being

being able to protrude a root downward, nor a plant upward, by reason of the closeness and pressure of the earth, from a plethory of the juices, it is necessary that an extravasation must follow, from whence a corruption must proceed. From hence I conceive it is, as Meagre writes, that primrose-seed, which is exceeding small, being sown in fine mold, some of the seeds will not come up under three, some under four, five, six, and seven years ; some of those seeds, I suppose, lay buried deeper, some shallower in the ground, and the juices that lie deeper require more time to be rarified than those lying shallower. — That seeds are more hardy, and can endure more than is generally conceived, Mr. Rudge of Portsmouth gave me an instance ; he affirmed, that until king William's time they did not use wormwood in their ship-drink ; but that of late they have used it with their hops, which are constantly boiled two hours, and then flung out on a dunghill, and that in those places now grow great quantities of wormwood at Portsmouth, where none grew before. And Dr. Bradyl of Leicester did assure me, that at a dyer's in that town, who used the attriplex baccifera, and boiled it in his dyes, after it had much boiling, and was flung out on the dunghill, there would grow up, in great quantities, from the seeds of it the attriplex baccifera : the berry of this plant is like a mulberry, and it's seeds are exceeding small. When Mr. Ray says the erysimus Neapolitanus (wild cress, or hedge mustard) did grow in that abundance after the fire of London, he adds, that this plant brings very small seeds and in great quantity ; therefore a hundred years might it lie without germinating, and not like to germinate then, unless it's tubes were put in action by the heat of fire. Sir John Floyer, in his Touch-stone of medicines, tells us, that poppies are very mucilaginous, and contain an oil, as ap-

pears

pears by a milky juice ; and an oil is pressed out of
poppy-seed : this seems to account for the great
length of time they are suspected to have laid in the
ground, where grass-lands after many years have
been ploughed up, and this plant has come up so
plentifully. Sir Thomas Brown also, in his Vulgar
errors, gives several instances of the lasting vitality
that some seeds are endued with. If Le Grand had
been acquainted with, and considered these instances, Of equivocal generation.
he would not, I think, have so readily asserted the
equivocal generation of plants : for his argument is
—If you dig up the earth an ell deep, it will, without
sowing, be fruitful the first year, but, if you turn
it up deeper it will not be fruitful till after a year or
two. ꜰ The seeds therefore of plants, says he, are
those insensible particles, which, by the agitation of
the subtle matter, acquire that situation, figure, and
motion, which are necessary towards the formation
of the first rudiments of plants : but this formation
is not so soon compleated, nor are plants produced
so quickly this way, as in the ordinary manner of
raising them from the seeds of plants.

Surely we have great reason to conclude, from
the instances above mentioned, that the earth does
not produce the most contemptible weed without a
seed ; and we find that even at the beginning God
took not that method, nor did the earth bring forth
plants in that manner when it was vastly rich ; for it
is said, Gen. ch. ii. ver. 5.—" that God made every
plant of the field before it was in the earth, and every
herb of the field before it grew ;" and it seems
as if Moses had said this to prevent an hypothesis,

ꜰ Plantarum igitur semina sunt insensibiles illæ particulæ, quæ,
per materiæ subtilis agitationem, eum situm, figuram, & motum
acquirunt, quæ necessaria sunt ad primum stirpis rudimentum ef-
formandum ; sed eorum conformatio tardius absolvatur, seriusque ex illis plantæ proveniunt quam ex seminibus plantarum. Le
Grand, p. 466.

that matter could act so nobly on matter; what is
recorded therefore in the preceding chapter, viz.
that God said, " Let the earth bring forth grass,
the herb yielding seed, &c." can only mean, that
God bad it come forth out of the ground. Patrick
will have those words above quoted, " before it
was in the earth,"——interpreted— before the seed
was in the earth, which if the Hebrew will allow of,
yet the foregoing words in that verse, " God made
every plant of the field," — shew the earth did not
produce plants, as causes naturally do their effects.

§. 9. A great advantage in summer-fallowing
for barley is, that your barley-land seldom is sufficient to provide for all the grasses you sow, and oat-
land will seldom knot fine enough to sow; but if
oats be sowed on the barley-stubble which was
summer-fallowed, in all likelyhood it will knot very
fine, and be fit to be laid down to grass.

To summer-fallow for barley, in order to destroy
weeds, you ought to fallow before the living weeds
run to seed, and yet so late, that the seeds of such
weeds as are in the ground may not have summer
enough to grow up and seed before winter come,
but as soon as may be (avoiding the latter inconveniency) is best; because when weeds are most
turgid with juices, by being ploughed up, their
roots are like to be killed by a plethory : for the
time of weeds seeding consult the herbal.

Lands lying to the north, being cold clay-lands,
should, if sowed to barley, be summer-fallowed, in
order to sweeten the ground, and sowed under
furrow, the middle of March, if the earth can possibly be got dry enough, that the barley of land exposed to the cold may be got ripe before the sun
leaves it, and frosty nights come.

§. 10. It ought to be observed by the husbandman, not only what grounds are cold and sourest,
but also what part of every ground is so; this he
will

*Of sum-
mer-fal-
lowing for
barley.*

*Of fallow-
ing poor
cold land
early.*

will eafily difcern by the grafs the cattle fhall refufe, unlefs hunger forces them to eat it: in the hill-country we may generally perceive thofe grounds, or parts of grounds, which lie upon a declivity from the fun, or are cooped up between hills, fo that the fun cannot freely irradiate them all day, and are not fo pervious to the air and winds, do bear a much fourer grafs than the fummits of the fame field; and it is refufed by cattle, efpecially at a time when grafs is plenty: I do advife in fuch cafe, that the hufbandman take hold of all opportunities and feafons to turn up fuch parts of a field early in the fummer to the fun, and alfo that he ftir it more in the fummer, thereby to fweeten it for grafs, and render it kinder for corn; for he may be affured, fuch ground as bears four grafs, however it may bear a burden of ftraw, will not bear a plump berry, but a thin coarfe fort, which will not fill the bufhel, as finer rinded or floured corn will do.

On my farm there is land, which tho' very cold, poor, and whitifh ground, or woodfeary, yet is very apt to run to four, rowety grafs, tho' it has born corn but the year before; on fuch pieces of land we ought to have a circumfpect eye, both in refpect of ploughing them very dry, and hot, and earlier than other lands, before they are run to grafs, fo as to nip the grafs, as it were, in the bud.

§. 11. I find the evil of white poor ground chiefly is, that all the fpring time it ploughs up too dry to bring up the corn, and tho' it be juft wet enough for mixed or clay-ground to bring up corn, yet that white ground fo foon dries, either by heat or the cold churlifh winds, which come at this time of the year, that the corn is checked in its * chiffum; therefore, if you fow fuch land on fallows upon a fecond ploughing, my advice is, that you fallow early; for ftale fallows will work moift. When you plough for fowing alfo in the hill-country, there

*Of winter-fallowing.*

* putting forth its roots.

are advantages in ploughing the poorer or mixed
land firſt, if it lies warm and in ſhelter, and the
ſtronger clay-land laſt; becauſe, when the ſeaſon of
the year for ſowing draws towards an end, the fallows being too dry for the corn to grow without
rain, the ſull, in ſtrong clay lands, that have a
depth, may, without damage, be carried lower than
the ſtale fallow, into the freſh mold, which will turn
up moiſt, (whereby you may have your corn all
grow) which, in hot ſummers, in the hill-country,
is the life of a crop.

Of winter ·    §. 12. If ground be ploughed dry, tho' ever ſo
fallowing   much rain ſhould fall after it, it will ſoon be dry
dry.      again, for the ſame paſſages the water found to wet
it, are alſo permeable to the ſun : but if ploughed
wet, it will not dry kindly again that ſeaſon, for
† mold.    the † grete is in a manner cruſt thereby, and blended ſo in a dab together, that the ſun cannot penetrate it ; but his rays are refracted.

I was obſerving to a certain farmer, that a certain
field did not produce me ſo good a crop of oats as I
expected, the ground having been fed to hop-clover
for two years. The farmer replied, he believed
the reaſon was becauſe the winter proved ſo wet,
and, that being a white ground, we ſtill went thither
in wet weather, becauſe ploughing in ſuch weather
did not that harm in white ground that it did in
other, but that white ground ſo ploughed bore the
worſe corn, which I believe to be true. Beware
however of either ſummer or winter-fallowing poor
land in the hill-country too dry, ſo that it turns up
deep, and breaks lower than the ſtaple : by experience I know, you impoveriſh ſuch land as much,
by jumbling the bad with the good, as a year's
dunging with the pot can do it good : and all the
experienced farmers I have conſulted, which are
many, are agreed, that tho' it is beſt to plough up
wheaten land in dry weather, (for if it is fallowed
wet,

wet, it will be apt to chill all the year) yet white land should be ploughed up somewhat wet ; for, when dry, it is apt to break up in too stiff clods, and turn up below the goodness of the mold. I have found by constant experience in our hill-country land, where the chalk in many places lies shallow, if, by reason of ploughing too dry, the chalk brush tears up, the corn will in that vein become defective some years after, tho' more manure be bestowed on it than on other parts of the same land, where the chalk has not torn up ; therefore fallow not such land too dry.

The air and watery parts in earth ought to have a free circulation, as in our human bodies, otherwise a corruption and poison of humours arises : the case is the same in earth ploughed up wet, which clings and holds in all the watery body, which then is very much, till it corrupts, and lets in no fresh air, dews, &c. Now earth should be always taking in and perspiring out, even as our bodies do.

If ground be worked wet in seed-time, the wetter it is, the less can a plough dispatch in a day ; for if it clings and sticks to the plough, and to the holder's shoes, it hinders the speed, nor shall the harrows harrow it so well at eight tinings as otherwise at four.

§. 13. If your ground be cold clay-ground, or sour ground, such as I have, take care to pursue the ploughing it up whilst the ground is in the most burning condition, and dry over-head ; and stop when either of those cases are wanting ; and either give your oxen play, or contrive some other work for them. When your ground is so ploughed up in fallowing, it will always turn up again rotten, and in good order ; and by such methods of never fallowing your grounds cold and wet, they will in some years time be marvelloufly sweetened, made healthy and kind for corn, and you will get a domi-

*Of fallowing dry in cold land.*

G 3        nion

nion over all common grasses and herbs of the field, so that such hill-country-ground, after it has lain down to clover, will turn up the second year knot fine, or fryable, which is a very auspicious temper to promise a good crop.

§. 14. The difference in practice amongst husbandmen is very great; to plough up many grounds in the winter, and let them lie so till seed-time, and then to sow them with oats or barley on one earth, i. e. drag the corn in without more ploughing, is a frequent custom amongst the hill-country-men, which the vale-men, when they are told it, are surprized at, and say, if they did so, they should have nothing but weeds, which I believe to be true; but, on the other hand, it is undeniable, that the hill-country-men, whose land lies cold, do this with good success. These different events seem to me to depend on good reasons, viz. high hill-country-land lying bleak and cold, and being somewhat poor, yet, if it be of a clayey kind, being ploughed up early, will not, by reason of it's barrenness, and cold exposition, produce weeds during the winter; the seeds of weeds in such cold beds lie asleep, till roused out of their lethargy by the warmer air and sun of the spring; whereas in warmer soils, which lie in the vale, where the land is commonly richer, the seeds of weeds, even during the winter, if the ground be hollowed up by ploughing, and mellowed by rains and frosts, will sprout and put forth a blade.

§. 15. I was saying to farmer Elton, it was the common opinion of farmers, that a team should be still going, in season, or out of season; but I differed from them; for when a season presented itself, and I was behind-hand, I should not scruple the hiring three or four days work of a plough, and, if a season did not present itself, should not scruple the going on somewhat towards a second year's crop.

He

*Different practice in hill and vale-country, in winter-fallowing.*

*Of ploughing unseasonably.*

He agreed with me, and said, 'twas better to be in the stable than to do things out of season, and said, there was a piece of one of his fields an instance of it ; they went to fallow there in a wet time, because they would not stand still, and that part of the ground has worsted three crops since successively, and made it run to weeds.

§. 16. It seems to me to be very wrong (tho' in the hill-country, where the earth is consequently dryer) to winter-fallow across the lands or furrows, if possibly it can be avoided, especially if the lands lie on a descent, and are of a cold clayey nature ; for the current of the water is thereby stopt, and the field lying the wetter for it is thereby soured and chill'd ; it seems therefore, that such lands should be winter-fallowed the same way the lands and furrows lie, if they lie upwards and downwards especially.

*Winter fallowing. —Not to winter fallow across the furrows.*

The ground generally winter-fallowed better in anno 1718 than had been observed for many years : the reason doubtless was the long, hot, and dry summer the preceding year, whereby not only the earth, through the drought, was made more fryable, but also the free growth of all weeds, and their roots, which matt the ground together, and harle in the clots, was checked.

The philosophers seem to agree, that in winter the air is fuller of nitre than in summer ; therefore a winter-fallow, to let in the nitrous particles of the air, must be beneficial.

§. 17. It seems the winter-fallows of every ground are then most seasonable, when you can make the furrows stand most upright, and so continue, with as little falling down as may be, that thereby the land may lie the healthier and dryer, and shoot off the rains ; whereas by falling flat it lies foggy, spungy, and cold. — Accordingly I was telling a very good farmer in my neighbourhood, that I thought it was better not to winter-fallow stiff land till the frosts

*When winter fallowing most seasonable.*

were

were near at hand; for, if one fallowed such lands early in October, they might settle too much before the frosts might come to hollow them. He replied, if it was lay ground, it might be as I said, but, if it was stiff land that was ploughed the year before, it was best, he thought, to plough it up as soon as I could, tho' the very beginning of October, before it had time to settle after it's last burden of corn; for then it would, when first fallowed, molder fine enough. — Tho' clay-lands however ought to be fallowed early for the better mellowing them, yet it seems to me no loss of time, but rather gain, to wait a little for the dry frosts; because in such weather you will better effect your ends. If the fallows should have been flatted by the rains, the frost having less power over them, they must needs be more inclinable to run to weeds; on the other hand, tho' fallowing should happen when the ground is very wet, yet if dry frosts follow, and not wet weather, such fallows may do very well. The reason is, because such frosts uphold the ground from falling, till it settles in the ridges in an upright standing, and consequently receives the benefit of the frosts: but this venture is not to be trusted to, lest wet weather should come after such fallowing, which is most likely, as the ground is already full of wet; and yet the farmers will plough and fallow in the wet, knowing, that they sometimes have had as good corn after a wet fallow as a dry one; but of the accidents, whereon it depended, they were ignorant; otherwise I judge they would not have done so. — On the like reason, in my opinion, depends the wholsomness of the summer-fallows; for, if the fallow be wet, it will be in danger of falling flat, unless very dry weather follow, to support the ridges: consequently the sun has less power over the parts, nor can it kill the weeds by it's burning heat, as in a dry fallow.

I gave

I gave a barley-fallow to a broad-clover field in
July: some said, it would not gain it's end, but lay
the ground chill for the whole winter.—By Michaelmass I found it full of all sorts of weeds green on the
ground, which when stirred would all be destroyed.
—Note, that fallowing land well carries a whole
furrow in the winter, and cannot be supposed to lay
a ground wet during the winter, but rather dry,
seeing the furrows have gutters between them, for
carrying off the water; but if the ground falls small,
then it may lie foggy and spungy. The harrowing
this ground after it was fallowed, made it fine, so
that it brought up weeds in abundance, which
would be stirred in, and so destroyed, and yet it lay
hollow underneath.

The reasons of early fallowings and stirrings, or
thwartings, seem to depend altogether on the nature
of the lands you have to deal with; for if it be probable that ground may work dry and mellow at
spring-seed-time, care ought to be taken to fallow so
early, that you may thwart early, I mean in January,
that your ploughing at seed-time may be moist;
but your fallowing, if the ground be not grassy,
may be later, especially your thwarting, viz. not till
March, if you are apprehensive your ground is like
to be too wet at seed-time; for 'twill plough much
the drier at seed-time for being thwarted late in a
dry season.

I fallowed a lay ground to grass in October and
November; I began very early to plough it, and
sow barley in it, viz. the 25th of March: notwithstanding the fallows were very stale, and, being
sowed so early in the year, one would think the
ground moist enough to bring up the corn, as by
turning up the furrows it seemed to be, yet the
ground ploughing very rough, being of a white
nature, and requiring ten tinings, it was a very great
disadvantage to the corn's coming up, there being

no

no rain; for the weather was hot, or windy and dry, when it was ploughed, and the tumbling it up and down so often with the harrows dried the ground too much : so therefore to order white ground, that it may harrow at four or five tinings, and thereby not lose it's moisture, is good husbandry.

Mr. Raymond says, the good husbands with them (in Wiltshire) fallow up all the lands in the beginning of winter, and finish by October, if they can, whilst their horses are at grass, and then lay them up at a cheap keeping all the winter : this they do in Leicestershire, as I have elsewhere noted.

Seeing the finer earth is tilted, the more each part of it communicates it's virtue to the grain laid in it ; I suppose the finer it is winter-fallowed (for the same reason) the more the winter rains and frosts communicate their virtue to the land.

**Of winter-fallowing for wheat.** §. 18. The finer the earth is made by often ploughing for wheat, the closer it lies all the winter to the roots of the corn, provided you sow corn in good time, so that the frosts come not to hollow it before it is settled ; for, not having time to settle, it is in more danger of being hollowed by the frosts. From my walking over the fallows, and observing how dry, and healthy, and exposed to the frosts, weather, and sun, the convex parts lay, and how the many small concave parts and hollows lay to receive the sun's strongest heats, I cannot but think it great husbandry to fallow up grassy, or strong clay-lands in the winter-season, for wheat, tho' one must give them an earth the more possibly in summer, by fallowing twice instead of once : indeed this cannot be done vice versâ to barley, by giving that a summer-fallow, because barley is sown after some corn that grew the summer before.

By winter-fallowing for wheat you have this certain advantage, that the fallows are so mellowed by the winter-frosts, that all the spring and summer
long

long they drink up the rains and summer-suns the more greedily.

In winter-fallowing for wheat there also sometimes falls out this advantage (as in anno 1705, when no rains fell from April to the second of July) that you have not only so much land fallowed beforehand, when no plough could follow in lay-lands by reason of the dryness, and consequently the farmers must be behind-hand; but you may also all that season stir the winter-fallows, for all that time they will work.

§. 19. Whereas in the strong deep lands of Buckinghamshire, and in some other countries, where there are strong lands, the farmers hold it ill husbandry to sow much barley, and they are restrained from it by their landlords, from an opinion that barley impoverishes their land beyond other corn. I am apt to think, if barley impoverishes such clay-land, it must proceed from the winter-fallowing it, and tumbling it about in cold raw weather, when it is wet, being cold clay-land, whereby it is chilled and soured; whereas I suppose they plough not up for peas and beans and oats till the spring of the year, when they are sown; and peas and beans hollow and mellow the ground. *Of winter-fallowing for barley.*

The first considerations, after wheat and vetches are sown, in order to a barley-crop, are of this nature, viz. to fallow up those grounds which you do not fold, and of them to fallow those first which are declivous from the sun, or by reason of high trees or hedge-rows are much shaded, or by reason of hedge-rows or declivities are skreened from the north and east; for all such grounds may and ought to be sown first with barley; and therefore the earth ought to be prepared first, and if such fields are to be folded, they ought to be folded first, in order to be fallowed as soon as may be.

§. 20. Mr. Edwards observes, the first thing the farmers do after harvest is to fallow for black oats; *Of winter-fallowing for oats,*

for

for the older the fallow is they sow black oats on they obferve it to be the better : but, if they sow white oats, they fallow but before they sow, for the later the fallow is for white oats, they count it the better, for white oats love to lie light ; and, said he, they never give two earths to black oats, but, if the ground be such as is run to grafs and a stiff ground, it is better, and will well answer, in cafe you sow white oats, if you give it two earths : nay, said he, **and for peas.** some of our clay-lands are so stiff, that it would very well pay if two earths were given to peas also, for it is impossible sometimes they should shoot their heads through. I said I never knew two earths given to peas before ; he replied, farmer Biggs, if I would talk to him, would tell me the fame thing ; and he was sure he loft half a crop for want of it.

It was the 16th of October, and farmer Biggs had fallowed for oats ; I asked, whether the land (he sowing on one earth) would not be too stale, and lie too hard at feed-time. He said, no ; if land worked light (for on this land he had sowed oats also the last year) it would be in fit temper enough at spring ; that he and others commonly gave a fallow to some oat-land by the very beginning of October.

## Of Winter-fallowing early for O A T S and B A R L E Y.

§. 21. On the 20th of October, 1719, I began ploughing a field of fifty-two acres for oats, which had been sown to corn, and chiefly to vetches, so that the stubble ploughed up so fine and small, that it might be well supposed the ground by the winter rains would fall flat ; I had finished ploughing these fifty two acres by the 20th of November. — Notwithstanding it was light and white ground, and fell so fine, yet at the oat-feed time, Feb. 20, the harrow

row tinings being good, the oats were laid deep
enough in the furrows or ſeams : for tho' they ſeemed to be cloſed, they were not ſo, but there were
cavities underneath, tho' the ſeams cloſed at top.
This ground was all harrowed off at five tinings,
which was the effect of early ploughing in the
winter. This method of fallowing light ground ſucceeded admirably well, and anſwered in every reſpect ; the oats were let in deep enough, and proſ-
pered in colour beyond thoſe I ſowed that year in
ſtrong land on two earths, and when I mowed them,
the 15th of Auguſt, they were in every reſpect great
oats, and the hop-clover I ſowed with them ſucceeded very well. I concluded therefore from this
and other experiments, that ploughing ſuch light
ground (which falls fine) thus early is beſt, ſince the
oats can be let deep enough into the ſeams, and by
that means the ground ſo ploughed, taking the
winter rains, will retain ſo much moiſture as to
bring the oats all up, the contrary of which is the
danger in all ſuch light grounds,—For the ſame reaſon I began fallowing ſuch light lands for barley as
early as the middle of October this year, that ſo
they, being beaten flat by the winter rains, and being drunk with them, might retain ſufficient moiſture to bring up the barley at ſpring.

In the beginning of November, 1712, I ploughed up four acres of a field conſiſting of fourteen
acres, which had lain down to broad-clover for two
years, during which it was mowed : tho' it was a
clayey ground, it broke pretty * knot by the * fine.
plough, and therefore, having much other buſineſs
in hand, I thought I might delay the tearing up the
reſt till the latter end of January, and that it would
harrow very well by the latter end of February,
ſowed to oats ; accordingly, the latter end of January I ploughed the reſt, and ſowed the whole field
with black oats the latter end of February : the
ground

ground dreſſed with the harrows very well ; only this difference I obſerved ; the four acres ploughed in November was broke by the froſts to duſt ; the other part ploughed laſt was not ſo fine, but worked very mellow. This experiment I made on conjecture that the four acres ploughed ſo early would carry the beſt oats, and my expectation was anſwered ; for the whole field from the firſt appearance gave me great hopes of a good crop : but by the latter end of May the four acres ploughed ſo early was diſtinguiſhable in colour, to lookers on, at a quarter of a mile diſtance ; for it was much the ſtronger, and darker in complection. June the 8th, which was nine days after, I took a view of another field, conſiſting of ſix acres, which I had ploughed in the winter in the former manner, viz. ――― I ploughed up four acres thereof in October, when the ground was very dry, and in January I ploughed up the two remaining acres, the ground being likewiſe then very dry. This field had been, as the other abovementioned, ſowed two years to broad-clover, and it turned up mellow in both parts, when ſowed to black oats in the latter end of February, and harrowed knot-fine, only with this difference, that the four acres ploughed up in October worked in duſt, or like aſhes. The conſequence of this huſbandry was as the former, viz.― June the 8th the oats in the four acres, ſo early ploughed, looked more proud, were thicker, and of a deeper green than the two acres ; and it is to be noted, that, in both the grounds, in thoſe parts which were ſo early ploughed, no graſs appeared during winter, nor at ſpring to prejudice harrowing.

Of fallowing for peas.

§. 22. I talked with ſeveral very experienced farmers concerning fallowing for peas : they all agreed that their crop of peas would be better if they did, and it would pay the charges, for ſometimes their crops were bad for want of it ; but it ſeems they had

ſo

ſo much other work for their ploughs that they could not allow time for it.

To ſummer-fallow for peas doubtleſs would be as proper as for barley; in which caſe you need not ſtir the ground again, but harrow down the roughneſs of the furrows before you plough for ſowing; your ground by ſuch ſummer-fallowing, or indeed by an early winter-fallowing, being laid curiouſly dry, will bear with the ſowing the peas earlier than otherwiſe, which has many advantages.

For this reaſon it is, that the vale-farmers ſow not their peas ſo early as we in the hill-country do, tho' they lie warmer, becauſe their land is wetter, and conſequently colder; but their barley they ſow a fortnight ſooner than we, for by that time the ſun has well heated their land.

§. 23. This year, 1702, happened to be a very dry year, and ſummer: an old farmer came to me, and lamented his bad crop of peas, and ſaid, they were worth little, and that they were ſo from his hiring his ploughing, which was of too little ſtrength; for, ſaid he, we had not horſes able to go deep enough; if we had ſtrength to go an inch or two deeper I had had treble the crop, for then I had laid them deep enough from the ſun. *Of ploughing for peas.*

From hence may alſo be concluded, that the later in the ſpring you ſow peas, the deeper you ought to go.

From what I have obſerved this year, 1715, it is evident to me, that, if I ſow peas in cold clay-ground, I ought to lay the lands round and ſmall, viz. after the rate of five, ſix, or at moſt ſeven furrows in a ridge, whether I ſow over or under furrow; for wherever the land lay flat, and pitched, or ſunk a little, there the peas failed, and did not come up, and thoſe that did, continued all the ſummer in an unthriving condition; and yet the ſpring after they were ſown was not ſo wet, tho' indeed we had often

cold

cold dry winds; the ground these peas were sown in ploughed up very mellow and dry, and was summer-fallowed. All these advantages give a plain proof to me of the profit of laying the lands in such grounds round, and I doubt not but where the ground was moſt healthy, and the peas more flouriſh-ing, yet both would have been more ſo, if managed as above ſaid. The peas, from which I made this obſervation, were blue peas, ſowed ſo late as the 19th of March, when the cold weather might ſeem almoſt over.

On experience I am very ſenſible, that if peas be ploughed under furrow, in ground where one ploughs up-hill and down hill, very great care ought to be taken that you do not bury the peas; for if the plough going down-hill be not took up, or held up with a good ſtrength, it will be very viſible at the time of their coming up; they will not come up half ſo thick in that half of the land that was ploughed down-hill, as in that half that was ploughed up-hill in every land reſpectively; therefore, in ſuch land, and eſpecially when ſo careleſsly ploughed, 'it muſt be evident there requires good dragging, and very good harrowing, to break and tear the furrows into ſmaller pieces, and to open them well, and hollow their compact coheſion, ſo that the corn may come through. Indeed no corn ſhould be ſowed under furrow, where the furrow turns up whole, or does not break well into ſhort pieces, but the drags ought to tear ſuch ground firſt, before it is harrow-ed; for in ſuch caſes the harrows do but ſcratch the back of the furrows, and when that looſe earth is waſhed away, or ſettled, the back of the furrows will appear intire and hard. I was plainly convinced of this in ſowing peas under furrow in the two for-mer years, but eſpecially in ſowing them ſo this year, 1716. From hence it is obvious, great care ought to be taken in well harrowing the ground, and that they, chey, who go with the harrows ought to be well over-looked. It also seems to me, if ground ploughs rough, so that it may require much harrowing, and yet is so heavy as to be in danger of treading, the best way is to drag it once or twice first before it is harrowed, because one turn of the drags will tear such ground more than three turns of the harrows; and it stands to reason the horses need go over it so much the seldomer; and so the treading will be the less; and it is to be noted farther, that, if a dry season falls out, and such peas, so sowe under furrows, are not harrowed well, they will have the more difficult task to get through.

§. 24. If ground be run to a sword, or run out of the sown grass, and fit to be ploughed up, in case the grete, or mold, is but shallow, and the chalk near the top, I think it is good husbandry to give such a ground, for wheat, a winter-fallow; for then you can take a leisure-time for it; and be sure to take a time when the ground shall be moist, wherein you may go as shallow as you please, and then may stir it to your own mind in summer; whereas, if you fallow such a ground in summer, and the season be dry, as it ought to be, it is odds but you turn up the chalk; for if the ground be dry, there is a loose spungy coat between the first coat and the chalk, which, being hollow, will suck in the plough, so that you cannot help ploughing up the chalk; and this method I believe will compensate very well for the loss of the grass.

*Of winter-fallowing chalk ground that is run to a sword.*

§. 25. A field of mine was very well dunged for wheat the summer 1713, and bore a good crop of wheat; in spring 1714, I sowed it to barley, having had a good season for winter-fallowing, as also a good dry season at spring for ploughing and sowing it, and a hot summer, and the barley came up well; yet I do not believe I had two quarters of barley on an acre —This ground is a strong clay-ground, and

*Manner of the hill-country in winter-fallowing for barley condemned.*

VOL. I.                    H                    it

it lies aſlope north-eaſt. — I am thoroughly ſatisfied
by experience, that the way of the hill-country-
huſbandry of ploughing and ſowing ſuch ground
four years together, that is, to four crops ; the firſt
of which is wheat, and the other three ſpring-corn,
for which laſt three they winter-fallow only ; I am,
I ſay, ſatisfied this cannot be good huſbandry for
ſuch ground ; for the firſt ſummer-fallow it receives
for wheat, whereby it is warmed, mellowed, and
ſweetened, can by no means qualify the coldneſs,
heavineſs, and ſourneſs it receives the three years
afterwards by the three winter-fallowings for ſpring-
corn ; nor can, I conceive, any other than the aforeſaid reaſon be given, why ſuch land ſhould produce
but two quarters of barley per acre, which in goodneſs and ſtrength was ſufficient to bear four quarters.
—There ſuch ground ſhould after the wheat-
crop receive one or two ſummer-fallows every other
year for ſpring-corn, before it will be in right temper
to receive a winter-fallow for a barley-crop, in order
to lay it down for graſs-ſeeds.

§. 26. To plough-in a good ſword of graſs by a
summer-fallowing ſeems to be of much greater conſequence to the improvement of the land than the
doing it in winter ; for the winter is too cold to ferment it, or to raiſe and fix thoſe bodies of ſalt thereby, which lie in thoſe graſſes ; it being eaſy to be
conceived that the moldineſs, and finnowyneſs of the
graſs ſo ploughed-in in ſummer muſt be much
greater than in the winter ; for which reaſon cow-
dung and horſe-dung, made in the fields by the cattle's ſoiling, falling ſo thin, is not of that conſequence ſome are apt to think, becauſe it never ferments, nor heats.

There is a great nitre and ſalt in roots, as appears
by Grew, wherefore the ploughing-in broad clover-
roots, which are ſo big and thick in the ground,
before they are dead, by a Midſummer-fallow, to
precipitate

*Summer-fallowing preferred to winter-fallowing.*

precipitate their rotting or fermenting, whereby
their falts are fixed, is of great confequence ; whereas by the infenfible decay of the root by canker it is
fo leifurely done that it has not fermentation
enough to raife a good body of falts.

When there is a graffy turf on ground it is obferved to bear much the beft corn ; the reafon of which
feems to be, becaufe the grafs and roots turned
down under furrow do heat, and thereby raife a
great quantity of vegetable falts ; for this reafon it
was I had fo great a crop of broad-clover by fummer-fallowing it's aftermafs, and do look upon it,
if a ground has a graffy turf on it, and not too rank
or poor for barley, it is beft to fummer fallow it for
barley ; then to give a winter-fallow for oats, and
fow them on the back ; becaufe in the winter-fallow, tho' the grafs rots, yet it does not fo heat, for
want of fun, as to raife from it's rotting fuch a quantity of falts.

§. 27. To plough a graffy ground in winter, Of plough-
when the fnow lies on the ground, or when it is a ing ground
wet feafon, is to bring up the weeds ; for the fword that has a
of the ground being turned in when wet, lies there winter.
fogging, and grows chill, keeping wet all the winter, nor will it eafily dry

Farmer Biggs ploughed up a fallow for peas,
being a lay-ground with a fword ; he faid, he would
fallow it as fhallow as poffible, which was very ju-
dicioufly confidered ; for undoubtedly, if a ground
be run to fword, and is to be ploughed againft the
winter, the fhallower it is turned up the more power
the frofts will have over the roots of the grafs, in
rotting them ; and there is no doubt, if the plough
fhould go deeper at fowing-time, but that the frefh-
er earth underneath will turn up mellow.

§. 28. A lay-ground having been fown to broad- Of fallow-
clover grafs two years, about the 8th of November ing head-
we began to fallow it ; and the 18th, when they lands in
                                                                    ftrong land.
had

had fallowed all save the head-lands, my bailiff said to me, that he believed 'twas best not to fallow the head-lands, for, being strong land and grassy, they would at sowing-time turn back again whole, which appeared very reasonable to me; so they were left unploughed. — From hence I do infer, that when grounds are large that are to be fallowed, and are strong lay-ground, it is good to plough round the head-lands at first hand of the year, though the plough should be carried out again for a month or two; there will be time thereby given for the head-lands to rot, that they may turn up mellow when they are stirred again. Nor will the trampling on them when the ground is fallowed dry, do any harm but good; this will make the head-lands sweet, and bear a good bodied corn.

§. 29. I was sensible by experience this year (anno 1714) that, if strong clay-ground have two earths given it to wheat, and after the wheaten crop is taken off, it lies the next summer to grass, and is ploughed up at autumn, tho' such ground be run to a thick matted sword, yet it will turn up rotten and mellow at plough-shear, so as to stir well in the thwarting at spring.

*Autumn-fallowing strong grassy ground.*

## Of the METHOD of ploughing for different sorts of CORN.

*Of plough-ing wet cold land to one earth.*

§. 30. They find by experience in the vale, that it is best to sow wet clay-land on one earth, for thereby the corn lies dry, whereas if they gave it two or three earths, and wet came, it would lie poachy, and cold, and thereby the corn would be chilled.

If lands are to be ploughed up and sowed to one earth, which have lain six or seven years to lain or grass, such ground will turn up with a much evener furrow, and a great deal more may be ploughed in
a day,

a day, in case you plough up the ground the same way the furrow went last.

I was asking the farmer who rented some lands of me, which I have lately taken into hand, how it came to pass, that a certain parcel of ground, which I had sowed to rye-grafs, run so much to erfhes, it seeming, when the corn was down, almost choaked up with rowety grafs. He replied, that those grounds had not been sown for three or four years last past but to oats, which having but one earth, and stiff land, the sword of the grafs and the root had not been killed, whereas, had it been sowed to barley, it would have been in as good tilt as any other land.

§. 31. It is plain why ploughing of poor land brings weeds; not only on account that the coulter in lay-ploughing cuts the roots of the weeds in many pieces, all which grow, but also forasmuch as those roots will emit stronger shoots than the corn can, which proceeds only from seed; and consequently, the weeds must over-top, and be more luxuriant than the corn. *Why ploughing poor land brings weeds.*

§. 32. Notwithstanding it was very white ground, I ploughed three earths, and then sowed French-grafs and barley in it: I had the evenest and best crop, I believe, that ground ever carried.—I sowed the ground when it was as wet as the plough could well go, which I believe is best for white mortar-earth-ground, which is not on a clay.—The reason why farmers sow white land on one earth, I judge to be from their great inclination to save charges, white earth being more capable of bearing a crop in that manner, as being less subject to weeds than clay-land.—The reason again they offer in argument for so doing is, and from experience too, as they pretend, because they have had worse crops on two or three earths than on one.—The true reason of which is, because they have never sowed such white land *Of ploughing white land to one earth.*

on

on two or three earths by choice and forecast, but by necessity, that is, when they have been negligent in taking their time for ploughing up such land, and have defer'd so doing too long, whereby it has worked rough ; then on force they have ploughed it again, or possibly the third time, to correct the first error, and all in vain, and so have had bad crops ; whereas, had they designed three earths from the beginning, and ploughed the first early, and acted uniformly in their second and third earths, I believe, they would not have repented it.

It is usually observed that the white land in our hill-country, if ploughed to two earths, and thereby made light, is very subject to poppy, which we call red-weed, but clay lands are not subject to it ; the reason of which seems to be this : the poppy-seed is an exceeding small seed, (Mr. Ray computes many thousands to lie in a pod) and for that reason is easily buried in clay-land, and less able to shoot it's seed-leaves through, because the clay soon settles and binds ; but through white land, made light by ploughing, it's seed-leaves easily pass : it is very likely therefore (the evil of red weed being so great) it may be better to sow white land on one earth.

There are several sorts of light or white chalky grounds in the hill country, which (when sowed to wheat) ought to be sowed on one earth, otherwise they will be subject to red-weed or other weeds ; so that there seems a necessity to give such land but one earth, whenever it is sown ; for it will not bear being torn to pieces, tho' it had lain many years to sword ; so care ought to be taken, that such land does not lie down too many years to grass, lest it should turn so stiff and tough, that drags will not tear up enough of the coat or mold to cover the wheat, and so it suffer on the other hand by lying too shallow, and on too stiff a ground. If such

ground

ground has lain so long to grass, as to be stubborn, there is a great hazard but it produces the less crop, especially if it be in a gentleman's hands, whose many avocations call him from home, and from a due attendance in the field whilst such land is sowing, it being very likely where much dragging is required, and labour to dress the ground, that servants will be sparing in it, than which nothing can in such a case be more prejudicial; and in all cases, it should be most the care of a gentleman, especially for the reason abovesaid, so to contrive the ordering his ground against the sowing-season, that, if possible, it should be in so good temper and order to receive the seed, that it should not be in the power of the ploughman to hurt him, unless he went wilfully so to do. — Such ground should be so nicked in ploughing up for wheat on one earth, as to turn it up when the furrow is a little inclinable to break, or be rottenish, especially when we may hope it will do so, and grow a little mellow by lying a while to sun and rain.

§. 33. In a burn-beaked ground I sowed barley and French-grass the 18th, 19th, and 20th of March under furrow; the residue of the month was very dry, and warm, but the month of April to the 20th, had every day dry, cold, and churlish winds, and the 17th, 18th, and 19th, there were hoar-frosts in the morning. On the 20th of this month I viewed my barley, and found most of it looked wan, and some of it yellowish, by the cold winds and hoar-frosts; but there happened in this ground to be a linchet ploughed up in the winter, on which barley had been sown on one earth; this barley, tho' the ground was new, did very manifestly complain, and was quite yellow, which proceeded from it's lying so shallow, and from it's disability to strike roots in the firmer ground of one earth's sowing. Barley sowed on one earth in other places I observed to be *very*

*Of plough-ing to one earth for barley.*

very yellow on the same occasion; I do therefore infer, that barley sowed under furrow will better bear cold than that sowed on one earth. Part of this white land, over which the sheep had often gone to fold, did not in the least complain; but the leaves kept broadly extended in their full verdure; whereas the others gathered up together, or lost somewhat of their colour. The French-grass sowed in this ground all this while did not in the least complain, or the seed-leaves abate of their verdure.

I find not only Captain Hedges, but Mr. Weston and others make some objections to my over-fondness of sowing my barley always, and my whole crop on one earth; saying, that in hot summers the ears will shrink and want nourishment, by reason the roots cannot strike a depth; but farmer Bachelour of Litchfield will by no means allow this to be an objection, for he says the contrary of this is true, and that in the driest and hottest summers his one-earth-corn flourishes and looks greener than his two-earth-corn. It must then necessarily be, that when Captain Hedges and Mr. Weston, &c. made this their observation, they ploughed their white land either too wet, or too late, when they sowed their one-earth-corn, whereby the frosts had not time to slat it, and shatter it to powder; and so the drags could not raise a grete to let the corn in deep enough.

Farmer Biggs assured me, that he had found by experience, that it was much the best way to sow barley on one earth, if it was poor white land; on such land he was weary of sowing on two earths, being satisfied he had thereby lost his crops.

In sowing corn, as oats or barley, to one earth, in the hill-country, I conceive these to be proper rules, and which I do practise, viz. to plough a narrow furrow (not a wide and broad one) that the winter frosts and rains may have the more power to mellow

and

and shatter the furrows against spring, whereby the ground will harrow the better, and the harrow tinings go in the deeper. To this end, that the ground may harrow the better, I always take a time of ploughing such ground not only early in the winter, but also in a dry season; and I take care to fence ground so ploughed, during the winter, and till I sow it, from sheep, lest they, by treading it, especially in the wet, should tread down the ridge of the furrows, and make it mortar.

§. 34. I see not why they, who sow wheat on one earth, should sow the earlier, as the custom is, unless on account that the drags cannot raise a deep grete; and so the corn must get an early root, lest it should be too much exposed to the winter: but provided your ground be in very good heart, and the earth mellow, that the drags may, when loaded, enter deep, I see not why such one-earth-corn may not be sowed at Michaelmass. Onploughing to one earth for wheat.

From the observation I have made these three weeks, on wheat now growing (May, anno 1712) I pass my judgment, that wheat, if sowed seasonably, i. e. between the 6th and 20th of September, when sowed on two earths, or on the second ploughing, will carry a better colour about the beginning of May, than the wheat sown on one earth; for the latter, tho' it might seem much the more flourishing, and of as deep a colour during the winter, till towards May; yet the ground sowed to one earth lying closer and harder than the other, the wheat could not move, nor strike so good roots as that sowed on two earths would do; when the spring began to grow dry and hot, it would give off it's support to the corn; which will then be apt to turn to a bright and paler colour, and the weaker tillows and branches, which made a show in the winter, will not come on, but starve; whereas the wheat sowed on two earths will, when hot weather comes,

flourish

flourish with a deep green, and fulfil all it's branches by nourishing them, it having a depth of mold, and mellowness in it to maintain the roots.    From hence it appears how necessary it is to plough deep, where the staple of the ground will allow it, and to lay the seed into a good depth of mold well prepared and shattered by being broke with the plough.

However white light lands, as elsewhere observed, are better sown on one earth; nor can a great crop be all sown in strong land, and on two earths, in cold hill-countries, because it cannot be in that manner sown time enough, and the neglect of that would be a worse evil than sowing on one earth.—I must also observe, that my land, which is more brashy and full of small stones, and of less depth of mold, though better supported with pot-dung than the parts which were only folded, brought less wheat than the other; for which no other reason can be assigned, but that the plough could not turn up a furrow of that depth as in the other part, and consequently the corn suffered by the weather in the summer-months, when it grew dry.    If it be objected to this observation, that barley sown on one earth is generally said to bear the hot summers better than that on two earths, it must be replied, that, when barley is spoken of in such a manner it must be intended of barley sowed on white land, or such light ground as would lie too hollow, if sowed on two earths : of such ground it is true also, that wheat sowed on one earth will endure the summer better than that sowed on two.

Of ploughing to one earth for barley after wheat in the hill-country.

§. 35. It is a common practice, in our hill-country, for farmers, the year after they have sowed light white land to wheat on one earth, to turn it up again early the next year, i. e. in October or November, to sow barley again on the back, or on one earth ; and this they do, because such land is poor, and will not answer the expences of two or three

three earths; and it is a question whether less than
three earths would most times make such ground
knot fine; because such white land in our country,
being sowed the year before to wheat on one earth,
is subject, especially if the summer prove wet, to
abundance more rowet and grass than our cold clay-
lands so sowed would be; consequently it would be
difficult to destroy it, and to make the couch tear
out at the third earth, tho' one ploughed it in early; therefore they endeavour to feed the rowet with
a great stock of cattle as soon as the wheat is off;
notwithstanding which, you will, if you have a
good quantity of it, have a hard task to get it eat
close time enough for your plough to enter. —— I
do not approve of this husbandry of sowing such
land the next year after wheat, as above said, on
one earth to barley, for the reason following, viz.
such land is commonly of a shallow grete or staple,
and therefore must be ploughed up shallow, and
the rowet, which is turned underneath such a furrow,
will not rot by spring, but the roots will mat and
hold the earth together, notwithstanding the frosts
may have considerably contributed to the tearing it
to pieces;—so that, what with the shallow furrow
you was obliged to plough, and the closeness of the
earth, your drags and harrows will not at spring be
able to get deep enough to give the barley a deep,
and an easy bed, and consequently the barley must
starve in summer.—I do therefore rather recommend
such land to be sowed to oats, in the same manner
as you would do to barley: oats being sowed a
month earlier, will have established a root, and put
forth tillows before they are pinched with hot weather, and will better endure to lie shallow than barley would do.

§. 36. It ought to be considered, if we suffer
poor shallow ground to run out of tilt, by letting it
run too long to grass, it will, if ploughed in summer,

Of one
earth to
wheat.

mer, be apt to spalt up below it's staple; and if, to avoid that, you plough it up in winter, when it is moist, and will plough shallow, in order to sow it to wheat on two earths, poor shallow ground will bear more weeds and less corn being sown on two earths than on one.——The best way therefore is always to plough up such land before it be run to too strong a sword; that you may turn it up to a shallow furrow, and be secure of it's working and tearing mellow under the drags at seed-time, when you sow it to wheat.

Farmer Biggs and his son, both assured me, that though white land did well with wheat on one earth, yet that they had always found it do better with two; but, said they, on about an acre or more of white land, to which this year (1702) we gave two earths, the wheat lies with it's roots out of the ground, there being but a little fibre or two at most that holds the root, and can feed it, so that it can carry no ear; for it is impossible it should have a full-grained corn, where there is so little conveyance of nourishment to it.    I asked farmer Biggs how that part of the white land sowed on two earths came to be so much worse than the rest. He said, because the land was side-long, and had a falling both ways, so that when at sowing-time they ploughed it up and down, one land having another falling against it, every other furrow, falling with the side-land and not against it, filled up without a seam, so that, the land working fine, the corn could not be buried.——The best way is, said he, to sow white land on two earths, and to sow the last under furrow.

But I have since found by experience, that, tho' two or three earths may be best for wheat on strong red clay-ground, (red-weed not being so apt to grow in that, tho' made never so fine) yet that either two or three earths is very improper for white light ground, or half red earth half white; for the finer such

such ground is made it is so much the more subject to red-weed, or poppies, especially if the summer prove cold and rainy, as in 1715.

The farmers of our hill-country say, they have found by experience, that it is best, when they sow wheat on one earth, which is always done early, to sow old wheat rather than new; because the old wheat is not so forward, and apt to run away to a grassy head, nor to be so proud as the new, which are faults at the forehand of the year. — This seems reasonable to me.

§. 37. Farmer Lake advised me by all means to give two earths to my peas: he said, if my land was like his, or the land about them, he was sure I should not often have a good crop on one earth.— Quære about this.—Farmer Biggs says, if it be lay-land, it will not come in tilt at two earths, but will turn up whole, and, if it be barley or oat-stubble, it will not need it; but he allows, it may be good practice as the ground may work, for sometimes such stubble-land may not work kindly under two earths. Farmer Elton afterwards told me what Biggs said was true, but it was upon land lying still a year or two that two earths was such good husbandry, and in that case it would come to tilt at two earths.

*Of giving two earths to peas.*

§. 38. If you give some of your wheaten lands three earths, if strong clay, it will turn much to advantage, but then such land must, if run to a sword, be fallowed in winter; otherwise the grass will not rot soon enough to be stirred: in such case you need not doubt of being able to stir such fallows in the driest time, when you cannot get the full into the grassy grounds you would fallow: by this means you will be able to cut out work for the most precious time of the summer, when farmers lie by, because they cannot easily plough by reason of the hardness of the ground.

*Three earths to strong land*

§ 39. The

Advantage of three earths to summer-corn.

§. 39. The advantage of giving three earths to summer-corn is in this very manifest, viz. that in a dry spring and summer, in any part of a ground that works rough, for want of making the earth fine by so much ploughing, in that part the corn will come up edge-grown, and later than the rest of the same ground where it worked finer, and apparently thinner in straw, and shorter in ear, as was visible anno 1704 in most grounds, which might have been prevented by giving three earths; — for if the corn in ground working rough comes up the later, it is consequently the backwarder, which is a great disadvantage in our cold hill-country, where it is of the utmost consequence to have our corn early ripe.

Custom in Leicestershire, and of the worm there

§. 40. In the inclosures in Leicestershire, where the land is fresh, the way is to have four successive crops without either dunging or folding; and then to lay down to grass, laying pot-dung on the last stubble: viz. they take three crops of barley and one of wheat; they harrow always on one earth; and plough not up for barley till January or February. — Because as I suppose, the land being deep, would be apt to run to weeds, on longer rest, before seed-time. — In these inclosures they never take a wheaten crop first: it seems in fresh broken-up ground both the wheaten and the barley crops are subject to be eaten by a worm, as the wheat in the Isle of Wight: to prevent which Mr. Clerk eats the grass as close as he can, for that being turned in, as he thinks, occasions the worm.

Of stirring poor land early for wheat.

§. 41. The workmen that were flinging out dung for me said, I might stir my land in the last stirring three weeks or a month before I flung in my wheat, and this was a frequent practice. I talked with an old experienced farmer about it, but he seemed by no means to allow it for poor land that had been often ploughed; for it would, by giving it it's last stirring so early in the year, be apt to

run

run abundantly to weeds; yet, said he, for fresh or lay-land it may do very well.

§. 42. I observe many farmers scruple stirring Of stirring land. their ground before seed-time (the success whereof nevertheless they doubt of without it) either out of covetousness, or a fancy of not having leisure to do it then, tho' at such times teams may be hired; and yet at seed-time, when time is ten times more precious, they shall bestow the same time in harrowing it, by reason of it's roughness, and, after all, the ground shall not work so well, nor lie down so fine as it ought to do.

If you propose to sow the ground you fold for barley the last in the season, have a regard to the stirring it, especially if it be a ground any wise inclinable to grass, for it is not to be supposed but the winter folding has established such a root of grass, by inriching it, as is not to be overcome by ploughing up the ground, after being fallowed so late as the latter end of April or May, by which time the grass must have gained a good root, which will not easily be torn asunder from the earth by harrows, and consequently will be apt to grow, and the ground not to work fine.

If you summer-fallow for barley, it is best to stir about two months before seed-time, to kill the roots of the green weeds that are come up, by turning them up to the frosts, and burying their leaves and stalks; besides such ground, being so thoroughly mellowed by the summer-fallow,- is so separated in it's parts, that it will not easily fall close and heavy before seed-time, tho' stirred two months before. — But if you have winter-fallowed for barley, and intend to stir, if the ground be still stiff, you should stir the earlier to mellow it with the frosts; but if the ground be pretty fryable before stirring, the later you stir it the better, for then it will break the smaller at seed-time, having the less time to settle;

and

and true it is, with the ancients, that land cannot be too fine for barley.

If ground, by spring-stirring and summer-fallowing, be made curiously mellow for barley at seed-time, tho' it will wet sooner than barley-land that has had but one fallow, so it will also dry vastly sooner; and if it be trampled on wet by the horses, yet the ground being so fine and mellow, the corn will come through; whereas when ground works rough and wet, the unbroken clods bind and cover in the wet, and keep the corn cold and wet all the summer, nor can it come through, but lies cold all the summer; besides, to work ground rough and dry at seed-time, tho' by much harrowing it may be made fine at top, yet it is to be considered, the corn has not a mellow soft bed, much of the land being buried in whole clods, as has been observed by the ancient writers on husbandry.

A neighbouring husbandman carried me into his wheat, and shewed me three or four lands that he had stirred, whereas to the rest he had given but two earths: the wheat he had stirred was as good again as the other, both in colour and thickness; the reason why stirring might be so serviceable was, that, when two earths only are given, the earth turned up to the sun in the first fallow, and thereby mellowed and impregnated, is for the most part turned down and buried underneath the corn that is sowed at the second ploughing, but on the third earth, it is sown again turned up to the surface whereon the corn is sown.

§. 43. The design of striking furrows after harrowing the wheaten land, is to strike the corn out of the furrows, wherein the corn generally dwindles, as as being chilled; to do this, when the fold is after to go over it, is needless, because the sheep tread it in again; but after the fold has run over it, it may be done.

*Of striking furrows after harrowing wheat.*

For

For want of drawing a furrow after harrowing in of wheat the reapers at harvest are at a loss how to measure, and for a guide to work by.

§. 44. Wet clay-grounds, that lie wet and soggy all the winter, will chop and grow starky all the summer, so that they will have peculiar infirmities in all seasons: in my opinion, abundance of, and very thick trenching of such lands will be a much cheaper, and more effectual improvement of them, than dunging; but indeed no improvement can have effect before they are laid dry.

*Of trenching wet ground.*

## Of the TILLAGE of different LANDS.

§. 45. *Mr. Hillman, a notable farmer at Thruxton, was against my picking up of stones, and said, it was certain ground would fall finer under the plough which had most stones. To which I answered, that it was true, lay-ground, or grassy ground, would break better on the first ploughing (at least if the ground was wet) the fuller it was of stones; for such ground cannot so easily cling, nor bind when ploughed up, because of the great number of stones; but ground, that has no stones, will be made to work as fine at three earths, as the ground that hath stones, and will plough with a much narrower and finer furrow standing upright and on edge than the stony ground will do, the furrow whereof must be carried broad, or else the tumbling of the stones will fill it up.

*Of ploughing stone land. * Vid. p. 87 v. §. 1. Of picking up stones. Arguments against it answered.*

§. 46. Quinteny says, to dry earths I allow a large culture or tillage at the entrance of winter, and the like as soon as it is past, that the snows and rains of the winter and spring may easily sink into the ground; but to strong and moist earths I allow but small tillage in October, only to remove the weeds, and stay to give them a large one at the end of

*Different tillage of dry and moist earths.*

April, or beginning of May, when the fruit is perfectly knit, and the great moisture is over.

Of ploughing husky, loose earth. §. 47. If ground be of a husky, wood-seary nature, in the parts of which is not a fit continuity, in such earth there is a porous adhesion, through which both cold winds and the sun may penetrate, and in which, being of a spungy nature, as light as it seems to be, the water will lie and chill the ground, as it does also in healthy grounds; to cure this evil, and bring it to a more solid body, the more you plough it the closer it will lie to the roots of the corn, and become more solid, being also rolled, or rather trod with sheep; for if in clay-land, notwithstanding the great room a post takes in a post-hole, the same earth will with ease be rammed in the same hole again with the post, and even more if need were, because in the digging it up the earth is broken into minuter parts, how much more is the husky land abovementioned so broken by ploughing; it being much more porous, and capable of being forced into a compacter and closer body in it's surface the more it is broken by the plough, and then trod with sheep, or rolled; whereas the roller, or sheep, if it be sowed on one earth, will not be able to compress the clods, nor squeeze the earth close in the hollows.

## Of the MANNER of PLOUGHING.

Of ridging land. §. 48. I observed this year, 1711, it having been a wet and cold spring, that wherever in my clay-lands there was a little sinking of the ground, on those flats there was little barley, and that thin in body, the ground being too wet for barley: from hence it seems to me, it would be very good husbandry to ridge and round up all the grounds that are cold clay on our hill-country, where the land is of depth to bear it; for as the delving parts of the grounds

grounds are much too cold for barley, so the very healthy and driest parts of cold clay would be the kindlier for barley, especially in so cold a country; whereas throughout this hill-country we all plough the grounds upon the flat, and thwart the furrows in stirring. It seems also to me, that this very good effect may proceed from such ridging up the lands, viz. that the lands will on that account plough so much the drier and mellower in fallowing, and consequently will at seed-time, (by turning up dry in fallowing) turn up dry and in powder; whereas, when the lands in fallowing are laid flat, they take in the wet, and lie wet all the winter, and when they come to be stirred at seed-time, they turn up too wet and cold for barley.

§. 49. There is a practice in husbandry of giving the last ploughing to grounds some time before sowing them; which is, when ground is not in a proper temper for flinging in the seed and harrowing; this is done when persons have a great deal to do, but, wanting a season, they would prepare their grounds against one may happen; but this practise commonly meets with very different events in wheat, or winter-corn, and in lenten or spring-corn; for winter-corn, when prudently done, it is very good husbandry; but seldom so, when practised for spring-corn, for the reasons following. The reason of doing it for wheat is, because the season of the year being far advanced for sowing wheat, and the land too dry to venture the sowing (for wheat is seldom long hindered from sowing by wet) the husbandman gives the last ploughing in order to sow wheat, that on the first rain he may commit the seed to the ground, and then harrow-in several acres in a day; whereas were he to plough for what he sows he could dispatch but little in a day: it is apparent this practice may be very good husbandry; for the ground in this case is supposed to be ploughed very

*Of ploughing some time before sowing, not good for spring-corn.*

dry,

dry, and confequently a fine bed, by breaking the ground with the plough, is not prepared for the growing of the feeds of weeds ; for no feeds of weeds can make advances to get the ftart of the corn till rain comes, and then the wheat will be fowed, and be able to fet forth as forward as the weeds; and hereby, when we are behindhand in fowing our crop of wheat, much time is gained ; which is a great advantage to a crop of wheat ; but in the other cafe, ploughing beforehand for barley, or fpring-corn, in order to fow it when a feafon comes, or the ground is in temper, muft in all likelihood be improper hufbandry ; becaufe, generally fpeaking, we muft in fuch cafe be fuppofed to plough beforehand, becaufe the ground was too wet or too moift for fowing barley, and then, a bed being prepared, and the fpring and warm time of the year being advanced, the feeds of weeds will grow, if the ground were ploughed never fo dry, yet if a glut of rain fhould come, which will hinder you from fowing, it will neverthelefs make the weeds grow.

§. 50 Mr. Edwards afked farmer Biggs, if he had not laid his ground too flat. Note, he had fown it to wheat.--Farmer Biggs replied, confidering what fort of ground it was, it could not be too flat, it being a lightifh fort of ground.—I afked, whether it was poffible to lay wheaten ground too flat in the hill-country of Hampfhire ; farmer Biggs replied, if it was clay-cold-land, they looked on it beft to round up the furrows a little,—and fo faid Mr. Edwards.

*Of laying the furrows flat in the hill-country.*

Mr. Garnam, of Prior's-court, Berks, was alfo of opinion, that, if ground was any ways wet and cold, laying it a little round for wheat not only favoured the corn in laying it the healthier in the winter, but alfo, when the fpring came, by lying healthier it would lie fo much the warmer, and fhoot away, tho' the fpring fhould prove wet and cold, and thereby avoid the blights the better ; for laying

laying corn dry forwards is as much as sowing early.

It is the heat and warmth of the earth, occasioned by the sun and dry weather, that opens, loosens, and refines the vegetative parts, and causes them to breath up in steams into the plants; nor does the earth want moisture for such a purpose, provided it hath just enough for a vehicle sufficient to convey those corpuscles; therefore all cold rains, or rains in cold weather, or wet sogging in the earth, are great enemies to that vegetative power, and do chill, check, and lock up (instead of loosening) those corpuscles from ascending up into plants, to the augmenting their bulks; from hence it may be collected, how reasonable it is to lay the furrows of wheaten clay-lands up round, tho' they are in the hill-country; but, if they should lie at all flat, yet so to contrive that they may not lie wet, longer than needs must be, under the cold winter or spring rains.

Lands being made very fine for wheat ought to be sowed the later; because, if early sowed, many seeds of weeds, more tender than wheat, and too tender to grow at the latter end of September, will grow at the beginning of that month; and the bed of earth you have made so fine and fit for corn, will, you must conceive, be also fitter to bring up the seeds of weeds; and the later you sow your wheat, if upon strong land especially, the more need is there to lay up your lands somewhat round, tho' the clay be of a healthy dry nature, for the drier the land lies the faster the corn will come away, and keep growing the better during the whole winter, it lying the warmer for lying dry; whereas cold and wet are certain enemies to vegetation.

§. 51. Mr. Edwards was saying to me, that it was a great error to turn up too large a furrow, and that ploughmen, that they might be thought to have done a good day's work, were very apt to do so, *Of large furrows.*

I 3 whereas

whereas it was more profit to turn up as narrow a furrow as they could, tho' less land were ploughed.—— Of this I spoke afterwards to farmer Biggs; he said, it was true; the smaller the furrow the better; but in lay-land, if stiff, it would not turn up small, but stand an-end, if the ploughman endeavoured to turn it up small; but, said he, in oat-stubble, or barley-stubble, that work light, the smaller the furrow the better.

Mr. Edwards having told me, that it was a great fault in ploughmen, out of greediness to seem to have done mnch, to turn up large furrows at seed-time, and it seeming good reason to me, because, the more and narrower the furrows the more the corn, the corn coming up for the most part in the furrows. —— I asked also Thomas Elton about it, a very understanding husbandman, and he said, he could never for his part see the sense of fallowing, and taking pains all the year, to lose a third or fourth part of one's crop at last by a large furrow.—— I asked him then, what furrow was best in fallowing; he said, if ground worked fine, a large furrow would do well and turn up small enough at it's second earth; but, said he, if it fallows up heavy and rough, and be turned up in a large furrow, it will not be brought to be fine by seed-time; therefore such land ought to be fallowed with a small furrow.

Quære, If the narrower the furrow in fallowing of stubble ground would not be the better for barley, as well as in the last ploughing in sowing-time? because the narrower the furrows the more power the frosts and dry weather would have over them, and the more upright the more hollow they stand; whereas the broader the flatter, and more apt to receive wet, and the more the furrow holds in breadth the less does it break. I know in whole land, that is grassy, it is otherwise, for, if such land be designed for a fallow, unless one furrow flap over the other, the

the grass will live between the furrows, and not rot, and if such land is to be sowed on one earth, if the furrows lie upright, the corn must fall between.

I ordered my head-ploughman to fallow for barley in a field, which being proper to be ploughed the same way again, as I fallowed it, I thought it might not plough so fine at sowing it, as if I had thwarted it ; so I gave him a caution, not to fallow it rough, but to turn up a little furrow. —— But he said, a large furrow would be best, because that will be split or divided in seed-time, but if he ploughed a fine furrow now, and ploughed the same way at seed-time, a narrow furrow could not be split in the middle, but turn back again whole.

I was sowing barley on wheaten-fallow, and, as you plough up-hill and down, the plough also goes alongside part of the hill ; as I was in the field observing this ploughing my bailiff said, the plough going on the side-long could not carry so narrow a furrow as otherwise it might, for, if they should go to plough a very narrow furrow, they could not hold the plough in, but the hill-side would be often casting it out ; on the other hand, when the plough turns, and the broad board goes against the side of it, it is as hard to keep a narrow furrow, the hill being apt to fling the plough off.

## Of PLOUGHING with HORSES or OXEN.

§. 52. My carter says, that wherever one ploughs stiff land, or lay-land, or hilly land, it is cheaper to maintain six horses, and drive them in the plough, than four ; for, says he, four cannot be supposed at most to plough above an acre in a winter's day, and six will go away so fast with it (it being so much easier to them) as to plough near an acre and half per

*(margin note)* Stiff land ploughed cheaper with six horses than four.

I 4 day

day; and then besides the horses need not that proportion of oats, their labour being easy. A farmer stood by and said, he believed the same; if so, the two horses will well pay for their keeping.

I summer-fallowed for barley, and hired a farmer to fallow with four horses, and I fallowed myself with other four; but the season being very dry, and the ground having laid two years to broad-clover, and being stony withal, I found they made but a slow riddance, insomuch that I believe, a plough and six horses would have ploughed as much as those two ploughs; and besides, they, by being weak, were forced to plough the ground scragling, inasmuch as the ploughman was forced to wriggle with the plough where the sull stopped at any stones, to help the weakness of the horses, by means of which we could not hold a steady and even furrow neither in breadth nor depth; and as his plough did consequently often jump out of ground, so he was at a great deal of pains and care to get it in again; whereas a plough with six horses goes through thick and thin, and will carry an even furrow by flinging and forcing up all stones in it's way; so note, against the next time, in like case, the advantage of ploughing with six horses.

**Advantage of oxen.** § 53. One advantage in a team of oxen is, that one of the men who go with them may go about other business when ploughing hours are over, for one man is abundantly sufficient to look after six oxen.

Mr. Baily of Wiltshire very strongly persuades me to keep a plough of oxen together with my horse-plough: he confesses an ox-team cannot go to market, in a country where horse-ploughs are kept, because of the ruts they must tread into, but for carrying out dung into the fields, ploughing, and harvesting, they will do as well as horses. He says the shoeing of an ox round, comes to 16 d. — but if the

inner

inner hoofs behind are not fhod, (which in our country they need not, not going on the roads with them)
four oxen in fhoeing are but the price of three. He
fays they will endure eight hours ploughing in the
day, in winter, with ftraw only, till towards Lady-
day, and then they muft have hay ; and if they are
kept up, they will go as faft as a horfe-plough. And
he fays, in the very winter they may be turned out
into the backfide to ftraw after their day's work, and
will not take cold ; but I believe in our country fuch
ufage would be too cold : Mr. Biffy was prefent, and
agreed to all this, ——and both of them held, that,
if fatting oxen ftalled were over-bound in their bodies, which by being kept hot they might be apt to
be, they muft be turned out to the air, for, whilft
bound, they will not thrive.

An advantage of ploughing with oxen is, that you
fummer-fallow the ftrongeft lands with them in the
drieft feafon (their chains being ftrong) by making a
plough of ten oxen, and adding a ploughman the
more to hold down the plough ; whereas, if at fuch
time you make a plough of eight horfes, they will
not carry fo true a furrow, and will break their har-
neis.

# HARROWING.

§. 1. THE Romans, after the feveral fallowings before mentioned, fowed their
grain, and, if they found occafion, harrowed it, and
then, as it feems to me, turned it under furrow, tho'
I do not remember that any of their writers fpeak
particularly of fowing under furrow, or on one earth ;
I think they are filent in thefe matters. When
this was done, and the corn was come up, they
proceeded to another operation, which they called farrition, a kind of harrowing or raking with
wooden

*Of the far-
rition of
the anti-
ents.*

wooden or iron rakes, for they are both either mentioned or intimated by Columella..—[b] This sarrition was performed in dry burning lands before the winter came on, and then they covered the blade intirely by raking the new earth over it, taking however what care they could not to wound or mangle the roots.—This, they thought, protected it from the cold, gave it fresh nourishment, assisted it in it's growth, [c] and made the roots tillow and spread. When the rigor of the winter was over in January, according to Palladius, and in February according to Pliny, and in dry but not frosty weather) they raked it a second time, in a slighter manner, or a different way;—[d] But in cold wet land they used only the spring sarrition, raking the earth so as not to bury the blade, lest the young suckers or tillows should be thereby destroyed——[e] The great use of this later sarrition was thought to lie in it's loosening the ground which had been bound up by the winter's frosts, and thereby giving an easier admission to the rays of the sun.——They made it a rule however, let the season be never so favourable, not to use this husbandry [f], till the corn was grown to that height as to equal the

[a] Ligneis rastris sarriendus. Colum. de medicâ—Ferro succisa emoritur. Id. de lupino.

[b] In agris siccis et apricis, simul ac primam sarritionem pati queant segetes, debere eas permotâ terrâ obrui, ut fruticare possint, quod ante hyemem fieri oportere, deinde post hyemem iterari.—Sic fieri debet ut ne radices satorum lædantur.

[c] Ut latius se humi frutex diffundat.

[d] In locis frigidis et palustribus plerumque transfactâ hyeme sarriri, nec adobrui, sed planâ sarritione terram permoveri.—Cum pullulare desiit frumentum, putrescit, si adobrutum est.—Columella.—Qui sarriat, caveat ne radices frumenti suffodiat.—Plin. lib. 18.

[e] Sarculatio induratam hiberno rigore soli tristitiam laxat temporibus vernis, novosque soles admittit. Plin. lib. 18.

[f] Cum sata sulcos contexerint. Columella. (Sulcos æquant sata. Virgilius.) Triticum sarritur quatuor foliorum, hordeum quinque. Palladius et Columella.—Faba et cætera legumina cum quatuor digitis a terra extiterint. Columella.

tops

tops of the furrows.——Wheat was thus harrowed
when it began to have four leaves, barley when it
had five, beans, and the rest of the leguminous kind,
when they were four fingers high.——The earlier sarrition would by no means be proper in our wet climate; [g] and indeed this method of husbandry, both
of the earlier and later kind, tho' in frequent practice
among the Romans, was thought by many to do
rather harm than good, inasmuch as it often wound-
ed the roots of the corn, or laid them bare to be
killed by the frosts.——When their sarrition was
finished, they pulled up by hand the weeds that
these harrows had left remaining, and this they
termed runcation.

§. 2. Mr. Hillman being with me, when I ordered
the smith to make tinings to my drags, he persuaded
me to have the tinings steeled, assuring me it would
five times over-pay.——Qu. why not steeled tinings
to harrows ?

*To steel the tinings of your drags.*

§. 3. It is some disadvantage that oxen will not
make any great dispatch in harrowing, nor will the
slow manner of their drawing the harrow about do
great service, if the furrow tear not easily ; for the
harrows drawn slowly slide over the hard earth;
whereas, when drawn apace by horses, they jump,
and whatever the tinings or teeth catch hold of they
tear through ; but in mellow rotten ground, where
the harrows easily enter, there you may make good
work with oxen.

*Of harrow-ing with oxen.*

§. 4. Sometimes in dragging-in of corn, especially by oxen, where the chain, which is fastened to
the drags, may be taken up and shortened, as the
ox-hind pleases, if you have not an eye to your ox-

*Caution against the fraud of ox-hinds in drag-ing.*

[g] Quidam negant eam quicquam proficere, quod frumenti
radices sarculo detegantur; aliquæ etiam succidantur, ac si frigora incesserint post sarritionem, gelu frumenta enecentur. Sub-
ungenda est deinde sarritioni runcatio.

hind,

hind, he will be apt to shorten his chain so, that it shall lift up a row or two of the hither or fore-tinings, and so but a small weight will lie on the hinder row of tinings, whereby the drag will, for the most part, be born up from the ground, so that the first row, and it may be the second, shall not enter the ground, nor the hindmost row go deep enough; and this the ox-hind will do, if not well looked after, for the ease of his cattle; because they draw abundantly less weight, when the foremost rows of tinings are lifted up from the ground, than when the chain the oxen draw by is so lengthened out, that every row of tinings may lie plumb and flat on the ground, and have liberty thereby, not being held up, of sinking in the deeper; whereby the corn is also laid the deeper, and the ground torn the better: the ox-hind's ill practice in favour of his cattle is ruinous to the master, and therefore servants are to be well looked after: an hundred pounds by this abuse may soon be lost in an hundred acres of corn sowed on one earth.

What number of harrows best for stiff land.

§. 5. Where land has been summer-fallowed for barley, two harrows will harrow it as well as four harrows will harrow land winter-failowed for wheat.

It is agreed, that three harrows will do more service than four going two and two, for the third harrow contributes much by it's weight in keeping down the other two.

Manner of harrowing stiff land.

§. 6. If furrows be starky and stiff, so that there may be danger of turning them back again, in thwarting them with the harrows, if one harrow them not directly athwart, but aslant, that danger will be prevented.

Caution against harrowing too wet.

§. 7. It is to be observed in harrowing, tho' the ground may harrow well enough at top, whether it may not be so wet underneath, as for the horses to tread the seed in too deep, and into such paste and mortar, that it cannot shoot it's blade through.

It

# HARROWING.

It is a common piece of ill husbandry, when the spring-season of sowing proves wet and rainy, and there may be a ground under harrowing that may want but the last tining or two, (perhaps an hour's, or but half an hour's work of being finished) when a hard shower of rain shall come, and the ground harrows wet, to continue harrowing, out of covetousness of finishing that ground, and unwillingness to leave so little behind undone, and to come again to that ground, when the next work they are to go upon lies perhaps a mile, or half a mile off; but servants should have most express charge given them, as a general rule, at the beginning of seed-time, immediately to stop and desist harrowing, if the ground harrows wet and dauby, especially in clay-ground; for, tho' the ground harrowed never so well before a shower of rain came, yet the taking one turn more with the harrows, while the surface is wet, will make it crust and bake so, that if dry windy weather come, the corn will have a difficult passage through.

§. 8. I sowed a field anno 1703 with oats, having fallowed it very early; the winter proved wet and rainy, which beat the ground very flat; but, being in good heart, it was apt by sowing-time to shew grass; and particularly in the bottom of that ground, that being very stony, as well as beaten flat by the great rains, the harrows could not raise * a grete; therefore, tho' in the hill-country such grounds are the best, yet that bottom brought me more grass than oats; wherefore it is to be remembered, that such bottoms be ploughed up again at seed-time, and care ought always to be taken, that such bottoms lie light, when to be sowed; that the harrow tinings may be let in.

Of harrowing stony bottoms.

* mold or staple.

I had wheat anno 1706, which I sowed on one earth, and tho' the bottom of the ground was as good as any of the rest, yet the wheat was not above half as good, neither as to thickness, nor the proof it was in: the

reason

reaſon muſt be, becauſe, the bottom of that ground being very ſtony, the tinings of the harrows rid upon the ſtones, and ſo the corn was never well healed.—— Therefore, when ſuch grounds are ſowed with wheat on one earth, I adviſe that the ſtony bottoms be ploughed ſome time before, ſo that they may come to be thwarted, and ſowed under furrow, when the other land is ploughed and ſowed to one earth.

*Much har-rowing, no cure for ground ploughed rough.*

§. 9. I can ſee but little cauſe for the ſatisfaction the farmers ſeem to have, in fancying if a ground works rough, that fault may be cured by much har-rowing; for thereby the lumps are buried, and, for the moſt part, the corn under them, there being only a fine ſmooth mold gained at top, by the ſcratching of the harrows.

*To drive ſheep over wheat raiſed out of the ground by harrowing.*

§. 10. Having harrowed a field of my wheat, and endeavouring to give it three or four tinings more, in order to fine off ſome of the rougher part, they brought up a great deal of grain, that in three or four tinings before they had buried: I adviſed with farmer Biggs, and propoſed to rake them in: he ſaid, the beſt way by much, and in ſuch caſes they uſed, was to drive their ſheep over the ground, which would prick them in.

*Of har-rowing peas.*

§. 11. It is beſt to let the furrows lie three weeks or a month, after ſowing peas, unharrowed; the fur-rows keep the cold and wet from the corn; whereas, if by that time the peas be rooted, they will not have ſprouted out, and then the harrows will not hurt them.

*Of drag-ging.*

§. 12. In talking with a notable farmer in Wilt-ſhire on the ſubject of ſowing broad-clover with oats, he told me, he always dragged them in with their country drags (which are not ſo big as ours, and have but ſix tinings on a harrow) and this he does, tho' his ground had been ploughed up but a fortnight before; but he commonly ſowed broad-clover on ground ploughed ſo long before as Candlemaſs, which never will,

will, tho' it works mellow, fall too close for the drags
to tear it.——Here note, if dragging does so much
better with them than harrowing, even in ground
that would, as we should think in Hampshire, tear
well with harrows, it must do better with us, because
we do not plough so deep as they do in Wiltshire,
nor will the tinings of the drags go so deep with
us as with them, on account of the stones, and so
we can be in no danger or fear of burying oats or
barley. The farmer says, he sows very little or no
barley without dragging it, and the like he does to
wheat too after he has sown it, tho' on a second
earth; nay, he often drags the ground once, when
ploughed the second time, before he sows either
wheat or barley, in order to break the furrows and
the seams, that the corn may come up the more
* suant; and on the backs of the furrows, which * Kindly.
are dragged after the corn is sown, there is no fear
but the drag-tinings will let it in deep enough. ——
To make wheat come up more suant, when sown
on one earth, or on stale fallows, he always drags
it first, before it is sowed, and then gives it two or
three tinings, and says, there is no fear but the
drag-tinings will let the corn in deep enough. ——
This method of dragging wheat and barley land, in
any of these respects, before you sow it, saves seed:
for you may sow less on an acre.—— It is a general
fault in Hampshire, that, having so much to do,
we slubber it over without dragging when it ought
to be dragged, and content ourselves with only harrowing the ground, and, when we either drag or
harrow, we do not bestow labour enough on it in
either respect.

*PICKING*

# PICKING UP STONES.

Advantage
of picking
up stones.
Vide §. 45.
Of plough-
ing.
† mold or
staple.

§. 1. THE advantage of picking up stones in clay-land is, that, the stones being picked up, the ground harrows much the better ; the number of stones and their bigness bearing up the harrows from reaching the † grete, and making the ground plough rugged ; nor can a weak plough turn it up but to great disadvantage, every stone being a harrow-rest ; besides, to plough such ground true, there must two men go with the plough, for a man and a boy are not sufficient, it being too tiresome for one man to hold the plough all day, a man's weight being necessary to keep the plough in the ground.-----It is to be noted that, where ground is trod much by cattle, especially that part of it that they go most in and out on, or where carting has been, the ploughing is very stiff.

The better raking up the barley is another motive for picking up the stones to be added to the former.

Another advantage of picking up stones is, that thereby the plough turns up fresh earth by going deeper : the very weight of the stones (where there are many) contributes to the settling and binding of the earth to great prejudice after rains.

The advantage of picking up great stones at least appears from the inconvenient rolling of wheat in March or April ; for the roller is always riding on one stone or other, which it cannot squeeze in, and in that case, is born hollow throughout it's whole length from compressing the ground.

Another advantage of picking up stones is, that, if it be clay-lay-land, and ploughed dry, which for wheat is to the advantage of the land, the plough-beam, sprinter, whippings, and traces must often break when they come against a great stone, as my

neighbour

neighbour experienced this summer (anno 1704)
who said, they broke in one piece of ground as
much plough-tackle (even their beam, tho' new,
&c.) as came to the value of every day's work.

Another advantage of picking up great stones in
arable land is, that a less roller, with fewer horses,
will roll the ground in seed-time.

Another advantage of picking up stones is, that,
at a day's notice, one may take the advantage of the
times in hayning up for mowing, after one has
waited for the fatting cattle on one's land, and
found by the markets rising they must be bought
in too dear ; but, if an hundred load of stones must
be first picked up and carried away, it will render
the method impracticable.

§. 2. To pick up stones from poor land, continued in that condition, I look upon rather to be im-
poverishing than improving it ; for thereby you rob
the poor land of it's only dependence, which was being kept moist ; for, if such ground has not moisture
to bring up the corn, it must fail, having no strength ;
of rich land I believe just the contrary, and that
such abundance of flints, which lie so thick, or are
so broad as to keep the dews and the sun from impregnating the ground, must needs be to it's prejudice.

Not to pick up stones from poor land.

If a multitude of small stones lie on light white
ground, the evil whereof is being subject to be too
light, it seems good to let them remain, that the
weight of them may compress the ground together
(for which reason they are prejudicial to clay-land)
and wedge themselves with the ground, which se-
cures it from burning, &c. —— But great stones are
every where pernicious.—[d] In Sicily, near Syracuse,
says Pliny, a farmer, who was a stranger to that

[d] In Syracusano agro advena cultor, elapidato solo, perdidit
fruges luto, donec regessit lapides.  Plin. lib. 17.

kind of land, and to the manner of husbandry in those parts, lost his crops by picking up the stones, and found it so great a disadvantage to his land, that at length, to retrieve his damage, he thought it adviseable to bring them back again. — The ground was light there, and, I suppose, they had not the use of rollers in those countries ; nor do I find that Cato, Varro, Columella, Palladius, or Pliny, make any mention of a roller for their lands, but only of a cylinder to roll their earthen barn floors hard, and a crates, or flat frame of timber, to draw over their corn, and level their ground.

**Stones hinder wheat from tillowing.** §. 3. Quære, whether an abundance of stones in a ground may not hinder the tillowing of wheat at spring, by bearing the root off from the earth, and hindering it taking fresh root, and not suffering the roller to press it to the earth.

**Keep the roots from the benefit of the sun.** §. 4. To the disadvantage of stones in grounds may be added, that though the corn under them comes up, yet, where the root is hindered from the sun, such corn must be thin ; and, when corn lies under stones, shaded from the sun, I suppose it not only to be thinner in grain, but shorter in ear, and to carry less and fewer tillows under the stones than if exposed to the sun and air.

Nor in the bottoms, where so many stones generally lie, do the sown grasses, such as clover, &c. come to any thing, tho' the ground is allowed to be much the best : if such a ground of twenty acres has such a bottom of two or three acres, and it should cost ten pounds ridding the stones, the advantage to the clover in those two or three acres would, I believe, pay the whole charge.

SOWING.

# SOWING.

§. 1. [a] THE best seed, says Pliny, is that of a year old; if you keep it to two year old it is not so good, but if to three, it is worse still, and if it be older than that, it will not grow. [b] For seed you should choose the heaviest corn, and fullest ears, and set them apart in the barn, and by no means admit those ears that are not full throughout, but have only grains here and there by intervals. Note the curiosity of the ancients, and it stands to reason; it is in danger of producing such ears.

Of choice of seeds among the ancients.

§. 2. [c] Pliny directs those that sow early to sow thick, as the corn will be longer in coming up; and the later sown corn, he says, should be sown thin, lest it should be destroyed by coming up too thick on the ground: but surely he must mean this of the spring-corn and not the winter-corn, for the direct contrary rule holds in sowing wheat.

Quantity on an acre.

§. 3. [d] According to Cato, cold wet land should be sown first, and the warmer and drier ground be reserved to be last sown.—This he must mean of a winter-crop. Pliny and Palladius give the like rule: see also a subsequent remark of mine on a passage in Columella.

Time of sowing.

K 2 §. 4. In

[a] Semen optimum anniculum, bimum deterius, trimum pessimum, ultra sterile. Plin.

[b] Ad semen reservandum est quod gravissimum: quæ spica per intervalla semina habet abjicietur. Plin. ——Quæ seges grandissima, atque optima fuerit, seorsum in arena secerni oportet spicas, ut semen optimum habeat.—Varro, sect. 56.

[c] Festinata satione densum sparge semen, quia tardè concipiat, serotinâ rarum, quia densitate nimiâ necetur. Plin.

[d] Ubi quisque locus frigidissimus, aquosissimusque erit, ibi primum serito; in calidissimis locis sementem postremo fieri oportet. Cato, sect. 34. fol. 8.— Sationem locis humidis celerius fieri ratio est, ne semen imbre putrescat, siccis serius, ut pluviæ sequantur,

§. 4. ᵉ In the month of November, says Palladi-us, we sow wheat and barley, and of wheat five mo-dii to an acre; Columella's directions are, four mo-dii of wheat, five or six of barley, three of peas, and six of beans, which I wonder at. So that a modius, as above, being near half a bushel, they sowed above two bushels and a peck on their acre; which is as much as generally we sow in good ground; but then it must be considered, that they sowed in November, and we in September and October.—— ᶠ But Palladi-us says in his calendar of September, In this month, in wet, barren, and cold ground, and in places shad-ed from the sun, wheat should be sown, in clear se-rene weather, about the time of the æquinox, that the roots may have time to grow strong before the winter. —— ᵍ Speaking of September, he says, This is the first season of sowing vetches to be cut up for food, and the quantity to be sowed is seven modii on an acre.——So that 'tis plain they sowed vetches two months before wheat, and sowed seven modii on an acre; which is above three bushels. But in his calendar of January he says, In this month we sow vetches for seed, and not to be cut up for food;——which seems to agree with what I have in ano-ther place observed, that the seed of a plant is the tenderest part of it.: and so Columella, lib. 11. f. 9.

sequantur, ne diù jaciens, et non concipiens evanescat. Plin. lib. 18. fol. 300.

Frigidis locis autumnalis satio celerior fiat, verna vero tardi-or.---Pallad. lib. 1. fo. 60.

ᵉ Novembri mense triticum seremus, et hordeum: jugerum seminis tritici modiis quinque tenebitur. Pallad.—Tritici qua-tuor, hordei modios quinque vel sex, pisi modios tres, fabæ sex. Colum. lib. 9. fol. 9.

In hoc mense, uliginosis locis, aut exilibus, aut frigidis, aut opacis, circa æquinoctium triticum seretur, dum serenitas constat, ut radices frumenti ante hyemem convalescant. Pallad.

ᵍ Nunc viciæ, cum pabuli causâ, prima satio est; viciæ sep-tem modii jugerum implebunt.

—— [h] Of the month of May Palladius says, At this
time most corn is in flower, and the farmer must
by no means suffer it to be meddled with. Wheat
and barley, and all seeds that are single, and do not
split, are eight days in flower, and afterwards forty
days in growing to maturity; but seeds that are
double, such as beans, peas, and the rest of the leguminous kind, are forty days in flower, and are coming to perfection during the same time.

[i] Columella, lib. 11. f. 9. has these expressions;
It is an old proverbial saying among the farmers,
(a) early sowings often deceive us, (a) late never.——
We lay it down as a rule therefore, that those places
which are naturally (b) cold, should be sowed first,
and those that are (b) hot, last.

As to the former expressions, (a. a.) they wholly
depend on the clime whereof they are spoken, viz.
Italy,———where they used to sow wheat and barley in
December: no wonder therefore, if an earlier sowing,
where the corn indures the whole winter, oftener
miscarries than a later sowing, where it indures but
half a winter: nor could they well sow too late, in
another respect; because their corn was ripe the beginning of June, that was sowed in December; what
harm then can ensue from it's being sown in January
or February? for then it will be ripe in July, which
is before it can suffer by a cold autumn.——It is plain

*Depends on the climate, and is no rule for us.*

[h] Nunc omnia prope quæ sata sunt, florent, neque tangi a
cultore debebunt.  Florent autem sic: frumentum et hordeum,
et quæ sunt seminis singularis octo diebus florebunt, et deinde
per dies quadraginta grandescunt, usque ad maturitatis eventum;
quæ verò duplicis seminis sunt, sicut faba, pisum, cæteraque legumina, quadraginta diebus florent, simulque grandescunt. Pallad.

[i] Vetus est agricolarum proverbium, maturam (a) sationem
sæpe decipere solere, (a) seram nunquam;  — Itaque in totum
præcipimus, ut quisque naturâ locus (b) frigidus erit, is primus
conseratur, ut quisque calidus, (b) novissimus.  Columella, lib.
9. fol. 11.

therefore,

therefore, it would be very dangerous to import this Italian maxim into England; because we may easily sow too late: for our ground being poorer, if we sow it in May, which is the latter season of English seed-time, it may often be so dry, as never to bring up the corn, and what may be brought up, if the summer be cold, will never ripen kindly; some sort of strong fat lands, and even some cold gravels, may carry it out so late sown.——The latter expressions, (b. b.) are also purely southern, and would deceive an Englishman; but no wonder it was best in Italy to sow their cold land first, whether for wheat or barley; for directions are given by Palladius to sow such wheaten-lands, in September and October;---and those months, and November and December, are drier months than January and February; therefore heavy strong ground may be expected to work better, and the flinging corn into a dry warm bed, especially if land be cold, is of great consequence, whatever weather may come after: and the season of sowing their hot land is as judiciously chosen in January and February, which are wetter.---But this general practice would be destructive to paying rents in England; for the beginning of our barley season being in March, and the beginning of April, and the grounds satiated with winter-rains, 'tis then commonly the wettest season, and consequently cold lands ought not then to be sown, but hot lands; and therefore with us, in that case, the order in husbandry is plainly to be inverted.

The antients sowed more corn on an acre than we do.

§. 5. If it be well considered, that a Roman jugerum is but little better than half our acre, and their modius a little less than half our bushel; we shall find that the Romans, see their Rei rusticæ scriptores, did seed their grounds more than we do, notwithstanding they sowed better land, and it lay so much warmer than our's.----A modius is 26 lb. 8 ounces.

Pliny

[k] Pliny orders to fow in an acre, (which is but little above half our acre) of wheat five bufhels, (each little better than half our bufhel) of barley fix modii, of beans a fifth part more than of wheat, of vetches twelve modii, which I think very ftrange; of chick peas, and chicklings, and peas, three modii, which is equally furprifing.

§. 6. Sharrock in his book of Vegetation, speak- *Time of ing of the feafon of fowing, fays, fol. 10. The moft *fowing.* natural time of fowing is that which nature itfelf follows, viz. when the feeds of their own accord fall into the ground.

§. 7. In the fecond volume of Collections of *Time of travels it is faid, that in Mufcovy, as well as in In- *fowing in gerland, Carelia, and the northern parts of Livonia, *the north-ern coun-they do not fow till about three weeks before Mid- *tries.* fummer, becaufe the cold, which has penetrated deep into the earth, muft have leifure to thaw, notwith-ftanding which, their harveft is over in Auguft, the fun, which remains fo long above their horizon in fummer, foon ripening their corn ; [l] but the Livo-nians are forced to dry their's by the help of ovens in the barns, after it is brought in, which is fubject to many inconveniencies, and makes their corn unfit for feed, whereas the Mufcovites carry in their's dry and fit to be threfhed. fo. 18.

§. 8. A feeds-man is much lefs apt to fow too *Of fowing thin going up and down-hill than on a level, becaufe, *up and when he takes his turn up-hill, his fteps are always *down-hill.* fhort, and his hand muft caft corn at every ftep ; again, going down-hill it is painful to take large fteps. My carter and feeds-man are very pofitive in this point, and to me it feems reafonable.

[k] Tritici quinque modios, hordei fex modios, fabæ quintam partem amplius quam tritici, viciæ duodecim modios,—ciceris, & cicerculæ & pifi tres modios.—Plin lib 18. c. 24.
[l] Of this fee Mr. Tull's and Mr Dubamel's account in note on Granaries. Article—Of preferving corn.

§. 9. IF your feeds-man in the caft of his hand
back drops pretty much of his feed, which is common to many, who are not right good feeds-men;
in the middle of each half of the land, which the
feeds-man walks on, you may perceive a thicker lift
or feam than ordinary, when the corn comes up,
as if it had been double fowed, as indeed it has;
and the other parts of the ground between muft
confequently be thinner fowed, by reafon of this feed
mifemployed; old feeds-men will often do this
when the wrift of their hand grows weak; but fuch
a feeds-man ought by no means to be fuffered to
fow.

§. 10. My feeds-man fays, he has many a day
fowed five, and fometimes fix quarters of oats or
barley per day; though it is a very hard day's
work; but wheat, he fays, is too heavy a grain to
carry fo much of, and that three quarters of wheat
per day is very good fowing.

Quantity
of feeds,
and why
farmers
differ in
this in the
hill-coun-
try.

§. 10. In our hill-country of Hampfhire fome
fow two bufhels and an half of wheat on an acre,
and fome fow four bufhels: I have been at a lofs to
underftand the reafon of this diverfity. In both
cafes, the ground being very poor, I do conclude, that
where but two bufhels and an half are fowed, the
land lies cold, and is alfo cold in nature, (as at Eafton)
and muft therefore be fowed early, as in Auguft,
whereby it has the benefit both of the autumn, and
of the fpring-tillow. But in warm, tho' poor land,
and lying on the open hills, yet much warmer than
at Eafton, fhould they fow early, it would run up to
fpindle; confequently they are obliged to fow late,
perhaps the latter end of September, or the beginning
of October;----whereby they lofe the benefit of the
autumn-tillow, and can depend only on the fpring-
tillow, which on poor land is not confiderable; therefore to fill out a crop they fow it thick, viz. four
bufhels on an acre.

§. 11. When-

§. 11. Whenever you see corn in flourishing Of sowing<br>ill or un-<br>seasonable. proof, and of a good colour, tho' never so thin on the ground, you may be sure the ground is in good heart, and would have born a great crop, had there not been some error in the managing it, either by under-sowing, or by sowing the ground out of order, in respect either to it's temper, or to the season when it was done.

§. 12. Being at Mr. Whistler's, a discourse arose Quantity<br>of seed on<br>new broke<br>up ground. about the quantity of seed to be sown in a new broken up ground, rich in heart.- -Mr. Whistler said, he always understood that such ground should be sowed thick.---And it is true ; this is the practice : but the intent of this can only be, and the only foundation this practice is built on must be, that the thicker the corn comes up the lesser the ear, and the shorter the straw, and therefore not in such danger of lodging as when sown thin ; for then the straw runs to a length, with a long heavy ear ; besides, when corn tillows much, as in good ground sowed thin it will do, many stalks or tillows on one root do not stand so firm as the same number of stalks do in the same field, where only one or two stalks stand on the same root.——But this method seems to stint the produce and power of nature, for fear of a worse inconveniency attending the corn by being * more- * loose at<br>root. loose, and so apt to lodge ;---whereas, in my opinion, this may be prevented by sowing great wheat, or battel-door-barley, or beans, which have stronger stalks, and are not in such danger of falling as vetches, peas, &c. are ;---and thus the increase of the ear will not, as in the former case, be diminished.

§. 13. The only reason, as I conceive, for far- Of sowing<br>small lean<br>seed in<br>poor<br>ground. mers choosing the smallest and leanest seed for their poor ground, such as ours in the hill-country, is, that the large seed has a posse in it to send forth more tillows than the poor seed, according to which power if the great seed should exert itself, and the ground by reason of it's poverty could not maintain

what

what it had brought forth in a green blade, then moſt of ſuch blades muſt die, or ſtarve ; in which caſe, it had been much better to have ſown ſmall ſeed, which would have brought fewer tillows, and thoſe have been well maintained.----What way ſoever, whether by brining or liming your ſeed-corn, or nicking the ſeed-ſeaſon, it is of great conſequence, and the firſt good ſtep to be made to get good roots from your ſeed ; for, tho' your ground be poor, the larger and fairer the ſeed ſtrikes it's roots, it has the larger compaſs of ground to draw nouriſhment from.

**Of ſowing under fur-row.** §. 14. It ſeems dangerous to ſow any ſort of corn under furrow in gravelly land, or ſuch ſtony ground as may bind after rain, tho' it ſhould work never ſo fine ; for the ground being inclined to bind makes the corn require a much longer time to come up, whereby it runs the greater danger of ſuch weather falling, before it can come up. as may deſtroy it.

**Of ſowing ſpring-corn.** §. 15. In the ſpring-ſowing-time, in our hill-coun-try, we may venture to plough and ſow our ground a little wetter in the beginning of the ſeed-ſeaſon than we may in the middle and latter end of it, becauſe at the beginning of the ſeaſon the air is cooler than at the latter end, and the ſun not ſo ſcorching ; and ſo the ground ploughed and ſowed a little too wet will have leiſure to dry moderately, and not be ſo ſubject to bake and bind as towards the latter end of ſowing-time, when the ſeaſon begins to be ſcorch-ing.

**Of ſowing ſummer-corn early on ground winter fal-lowed dry.** §. 16. If ground, be it clay or other cold land, has been ploughed when dry in winter, and ſo early, that the rains and froſts it has ſuſtained have ſlatted it to powder ; ſuch lands no one ſhould be afraid of ſowing to barley, oats, or peas, a fortnight ſooner than uſual, in caſe the ſeaſon be very dry, ſo that it will harrow on one earth in duſt, or ſtir up in like manner by the plough ; for if the earth be in ſuch temper, no froſts, even the very hardeſt, following

immediately

immediately on such sowing, can freeze the ground, because there is no watery substance in it to be frozen, and the seed, being put into the ground dry, cannot freeze, and so must lie in a warm dry bed.----But again, supposing rain should immediately come, and hold for a fortnight after such sowing, yet the ground so ploughed and sowed, as abovesaid, will lie very light and hollow, for the air, and winds, and sun to dry it apace, and will not lie cold to the corn, as cold clays fallowed and sowed heavy would do, so that your corn will then lie safe: again, when corn is sowed in such ground in dust, a moderate rain will not throughly wet it, but the ground, when so dry, will take it without being glutted; and if such rain should continue for many days, time is gained, and the spring, by the end of those days, will be much nearer advanced, which is a great point gained.——But supposing the worst, that after many days rain, when the ground is throughly wet, a smart frost should come; neither in this case would corn, sown when the ground was in such order, take harm; for first, it is to be considered, that towards March the sun has got some strength, and that frosty weather is usually clear weather, when the sun shines by day, and thaws as deep as the frost went by night, which frosts at that time of the year seldom go so deep as the seed lies, in ground working in dust when sowed, which falls in deep; but supposing the frost should go as deep as the seed sown, it must still be allowed, the roots of the seeds strike downwards, and first form themselves before the spear peeps out of the rind, or shoots through the skin of the corn; so that to hurt the roots the frost must go deeper than is common at that time of the year; but to prevent all possible evil from frosts by sowing corn so early, when the ground invites you to it by so excellent a temper (which I do not easily foresee can happen) the person

so

so sowing his corn may do well to roll it immediately after sowing, whereby the ground so compressed, if rains should fall, and then hard frosts happen, would be able, by being more compact and close, much better to resist the frosts.

**Bad custom among the farmers in their sowing.** §. 17. It is the custom of farmers too frequently both at autumn-seed-time for wheat, and at spring-seed-time for barley, to plough up several acres of each sort a fortnight beforehand, in order to sow and harrow them in immediately, whereby they think, who have a great deal to sow, that they make a mighty dispatch, having prepared so much land beforehand, and kept themselves thereby beforehand in their business, and out of a hurry; but I take this method to be very improper and ill husbandry, for I have always observed such sowings to be full of weeds.----The reason of which I conceive to be, because in August, and at the beginning or in the middle of September, and in the middle of March, when these beforehand-ploughings are performed, the season of the year is warm enough to set seeds on growing, and the earth moldering under the plough is well prepared for that end, whereby the seeds of weeds begin to chissum or set forth their roots, and to germinate in such land so ploughed up before the corn is sowed, the narrowing-in of which when sowed will not prejudice such seeds so as to choak them; no wonder then if you have another crop of weeds along with the crop of the first ploughing, and by harrowing-in the furrows fresh seeds of weeds are moved;---but if any ground may be so managed it seems that for peas may, because in such case, if one plough barley-ersh for peas beforehand, we plough it about the latter end of February, which is before the season of the year is so far advanced, as to make the seeds of weeds put forth either root or branch, and therefore, in this case, I have known it often done successfully.

§. 18. Those

§. 18. Those lands that before harvest, on the sun's withdrawing from us, give-out in nourishing and supporting the corn, as, amongst others, cold, loose, hollow, wood-sear land will do, such lands ought to be earlier sown at autumn for wheat or vetches, because in such ground the corn will come but slowly on to establish a root before winter, for the same reason that it gives-out the following autumn before harvest; but such ground ought not therefore to be sowed early in the spring with tender grain, such as white oats, barley, &c. the ground being too cold; such ground also springs later with grass, and against winter grows sooner rowety.

Cold loose land to be sowed early, for wheat or winter-vetches.

§. 19. There is no article in husbandry of higher regard, and of greater consequence, than the rule of difference and distinction we ought to make between the seasons of sowing light, white, and chalky earth (of which we have abundance in our hill-country) which is generally very poor, and other sorts of earth. By the constant experience of my neighbours husbandry, and my own bought experience, I find, that, if such chalky white ground be sowed very wet, the whole crop is like to be very ordinary, tho' the ground was put into the best heart; for such grounds ploughed wet, to the degree of fatness or dawbiness, will certainly bind, and grow obstinate to a greater degree than the stiffest clays so ploughed; so that little corn will be able to come through, nor shall the corn which grows be able to strike roots freely, by reason of the strong union of the white earth; and successive rains, after you have sowed white earth in such condition, will sooner loosen and open and mollify the parts of clay-earth, so as to let corn through, than of white earth; therefore ploughing such ground wet at seed-time (for fallowing it wet cannot be amiss) or harrowing it wet and dawby, is most pernicious : yet it is a common thing for the farmer, when the rainy seasons make it too wet

at

at feed-time to plough other grounds, to plough
and fow in the white lands, being deceived by the
mellow breaking of fuch earth, which feems to fall
in pieces, all which foon clofe into a folid compact
fubftance; nay, the very beft of the farmers, who
are afraid of, or avoid the former evil, will in fuch
cafe run into another, when the white earth is too
wet to plough and fow at the fame time, viz. they'll
plough up fuch lands, and take the opportunity of
fowing them when they are dry; but this is bad
practice; for the inner parts of thefe lands bind and
fquat together below the harrowing tinings, fo that
the corn cannot ftrike roots, and if rainy weather
continues two or three days after it is thus ploughed, the top of the earth will bind and fquat alfo; fo
that the harrow tinings will never heal the corn, nor
open the ground, tho' they go twenty times over it.
The farmer will alfo, through difpatch, in a hurry
of much bufinefs, fow his ground in this wet condition, which brings commonly an additional affliction,
for, if wet weather follows, his corn muft lie above
ground, unharrowed, expofed to the birds, and will
foon grow, which will oblige him to harrow it
in more wet, and unfeafonably, than otherwife he
would; and thefe are the confequences of fowing
fpring-corn in white-land, either over or under furrow.

**Of fowing white earth that is graffy.** §. 20. A crop of corn fown on white earth, after
it has lain down long to grafs, is hazardous, if there
come a hot fummer after it; a fecond crop does
better; your corn may then with drags and harrows
be let in as deep as the plough goes, and, being
rolled, will endure the heat and want of rain.

**Rule for fowing fpring-corn.** §. 20. It is much in the power of farmers to
make a fhort harveft every year, which would be
much to their advantage. This might be effected
by the order of fowing the different forts of corn,
viz. to fow the rath-ripe and earlier corn fo in order,
that

that they might be ripe nearer together, and as early as poſſible. To do this it is but employing the more hands in a ſhorter time, whereas there are too many farmers, who, for want of this contrivance, or out of a delight they have in employing but a few hands, ſo ſow their ſeveral ſorts of corn, as to cut them with the feweſt hands in a lingering manner, not conſidering how much is loſt by the thinneſs of the corn in meaſure, in a backward harveſt, beſides the too frequent damage by rains in being late.

## Of ſowing SUMMER or WINTER-CORN early on one Earth.

§. 22. The reaſon of ſowing ſummer or winter-corn earlier on one earth is, becauſe the ground being cloſer and firmer underneath than land often ſtirred, the corn cannot ſo eaſily enter with it's roots, and gain a depth before winter or ſummer advances

§. 23. There is a great advantage in ſowing early, where it may be done, by ground being in it's nature warm, and lying warm, and being ſkreen'd from north and eaſterly winds. It is no ſmall inducement to it alſo, where it may be done with good huſbandry, in conſideration that the ſtraw of the corn will be ſo much the ſhorter, whereby it is evident the ſtrength of the ground will be ſo much the leſs exhauſted.

*Advantage of ſowing early.*

§. 24. Such land as was hard ploughed, and thereby ſubject to weeds, or was pot-dung'd, a farmer, of whoſe judgment I have a very good opinion, ſaid, he choſe to ſow about Michaelmaſs, becauſe the ſowing ſuch land of the firſt ſort early made it ſubject to weeds, and if pot-dung was laid early on ground it would be apt to breed weeds.

*What land not to be ſowed early.*

— I aſk'd him how the early ſowing of land hard
ploughed

ploughed made it subject to weeds. He replied, that much ploughing brought weeds; I suppose cutting the roots into pieces that grow, as it is by colts-foot, which being ploughed-in early gets a-head before the winter comes, but being ploughed late is apt to be killed by the winter.

**Of change of seed.** §. 25. ᵐ Though white and clay-land may bring corn of very good change for each other to sow, yet in a cold country, where both those sorts of land are cold, and consequently bring a coarse and thick-rinded corn, I do by no means allow of such seed for change, as before hinted. The change of earth to seed is not of that consequence to a crop of corn, as is the flinging in of seed in perfection into a cold ground in a cold clime.

So much depends on the goodness of your seed, that Mr. Hillman of Berkshire, a gentleman of great experience in husbandry, said to me, I verily believe a farmer, that sows clean seed and good change, may live as well upon his farm as the land-lord could do, that had that only farm, and kept it in his own hands, but sowed foul seed, and was careless in his change; for what signifies it to give one shilling in the bushel extraordinary for fine seed-wheat, when three bushels will sow an acre, the produce of which may be supposed to yield twenty bushels that will raise twelve pence per bushel extraordinary; besides, if foul seed be sown, the burden cannot be so large; for a great deal of it will be taken up in weeds.

ᵐ The common opinion, says Mr. Tull, is, that the strong clay-land is best to be sent to for seed-wheat, whatever sort of land it be to be sown on; a white clay is a good change for a red clay, and a red for a white; that from any strong land is better than from a light land, and that sand is an improper change for any. But from whatever land the seed be taken, if it was not changed the preceding year, it may possibly be infected with smut; and then there may be danger, tho' we have it immediately from never so proper a soil.

It

It is however to little purpose to sow the cleanest of seed in the common-field-lands; for it will never come out fine again, because the neighbours in sowing cast over some of their seed into each other's land.

§. 26. Any wound to the nib of any seed, where-in the smallest fibre is damaged, grows up and in-creases with the plant, as a wound in the bark of a tree : any imperfections in the leaves of bean-stalks. when they first come up, or other-seed leaves, seem to owe themselves to this cause. *Of wounds in seeds.*

§. 27. Towards the latter end of May (1707) I sowed garden-beans in a piece of strong clay-land in my garden ; the ground being in heart, I expected a crop of beans in the beginning of August. The seed-beans were * finnowy, and somewhat damaged withinside (for I broke many of them) being laid in a dampish place ; the halm or stalk came up well, and they blossomed well enough, but not one kid came of all the blossoms, tho' I sowed a spot of ground two or three lugg-square : the chief end for which I instance this is it's relation to a preceding observation, that defective beans proceeded from defective seed.——And this is the more observable, because in the blossoming-time frequent and great showers of rain fell, and continued so to do till Au-gust, so that this failure could not be attributed to any blight, or want of moisture, but to the defect of the seed only.——I also had this spring some summer-goar-vetches, that had been harvested wet, and lain all the winter sodden in their kids, and when thresh-ed they were finnowy and stunk : I doubted whe-ther or not they would grow ; I made a trial of them in the garden, but not half of them came up ; so I sowed about two acres of them in a treble quanti-ty, but having ten acres to sow, I bought seed for the other eight acres, and I observed, tho' I know the whole ten acres were of equal goodness, that the

*Defective beans come from defective seed.*

*\* moldy.*

vetches of the damaged feed did not produce one tenth part of the kids the found feed did, tho' the halm of each was much of the fame goodnefs.

Mr. Bobart, of the phyfick-garden at Oxford, gave me fome Smyrna cucumber-feeds, of which very few came up, but none of thofe came up which he referved for himfelf: the reafon was, as Mr. Bobart fufpected, becaufe he kept his too long in the mucilage, after he had taken thofe out which he gave to me; and I do fufpect that mine alfo, though not kept fo long in the mucilage as to perifh wholly, had however in the feed of the feed received a perifh, becaufe, tho' the fruit came up very fair, being twelve inches long, yet every feed of fome hundreds of them wanted a kernel. The like defects I have already obferved in beans, whofe feed hath been defective, and bore no kids, tho' they bloffomed, and others I have had bearing kids and yet not feeds; all which, as well as that of the cucumber, proceeded from the defects of thofe parts of the plant, which had been formed perfect and compleat in the feed, but had, while in that ftate, received fome damage, fo as to occafion a putrefaction in them, more or lefs, according as they were more or lefs tender; for, as the plant by glaffes is to be feen perfect in the feed, fo the refpective parts of flower, pods, and feed of the pods, tho' fmaller than a mote in the fun, may for as much reafon be conceived to be fully formed in the feed: it is plain the kernel of the feed is not fo tough or firm a body, as the plant itfelf, or as the pod, or the fkin of the feed, the kernel being at firft but a thin gelly or mucilage, and therefore more liable to be damaged. It may be refer'd to the above obfervation of the Smyrna cucumbers, that, of thofe exotic plants, which come from warmer climes than ours, though they are of a ftrong nature, and grow well with us, yet many will not bloffom with us, and fome that
will

will blossom, will not seed ; because, as the blossom
is more tender in the seed than the plant, so is the
seed of the seed more tender than the blossom. Lu-
cerne grass rarely seeds with us, tho' it flowers, but
the jessamine never ; and it is very probable there
are such defects in mulberry, grape, and fig-seeds
here in England, that from the seeds of the fruit
growing in England they can never be propagated
in England, though from their seeds they may be
propagated in other countries ; this also may seem
to account for the degeneracy of the foreign coli-
flower-seed, when sown in England, from whence,
in two or three years time, if sown from seed raised
here, no flower will proceed, but only a cabbage-
head. Thus apple and pear-trees have been known
not to produce kernels, which I suppose was from
the damaged seed ; and I do therefore believe the
cyons or cuts of such trees will not produce kernels ;
of oranges, &c. likewise it is supposed the first failure is in the seed : Mr. Bobart says, oranges rarely
seed in England.— Heat and drought, as well as
cold, will, I doubt not, hurt the seminal juices of
a plant before any other part ; for in the very hot
and dry summer, in the year 1705, I found few ap-
ples that had any kernels in their seeds, tho' the co-
tylidones seemed perfect enough, and I question
whether under the tropics, or near them, the ap-
ples bear seeds, or the husks of the seeds kernels.
Seeing therefore that fruit is never the less perfect,
tho' it has no seeds, quære whether the stamina farinacea in the flower does not contribute to the well-
being of the fruit as well as the seed ; (God having
intended the fruit for the use of mankind, as well as
the seed for propagation); otherwise the blossom that
proves seedless ought to fall, as it is observed to do
when the stamina farinacea are wanting : for then
the whole design of nature is defeated, both in re-
ference to fruit and seed.

L 2                    §. 28. The

Change of
feed.

§. 28. The farmers of Crux-Easton, and this hill-country, buy their seed-wheat from Newbury and that country, becaufe there they are on a white earth, whereas Crux-Easton is on a red earth; and the country about Newbury buy their feed-wheat of us, becaufe to change is thought beft.—The changing the feed of all grain whatfoever is of as much ufe and fervice as half the dung fufficient for a crop; therefore the farmers are often to blame for not changing fo frequently as they ought to do; if their corn prove good and fit for feed they will fow it a fecond year, and fo it may do tolerably well, but longer it will do very ill.

I have a great opinion of the advantage of changing feed every year rather than once in two years; for I fowed barley of the laft year's feed in the beginning of April, and I fowed part of the fame ground, but a clayier piece of land, with frefh feed of this year's change on the laft day of April, which ought to have been the coarfer barley, whereas it proved full as white and fine, if not finer than the other.

The order in which different crops fhould fucceed one another.

§. 29. [n] Pliny takes notice, that the rule laid down by Virgil is, to let the land lie fallow every other year, which, if the farm be of fufficient fize to admit it, he thinks is a very good way, but if you are ftraiten'd in conveniency of this kind, he advifes to fow wheat after lupines, vetches or beans, or any other grain that has the quality of fertilizing and enriching the ground.—This is to be well noted, becaufe in England, where our land is worfe, the farmer if he pays twelve fhillings an acre, will not imagine rent can be paid, unlefs he fows it every year, and he will not lay it down to grafs.

---

[n] Virgilius alternis ceffare arva fuadet, et hoc, fi patiantur ruris fpatia, utiliffimum proculdubio eft; quod fi neget conditio, far ferendum, unde aut lupinum, aut vicia, aut faba fublata fint et quæ terram faciant lætiorem. Plin. lib. 18. fect. 10.

§. 30. Some

§. 30. Some farmers approve very much of sow- ing peas after wheat, and then barley, and say, it will make a better tilth for the barley, and be the lighter, inafmuch as the ground lies down a year with wheat, and but half a year with peas, there-fore better to fow barley after peas than after wheat; but it feems to me the beft way is (inafmuch as it may fuit other circumftances of conveniency) to fow the clay-land to peas, and then to barley, be-caufe the clay-land will be the better mellowed thereby for barley, and the whiter and mixt land to wheat, and then to barley, becaufe the whole year fuch land goes with wheat will not prevent it's working kindly for barley.

§. 31. The country people fay, peas do beft on a barley-erfh, and of this I have fpoken more at large under the article Peas, to which I refer the reader.

§. 32. Farmer Wingford falling into my com- pany, I told him I propofed to fow my clay-land to peas, and then to barley, and lighter land to wheat and then to barley: he reply'd, I might alfo very well in my clay-land fow wheat after peas, which I remark, becaufe I think it properly faid; for peas will be a manure to wheat on fuch land, and not make it fo light as to be fubject to blight, and clayey heavy lands in Wilts are fo managed.

I afk'd farmer Elton, why I fhould not on the ftrong clay-land of Crux-Eafton fow wheat after peas, feeing ftrong clay-land could not by being lightened by the peas-ftubble be fubject to blight, and it was the method of many countries, where their land is of a ftrong heavy clay, to fow wheat on peas or vetch-ftubble; he replied, they had on the clay-peas-ftubble fowed wheat the fame year at Crux-Eafton, and it had fometimes come well, but for the moft part ill; for the worm had in October, November, and December fallen on it, and eat it up. I put afterwards the fame cafe to farmer Biggs,

and

and he said, if the season proved dry for sowing
wheat after peas, the wheat generally proved well on
clay-land; but, said he, if the peas-stubble be wet
when ploughed, the land being hollowed by the
peas-stubble will lie very cold, hollow, and wet, the
whole year after, and the wheat, if a bad winter, die
away. I replied, when I spoke of sowing wheat
after peas, I did not mean the sowing it till the year
after. He said, he thought there could be no better
husbandry than that, and free from the before-men-
tioned inconveniencies.

I observe, in Wiltshire, where the said husbandry is used of sowing wheat on the same year's peas-
stubble, that the ground is of a heavy malmish sort
of clay, and consequently not subject to the inconveniency of our hill-country strong clay, which is apt
to be hollowed too much after peas-stubble; again,
such husbandry is practised often in common-fields,
where people will not be at chargeable husbandry;
it is also practised (instead of manure) where lands
lie at a distance from a farm-house, and in deep
baning lands, where the husbandman dares not trust
to his fold.

If one would sow a large quantity of wheat on a
peas-ersh, it must, in the hill-country, be with a
proviso that harvest does not fall out very late; for
in that case a large quantity of ground cannot be
sowed on a peas-ersh early enough, but a considerable part of it, especially the poorer sort, will be
obliged to be sown to barley.

§. 33. It had been a mighty wet winter and spring,
whereby the fallows were well wetted: I had that
year a great crop of oats, and but a middling crop
of barley, which I impute to the barley's lying
wetter, by being buried deeper in the cold earth;
whereas the surface of the earth, in which the oats
were sowed, was soon and easily rectified, the sun
having full power to penetrate that, and to move
the

*Oats may succeed wheat bet-
ter than barley can
in wet years.*

the salts, &c. for which reason, in such wet years, the husbandman should alter his measures, and sow his barley-fallows on one earth to oats.

§. 34. Mr. Byssy of —— near Bradford in Wilt-shire, ploughed up a piece of French-grass ground worn out, and sowed it on one earth, and said he had excellent barley; and the next year he ploughed it for wheat, which whilst he was doing, farmer Sartain came by, and said, that ground would fool.him, for he would have no wheat;—and I having observed a wheat-stubble of his to be very indifferent, asked him, how it came to pass his crop was so ordinary; he said, that was the ground abovementioned, and added, that the corn all blighted; he thought the roots of the French-grass, being not sufficiently rotted, or rather too rotten, but yet not converted into mold, made the wheat * more-loose, which I believe reasonable, and therefore such ground is to be well considered of before so husbanded.

Sowing wheat too soon after French-grass, condemned.

* loose at root.

§. 35. Mr. Raymond of Puck-shipton in Wilts, broke up ground of 30 s. per acre to destroy the ant-hills, and the first crop he sowed was white oats; for, said he, if it be sowed with wheat it will be mad, and come to nothing; the second crop he sowed was some sort of great wheat, whose straw is so large and strong, that it is not subject to lodge; whereas, said he, if sown with any of the smaller wheats, such as red straw, &c. the straw of those are weak, and would certainly, being rank, fall down and lodge; the next crop, said he, I will sow red straw; for by that time the ground will be tamed; and this is the approved method in that country, where rich lands are broken up.

What succession of grain on new broken up rich ground.

§. 36. The whole method of husbandry in the Isle of Wight is, upon the first tilth of land to sow peas; on the next wheat, and then barley. In Hertfordshire the method is to sow, first wheat, next peas, and then lay down to fallow for a wheat-

Order of sowing in the Isle of Wight, Hertfordshire, &c.

L 4                                                        en

en crop, or elſe ſow oats after the wheat, and lay down to graſs-ſeeds.

In Eſſex, and ſome other places, eſpecially where the ground has been improved by chalking, they firſt ſow wheat, then beans, which, being kept clean by the hoe, they reckon equal to a ſummer-fallowing, then wheat again, ſowing broad-clover on their laſt wheaten crop.

About Holt, it is a great practice to ſow wheat after peas, and then peas, and wheat again, not having in thoſe parts ſo much land as to afford to let a ground lie ſtill for a ſummer-fallow. They reckon that a peas-crop does the wheat as much kindneſs as laying it to a ſummer-fallow.

In Leiceſterſhire they ſow a wheaten crop the laſt, and lay down to graſs ; the reaſon they give is, becauſe, the ground having a twelve month to grow to graſs, the year following they may expect a very good head of graſs ; and ſo gain a year by it ; whereas, if they ſow it with a ſummer-crop, they can expect but little ſhow the firſt year ; and Mr. Clark ſaid further, that they counted the wheaten ſtubble kept the graſs warm in winter, and, as it rotted, the worms drew it into the ground, which made much for the graſs [o].

§. 37. I am fully ſatisfied on experience that whoever keeps land poor, and ſows it with wheat, which grain requires land (according to it's nature) in good heart, it will not only produce a thin crop in ſhow, but alſo a crop that will fall ſhort in reſpect of yielding.

§. 38. Whatever the practice may be to the contrary, I hold it improper to ſow wheat on the green ſtubble of goar-vetches cut for horſes : this ſtubble being ploughed in with the wheat will finnow, and

[o] See the author's obſervations on Corn in general, where you will find ſome particulars relating to ſowing.

heat,

heat, and moldy the ground, and be so far from feeding the wheat with a sweet dish that it will make it
produce but small ears, and weak tillows, and thin-
bodied corn.

§. 39. No wheat can be ensured to be clean seed *Wheat*
from oats, if oats be sown in the next adjoining *near oats brings foul*
ground, for the rooks and small birds will carry *seed.*
them into the wheat-land.

§. 40. I have ventured to sow some grounds *Of sowing*
with wheat after a wheaten crop the time before, *wheat after wheat.*
being summer-fallowed the year after for the second
crop, and have found by experience that strong
land will bear an excellent crop of wheat after wheat,
provided it be summer-fallowed the second year,
that is, let the ground rest one year, dunging or
folding it for the second crop; but by experience I
find, that shallow light ground will produce but
thin wheat, and a small ear, if sowed to wheat after
wheat, and a summer-fallow taken between; though
the ground be dunged for such second crop, especially if the spring prove cold and wet; for shallow
or weak ground being unkind for a crop of wheat
so managed, if the spring and summer prove un-
favourable to this grain, such ground will shew it's
passiveness, and tokens of such inclemency, much
more than ground of but equal strength, when
sowed to the first crop of wheat.

## Of S O W I N G W H E A T.

§. 41. [p] Lord Bacon, in his Natural history, says, *Of steeping*
he sowed wheat steeped in urine and dungs of several *corn. See*
sorts, chalk, &c.——And that the corn steeped in *Wheat, §. 14.*
urine,

[p] In contradiction to this, Mr. Tull asserts, that, if seed-wheat
be soaked in urine, it will not grow, or, if only sprinkled with
it, it will most of it die.---A very knowing husbandman, whom I
consulted on this occasion, confirmed the former part of Mr.
Tull's

urine, and fowed in the fame earth with the reft, came up, and grew bolder than the reft. —Therefore it feems of confequence that fheep and other cattle have plenty of water. —But he fays not that he let it grow till it came to feed.

Of fowing wheat under fur-row.

§. 42. I had wheat fowed under furrow in a ground which I had ploughed, thwarted, and dragged, after which I ploughed and fowed the corn in the moft hufbandlike manner I could; and indeed the wheat came up in the furrows in uninterrupted parallel lines, and without any weeds between the furrows.—— But farmer Ginneway faid, that the ground at feed-time working fo curious fine fhould have been fown one caft over the other under furrow, and then the ground between the furrows had been filled, which I believe to be a good way.

By the confideration of a ground where I have wheat fown this year, 1706, where the ground had been winter-fallowed, and brought to a curious mold, I am apt to believe, that in our cold clime, wheat in fuch earth fhould be fown under furrow, that it may lie the deeper; for this crop on the 24th of April was miferably thin, and what blades grew feemed fomething towards an ink-blue, and the roots feemed matted on the furface of the ground; which makes me believe, that the winter-corn was not buried deep enough; being fown, as this ground was, not till the 25th of September, it lay too much expofed to cold; for, where ground works fine, the earth crumbles in at the firft tining, and fills up the furrow; and three or four tinings finifhes it, in which cafe it is not poffible it fhould be well buried. —If ground work well, it is alfo beft to fow vetches under furrow, the dung in that cafe being laid on the ground

Tull's affertion, and affured me he had found it fo by experience, but added, if the urine were mixed with fomewhat more than one half water, it would make excellent brine for feed-wheat. See more on this fubject in the author's obfervation on Wheat.

ground after the thwarting it. At sowing, the ground working so fine, the seed was not easily buried, but lay on the surface, which was inconvenient.

Some consideration there ought to be, whether you sow under furrow at two earths or three. It seems, if no reason offers to the contrary, that wheat folded on fallows should be sown under furrow on the second earth, because the strength of the dung is turned down to the corn, but, if folded on the second earth, then, for the same reason, to be sown under furrow on the third earth; but if the winter-fold for barley was on lay-ground, the barley should, for the same reason, be sowed under furrow on the third earth.

September 14th, 1699, I observed a close ploughing up in Leicestershire, and the corn sowing under furrow; the ground had been limed, and so strangely run to weeds, that I wondered at the boldness of the husbandman, and went up to him.---He was sowing his wheat steeped in lime; I observed the grain was plim and very large; I told him in Hampshire we esteem the lesser wheat the best; he said, in the common-fields, where they gave three earths, which laid the land light, they usually sowed of the smaller seed, but (said he) here we choose a large seed, as supposing it has strength to shoot forth it's stalks through the clots and earth it lies under; for it now lies deeper, and the earth closer and heavier upon it than if it were sowed after the plough, and harrowed-in; besides, if very wet weather should fall upon it, so as thoroughly to wet the trumpery of weeds we turn in, a small grain would be sooner chilled than this large sort.—— I asked him, how many bushels he sowed; he said, three to an acre.

Mr. Byssy of Wiltshire being at Easton I told him of my new husbandry of sowing my wheat under furrow, and ridging it up.—He said, if I sowed ::

under furrow fo, I muſt take care to be ſure that the ground was ſo thoroughly moiſt that the corn might grow from ſuch moiſture, though no rain ſhould come ; for he had known crops often loſt, by ſowing dry under furrow,—and I remember my carter had told me the ſame thing.

In North Wiltſhire, when they ſow under furrow, I find by the account of many experienced huſband-men, that they aim to ſow the laſt of their crop that way, and to ſow it on mellow earth, ſuch as peas-erſh : the reaſon why they generally ſow the laſt of the wheat ſo, is, becauſe it is the latter end of autumn, for the moſt part, before the ground is well wetted, and in order for it ; for it is the great-eſt caution they have not to ſow dry under furrow, but, on the contrary, to ſow ſo wet that they may be ſure the corn will grow : but I find they all agree, provided the earth be wet enough, the middle of Auguſt would not be too ſoon to ſow under furrow.

§. 43. It ſeems to me in early harveſts, occaſioned by hot and dry ſummers, at which times the wheat is alſo very yellow, and ripens to perfection, there is no need to ſow ſo early as in cold wet ſummers, when the harveſt is backward, and conſequently the wheat more horny ; for the ground be-ing heated, or in a manner burn-beaked by the hot and dry ſummer, and the flour of the wheat dry and mellow, it will come up and ſhoot away at an in-credible rate, and the aftermaſſes of all graſſes in the autumns of ſuch ſummers carry a ſtrong deep green, a token of the ground being impregnated with the heat, and a proof likewiſe that it has not been exhauſted of it's ſpirits, for they were not tranf-mitted into vegetables, being bound up for want of a vehicle to infuſe themſelves into their roots by rains ; but after cold raw ſummers the autumn-aftermaſs of graſs has a weak pale verdure.

*Time of ſowing wheat.*

§. 44. It

§. 44. It was May 12th (anno 1700) and time to consider what to do with the wheaten fallows. Several good farmers were of opinion that it was time enough to sow my fallows a fortnight before Michaelmass, because I had dunged them; but, said they, in case one sows a light and poor ground, or a cold ground, without well maintaining it, such ground ought to be sowed the beginning or middle of August.

§. 45. To sow summer-corn dry, and wheat *To sow* wet, is accounted best for different reasons, viz. in *wheat wet.* the spring there is no doubt but rain will come enough to bring up the corn, and in September, when wheat is sown, there is little danger at that time of the year of so much sun as to harden a crust on the earth, so that the corn cannot get out, tho' ploughed and sowed wet. —— It may not be amiss however, if one sows wheat at the latter end of the year, suppose at Michaelmass, to sow it when the ground is dry; for that time of the year grows cool, and large dews fall, nor can it be long before rain will come; and, if it be cold land, and sowed at the latter end of the year, when the ground is very wet, it will be the apter to chill.

§. 46. In the beginning of August, 1697, I ask- *Time of* ed a husbandman when the farmer intended to sow *sowing* a certain field to wheat; he said, in the latter end *wheat on* of August. I asked him how that came to pass, *various* seeing he was already sowing the field adjoining with *soils.* wheat.

---

*It is a general rule, says Mr. Tull, that all forts of grain and feeds profper beft, fown when the ground is fo dry, as to be broken into the moft parts by the plough. The reafon why wheat is an exception to that rule is, becaufe it muft endure the rigours of the winter, which it is the better able to do, by the earth's being preffed or trodden harder or clofer to it, as it is when moved wet. For this reafon the farmers drive their fheep over very light land, as foon as it is fown with wheat, to tread the furface of it hard, and then the cold of the winter cannot fo eafily penetrate, to kill the roots of the tender plants.*

wheat. He replied, it was becaufe that was fuch
light ground, that it muft be fown early, that it
might get root before winter came on; otherwife
it would be in danger of being killed; but, faid he,
the former is a clayey heavy ground, into which the
winter could not foon penetrate, fo as to kill the
corn; befides, if that were not fown late, the weeds
would get ahead.

On the other hand, December 19th (anno 1700)
I faw ground of farmer Farthing's in the Ifle of
Wight fown to wheat, which was malmed, and it
was not come up; alfo I obferved fome other perfons fowing then; I thought it very late, and afked
the farmer about it. He faid, that, in their country
(the winter being milder than with us at Crux-Eafton) if fandy and poorifh land be fowed early, it will
have fpent it's whole ftrength on the halm, or green
wheat, before the fpring and fummer comes, and
will not then be able to maintain the crop.

The fowing of wheat in the Ifle of Wight late,
that is, at the latter end of October, and all November, efpecially if land be poor, is very good hufbandry, (but it feems it ought to be well trod, left it
fhould blight by being too loofe) becaufe that country is warm through the vapours of the fea, and it
would fpend itfelf too faft, in cafe it was fowed in
September; but it is quite otherwife in many parts
of Hampfhire, becaufe the cold lies fo hard there,
that the wheat cannot be too rank before winter, and
will fettle the better; yet, in cafe the winter fhould
prove fo mild, that it fhould by being fowed early
run to be rank, it ought to be refrefhed in the fpring
by pigeon's dung, or fome fuch contrivance; otherwife a fmall and weak ear with a weak fpindle muft
be expected.

Early-
fown wheat
does not til-
low fo
much in
the fpring
as late
fown.

§. 47. The Hampfhire farmers obferve, it is not
to be expected, that wheat fown fo early as the beginning of Auguft fhould tillow fo much, when
fpring

spring comes, as wheat would do that is later sown;
because wheat early sown has already tillowed and
too far spent itself in the forehand of the year.

I struck in with a notable farmer in company Of wheat's tillowing.
with Mr. Hillman; it was July 24th, anno 1701;
I asked them, whether some in their country were
not sowing wheat: they said, many talked of beginning; but, said the farmer, I think they had
better let it alone; for our's is a light and sandy
ground, and the summer has been very dry and hot
(for not above a shower or two of rain had fallen
between May and that time) therefore, said he, these
last two days rain (for it had rained plentifully for
two days) the corn by virtue of the great heat of the
ground will rise up very quick and fast, and run itself out of heart before winter, and dwindle all next
summer, for it is in a manner carrying a double
crop:—so said Mr. Hillman also.

Many of the hill-country of Hampshire are of
opinion, that a fortnight before Michaelmass and a
fortnight after are the prime times for sowing wheat
in the hill-country,—but I do think all wheat should
be in the ground by Michaelmass day.— It is true,
too many of the hill-country do not husband so well
as they ought to do; for poor land sown early, if a
mild winter should come, may spend itself so much
that at harvest the spindle may be but weak; but
if the land were better husbanded, it would bear the
running to rankness in the forehand of the year, tho'
the winter should prove mild, and have strength
enough not to abate of it's crop in the spring.

It was the 15th of September (anno 1702) when
farmer Hawkins told me, that no wheat had then
been sown with them about Andover; for, said he,
our ground puts very forward in the spring, and
wheat sowed early would then be too proud.

It seems, that in the hill country of Hampshire In the hill-country.
we ought to take care not to sow strong clay-land
too

too late with wheat; indeed, the beginning of September seems not to be too early, for there is no danger of clay-land, lying so cold, being too proud, the dews and cold nights in September and October, the frosts and cold rains in winter, and the cold spring will keep it back; so that it seems in cold clay-land wheat ought to get some good root before the cold seasons come on, that it may be in heart to bear up against the winter; whereas earth of a mixture between white earth and clay being of a drier, warmer, and healthier nature, and in every of the foregoing respects capable of thriving both in October, and all winter long, how wet soever, as well as in a cold spring, if such land be in good heart, it need not be sowed till the last of all your land.— The mere white earth-chalk might also be sowed as late, but that it is rarely in heart enough.

I was observing to some farmers of Holt in Wilts, it being in the month of March (anno 1702) that their wheat looked much greener than our Hampshire wheat at this time of the year. They said, it was because it was sowed so much later, and that their's would lose it's beauty, and it's first leaf would die and look rusty were they to sow early.

In Leicestershire. Mr. Clerk of Leicestershire says, if the season be mild, they often sow wheat at Christmass, and that Mr. Chestlin has sowed wheat this year (1699) which is not out of the ground, it being the 12th of February; that if they should sow wheat as early as we do in Hampshire it would be destroyed by weeds, as well as be too rank.

Wilts. Mr. Raymond of Puck-shipton, Wilts, tells me, the notable men, who make their observations in the vale, say, though they should not have a season to sow their wheat so early as they would, by reason of the wet, and are forced to sow late, suppose the middle or latter end of November, yet they find such wheat will do very well, if very hard frosts do

not

not come before it has made a pretty good spear un-
der-ground; no matter whether it has first put forth
a blade or not, for by the time the spear is shot un-
der-ground the corn is well rooted.

I have eight or nine acres of brashy ground, tho'
redish and clayey, occasioned chiefly by the abundance of stones, which mixing with the clay make
it hollow; this ground was fallowed up pretty late
in the summer, viz. the latter end of July or beginning of August, with intention of ploughing it again,
and sowing it with wheat; but viewing it September the 30th, after a good shower of rain, I found
it would work and tear very well on one earth so as
to harrow off at six tinings at most: so, tho' the
ground was designed for two earths, yet I sowed it
on one earth; for it is of that consequence to get in
corn in good season, if the ground will work well,
that in the hill-country, where we have a great crop
of wheat to sow, no opportunity of sowing may be
lost after this time of the year; for it very rarely
happens but wheat early sown in such ground as
above described, and in the hill-country, comes off
better, and produces a better crop than the last sown
wheat, tho' we were sure of a season for sowing it.

I observed, that a few lands of the abovemention- *In ground
ed ground had a pretty deal of grass come up in *run to
them, and said to the man, who was there sowing, *grass.
that I thought such grass would tear up pretty well
with the harrows, the ground being hollow, and having lain down but one year.—He said, that he
thought also the grass would do no harm, because
the ground would be sown early, and so the wheat
would out-grow the grass, and top upon it,—which
I thought a good reason.

§. 48. *The old custom in the hill-country in *The earlier
Hampshire has been to sow two bushels and an half *wheat is
*sowed the

* Mr. Tull observes, when wheat is planted early, less seed is *less seed is
required than when late: because less of it will die in the winter *required.
than of that planted late, and it has more time to tillow.

of wheat on an acre in the ground early sown, but in that later sown three bushels and an half on an acre.—The reason they assign is, that the earlier the wheat is sown the more it will shoot out in blades and tillows, and spread farther, whereas the later sown corn will not spread, the cold winter coming on it, and very likely give but one blade only.

One Parker came to see me with farmer Biggs; he was speaking of the great fatness of their land for wheat, and said, that at the latter end of November they sowed but one bushel on an acre, and, if in January, but a peck more; therefore, said he, tho' we give fourteen shillings per acre, we sow a bushel less on an acre, nay a bushel and three pecks less than you when we sow late, for then, said he, you commonly sow three bushels; so that the bushel of seed you exceed in, or a bushel and three pecks, will abundantly recompence for what we exceed in rent, especially when wheat is at six shillings per bushel; but then, said he, we give three earths.

I was telling Mr. Bachelour of Ashmonsworth, that I found I had underseeded my wheaten crop that I had sowed in my clay-lands in September and October this year (1705), and yet I sowed three bushels on an acre. ——— To which he replied, that of late years he and others had by experience found, that at that time of the year it was best to sow at least three bushels and an half; nay, said he, the ground at that time will take four bushels, and we find 'tis best to sow four bushels and an half of barley, and five of oats on an acre.

As most farmers, who sow any quantity of wheat propose to buy every year a load at least of seed-wheat for change, so it is adviseable to sow the said load of bought feed so early, and in such forward ground, that they may be likely to house and thresh it time enough for sowing the next year's crop, which, in the hill-country, is by the middle of August.

One

One ought to contrive to have the clean feed-wheat for a change as early as may be, becaufe it is much dearer than common wheat, and the earlier it is fown it will go the farther, becaufe lefs need be fown on an acre; again, it is proper to contrive to fow the choice clean wheat in good land, becaufe the increafe will be the greater, whereby you may have the more to ferve your own occafions, or to pleafure your neighbour.

§. 49. It feems to me cheaper and better to buy middling clean wheat for feed, and hand-pick it, than to buy clean feed, becaufe it cofts lefs to hand-pick that wheat than what one muft give over and above for clean feed, which is never that I know of clean, though pretended fo to be. *Of hand-picking-feed-wheat*

§. 50. It is a common expreffion in country-men's mouths, that old wheat is not fo fubject to blight as new,—but, as I take it, the blight is not founded either on the newnefs or oldnefs of the corn, but inafmuch as old wheat is generally fowed be-times, and before new wheat can be had, therefore fuch land is lefs fubject to blight is true. *Sowing early prevents blighting*

Again I judge, that, whereas it is faid, that wheat fowed early is lefs apt to blight, the ground having more time to fettle, the main reafon is, not that the time that latter fown ground hath to fettle is not long enough before the burning weather and blights come ; but that, when ground is fowed early, it has time to fettle before the frofts come, which keep heaving and hollowing it, and hinder it all the year after from fettling.

§. 51. It is obferved, that new wheat and old wheat being fowed at the fame time, the new wheat will at the end of the firft three months be above a week forwarder than the old : for this reafon I ad-vife to fow old wheat at the firft and earlieft fowing, *Different times of fowing new and old wheat.*

if

if you fear winter-pride, but new wheat, if you fow
late, and fear it will be backward in tillowing [t].

Of plough-
ing in brit-
ted wheat
for a baf-
tard-crop.

* brit fhed.

§. 52. In a hot fummer, when harveft comes
early, before the ftrength of the fummer be far
fpent, when the wheat is yellow, tho' not hardened and thoroughly ripe, it is incredible how
foon, if the ground be wet, * britted corn will grow.
I had fome acres this fummer (1714) blown out by
a high wind, enough to feed the ground for a baf-
tard-crop; and what fell in criveffes and chinks, the
wind coming with rain, grew to be five or fix
inches long in ten days time; fo that in fuch cafes,
if you think to drag or plough it in, the fooner the
better; and, if you plough it in, the fhallower the
better, and the furrows as narrow as may be; that,
if it cannot get through the furrows, it may have
the lefs way to fhoot flantwife before it meets a
feam to come out at.-----The lefs graffy any ground
is, and the more knot-fine, fo much the narrower
will the furrow turn up, or break by the plough.

## Of S O W I N G B A R L E Y.

§. 53. " Sow barley in the drier lands, fays Varro; fo that, in thofe hot countries, they did not
look on their land too hot for barley.

Time of
fowing
barley—
fhould be
early fow-
ed.

§. 54. It was Chriftmas (anno 1702) and farmer
Biggs, farmer Crapp, Mr. Bachelour, and farmer
Hafcall were with me: I propofed to them the
advantage of fowing barley and fummer-corn earlier than they did by a week or a fortnight, in cafe
the land was in any good heart, and in duft, for the
damage by what might die by bad weather would
not come to fo much as was always loft by drought.
----- Farmer Biggs and farmer Crapp were of my

---

[t] See the author's obfervations on Wheat.
[u] In aridiore hordeum potius quam far ferito.   Varro, fol. 4 3.

opinion,

opinion, but Mr. Bachelour differed from us, which seemed to arise from his sowing poor land early, but I grounded the supposition on the land being in good heart; however we all agreed, that the earlier barley was sowed the finer it was, and the later the coarser, which must arise from the first having it's growth from it's earing in a hotter time, whereas that sowed later has much the colder time; so rath-ripe barley is generally the finest. Farmer Biggs said at another time, that a week's sowing earlier than ordinary was of great avail to the fineness of the barley.

Considering therefore the small dispatch in plough-ing the second earth in the spring, and the danger of being late, and also caught in the wet, it seems to me most reasonable to hire ploughs to help, the first dry season that offers, and not to trust to the con-tingency of dry weather; for, tho' you should con-tinue hiring the whole barley seed-time, yet you will be well repaid for it by putting your corn in early, which will carry the finer and larger body.

Captain Tate of Leicestershire says, that it is al-lowed that their early sowed wheat and earlier sowed barley are the best, and that, if the season permits, they begin to sow barley the beginning of March; —to that therefore I must attribute the fineness of the barley of the north, seeing they lie wetter than we do at Easton, and seeing that we at Easton have finer barley than at Burclear, &c.—where they are on the clays, they sowing as late as we do; yet there should be some difference in soils, seeing Cap-tain Tate named a place in Yorkshire, where he said was the finest barley in England, which would be ripe and in the barn in eight weeks time. *In Leicestershire.* *In Yorkshire.*

§. 55. At seed-time, in flinging the barley into the ground, the farmers are much governed by the season of the year; for, unless the ground be very dry, and has had warmth by some good weather preceding, *Time of sowing barley on different kinds of land.*

M 3

preceding, they hold it not proper to sow their barley, in fallowed land that they stir again, till about a week in April, because, if much wet should fall on such land after sowing it would lie sodding, and be apt to chill the corn, but on white land which they sow on one earth, if the weather be dry, they often sow a week before Lady-day; for from such land the water runs off and sinks down the better; besides land so sown is usually white land that is naturally dry and warm.

Mr. Worlidge in his Kalendarium Rusticum, fo. 270, says, About the end of March or earlier you may begin to sow barley in clay-land, but not so early in sandy-land.—The only reason of which, as I apprehend, is, that hot weather coming on apace at that time of the year, the clay-land is very subject to bake; therefore it is best to sow barley there before the sun has such power, whereas the light land is in no such danger; and since, as above, you find that barley to prove the finest that is sowed earliest, so, as clay-land naturally brings the coarser corn, sowing it the earlier may much mend it.

**Why weeds abound in early-sowed barley.**

§. 56. It is observed by many, that, when they have sown their barley very early, the crop has been almost eaten up by weeds; the only reason to be given for weeds in early-sown barley more than in that sown later is, because many weeds and their seeds are of a more hardy nature than barley, and will grow early, whilst the spring is as yet cold, and may get the forehand of the barley, and over-top it.

**Time of sowing barley in Leicestershire.**

§. 57. February 1st, (anno 1699) I observed a close of about twenty acres belonging to a farmer of Hawthorne in Leicestershire, which had been fallowed up but the week before, was sowing to barley; thinking it was very early I asked the farmer, who was in the field, whether it was common in that country to sow so soon. He answered, that they generally found the barley first sowed proved best,

and

and so said others whom I spoke to about it.---This ground kirnelled very fine, and was of a curious fat-light mold, lying very warm amidst the barns and houses of the town, and upon a shoot, that neither rain nor snow could lie long on it.---I spoke to Mr. Clerk of it, and he said, by the middle of February all the common-fields and inclosures would be sow-ing with barley: this was as warm a winter as had been known.---He said their grounds were very apt to bind by heat, and therefore the barley was better if it was pretty high; whereby it kept the ground cool against the time the hot weather came upon it. ---He said, the snow at this time of the year never laid long with them, but he approved of late sow-ing where the snow lay long.---He added however, that the farmer abovementioned sowed his barley a fortnight the earlier in hopes it might be reaped the sooner, and so he might be the forwarder in his turnip-seed-time.

§. 58. My opinion is, that such grounds as are early-sown in a cold hill-country; the land itself being also cold or clayish, ought to be sown with a late-ripe barley, especially if such land be declivous from the sun, or hidden from it by hedge-rows; for the straw of rath-ripe barley being in it's own nature weak, will be much more so where it has not it's share of the sun, and where the cold clay-ground gives off it's strength sooner, after the sun's passing the solstice, than other ground; on this account the straw of the rath-ripe barley, for want of being sup-ported and nourished to it's maturity, rather withers than ripens, and then the straw must needs crumble or fall down; and the grain will plim no farther, but dry away and be very thin; but the straw of late-ripe barley, being bolder and stronger, will stand the longer; and, tho' the sun should be with-drawn, and the corn should lie under a shade, yet, so long as it stands upright, the straw will convey so

*What kinds of barley to be sown on different soils.*

M 4 much

much nourishment to the grain, it being sown early, as to ripen it kindly, even notwithstanding the disadvantage of being shaded from the sun.——Yet, if I may advise in this case, I should rather propose in such ground as lies from the sun, or is shaded, especially if it be clayey and cold in it's nature, to sow white oats; for they will have finished their course sooner, if sown pretty early, and will ripen before the strength of the sun shall be much declined.—— If to avoid the aforesaid mischiefs late-ripe barley be not sown, and there should come a cold wet summer to add to the evils aforesaid, rath-ripe barley being sown will fall much the sooner, even while the straw is green, and will then never come to maturity, but from the roots new tillows will shoot forth with green ears, which will neither ripen themselves, nor, by drawing away the nourishment, suffer the first and elder ears to ripen.——The reader may see more relating to this subject in my observations on Barley, where I have treated more largely of the nature and qualities of this grain.

**Quantity of barley on an acre. ---Hants.** §. 59. Four bushels of barley is generally the quantity allotted to be sown on one acre, but, if the ground is very good, they may sow five bushels.

**Leicestershire.** Mr. Edwards of Leicestershire sowed this year (1699) four bushels of barley on an acre, because his barley was not good; when his seed was good he used to sow but three bushels and a peck at most; upon which he argued much to prove, that it was most profitable to sow the best seed, for what of the other will grow, said he, nobody knows.

**If the fallows are dry, barley and oats may be sowed earlier.** §. 60. If the fallows are very dry, barley and oats may be sown somewhat the earlier; for it is a great matter to throw seed into a dry bed, especially if cold and wet should come after. Summer-corn may be killed two ways by cold, 1st, by the chill and coldness of the earth; 2dly, by the fierce season and coldness of the air:—Now, if corn be sowed

when

when the land falls into powder, tho' cold rains should fall after, yet the land will lie so warm as not to chill the corn ; and if the root is not starved, tho' the blade should be taken off, that will grow again ; but if ground be ploughed wet, and such weather should come, the corn will be in danger of being killed both ways.

§. 61. The general proverbs or wise sayings of our ancestors relating to husbandry, seem rather to have been calculated for the vales than the hills ; for the hill-country was of less consequence till the late improvement by sowing grass-seeds. The ancients used to say, " barley should leap on the ground, " when sowed out of the hopper,"---which exactly suits the condition of the vales, where commonly they begin to sow their barley at the latter end of February or the beginning of March, when it is impossible such deep lands should at that season be too dry ; they are rather subject to the other extreme ; but in the hill-country, where the lands are light and poor, I have often experienced, that we have sown in the spring, when the ground has been so dry that there was no likelihood, except rain came, of seeing half the corn come up, and we have often waited a month for rain ; the consequence of which has been thin barley, and an edge-grown crop ; therefore, if my ground be rightly prepared by seasonable fallowing, so as to work fine at seed-time, I never fear sowing my barley too wet, provided the ground be not in danger of treading [x].

*Different seasons of sowing barley in the hill and vale-country, in regard to wet and dry.*

## Of S O W I N G  B A R L E Y and O A T S.

§. 62. How much cold is an enemy to vegetation may appear from the seeds being put into a glass

---

[x] Of barley's degenerating, and cautions to choose the fullest and best bodied seed, see our author's remarks on Barley.

glafs of water; for many days they will not * chitt-
fum, nor imbibe the water; but their pores will rather
be clofed than opened by the water, it being cold;
for which reafon I conceive it not to be good to fow
the lenten corn in cold clay-lands, efpecially barley,
early;---for it feems not to be good to check feeds
in their progrefs to vegetation, for not proceeding in
that cafe is going backward, and fuch damage may
the feed receive in a few days, when firft fown, as it
can never after recover.

§. 63. I cannot find in the four ancient authors
De re rufticâ, that any of them give any directions
about fowing oats: it feems they had an opinion,
that they were a grain to be neglected, being, as
Virgil has it, of a burning quality, and exhaufting
the land, and they having other variety of corn for
their cattle.---On review I find the following brief
directions in Columella. ʸ Oats are fowed in autumn, and partly cut up green for food, and partly
referved for the fake of the feed. The feed here to
be laid up feems intended for feed again; for I cannot find any directed for feeding horfes, &c. in thefe
authors. If thefe oats were to be cut green, no
wonder they preferred other forts of leguminous
corn.

§. 64. I inquired of a farmer in my neighbourhood about feed-oats: and whether he had any to
fell: he afked me, if I thought it not too early to
fow them yet, it being March 27, (anno 1703) for,
faid he, I once fowed oats at this time of the year,
and in good land that I had defigned for barley;
but cold dripping weather came, and I had not two
bufhels again in an acre.

§. 65. A field of mine having born three crops,
the laft of which was vetches, I fowed the fourth

---

ʸ Avena, autumno fata, partim cæditur in fœnum, vel pabulum, dum adhuc viret, partim femini cuftoditur. Columella, lib.
2. c. 11.

with

with white Poland-oats; the ground ploughing very fine, and harrowing in dust, I was the rather inclined to harrow them in on one earth, since I could lay them in a warm dry bed, the ground being very dry, which induced me to do it so early as the 9th and 10th of March, though it was sooner than I had ever known them to be sown.—There followed a very dry cold spring (anno 1713) without rain till the first of May, when there fell a plentiful rain, which went to the roots of all corn ; one fourth part of the oats sown never came up, and those that did, looked spiry and weak till about the 20th of May, and then, warm weather coming, they thrived wonderfully in tillows, rankness, colour, and breadth of blade, so that it was plain the ground was in sufficient heart ; but they were sown too early : it further appears that they were only sown too early, because the upper part of the ground, though by much the best, had not half the crop of oats the lower part of it had ; the reason of which was that the upper part lay most exposed to the cold.—From hence it is plain, that two or three days before the end of March, or after the beginning of April, is the time for sowing white oats, and, if the ground be ploughed just before sowed, they will lie the deeper and warmer.

§. 66. Five bushels of oats is the quantity they sow in the hill-country on an acre ;— but, if there be a strong elbow-wind at the time of sowing, there must be half a bushel extraordinary allowed to an acre, whether oats, barley, or wheat, but a face or back-wind signifies little, nor the elbow-wind neither to peas or vetches.—There are some farmers among us who sow but four bushels, but that quantity is not sufficient to seed an acre properly : though the seed be very good they ought not to sow less than four bushels and an half.

*Quantity of oats to an acre in the hill-country.*

§. 67. Hugh

Quantity
of wheat
barley and
oats sowed
on an acre
in Leicel-
tershire.

§. 67. Hugh Clerk of Hawthorne in Leicester-shire, and Mr. Clerk of Ditchly assure me, that, on light lands in the common-fields, they sow six bush-els of barley in a lugg, that is a chain-acre, though but four in clay-land in the same fields.— I asked Hugh Clerk the reason of it; he said, because, if the light land was not filled with corn, it would be full of weeds. I asked him whether the clay-land would not be the same, and if so, why he did not sow as much on that; he said, the clay-land would have as full a crop with four bushels as the other with six, for from one grain the clay would put forth three, four, and five stalks, whereas the light earth would not yield above one or two stalks.—I saw this sort of clay-land last abovementioned, and I thought it was half clay half sand. —— On the light-er land they sow three bushels of wheat, on the hea-vier but two, and of oats not above four bushels on the light land, for, said he, there is more of that grain goes to a bushel.

§. 68. At Whitchurch farmer Perry and Mr. Bunny had discourse with me about the nature of white oats:—they both on their own experience a-greed that they were to be sown very thick, because they would not tillow nor multiply like black oats; — therefore, said they, five bushels ought to be sow-ed on an acre.—Farmer Crapp agreed afterwards that they would not tillow like black oats; but others I find are of a contrary opinion, as I have noted in my remarks on Oats. [a] Mr. Ray says the white oat will degenerate in poor ground, and be-come a black oat.—— See my observations on Oats.

[a] Si ager paulo sterilior sit avena nostra alba in nigrum dege-nerat. Ray, fol. 42.

## Of SOWING BEANS.

§. 69. [b] Palladius tells us, it is a rule laid down by the Greek writers, that all corn of the leguminous kind should be sowed dry, except beans, and they ought to be sowed wet.

§. 70. In Wiltshire they sow beans in December and before Christmass.—— Farmer Miles said, it was observed that those beans kidded best, and he thought the reason to be, because such beans, being checked in their stalk by the cold weather, did not spend their strength, when at the same time their roots were getting a fastening in the ground, whereby they so much the better fed their stalks when spring came; whereas the beans sown late, having no check, run into halm, and draw faster from the root than it can afford, and so the root has the less strength for kidding.

§. 71. August 30th (anno 1721) I shewed farmer Sartain of Broughton in Wilts the two acres and half of beans I had sowed; the strongest and best part of the ground bore the worst beans, and the lighter land by much bore beans excellently kidded. —— I had been at a loss for the reason of it, but as soon as the farmer entered that part, which was the strong and cold land, he said, those beans looked as if they were sown too wet.—— On reflection I well remembered, that I feared, when they were sown, that part of the ground was too wet. Why, farmer, said I, should beans be sowed as dry as peas? he said yes, if ground be strong-clay-ground, one need not fear sowing them too dry in February or the beginning of March, for so early

*Time of sowing beans in Wilts.*

*Beans, if sowed early on strong clay-land, to be sowed dry.*

[b] Omnia legumina Græcis auctoribus seri jubentur in sicca terra, faba tantummodo in humida debet spargi. Pallad. lib. 1. sect. 6.

in

in the spring the ground could not but be moist enough to bring up the beans.

**How to plant horse-beans in stony ground.**

§. 72. I was asking farmer White of Catmoor in Berkshire, how he would advise me to sow horse-beans, whether to plant them or sow them; he said, he thought in our country we could not well plant them, because, our land being very stony, the stick for the most part would not enter the ground, and it would also be very difficult to hough them; — but Major Liver did not apprehend these to be objections, and said, if I planted them, I must plant by a line across the furrows, because there is no good houghing with the furrow, the earth not being well raised about them. — About Catmoor they often sow beans and peas together.

**Of the seminal leaves of seeds.**

§. 73. Mr. Ray supposes, that the seminal leaves first swelling do afford the first nourishment to the nib or radicle to shoot, which having gotten root does again nourish the seed-leaves, which do again communicate their oleous and salt particles to the plant; but, says he, in seeds, whose leaves or seminal lobes do not rise above ground, as in beans, peas, vetches, and other legumens, the radicle, as far as I have observed, does afford no nourishment to the lobes, which therefore cannot properly be said to increase and augment, tho' they swell very much, occasioned by the watery humour that insinuates itself into their pores, as into a sponge. Ray's Proleg fol. 28. For this reason the seminal leaves or lobes of these grains may not be much the worse for sowing tho' the lobes are partly cut off. The root of every

**The root shoots first.**

plant makes a beginning, and shoots downward before the plume stirs and advances upwards; for the plume is included between the lobes of the seed, and so the moisture or vegetable parts of the earth cannot come immediately to it, and lend their assistance, as they can to the outward part of the nib,

which

which fends forth the root, and therefore the root
muft make it's firft advance.[c]

## Of S O W I N G P E A S.

§. 74. Many good farmers I have converfed
with on the fubject of fowing peas, agreed, if the
ground was very dry, and worked pretty fine, it was
beft to fow peas under furrow;—but, if they were
fowed under furrow when the ground was wet, and
a dry feafon fhould come, the ground would be fo
ftarky that they could not come up.—By fowing
under furrow there is this certain advantage, that
the peas are fecured from pigeons. *Of fowing peas under furrow.*

Feb. 12th, (anno 1699) they were fowing peas
under furrow in the common-fields in Leiceftefhire,
and alfo harrowing fome in.——I afked Mr. Clerk
what rule he went by for harrowing-in peas, or fowing them under furrow ; he faid, if the land was
light, they fowed under furrow ; but if heavy, they
ploughed and harrowed-in ; or though the land was
clay and heavy, yet, if it had had a frofty winter,
whereby it broke and crumbled well under the
plough, they fowed under furrow, or fometimes,
though land in it's own nature light, having had an
open wet winter, fhould work heavy, they have
neverthelefs fowed peas under furrow. *In Leicef-terfhire.*

The great danger of fowing peas under furrow,
the ground being wet, is, if rain fhould come upon
it, and after that a baking fun, the earth will have a
glazy cruft at top ; now a pea will fhoot forth a
ftem or wire, which fhall work upwards, tho' a foot
under ground, but the danger is left the bud, or
leafy fubftance it fhoots out when near the top,
being broad and tender, fhould not be able to get
through the faid cruft, and fo be buried.

[c] See the article Beans.

Farmer

Farmer Lake of Faccomb, a very underſtanding huſbandman, is not fond of ſowing peas under fur-row ; he ſays, they are ſo long in coming up that the knap-weed, and other weeds get up before them, and are apt to ſmother the peas, and if the land lies on a ſlope, it is hard to plough ſhallow enough, and ſo the peas may be buried.

Farmer Carter of Cole-Henly being with me, we were talking of peas ; he ſaid, he had always ob-ſerved, when peas are ſowed under furrow, if the furrow ploughed heavy and cloſe, ſo that the peas could not ſhoot upright, but were forced to ſhoot aſlant for a good length before they could get out, that, tho' ſuch peas halmed well, yet they never bloſſomed nor kidded well. ---This is very probable, and agrees with what has been already ſet forth, viz. That where a plant receives any injury, the firſt is in it's ſeed, as being the moſt tender part, the next is in it's bloſſom, &c. Note, It is very obvious, that, where the pea runs ſlanting under a furrow before it can get out, it muſt ſpend itſelf, and it is alſo viſible, that it loſes of it's health thereby in it's being whitened and blanched.

In Wilts.     The wet ſpewy clay about Holt in Wilts, of which ſort that country does much conſiſt, if kept in arable, is mad by much rain, if heat or winds fol-low ; for which reaſon the countryman is forced to ſow his peas under furrow, and to leave the ground and furrows rough upon them, without harrowing-in the grain, in hopes that, if rain come, the ridges will molder and tumble down, and then grow mel-low, that ſo happily the peas, if the ground breaks kindly, may come through the earth under which they are covered, and, if the earth be too cloſe, that they may notwithſtanding come through the ſeams of the furrows ; thus their lands when finiſhed lie like ſummer-fallows for wheat, for the finer they make their grounds the faſter they bind, if rain

ſhould

should come and dry weather follow, so that no peas could come through; whereas in the rough manner (above described) in which it lies, the heat and rains together contribute towards the moldering of the earth; though this way is subject to many inconveniencies, (as before set forth) yet under the circumstances abovementioned I know not how the countryman can do better; but where such lands do abound, those parts of England will never get the name of corn-countries.

Farmer Reynolds, of Laverstock in Hampshire, speaking of sowing peas early under furrow said, —— it was an old proverbial speech, that

" The longer peas lie in their bed
" They will rise with the better head.

Which observation I have found to be true.

§. 75. February the 3d and 4th (anno 1713) I sowed four acres with Cotshill-peas under furrow. —February 5th to 10th I sowed under furrow ten acres with great grey partridge-peas; 'tis true, we had no stinging sharp frosts to endanger them that way, but we had a very long cold dry spring with easterly winds, yet I could not observe that either of these peas suffered by being sowed so early, but flourished much the better for it. *Of sowing peas early under furrow.*

Iles, my tenant in Wilts, and Smith of Dead house, had sown the same grey partridge-peas under furrow the 25th of January in mellow good ground, and throughout the spring I observed the halm to flourish very well, but at harvest, there having been an exceeding dry spring and summer, they, like the generality of the peas of that country, bore very short and but few kids, whereas I had long ones, and my halm extraordinary well kidded, not only of this sort, but all the sorts of peas I sowed, viz. blue peas and poplings, early in their season, which I attribute to the summer-fallowing my ground. *In Wilts*

# SOWING.

To plough
up the
ground in
the hill-
country
some time
before you
sow rath-
ripe peas.

§. 76. I am clearly of opinion, that in a cold hilly country, and more especially if the soil be clay, which is therefore the colder, if you sow any of the rath-ripe peas, which are the tender sort, such as poplings, blue-peas, or Henley-greys, it is prudent to plough up the ground a fortnight or three weeks before it be sown, that it may be dried and mellowed by the air, wind, and sun, and then to take an opportunity of sowing the peas when the ground is in the temper above described, which cannot in such a situation be too nicely regarded; for the common way of sowing after the plough the latter end of February, or beginning of March, especially if the grain be tender, is still the more improper, because the earth will at that time turn up a little moist and cold, which so early in the year chills corn; whereas by turning up the ground a fortnight or even a month before you sow it (according as your ground may require time for mellowing) you'll be able to command a fit time to sow your seed in, a few dry days rendering land chastened, dry, and friable; nor will land ploughed up dry in a cold country so early as January or February be apt to bring weeds by lying fallow.——I would also recommend the same way for oats or barley, if sowed by the middle of March, before the weather is warm enough to set the seeds of weeds a growing by the earth's lying in such a manner tilled.——But when I recommend the ploughing up of land a fortnight or even a month before it is sown, it is not meant of strong land; which will not by such time be brought to harrow, nor of light ground, which works knot-fine; for, if rain in the interim should come, such ground will quatt, and the furrow will fill up, and lie soggy and wet long after; but such ploughing beforehand is meant of ground, which for the most part will hold a furrow, or plough with some roughness, yet so mellow as to shatter either by dry or rainy weather.

§. 77. Being

§. 77. Being in Wiltshire I inquired of the far- Difference
mers, viz. farmer Earle, Mr. Smith, &c. why they of peas in
did not sow popling or grey Burbage-peas : I found hardiness.
they thought those peas too nice to sow in their cold
lands, and said they did not do well with them, but
that the hot and sandy lands about Scene and the
Devises might be very proper for them. —— Note,
It is my opinion, when any pea is sowed early under Best to let
furrow, if the land be somewhat mellow and friable, the land lie
as in that case it ought to be, and also to be very unharrow-
dry when the peas are sowed, the best way is, after ter sowing
the peas are sowed, to let the furrows lie unharrow- peas.
ed for some time, it may be for three weeks or a
month, for the roughness of the ground will be a
great means to keep the peas warm from frosts and
winds, and dry from rain, whereas, if such land be
harrowed off fine, immediately after the peas are
sowed, it will lie wet and cold a long time in January or February before it can dry again, that being
the wet season of the year, and no sun to dry it; but
if such land be harrowed only two or three tinings a
month after sowing the peas, they lying deep will only
have rooted, but not sprouted, nor will any of them be
torn up by the harrows; this method will protect the
peas from cold till the fierceness of the season is over,
and secure them a warm bed at first putting in by
the furrows covering them and shooting off the rain,
which is of vast consequence to all sorts of corn.

§. 78. A neighbour of mine sowed peas on fal- Peas chil-
lows, being dry and in good order, but, before he led by
could finish the harrowing them, came a snow; af- being sow-
ter the snow was melted, which was in a day or two, snow.
he sowed more in the same ground, being of the
same goodness, and harrowed them in, the ground
working pretty well, but not so well and mellow as
the former : of the peas of the first sowing he had
treble the crop he had of the latter sowing. —— I
conceive, for the solving these two notable instances,
we may compare corn to an egg, which has the san-

N 2                                              guinea

guinea gutta, of which Pliny says, "certò saltat pal-
"pitatque," and the many damages that sanguinea
gutta receives on the first incubation, either by
thunder or shaking, or chill the egg takes, are
reckoned up by the Roman writers. Now, in like
manner, in the germen of corn there is a punctum
saliens, a minute vital principle, which moves, and
which receives an immediate check, if laid in a cold
bed, which has a notable ill effect throughout it's
whole progress of vegetation afterwards; and a
warm dry bed, which enlivens it, has, on the contrary, a good effect. I think there is no room to
doubt but that there is an innate action in seed,
more than is merely mechanical, implanted in it by
God Almighty, (it is this, which in it's punctum saliens, inclines the root to take downwards, and the
stalk upwards; otherwise the first conduct in vegetation is unaccountable) and that the seed has this
power of action seated in itself purely relative to the
thing it performs, and confined only to that; nor
is this strange, seeing the union of the soul and body
in man cannot be resolved without flying to Omni-
potence; it is the same of the animal life with the
body of brutes, and it is plain the things of this crea-
tion move within peculiar spheres of subordinate
gradations; we may therefore well believe there is a
power of action thus confined, which partakes not
of any agitations; this may be termed a moving
spring, elater, or pulse; nor is it rash to affirm such
a motion we cannot see; for who can see the motion
of the index of a clock? and yet, that a motion can
be a thousand millions of times less, none can deny.

§. 79. On lightish or whitish ground, or such
ground as one may suspect to be too light for peas,
in my opinion they ought to be drilled when sowed,
and drilled at a tolerable distance, that a sufficient
quantity of earth may be houghed up to cover the
roots of the peas, in order to keep them moist, and
to break the scorching heat of the sun, which

bring

Of the
punctum
saliens in
seed.

Of drilling
peas on
light
ground.

brings blights, choaks them up in bloſſoming-time, and occaſions other evils, which may be the chief reaſon of drilling about Burbage.

§. 80. I aſked ſeveral knowing farmers when was the beſt ſeaſon to ſow peas. In this country, ſaid they, peas as well as vetches require to be ſown early and when the ground is dry; if they are ſowed when the ground is very wet, or if much wet falls upon their being ſown, they will be apt to burſt, and ſwell out of the ground, ſo that they'll lie above ground. — I aſked them, how it could be that a pea could ſwell out of the ground; they could not tell that, but one of them ſaid, he believed there was no more in it than that the rain waſhed the earth from them. — I aſked them, what they meant by an early ſowing, and when was the beſt time to ſow peas; the farmer laſt mentioned ſaid, he thought the latter end of February;—the reſt agreed to it, and ſaid, if they were ſowed ſo early they would be likely to kid before the blight came, which otherwiſe would breed a catterpillar that would eat them up.—They told me little yellow worms ſometimes would ſwarm on them.

Where elms, maples, and furze are, the butterfly, that breeds the catterpillar, lays her eggs, rather than in the peas, which ſhews inſtinct for the good of her kind; for the butterfly chooſes what is beſt for the nouriſhment of her brood, not herſelf, who is fed by the juices of flowers, and the honey-dews.

It was January the 18th when my bailiff aſked me when I would ſow the farther part of a certain field to peas; he ſaid, he would not adviſe me (unleſs I ſowed them under furrow) to ſow them till a week within, or the middle of March; for, ſaid he, the land has been hard driven, and is but poor, and if ſowed too early, the peas may come up and receive a check by cold weather, which they will hardly recover; it is the ſame with oats; therefore, ſaid he,

*Peas—the ſeaſon of ſowing them.*

N 3 about

about the middle of March is the best time for sowing peas in poor land, but, if you sow them under furrow, they may be sowed the latter end of February, because they will require a longer time to come up. — Ashmonsworth-down is poor land, and they are ignorant when to sow it, and commonly they sow it too early, whereby I have known that ground to have had three starts, and as many checks by the cold weather, which has brought their crop to nothing ;---it is true, added he, farmer Bond sows peas the latter end of February, but then his ground is good ground, and lies warm.

*To be sown early.*    I find it is the opinion of the best husbandmen in these parts, that a good crop of peas depends very much on the early sowing them.----Major Liver says he never missed of a good crop, if he sowed early, tho' in the coldest part of the whole farm.----He said, it being then February the 12th (anno 1701) if the ground had been dry enough he had sown peas before that time.

Mr. Edwards assures me that on Christmass-day farmer Elton sowed the Cotshill-peas, and never had a better crop.

*The hotspur pea to be sown late.*    If you sow hotspur-peas in the field, says Mr. Randal, you must not sow them till May, because, if they ripen before other corn, the birds will devour them.

*Of sowing different sorts of peas.*    This year (1715) I sowed an hundred acres of peas ; part of the land I sowed with great partridge-peas, both under and on furrow, from the beginning of February to about the 20th day : these peas were sowed dry, and they flourished exceedingly, holding their own, and prospering throughout the summer.----March 19th I began to sow the rest of the land with blue peas and poplings ; these peas were all stunted, and continued in an unthriving condition, with a small leaf, and pale of colour, till about the 8th of June, when by means of warm
weather

weather they grew eftablifhed, and mended in all
refpects, and got into a thriving way; yet thefe
peas were fown when the earth worked well, and was
in feafon, all the peas-land having been fummer-fallowed. The reafon of this difference between the
profperity of the great partridge-peas, and that of the
blue peas and poplings, I take chiefly to be this, that
cold dry churlifh winds coming, and cold rains
falling from the latter end of March till the middle
of May; though they had very little or no ill effect
on the great partridge-peas fowed the beginning of
February, becaufe their roots were not only well
eftablifhed, but the ground was alfo by that time
fettled to them, yet the blue peas and the poplings
had not eftablifhed their roots, nor was the ground
fettled to them, and fo they became paffive both to
the cold winds and the cold rains.---If it be objected,
that the great grey partridge-peas are much hardier
than the blue poplings, and that the difference
might lie in that,---I anfwer, 'tis admitted that the
great partridge-peas are a hardier fort of peas than
the blue peas or the popling-peas; but there being
at leaft five weeks difference in the time of their
being fowed, that fets them on the level with each
other in refpect to their hardinefs and tendernefs.----
And if it be farther objected, that cold churlifh
winds and cold rain might as well have fallen on
the former as on the latter fort of peas, foon after
the great partridge-peas had been fown.---I anfwer,
we had a great deal of fuch weather then alfo; but
by conftant experience I have obferved, that peas
fowed very early, the ground being dry, and in
good order at the time of fowing, do bear the
cold weather, cold rain, and cold wind, which then
happens, better than the peas fowed from the beginning to the middle or 20th of March do bear the
fame fort of weather, which ufually falls about that
time of the year, without refpect to the tendernefs

of

of any particular sort of peas, (for I have sown both
blue peas and popling-peas the latter end of February) because it fares with grains, cæteris paribus, as
with our bodies, viz. that cold rains, cold winds,
and cold air in the months of April and May pinch
us, and make us more sensible of their effects than
those of February and March, when our pores are
closer, and the capillaries hardened; for in April
and May the sun-beams play on us by lucid intervals, and open and soften the pores and capillaries,
whereby the cold penetrates deeper, and we are more
sensible of it; and thus stands the difference between the young tender roots of the latter-sowed
peas, viz. the blue and popling-peas, because they
are tenderer, and the great grey peas sowed earlier,
because they are hardier, and so their roots are
hardened, and struck down deep into the earth, and
the earth is well settled about them before the sun
from April to June acts by fits on the ground to the
prejudice abovementioned, whereas otherwise, as
hardy a pea as the great partridge-pea is, the stalk
and leaves, if sowed at the time the other peas were,
would sicken also upon the same occasion.—It may
be demanded now what remedy can there be prescribed to help this; I answer,—By all means roll
these latter-sown peas the first opportunity of dry
weather you have, after you have sown them, the
ground being then also dry; those sowed the beginning of February need it not; but be sure to
roll the latter-sown peas as soon as you have half or
a whole day's work for a team cut out, (which we
commonly reckon from ten to twelve acres) and delay it not out of impatience to sow your whole crop
of peas first, for such delays are fatal; a team that
rolls ten or twelve acres m a day, can in lieu of it
plough but an acre —Note, I and the whole country neglected snatching this opportunity on account
of dripping weather, but dearly paid for it.

Caution—
to roll the
latter-sown
peas.

§. 81. Of

§. 81. Of the great grey Cotſhill-peas three The quantity of peas on an acre. buſhels and an half uſed to be ſown on an acre, but the ground about Crux-Eaſton is not good enough for them ; of the grey partridge-peas they ſow here three buſhels on an acre.

This year (1700) peas being houſed dry, the more will go to a buſhel ; ſo poſſibly three buſhels and a peck may do to ſow an acre ; otherwiſe it is beſt to ſow four buſhels ; for peas, according to the countryman's obſervation, never thrive well till they can take hands with one another, that is, by their ſtrings, which they can never do if ſowed thin : when they can climb up by one another they ſhade the ground.

July 20, 1701, I obſerved my peas, being well kidded, were fallen on the ground about three weeks before they ought to be hacked, from whence I did infer another benefit from ſowing them thick, viz. that, by handling one another, they were able to ſtand up the longer before they were pulled down by the kids, whereas by being pulled down too ſoon, if wet weather ſhould come, both kid and halm might rot. Farmer Biggs ſays, he had a ſervant that one year ſowed five buſhels of peas on an acre, for which he was very angry with him, but however he never had better peas.

Palladius tells us, and Columella and Pliny agree with him, that peas are to be ſown the latter end of September, in light, mellow earth, and in a warm moiſt ſituation, and we have ſeen indeed, that this dry ſummer, 1705, has been more ruinous to peas than any other ſort of grain. The quantity Palladius preſcribes to be ſown on an acre is four modii, or three, he ſays, may be ſufficient ; whereas we ſow four buſhels, that is eight modii, tho' we begin not till March, and of vetches we ſow not ſo many as the Romans .

ᵈ See the article Peas.

Of

## Of SOWING VETCHES.

§. 82. Palladius says, vetches should be sowed as early in the morning as the dew is off, and should be covered in before night, for otherwise the moisture that falls in the night may corrupt and destroy the seed.

**Winter-vetches to be sowed dry and early.**

§. 83. Farmer Elton told me, it was agreed to be best to sow winter-vetches dry; the ground could not be too dry for them; he said they were a ticklish grain, and it was good to sow them early, by Michaelmass;—but, said he, I once sowed them when it was so deep in wet that my horses trod as deep as the plough went, being loth to let them lie still, and people who came by thought me mad, but I never had a better crop of vetches.—Three days after I dined with Mr. Whistler, and, speaking about vetches, I said they were a ticklish grain; yes, said he, but they need not be so, if people pleased; for I was told it by a wise husbandman forty years ago, and have found it true, that, if you sow vetches very early and dry, you'll have vetches enough.—What, by Michaelmass would you have them sowed? said I.—Ay, said he, by the first of September if you can; the winter then will never hurt them; they are to be sowed at a leisure-time, when the ground may be too dry for sowing wheat.

**To be sowed dry.**

Between the 29th of August and the 4th of September, 1719, I ploughed and sowed to vetches eighteen acres of a barley-stubble, which had been sowed to corn for several years before: the whole summer having been exceeding dry, the ground ploughed in ashes, and had no moisture to bring up the corn; I chose however to sow it in this condition, (tho' I had no prospect of the vetches growing without rain) because I was apprehensive, that, if rain came, the ground might fall so flat, and so close together,

together, that I should not bury the vetches. By
the fourth of September aforesaid I had sowed to
vetches another field of fourteen acres, a wheat-
stubble, it being also all in dust. After sowing I
trod them both with sheep. Notwithstanding this
great drought, yet by the 19th of September the
vetches in both these fields were come up, thick
enough for a crop; so that it must be concluded, by
the beginning of September there is, by night, a
coldness and moisture in the air, which enters the
earth, sufficient to make a vetch grow: barley also
is of the same nature, for the barley by this time
came up very thick in the first-mentioned field
among the vetches, I having ploughed-in the barley-
stubble.—The sowing of vetches in this manner succeeding to admiration, for, as they came up at first
extremely well, so they held their own all the
winter, and when I viewed them the 7th of June
(the time of noting this observation) the whole
crop stood as thick on the ground as the ground
could well bear, insomuch that it was not only the
most flourishing but the thickest crop I ever had;
for, judging from their thickness, one would conclude that every vetch took root and grew.

Mr. Edwards ploughed for vetches about seven
or eight days within September, but it happened to
be so wet he could not sow, nor could he harrow
till the 24th of October, when he told me he would
not sow them till towards Candlemass, for that the
middle time of sowing vetches (about St. Leonard)
was the worst of all; he allowed the early sowing
was the best; but, said he, the middle sowing,
which is about the beginning of November, and so
on, is the worst, because there is warmth enough in
the earth to bring up the vetch, which will in all
likelihood be tender when the frost comes, and so
be cut off by it, whereas what is sown the latest,
suppose before Candlemass, when the ground is cold,
will,

*Or, for want of an early sea-son, to be sown very late.*

will, if froſt and cold weather come, lie buried without coming up, and ſo take no harm. This to me ſeems to ſtand to reaſon.

Seaſon of ſowing goar-vetches.

§. 84. I have found by experience, that it is not good to ſow goar-vetches ſo late as the beginning of May; for they will not, if it ſhould prove a wet cold ſummer, come to a good growth and bulk, and yet will be very groſs and ſappy, and unfit for horſes, eſpecially when the heat of the ſummer is going off, as towards the latter end of Auguſt; and, if you deſign them for dry fodder, they will be ſo late ripe, that their groſsneſs will occaſion their lying out ſo long, as to be in great danger of being ſpoiled.

Miſchief from ſowing winter-vetches wet and late.

§. 85. At autumn (anno 1719) I was ſo late in ſowing that I could not ſow winter-vetches till the 18th of October, and got finiſh'd by the 24th. —— The ſeaſon was too wet, and the ground ploughed and harrowed as heavy, but not heavier, than we generally deſire it ſhould for wheat, not ſo wet as to tread in when harrowed; the winter continued very mild to the beginning of February, when there came a little froſt; yet the vetches never thrived, but looked very dwindling, and of a ruſſet colour, which I imputed to their being ſowed ſo wet, and ſo late in the year: I believe, tho' the ground had been as wet as it was, they had not ſucceeded ſo ill had they been ſowed five or ſix weeks earlier; and yet this ground was in a very friable condition, not clay, but a mixed land, and lies on a deſcent to the ſouth-eaſt. The vetches continued in an unthriving way till the firſt of February, when a hard froſt came with an eaſterly wind, which held for a month, and it killed the whole crop root and branch.

Ground ſloping to the north to be ſowed early for winter-corn.

§. 86. If a ground lies aſlope to the north or weſt, the earlier you ſow it for winter-corn the better; becauſe in Auguſt and September the days ſhorten apace, and ſuch grounds have but little ſun then, not ſo much as to make early-ſown corn win-

ter-

ter-proud; besides, such corn will ripen the sooner, before the sun loses it's strength over such grounds the following summer. —— I sowed at the latter end of September, 1702, vetches in a field that lies from the sun, the ground being also poor; they kept blooming to the last of August, and yet were very short, and the land was white land. I sowed wheat, just by the said vetches, after Michaelmass, which ripened as early as any; but then the ground was very well maintained, which must make the difference.

§. 87. If vetches be dry they sow two bushels on an acre; if swelled with being moist, two bushels and an half, because they take up more room. *Quantity of vetches on an acre.*

Three bushels of winter-vetches on an acre is more than is commonly sown, especially on white land, because they generally kid well on such land, but I think three bushels not too much for red land, because they may kid the better for it, and not run so much to halm.

§. 88. It is good to have such plenty of winter-vetches, as to be able to save seed in halm for sowing the next year; because it is best to sow them early, i. e by the beginning of September, vetches of the same year's seed being seldom ripe so soon, nor can they be got to be threshed till Michaelmass. *To save seed for sowing the next year.*

§. 89. A neighbour of mine was imposed on, and instead of the winter-vetch bought the summer-pebble-vetch-seed, which he sowed, and, though the winter proved mild as ever winter did, yet in March they were all dead, and the land was ploughed up again; which I mention as a caution to others. The pebble-vetch is a summer-vetch, different from the goar-vetch, and not so big; they call it also the rath-ripe vetch. *Care not to be imposed on in buying seed.*

§ 90. I was telling farmer Pocock of —————— near Hungerford, that I had sown winter-vetches two year old, being well housed, and that they came up *Vetches two year old will grow, also peas.*

up well.—He replied, that he had fown great partridge-peas the fecond fpring after the harveft, and they grew very well ; but, fays he, I kept them in the mow till near the time I fowed them, for otherwife, as he fuppofed, had they been threfhed long before feed-time, they would not have grown fo well

## Of SOWING TILLS.

**Tills—beft on good land.**

§. 91. Going from Crux-Eafton to Holt I obferved in the fat ftrong clay lands between Pewfey and Devifes beans on one ridge of land, and tills on another, and fo to continue interchangeably for fome miles.—-I thought tills had always been fown on light and poor land ; therefore I afked a farmer I met whether tills grew well on fuch land ; he faid, the ftronger the land the better the tills.——— I afked him if they fowed not tills on two earths, the ground being fo heavy ; he faid, fometimes they did, and fometimes on one earth, as the land worked.

**Time of fowing.**
**Quantity on an acre.**

Again I afked him, when they fowed the tills, he faid before their barley, that is in March. I found by him that two bufhels, and two and an half, were fowed on an acre : the tills on that land were the beft I ever faw.

**To fow barley with tills.**

§. 92. I was advifed by the country-people, where tills are much fowed, to fow a bufhel of barley in every acre of tills ; they faid it would ferve the tills to climb up by, and the rudder would eafily feparate them.

**Quantity on an acre.**

§. 93. I told my neighbouring farmers that between Pewfy and the Devifes, in mighty ftrong land, they fowed two bufhels, and two bufhels and an half, of tills on an acre. They replied, it muft then be becaufe, their land being fo ftrong, if not fowed

e See the author's remarks on Vetches.

thick,

thick, they would run too much to halm, but in poor land they thought a bushel and a peck on an acre was sufficient.

## Of SOWING GRASS-SEEDS.

§. 94. That seeds will not grow unhulled, or extra cotyledones, see the Experiments made by Malpigius in beans, lupines, &c. yet quære; for we know hop-clover unhooded grows well; but then that hood seems the pod rather than the rind or cotyledon, the rind going and growing with the seed still. The bran or cotyledon is taken off of oatmeal; quære of that therefore, and whether it will grow.

§. 95. James Young my tenant in the Isle of Wight and I were talking of clover-seed: he said, he had been acquainted with a husbandman who lived about Guilford in Surry, who told him, the method of sowing it there was, after the barley was sowed, to roll the ground, which laid it so smooth that the clover-seed might be delivered as even as you pleased, and then to sow it, and give it a tining-in.

*Method of sowing clover in Surry.*

§. 96 My bailiff, who was many years a farmer, assures me, that in the hill-country of Wiltshire he has often known hop-clover and broad-clover-seed sowed with wheat, and it has born the winter very well; he has likewise sometimes known clover-seed sowed among green wheat in March, without harrowing it in, with good success.—Another, a Wiltshire farmer, told me he had often known hop-clover sowed with the wheat in Wiltshire, and he thought it the best way, especially if the ground was out of heart; for then it would pay better than taking a crop or two of corn after the wheat; one gets a year's forwardness of the clover by it.—He says likewise, that not far from Puckshipton. where the ground is pretty rich, he has known the hop-clover,

*Of sowing clover-seed with wheat, barley, &c.*

clover sowed a month after the barley, lest it should prove too rank.

§. 97. In September, 1719, I sowed broad-clover-seed with my wheat on twenty nine acres of land; I dunged about seventeen acres of it with cow and horse-dung, and the rest with the fold, or with pigeons-dung, or malt-dust; I laid, I believe, near forty load of pot-dung on an acre: it proved an exceeding mild winter, with a cold and wet spring and summer, insomuch that near a month before harvest the wheat lodged: I had a very great crop of wheat, yet, notwithstanding the dunging and the mildness of the winter, and the frequent rains throughout the spring and summer, the broad-clover did not at all injure the wheat, though the wheat-harvest did not begin till the 20th of August; then I began to cut this wheat, but the broad-clover was neither rank nor high, so as to prejudice the wheat, but seemed rather to be too thin set on the ground, nor had it made any effort towards flowering; yet by a fortnight after the wheat had been cut the broad-clover appeared very thick on the ground: even so as in many places to be matted; the leaf also was very rank, fat, and gross, notwithstanding natural grass grew up with it.---What deserves farther to be observed in this case is, that in the spring of the year the wheat came so very gross, that, for fear of a lodgment, I was forced to put my whole flock into it for three mornings to feed it down, and they without doubt fed on the young broad-clover as well as on the wheat, yet it seems such feeding did the broad-clover no harm.

§. 98. The 10th of October (anno 1720) I went into my neighbour's wheat-stubble to view the broad-clover he had sown among his wheat in the preceding spring, and before he had rolled it. —— He was of opinion it succeeded very well.——I found the broad-clover to have come up very thick, but it had

a very

# SOWING.

a very small leaf, and was less sappy than my broad-clover sown when I sowed the wheat, which makes me conclude, that the seed sown so late could not penetrate with it's root into the ground so well as mine, nor find nourishment and maintenance like my broad-clover sown with the wheat, when the ground was new harrowed; therefore it is my opinion, that, when spring comes, the late-sown seed will decline and fall off.—I also observed his clover thrived better where the ground was mere clay than where it was mixed earth; and note, this had been a very wet spring and summer; otherwise, sowing his clover as he did, he would have had but little come up.

§. 99. This harvest (anno 1720) farmer Crapp of Ashmonsworth, Hants, assured me, that, it having been a wet and cold spring and summer, he was worse in his barley by 40 l. for sowing broad-clover with it; for four or five weeks before harvest the broad-clover had so eat out the barley, that the straw dwindled, and carried no substance, and the barley had but a thin body, and, when it comes, said he, to be threshed on the floor, it will thresh so heavy, that there will be no threshing it out for the broad-clover, which will deaden the stroke of the flail.—He says, if broad-clover be sowed with oats, it does not do well on one earth. *Broad-clover damages barley, if a wet spring and summer succeeds.*

It seems to me, that since broad-clover must be sowed in good strong clay-land, the rath-ripe barley is the fittest to be sowed with it, because it also requires good land, but more especially because it will be early ripe before the broad-clover can grow to that height as to prey much on the barley, or so that swarths of it must be cut with the barley, which may occasion the corn's lying out the longer, for the broad-clover to wither; it will also be cut before that time of the year, when the dew falls in great quantities on the broad-clover-grass, which would *Of sowing it with rath-ripe barley.*

revent the barley from being dry enough to be housed.

Since so much has been said of the damage that broad-clover often does to a crop of barley, for the better security against such evils, it seems reasonable to me, to lay down to broad-clover with a crop of oats: first, because, being sowed earlier with oats than with barley, it will not be in danger of growing so rank.—Secondly, tho' it should grow rank, it will not prejudice the oats as it would do barley, because oats may lie abroad a week after they are cut, and take rain without damage.— Thirdly, the ground laid down to oats is commonly in a poorer condition than ground laid down to barley, and therefore the broad-clover will be less liable to grow too rank.—Fourthly, oats are generally ripe before barley, and housed before the feeding weather of autumn comes, especially on the latter-sown barley, which sets the broad-clover a growing, and makes it very rank before the barley can be cut.

The farmers of Wiltshire choose rather to sow broad-clover with black or white oats than with barley, provided the ground works up mellow, and they say, the broad-clover will be the better crop, and the more certainly so, for being sowed so early as the oat-seed-time, nor will it ever hurt the oats.

* One of them, a very understanding man, speaking in relation to his sowing broad-clover with his oats, told me, that he always dragged them in with their country-drags (which are not so big as our's, and have six tinings on a harrow) and this he does, tho' his ground had been ploughed up but a fortnight before; but he commonly sows broad-clover on ground ploughed so long before as Candlemass, which never will, tho' it works mellow, fall too close for the drags to tear it.—

§. 100. Mr. Randolph and Mr. Short Baily of Wiltshire discoursing with me about hop-clover-seed,

Mr.

Mr. Baily affured me, that having once two or three quarters of hop-clover-feed by him, and having a wheat-ftubble, which he obferved the following fpring to be pretty clear of weeds, and pretty hollow, he flung in his hop-clover-feed without harrowing it, and had as good a crop as at any other time. This he faid on an occafion I gave him, by faying, I would try an experiment on my fide-lands by fowing them with rye-grafs at fpring, on the oat ftubbles, harrowing them in.

§. 101. A noted farmer near Uphaven, informed me, that it was the beft way to fow hop-clover with French-grafs; that he fowed feven bufhels of French-grafs on an acre, and with it a good fprinkling of hop-clover; the advantage of which was, that it filled up thofe fpaces that miffed between the French-grafs, and kept down the weeds till fuch time as the French-grafs could overcome all. *Of fowing hop-clover with French-grafs.*

§. 102. It is my opinion, that, if the ground works light and fine, French-grafs-feed ought to be fown under furrow, becaufe (as I have elfewhere obferved) if it be fown on furrow, it is apt not to be healed.--- To which add, that French-grafs-feed in it's hufks, being very prickly, is not apt as the harrows move, to fall deep into the earth, and tho' fallen deep enough, yet by means of the prickles which catch hold of the earth, it is apt to be harrowed up again. *Of fowing French-grafs and clover under furrow.*

About Crux-Eafton the farmers think they cannot fow grafs-feed too deep, fowing it often with corn, and harrowing it in afterwards; and I have known hop-clover mowed for feed, which, ftanding too long, fhattered, and after the grafs was mowed, wheat was fowed under furrow; the ground was harrowed fine, and the hop-clover came up with the wheat as thick as could be defired, fo that I am fatisfied, if the earth be light at top, there is no danger of burying it.

March the 12th (anno 1707) I fowed French-

grafs

grass-seed under furrow : no rain material fell till
the 22d of May, being near ten weeks, during
which time the sun was very hot with dry winds
and cold nights : in this dry time I often scratched
up the ground, and found the lobes or seed-leaves
out under ground, but, tho' sown under furrow, at
a perfect stand, not able to advance farther without
rain, and before rain came, the seed-leaves did a
little languish, and seemed to have spent their stock
of juice, so that I began to fear the crop would die
under ground ; but plenty of rain coming, I did
between the 30th of May and the 3d of June observe the seed-leaves coming plentifully out of the
ground, which was near three months after sown. I
likewise observed some oats, sown under furrow the
18th of March, appearing the first of June ;—I also
observed many stems of these French-grass-seeds to
be bit off under ground, by worms, they not being
able to get food above ground by reason of the
drought : the insects of the field are a great prejudice.

*Damage from worms.*

§. 103. Many have sown grass-seeds when fallows have worked wet, and have had no grass,
which might as well happen from the wetness of the
ground as the badness of the seed ; for if barley,
which carries so strong a blade, can hardly get
through ground that binds by wet, how should it be
expected of grass-seed so sown, the blade of which is
so much weaker and tenderer ? I alledged this to a
good farmer of my acquaintance ; he replied, that,
as he thought, grass-seed could not fall in so deep as
to be bound.---I answered he was mistaken, for the
last tining of the harrows let in the grass-seed as deep
as the first did the corn, of which I convinced him
by going out and digging up the seed.

*Grass-seed may fail by sowing it on wet fallows.*

§. 104. I hold, that in the hill-country, broad-
clover ought to be sowed thick, because the grass
will be finer for sheep, not so gross as otherwise
it would be, and consequently, if rain falls, it will
quickly

*Broad-clover, &c. to be sown thick.*

quickly be dry, and, if rain should not fall, the hay, when mowed, will be the sooner made by four or five days, and being cut in it's juice before the flower dies, it will not take the damage that it would do, provided it was cut ripe.

I was complaining to farmer William Sartain of Broughton in Wiltshire that my broad-clover at Easton was very sour, occasioned by the coldness of the land---He said, if I sowed twenty pound of broad-clover on an acre instead of twelve or fourteen, I should find it the sweeter and finer for it, and it might be farther improved in sweetness, if I fed it very close, and did not let it grow to any height.

In discourse with Mr. Randolph, and Mr. Short Baily of Wiltshire, Mr. Randolph highly commended the sowing all grass-seeds in a greater quantity than was practised, especially, said he, French-grass-seed; for, if it be not sowed thick, if a hot summer comes, it will burn, and other grasses, if they be not sowed thick, will grow gross, and then, if at mowing-time a difficult season should come, the crop must stand till it is a little over-ripe before it be cut, and so it will lose it's goodness, whereas, had it been fine by means of sowing thick, it would take little damage. —— In Wiltshire they generally sow three or four bushels of rye-rass-seed upon an acre, and Mr. Raymond advised me by all means to sow no less than three bushels of hop-clover on an acre; for, said he, if you sow but two bushels, you will find abundance of vacancies, which would have carried grass, had the seed been dropped there, the vacancy not being for want of strength in the land, but because it had no seed fell in it.

§. 105 Seeds or kernels that are conical, as much *Of conical* as I have observed, have their root and spear at the *seeds.* narrow end, whereby, when they fall, that end inclines most to the ground. [f]

[f] See our author's observations on Grasses.

## EXPERIMENTS on the GROWTH
## of SEEDS.

Of the
pearly
drops on
barley, and
their use.

§. 106. I had often obferved in the fpring-time,
when the blades of barley firft began to fhoot out of
the ground, dewy drops ftanding every morning on
the points of the blades, even when the grafs of the
field, which was run into leaf, had fome mornings
no dew thereon; this made me believe they proceeded not from the defcending or circumambient
vapours of the air, but from juices drawn up by the
roots, which paffed upwards through the tubes and
iffued out at the top, which according to my conjecture was true, as appears by this experiment I
made.--I took a pot of fine garden-mold, and placed
it in my ftudy; the earth was but moderately moift,
and I put into it a handfull of barley; when the
barley fhot up about half an inch or an inch, at the
end of the points appeared the faid pearly drops; I
wiped them all off, and carefully took up half a
dozen of the blades of barley by the roots, then with
a pair of fciffars cut off the roots clofe to the grains
of corn, and covered them in the fame earth again;
the next day I looked on the blades, and found the
pearly drops of water fettled on the blades as before;
but on the tops of thofe blades, whofe fibrous roots
I had cut off, not the leaft moifture appeared, tho'
the blades continued in a good verdure through the
moifture of the earth they were put in; this fhews
plainly, thofe watery globules are not collected from
the moifture of the outward air, but from the juices
drawn upwards from the roots. I again wiped off
the faid drops, and within three hours after found
the tops of the blades were fupplied with frefh
drops, which trickle down the ftalks when they
fwell to fuch a bulk as to break, and again foon re-
new themfelves. This experiment was made in a
mild

mild time in December. From hence it appears that moisture must hold proportion to the roots; and it gave me farther occasion of admiring the wisdom of God in this appointment; for observing that these exsudations are, as soon as the sharp-pointed blade appears, continually sent forth, we may ground our judgment on reason and probability, that this moisture immediately begins to discharge itself, as soon as the spear is shot thro' the end of the barley-corn, which softens the earth upwards, as the blade pushes forward, and facilitates the easy passage of the spear: I conjecture it is the same in all the grassy sharp-pointed plants for the same reason. The roots of corn and beans also terminate in a sharp point, as they tend downwards, and, seeing it is so in the spires which ascend, I do very presumptively suspect, that there is a continual exsudation of a moist liquor from the points of the roots, to moisten and soften the earth before them, the more to facilitate the roots penetrating downwards, as it helps the blade to push upwards.

§. 107. Tho' this last summer (anno 1711) was a dry summer, yet it was not a hot summer by any means: I malted barley in November which had taken no wet in harvesting, and was seemingly very dry and hard: I wondered to find in every handfull I took in the malt-floor at least one hundred grains that did not come: I stayed till it came round to the kiln, and then took twenty of the grains which did not sprout with root, and put them the third of November into a flower-pot with very good mold, and set the pot in my study. Mr. Raymond came to see me, and, he being present, on the 13th I opened the earth in the pot, and found fourteen barley-corns of the twenty had put forth roots, but had not speared: the other six had not in the least made any proffer towards putting forth a root, which I concluded were dead corns. From hence we may easi-

*A cold soil will not ripen corn so as to make it fit for seed. Experiment on barley.*

ly

ly judge how my land, being cold in nature, and
coldly situated, ripens not barley to perfection but
in the hotteſt ſummers, and that this barley, which
came not till nine days after it had been taken from
the laſt floor, would have proved very coarſe and
edge-grown barley, had it been ſown in the field ;
it alſo ſeems plain from hence, that not only when
the barley takes wet in harveſt, and is cold by reaſon
of a wet ſummer, but even in all but the very hotteſt
ſummers our barley ſhould be ſweated on the kiln
in order for malting.

It is now further to be obſerved, that the very
ſame barley, out of the ſame field, and of the ſame
goodneſs with the twenty grains abovementioned,
and which alſo had not taken wet in harveſt, after
the floors had been ſeaſoned with drying off two
kilns, did ſo far root, that out of a handfull of it,
when it had ſo paſt the floors as to be within a week
of the kiln, I did not find above thirty grains,
which did not ſhew a root. Note, it is to be underſtood, that by drying off two kilns, and carrying the
malt through the floors, the floors and houſe had
been ſo warmed, which is very ſenſible to the ſmell
and feel, that thereby the vegetative powers of the
barley were forwarded and more exerted by ſuch
heat : this experiment ſtill ſhews how wrong it is to
ſow ſuch barley, eſpecially in a cold ground and cold
country, to the growing of which warmth is more
neceſſary ; and tho', as I obſerved, moſt of this barley did come, yet much of it did lie ſo many days
backward, that it might be doubted whether it
would make above half malt ; it is to be believed
therefore it might prove, if it came up in cold land,
an uſtilago or burnt ear.—*From hence I conclude
that wheat, if it handles cold and heavy, will do
better the earlier it is ſowed, whilſt the ſeaſon is warm;
for if ſowed late, by reaſon of it's own innate coldneſs, it will grow much worſe, and be longer coming
up ;

*Inference,
that peas
alſo and
wheat,
from a
cold ſoil,
are not
good for
ſeed, or
muſt be
ſowed
early.

up; from hence I also conclude, that peas cold or black by reason of a wet harvest, and cold oats, ought by no means to be sowed in cold land.

§. 108. I took nineteen grains of barley out of a heap that past the floors of my malt-house, and was to be dry'd off in a week's time, which made no shew of a root, and on the 17th of November I put them into a flower-pot of earth; I observed three of them had shot blades in five days time above the earth, and on the 27th of November, which was ten days after I had put them in earth, I took them out, and found four more grains were speared under ground, and had not yet appeared, the spears being short; and I found the ten remaining grains rooted with four or five roots, but not speared, as yet appearing; but on opening the rind found the spears alive, and that they had run near the length of the grain under the rinds: these instances plainly shew the different degrees of virtue in the stamina of seeds, and how far some stay behind others, which must be of ill consequence when grain of the most perfection is not sown, especially when such indifferent seed is committed to cold ground in a cold clime.

§. 109. In order to make a fuller experiment of this matter, I tried different grains from different soils.

February 8th 1711, I put into a flower-pot two hundred grains of black Poland-oats, marked numb. 8.—The same day I put into a flower-pot two hundred grains of Easton-oats, marked numb. 9.— March 16th both these and the Easton-oats were come up an inch in spear; by the eye I could discern no difference in the number of each come up; (they seemed to be all come up; viz. two hundred of each) but, on examining with the eye only it was plainly discoverable that the Poland-oat came up with the stronger spear, and March 27th, after both sorts of oats had been some days in blade and

*The different degrees of virtue in the stamina of seeds.*

*A farther experiment to shew the necessity of sowing good grain and from a good soil.*

leaf,

leaf, it was as difcernable, that the leaf of the Poland-oat was fomewhat broader than the leaf of the Eafton-oat, and the ftem proportionably ftronger.

February 8th 1711, I put into a pot two hundred grains of barley, being very coarfe, cold, and thin corn, marked numb 5.—And in another pot two hundred grains of Weftover barley, marked numb. 6.---And in a third pot hundred grains of my beft barley from the down, marked beft, B. numb. 7.

March 13th there appeared but five of numb. 5, in blade, whereas of the Weftover and my beft barley appeared half an inch above ground almoft all that were fowed.

March 18th of the worft barley appeared as near as I could reckon eighty-five blades.---Of Weftover barley I told above double the number, which being thick I could not eafily count right, but believe very near the whole two hundred grains were in blade.---Of my beft barley I believe I might not have by thirty blades fo many as there were of the Weftover : ---it was alfo manifeft that many more of the blades of the Weftover barley, and my beft barley, had from time to time dew-drops on them than had the blades of the coarfe barley ; alfo the drops of the former were larger.—I could alfo eafily difcern, if I looked attentively, that the Weftover barley carried a broader blade than my beft barley, tho' my beft barley feed feemed as full bodied as the Weftover.

March 27th I opened the three pots of barley, and was furprized to fee how the Weftover barley and my beft had ftruck roots down to the bottom of the pot, the tap-roots were above eight inches in length and had matted in the bottom, wanting depth to ftrike deeper ; moft of the roots of the Weftover barley had ftruck feven, eight, and nine roots ; my beft barley did not fo often run to feven and eight fibres or roots, but more frequent than the Weftover to five or fix.---The coarfe barley very rarely run

to

to seven or eight, but more commonly to four and five;——and I commonly observed some of the collateral fibres or roots to be very short.

From all the experiments I have made by sowing wheat, barley, oats, and peas in flower-pots within-doors, I found that, though the earth was rich and well moistened when I first put the corn in, yet all the said grains would hasten up to spindle with a maiden spear, without tillowing; which shews that when ground of the field wants either strength, thro' poverty, or convenient air and moisture, it will do the like, and when corn in the field does so, it is a certain sign of some deficiency; for the tillowing of plants proceeds from a redundancy of humours, or a good quick air that agitates them, whereby the maiden stock being sufficient to receive the vegetable juices, there must be an irruption into collateral branches. — I cannot but in a great measure impute the abovesaid defects in the seeds I sowed in the pots in my study to the want of, and the stagnation of the air; because the earth, when I examined it, did not seem so very arid and exhausted of juices, but that the plants might have better flourished, considering the goodness of the mold.——But I believe the collateral branches to be as perfect as the maiden plant in the seed; and this vegetation to be no new formation, but an extension of parts only.

As the experiments I have made therefore of sowing corn in pots of earth were within doors, where it seems to me, for want of motion of air and a quick succession of it, the juices stagnate in the plants, and are not pushed on to tillow, but run to spindle, and as by the experiments of malting barley, which in windy weather, when the air is plentifully forced into the bodies of plants, runs out to root and to spire in a hasty manner, [g] I doubt not but, when I can make

*Conclusion.*

[g] Of the great quantity of air contained in vegetables, and it's various uses, see the articles Air and Seed in Mr. Miller's dictionary.

make the experiments of fowing corn (as before within doors) in pots of earth placed out in the air in the month of April, when the earth fhall be the fame, the water which waters both forts of pots be rain, the inlet of the foutherly fun through the glafs window the fame pofition, and the warmth within doors rather greater, I fhall then better difcover the beneficial powers of air to plants, by comparing the difference ; from whence juft reflections may alfo arife of how great confequence falubrious and plentiful hauftus's of it muft be to our human bodies.

§. 110. It is a difficult tafk to unfold and afcertain the complicated principles of vegetation (as they are more or lefs in all forts of earth, and as they not only quicken or impregnate the feed, but carry it on through all it's gradations, of woody, leafy, flowery, and fruit fubftances) fo as to know how to proportion them, or fay in what manner and proportion they act and perform their feveral offices.

*Of vegetation in general.*

For though experiments have been made of nitre, blood, foot, &c. all which have been found great forcers, fo as to bring forward the leaves and branches of a plant, yet it may be the flowers or fruit, either in bulk or number, may not equally fucceed by fuch mangonifm ; few I believe having had the patience to make an exact experiment

ary.—Lettice-feed, that was fown in the glafs-receiver of the air-pump, which was exhaufted and cleared from all air, grew not at all in eight days time ; whereas fome of the fame feed, that was fown at the fame time in the open air, was rifen to the height of an inch and an half in that time ; but, the air being let into the empty receiver, the feed grew up to the height of two or three inches in the fpace of one week.—When feeds are packed up for exportation, great care fhould be taken, that they are not fhut up too clofely from the air, which is abfolutely neceffary to maintain the principle of vegetation.

Seeds fent from abroad in fealed up bottles would not grow when fown.

Seeds being hung up a year in bags, and others from the fame parcel being kept a year in bottles fealed hermetically, the former when fown grew well, but none of the latter came up.

throughout

throughout the aforesaid course of vegetation, or if they have, they may not have rightly considered what other mixtures there are in the earth wherewith these menstruums may co-operate.

To make a just experiment of this kind, I conceive the naturalist ought to take earth very much emaciated by hard ploughing (if it were reduced to a caput mortuum it would be much the better) and to lay some loads of it in different heaps apart, and to impregnate each heap with a different and most simple manure, and by equal measure, and then to plant it with the same seeds; it would be also proper that one heap of this earth should be left in it's natural strength, and seed sowed in it, to see the difference.

I should also propose that many parcels of the same earth were taken out of a corner where the plough cannot come to stir it up and impoverish it, and that the same experiments were repeated, and a trial made as before what a parcel of this earth could do by it's own virtue;

Also, that in the like parcels of earth different mixtures were made and blended together of the said menstruums, in order to see the success of such compositions;

And when all this is done, if I may be allowed to anticipate the event, I may venture to pronounce the project will be in a great measure fruitless; for though by this means may be in a great measure discovered what are spurs to nature, and what will produce the desired increase, yet to transfer such discoveries into the course of husbandry will be impracticable, by reason of the expence, nor will it explain and discover the principles of vegetation, as to the cause, so as to make a person the wiser, though we know whereby to give the production; because I conceive these menstruums taking in with them the latent and concurrent powers and virtues of the air, earth,

earth, water, sun, and temperament of soil with which they are blended and digested, make a certain union and texture so incorporated and interwoven, that they are not easily separable (unless by fire) from whence results a third principle, or quinta essentia, which performs these mighty wonders of nature; so that from these happy mixtures does arise a specifick which God wills shall do, and therefore does these great things.

Wherefore by experience we say of principles in vegetation with physicians in medicaments, that, as such and such simples are of themselves profitable towards curing particular distempers, so when taken in composition (as Sydenham professes) their efficacy is much greater.

This vegetable balsam, tho' so difficult to say wherein it consists, yet it may be averred, is as easily to be seen as understood; for tho' almost as subtil as a phantom, yet it's marks are easily discovered to the diligent husbandman conversant about arable land: we can easily perceive by the different colour of our land (as it turns up under the plough) whether it has born one, two, three, or four crops, and how in proportion the virtue is gone out of it; and as sensible we are by it's rest, and lying to pasture, how with it's vigour it renews also it's colour; we do not better see and know when the plumb or grape is covered with or has lost it's bloomy blue, than we know by the colour the fertility of our soil, which colour arises from the principles before intimated, of dung, air, fire, earth, &c. mingled together, which by often sowing are absorbed into the corn in too liberal a manner to be renewed by a daily recruit from those elements.

*Cause of good land's soon recovering it's strength, and bad land not doing it.*

§. 111. There is one thing not easily reconcileable, and which may well afford matter of speculation to the curious, which is, that very good earth, tho' exhausted never so much with ploughing (so

that

that it will not bear a crop of corn) yet will in
a few years recover by reſt; whereas land poor
by nature, and yet capable of bearing as good a
crop as the land good by nature, when it's ſtrength
was at loweſt by being over-wrought by the plough,
ſhall make but a very ordinary improvement in proportion to the other land, and never exceed a certain fecundity, which is it's ne plus ultra; and yet
both theſe ſoils equally exhauſted one would think
ſtarted fairly together, and ſtood on equal terms and
advantage of imbibing the aforeſaid elements, and
theſe are all the materials and talents they have to
improve from.——I am at a loſs what ſolution or
tolerable account can be given of this phænomenon,
unleſs I ſay, the earth, which was good by nature,
conſiſting of a juſt and happy texture of parts, fitted
by a due continuity and unity to receive the aforeſaid elements, and yet not ſo cloſe as to retain and
impriſon the watery and firey parts till they putrify
and corrupt, but till by a kind fermentation the ſpi-
rituous parts are converted into fixed ſalts, do then
let through, and ſuffer the fæces to be waſhed away,
or to be purified by the continual free acceſs of the
elements; whereas, on the contrary, the abovementioned poor land, either by too ſtrict a bond of union
(as clays, before they are friable by art) are too compact and conſolidated to admit the benign influences
of the elements, or elſe they retain and impriſon the
immiſſions, till, for want of ventilation and circulation, the ſtagnating juices grow ſour and acid, and,
by reaſon of the coldneſs of the earth they are ſhut
up in, are not capable of a ſufficient fermentation to
be converted into fixed vegetable ſalts.

The other ſort of poor land, which being once
impoveriſhed is a long time before it recovers, runs
into a contrary extream, viz. that of too looſe and
light a mold, which may be compared to a perſon
under a dyſentery, who has no retentive faculty;
through

through this the nourishment passes with that precipitation as not to abide long enough to receive a fermentation; but the spirits, and all the fat substance received is washed away and carried downwards undigested, and so such ground can receive but slow recruits from the elements.

Or shall we say, the recruit good land receives, after it is impoverished, seems in a good measure to arise from the effluvia of the layers or beds of earth, many feet deep, which are exhaled into the upper surface, and by the heat of the sun converted into fixed salts; for generally the better and richer the upper coat of the soil is, the lower veins of earth are in some proportion answerable and correspondent thereto.

# ROLLING.

No roller amongst the antients.

§. 1. I Cannot find, as I observed before, by any of the Roman writers, that they used a roller in their husbandry, but only a crates, that is, a hurdle or flat timber, to draw over their corn, to level the ground. See Columella, lib. 2. cap. 18.

The Spanish instrument like the crates.

§. 2. In Spain, after their summer-corn is sown, a horse draws a broad board of about ten foot long, a boy standing on the board, and driving over the corn, which serves instead of a roller.

Whereas above, the long plank is described to be drawn as a roller, Lord Pembroke rectified my notion, and told me, that the plank is drawn at length after the horse, as he has seen it; for, said he, otherwise a horse could not draw it, and this way there is an equal weight on the earth for the space the board covers, as there is on the breadth of earth covered by a roller, whereas, had the plank covered the earth, and been drawn the same way as a roller, it would be too light to signify any thing.

§. 3. Treading

§. 3. Treading wheat, after it is sowed, by fold- ing sheep on it, is allowed to make it closer than rolling it, in regard rolling only lays the ridge of the furrow flat, but the sheep's feet find every little hollow place, and tread it close.

I asked Mr. Edwards whether the farmers in Leicestershire rolled both barley and oats ; he said, yes, they always did, and wheat too, except they folded it, but he never knew them roll peas.—I asked him why they rolled not the wheat they folded ; he said, because that needed it not, for the fold trod it harder than a roller could press it, for which reason they endeavour, as much as they can, to fold on the light land. He said a roller could not be too heavy, tho' it was as much as five horses could draw; that the land by good rolling, if there wanted rain, bore the hot weather much the better ; the roller also broke the clods, and made way for the corn to to come up through them.

§. 4. If corn be come up, and then rolled with a very heavy roller, the five or six horses that draw it, going all in a line, and treading in each other's steps, often bruise and hurt the corn very much, for which reason it is adviseable to draw such a roller with horses on breast, side by side.

§. 5. They are forced to make use of very heavy rol- lers in our hill-country to roll over the flints among the barley and oats, otherwise there would be no mowing them ; they often use them likewise in March to press the ground somewhat closer to the corn.

§. 6. Major Liver says, he rather approves of two rollers, that may be drawn by three horses apiece, than one heavy one that requires six ; for, said he, the light ones make double the dispatch ; besides, if the great roller be used in clover-grass it will be apt to bruise the bulbous root too much, and if used on corn-ground, tho' never so dry, (whereon it will do most good) the horses will break it up so much with their heels in straining, that it will not be healed again by the roller's coming over it.

As it is of great consequence in the hill-country, at seed-time, in dry seasons, to break in the earth after the sown corn, the same day it is sown, with a couple of harrows, so I think it is of as great consequence that a roller, or a couple of a small size, such as one horse, or two at most may draw, be kept in readiness, to settle the mellow and hollow earth close to the roots of the corn, without compressing it too close ; for tho' corn loves to lie easy, it loves also that the earth should lie close about it, that it may go immediately on it's work of shooting forth it's roots to the best advantage. If the ground works any ways dry, or in powder, this will be found to be the best way in the hill-country, to prevent the sun's penetrating too deep by reason of the dry and light mold,—and then, after the corn is well come up, the great roller may go over it as usual.

Of rollers with nails in them.

§. 7. My bailiff said, he had seen rollers, on which nails had been drove as thick as it could hold to save it from cracking, and from wearing with the stones ;—but I think such a roller could not do well to roll stony land, when the corn is come up, because the nails would be apt to cut off the corn.

Rolling saves seed, a less quantity will do.

§. 8. In conversation with several farmers on the subject of rolling, and in speaking in commendation of rolling after the corn was sowed, they said, that half a bushel of oats might be saved in sowing an acre by securing the earth, and laying it close to the corn ; if a rascally team, said they, were bought for that purpose, and sold off again, it would pay the purchase of the horses.

*Spungy, ferny, loose.
A heavy roller for woo l-feer ground

§. 9. I believe that a * wood-seer ground should have the great roller, if it be never so big, go twice or three times or oftener over it, after it is sowed to summer-corn, and after rains, to consolidate, if possible, an iron-mold-ground, consisting of coarse harsh disjointed

disjointed particles ; for both cold and heat penetrate it, and, by changes, make the corn die to the root, but at length, getting more strength by this compression, the root may be enabled to live, and maintain it's blade.

§. 10. In harrowing after sowing, it should chiefly be considered how smooth and fine your ground lies, in order to settle, and, if any of your ground lies rough and knobby hard, it seems that the smooth loose land should be first rolled, and the rough knobby land be deferred in hopes of a shower of rain to mellow and loosen it, not only because the knobbs will then break, but also because their being so hard may bruise and cut off the tender blades of corn. *What sort of ground to be first rolled after sowing.*

§. 11. Rolling as soon as possible after sowing summer-corn will in a great measure prevent edge-growing, in case of a dry season ; for the lower corn laying moistest, would, unless rolled, come up long before the other ; but that which lies shallower, the crust of the earth being scorched, could not get away without a good shower, and perhaps be malted first, whereas rolling soon, if it be dry, brings it all up together. *Rolling soon after sowing prevents edge-growing.*

§. 12. When the ground is wet, or after a little rain fallen, it is not proper to roll, because the earth will cling and gather to the roller ; and also when land is wet, rolling after sowing may be ill husbandry, because it keeps the moisture so much in the ground, especially if early in the spring, that thereby the corn will be chilled. *Not to roll wet ground after sowing.*

§. 13. If corn be well come up, and wet fall, it is generally proper to roll the last sowed first, because such corn has less dew, and the earth dries fastest. *What corn to roll first when come up.*

§. 24. They seldom roll their wheat about Holt in Wiltshire, and observing the surface of the wheat-ground to lie very hollow and dry, and one's feet to sink deep into it, it being in March, I wondered at it, and spoke to Mr. Randolph about it.——He said, in their country they seldom found their wheat suffer for *Why they roll not their wheat about Holt in Wilts.*

want

want of rolling, becaufe they ploughed round furrows, and laid their corn in deep :——on which he
and I went into Mr. Byffy's wheat, and I found, tho'
it was hollow, yet the corn lay about four inches
deep, and from thence took root downwards ; however we both thought rolling would not do amifs.

Of rolling
wheat foon
after fown.

§. 15. Mr. Carter of Colehenley and Mr. Long-
man affure me, that they have rolled their wheat foon
after fown when they can get a feafon for it, and it
has always been much the better for it ; and farther,
that wheat fo rolled has this advantage, that there is
generally more leifure for rolling foon after fowing
wheat than after fpring-corn and it clofes the ground
to the roots, and prevents the winter-cold from penetrating, nor can the worms fo eafily turn up the
earth from the roots of the corn ; and by experience
it has been found, that fuch grounds bear the high
winds the better for being fmooth ; for the wheat itfelf breaks the wind, and each blade fhelters the
other, and more efpecially fo the lighter the ground
was before rolling, juft as a drab-coat is warmer to
us than a fpungier cloth of the fame thicknefs ; and,
when the March-winds blow, the earth of fuch rolled
ground is not fo eafily carried away from the roots
of the corn as that of rougher ground is. Mr Carter
fays, about Bafingftoke they always roll in the fame
manner.

At a meeting of feveral good farmers I difcourfed
with them on the fubject of rolling wheat foon after
it is fowed, and faid, I could not fee any inconveniency in it, but that it muft be good hufbandry ; for
I could not apprehend how by laying the land flat
the wheat fhould lie the colder, or, if it did, what
fignified the blade being taken off by the winter cold
fo long as the root was well fortified by the earth's
lying clofe to it ; yet I fhould not always approve
of rolling till I faw the approach of winter, left by
rolling too foon after fowing, efpecially if the beginning

ning of winter proved mild, it might bring the wheat away too faft, and make it rank. To this they all affented.

§. 16. The autumn anno 1715 was fo very wet, the country people could not fow their full crop of wheat, and, whereas I intended to have fown one hundred and fixty acres, I could fow but one hundred and twenty,——and one third part of that I could not get into the ground till between the 10th and 20th of October. The winter proved extream cold and fnowy, and the fnow lay deep and long on the ground: the wheat of the country in general, as well as mine, was pinched by the cold, and ftopt in the ground during the whole winter, efpecially the latter fown, and in the fpring, when the fnow went off, from the end of January to April we had no rain, but drying churlifh cold winds with frofts; fo that towards the end of March the wheat was very poor and weak, infomuch that a traveller, could hardly take it to be wheat.——Being fenfible the ground muft lie hollow from the roots of the wheat through fuch extream frofts, and alfo want moifture by reafon of fuch dry winds and want of rain, I rolled my wheat at a time I could ill fpare my horfes from fowing fpring-corn, but it was wonderful how much it began immediately to thrive after fuch compreffure of the earth to the roots of the corn, and how much it contributed to the colour, which was vifible in a day or two after rolling, and it continued to improve proportionably, though the cold winds and drought ftill continued.

If wheat turns yellow, or looks unhealthy in winter-time by wet, it is to no purpofe to fay, the ground will lie too fmooth and cold, if fmoothed by rolling, the prefent diftemper is to be confulted, and the ground, as foon as dry enough, ought to be rolled.

§. 17. As wheat fhould not be rolled too early in the fpring, left the frofts fhould hollow it again, fo it ought

*Of rolling in the fpring and after a hard winter, wheat that was fowed late and wet.*

*Beft feafon of rolling wheat in the fpring.*

ought to be done foon enough to give it the advantage of tillowing ; for doubtlefs the finking the roots of the wheat deeper into the earth by rolling, and the clofing the earth to the mores and knees of the winter or autumn-tillows makes them tillow afrefh, and if rolled by about the eighth or middle of March, that will, as I fuppofe, be the beft feafon for rolling in the fpring ; neverthelefs wheat may be in that unthriving condition, that it may be neceffary to roll it fooner.

**Of rolling barley.**

§. 18. The firft week in May (anno 1703) I fowed rath-ripe barley, and on the firft of June I faw the barley falling off, and declining ; the ground was very hollow, and as I thought needed rolling again ; fo I ordered it to be rolled where it was lighteft, as on the head-lands, &c. —— The barley had a good ftem, and in going up the hill, the horfes being forced to ftrain on their hoof's points in many places actually cut off the barley at the ftem, infomuch that I could in fome places take up handfulls ; but examining it, and opening the valves, I found nothing but leaves rolled together, and that the ear of the barley was feated lower, and not yet fhot above ground ; however I ftaked down a ftick or two in the places that fuffered moft, to fee how the ears there proved.—In the evening of the next day walking in the ground I obferved the barley to look much refrefhed, and to be greatly improved in colour, which feemed ftrange in fo fhort a time ; but what wonder if a plant revives in twenty-four hours, when, being gathered, it languifhes in one. The confiderable benefit it received was by compreffing the ground, which by it's fpunginefs had taken a great deal of wet, but the roller, by compreffing it, fqueezed it from the roots of the corn. — The corn I had marked with fticks came up well alfo, and carried as good ears as the other.

§ 19. Oats

§. 19. Oats early sowed, if not rolled till towards the end of or after seed-time, ought, for the most part, to be rolled with the heaviest roller, for a light one will make but a small impression where the ground has been so long settled.

§. 20. I observed the great grey partridge-peas sowed in February had very little charlock among them, tho' not rolled: it seems to me the ground ploughing heavier then, than it did in March, and the coldness of the season obstructed the germination of the charlock-seed, and by that time the spring came the ground was pretty well settled, and become too close and hard for much of the charlock-seed to push through;— but the blue peas sowed in March had abundance of charlock amongst them, especially where the ground had been dry and worked fine, to the prejudice of the peas, these peas not having been rolled neither; wherefore I conceive, that rolling of peas as soon as the ground is sown, or soon after, would bind and press it so close, as to prevent the charlock-seed from coming up, and I do therefore hold rolling to be good to prevent the growth of this, and many other sorts of weeds.—— And barley and oats, which with us are rolled, do doubtless thereby much more escape being infested with weeds:—— but, as the coldness of the ground in February, and the moisture, is a check to the growth of charlock, (for all moisture at that season is cold) so moisture and wet after the middle of March, and in April, is productive of charlock and other weeds, because such moisture, is then tolerable warm by the power of the sun acting on it.

§. 21. To roll winter-vetches when first sowed seems to me to be as proper as to roll wheat when first sowed: as before noted.

§. 22. In light land, where clover is sowed, if in the winter-time the great roller was drawn over it, it would fasten the ground, and make the clover hold much better and longer.

Of

## Of CORN in GENERAL.

§. 1. ᵃ COlumella tells us, that, except we take care to change the feed, corn will degenerate much fooner in a wet foil than a dry one, and, after a third crop, wheat will become what he calls a filigo, a fort of corn fair in colour, but poor in fubftance. Palladius fpeaks to the fame purpofe.

§. 2. Evelyn, as before hinted, reports that diverfe ears may grow on one ftalk, which is what I have never obferved, except in Pharaoh's dream, (Gen. xli. 5.) where we read of feven ears of corn that came upon one ftalk.

Heylin, lib. 2. fo. 133.—fays, in Rezan, a great and goodly province in Ruffia, fituated between the river Tanais and the river Occa, the moft fruitful country of all Ruffia, and (if report be true) of the whole world, it is credibly affirmed, that one * grain of corn brings forth fix ears, the ftalks whereof ftand fo thick that a horfe may pafs through, or a quail fly out of them, but with very much difficulty. This author alfo gives inftances of the vaft fruitfulnefs of Padolia in Poland, fo. 144.

Mr. Bobart of the Phyfic-garden at Oxford told me, he had in his herbal a barley-culm with three fair ears thereon, but the two outermoft were fhorter than the other ; he infcribed or under-wrote this plant Thus ; —— Hordeum fpica multiplici,

Found plentifully growing near
Sutton by Cranborn in Dorfetfhire,
By Mr. Crop of Chrift's-church-college, an. 1697.

---

ᵃ Celerius locis humidis quam ficcis frumenta degenerant, nifi cura adhibe atur renovare femen. Columella, lib. 8. f. 102.— Nam omne triticum folo uliginofo poft tertiam fationem convertitur in filiginem. Columella, lib. 8. fo 102.—Locis humidis femina citius quam ficcis degenerant. Palladius, lib. 1. fect. 6.— Et infra dicit, omne triticum in folo uliginofo, poft tertiam fationem in genus filiginis commutatur.

Concerning

Concerning the above field of corn Mr. Bobart said, the story was, that a charitable woman in time of great scarcity had relieved the poor, and God gave this return.——The same day I saw doctor Frampton of the abovesaid county, who told me, he had never seen the field, nor any such ears of corn; but had heard of the thing, and the story.—— However I give not much credit either to the fact, or the cause. ——Mr. Bobart also assured me, he had once seen a wheat-stalk with two ears on it. Some time after this I sent him a spike or an ear of smooth-crested-grass, which divided itself in this manner ϒ, so that there were two compleat ears nearly on one stalk. Refer this to Mr. Evelyn's prodigy of wheat.

§. 3. Mr. Ray, in his Prolegomenon to his first volume of plants, quotes the opinions of several authors, that barley ears have here and there carried grains of oats, and other grains of different corn from it's species; but they, who made such observations, it seems, were bookish men, who were misled by the appearance to their eyes, and unacquainted with what is commonly observed in husbandry; it being true, that, in wet years, when barley runs thin, it is common for a grain, here and there in a barley ear, to have a deep crese along it, and to be as thin as an oat, and to resemble an oat very much, but in truth, if unrinded, has no oat-hull, but a barley rind on it; and doubtless, in case such oat they pretend to grow on the barley ear was sowed, it would produce a true barley ear. *Of barley bringing grain of a different species.*

§. 4. In the hot countries, where little rain falls, the dews fall in vast quantities, on which the herb of the field has great dependence for being watered; this was reckoned in those parts amongst the greatest blessings in the gift of the Almighty, and so Isaac blesses Jacob (Gen. xxvii. 28 and 29) God give thee of the dew of heaven, and *Benefit of great dews in hot countries.*

Mr.

Mr. Garret who lived many years at Madrid affures me, their crops of corn in Spain are much thicker fet than ours, and yet their ground is very light, at which I wondered, their country being hot. —He replied, they fowed very early, before the fun grew hot, and that the dews were very great.

§. 5. This year (1707) the fpring proving very dry till June 13th convinced me, that not only peas, but all forts of corn alfo late fowed for feed will not feed well; for in our hill-country the oats and barley, &c. tho' fowed early, yet not growing till the abovefaid rain fell, had all fhort ears; the fort of land could not bring on the corn faft enough, tho' the fummer all-along afterwards had plenty of rain.—In very rich lands, it is likely this year the fame defect was not obferved.

Late fowed corn will not feed well after dry fprings in the hill country.

§. 6. It feems to me, and was apparent this cold wet fpring (1708) that, if the month of April be wet and cold, the wheat will not tillow, or multiply it's iffues, but the winter-fpindle or fhoot will run up; for that winter-ftalk being hardened will keep growing, whereas, to form collateral buds, which are tender, warmer weather is required, not too quick growing weather by means of hot gloomy rains, but mild and mellow weather; for, when the flufh of fap is impetuous by gloomy heat, it rifes fo faft upwards into the firft maiden-ftalk, that in it's hurry it ftops not enough to fling out fide-branches; as in the fmall pox, if in the firft fymptoms the patient's blood be high inflamed and feverifh, it hurries the morbific matter fo furioufly along the veins, that (unlefs by bleeding it be qualified) it is fo carried on in a torrent as not to have leifure to kick out the puftules and the diftemper; fo then a hot wet feafon or a cold wet one are both unkindly for great crops of corn.

Wheat will not tillow well in wet cold fprings.

§. 7. The great fertility of Ægypt fhews no country can be too hot where the land is very fertile;

No country too hot where the land is fertile.

tile ; for our clays and mixed earths, that want the impregnating heat of the sun, are often burnt up ; but their lands are so rich, that if there is but the least moisture at the bottom of the full, when they sow, their corn will be brought up in twenty-four hours time by vertue of that moisture, before it can be dried up, at which instant it strikes it's roots into the moister earth, as before mentioned in corn sown in sand ;—whereas in our country, where corn requires a week or ten days time to strike root in, the moisture may be dried up before the grain can be impregnated, and so, if rain comes not, it often lies two, three, or four months without striking root, as it did this dry summer anno 1705 —— and began but to grow just before harvest. If corn once grows, we see it is not easily check'd by drought in good land : in the hot countries they have great dews.

§. 8. By the effects of this very dry spring and hot summer (anno 1714) from March to July the 23d, when we had a day's rain that went to the roots of the corn, I am sensible that winter-corn, as wheat and vetches, do bear up much better against the mischiefs by drought than the spring-corn, as peas, barley, and oats, the former being well established at the roots, during the winter, and the ground better settled to them.

*Winter-corn bears drought better than spring-corn.*

§. 9. Being in the north (anno 1706) I had a mind more thoroughly to be informed what was most prejudicial to their lenten crop ; so I asked an excellent husbandman in Leicestershire when rain fell most unseasonably on their summer-corn ; he said, in May ; if it proved a wet May they had always a bad crop of barley ; for rain then, either killed it, or starved it, and made it look yellow. —— I asked him what reason he could give for it ; he said, about the beginning of May was commonly the time that their barley took it's weaning, that is, said he, when the leaves of the barley begin to die, having till that time

*May, a critical time for the lenten crop in the north of England.*

time been for the most part nourished by the milk and flour of the corn : but then it begins to put forth new roots, and new leaves, and to betake itself wholly to it's roots for nourishment : though the weather should prove never so good, at this crisis it receives a stop and check, like a child taken from nurse, with whom it goes much harder if the nights are cold and long ; so, if wet and rainy weather comes then, the barley will be so dashed, that it will never recover it, let what warm weather soever come after ; for, said he, after such rains, the sun having baked the top of the ground does thereby so bind it, that the heat cannot penetrate to the roots of the corn, which by that means lie all the summer in a cold bed ;——but a cold and dry May, said he, I never knew to hurt us, but rather do us good : —— according as the spring proves forwarder or backwarder, so does this crisis of the corn's taking it's weaning come earlier or later, but generally about the beginning of May, unless the spring be very warm ; but a wet May used not to hurt their wheat excepting that it made it weedy ; for, said he, if we have a good season to sow our wheat in, that seldom misses.——— Mr. Clerk said afterwards, their having a season to lay their barley into the ground dry, and having a dry bottom the depth of the full, for it to take root in, was of great consequence towards a good crop.

**Corn does not spindle well in hot countries.** §. 10. Lord Bacon in his Natural history says, that in the hot countries it is a frequent calamity, that the corn will not spindle, that is, will not come out of the hose, by reason of the great heat and drought ; and he is of opinion, that on this account the latin word *calamitas* was derived from *calamus*.--- But I rather believe it also signifies any other misfortune belonging to corn. Pliny and Columella, speaking of blights and smuts, say, Hordeum omnium

nium granorum minime calamitofum;—but not
fpindling is a defect we feldom find in England.

§. 11. From conftant experience of fucceſſive
years I find, that wet years make the ftraw of all
corn weak, fmall, and thin, infomuch that it is apt to
lodge and crumble down, which in the country we
call being knee-bent; on the other hand in dry hot
fummers all ftraw is thick and ftrong.——The ftraw
in wet years runs the coarfer, and that in dry hot
years the finer, and then it has the more fpirit in it;
which is the reafon why in hotter countries than
England the cattle eat ftraw fo much better than
with us, and almoft as well as hay.——As cold wet
feafons make the ftraw run coarfe, fo cold wet land
has the fame effect; therefore, when both thefe
caufes concur and contribute their force, the ftraw
will run very weak, thin, and coarfe; as particularly
this year (1717) the rath-ripe barley did at Crux-
Eafton, where the land is cold and wet, as was the
year—, and rain more than ufual falling on the barley, about a month before harveft, lent a helping
hand to the beating it down; fo that the barley-
ftraw in a manner broke off a little below the ear,
and before the grain was full plimmed or hardened,
from which time all communication of nourifhment
ftopt, and the corn rather fhrank in than ripened,
and confequently the barley as well as the ftraw in
our cold lands ran very thin and coarfe.——However I efteem it beft on our cold lands to fow one
half of the crop rath-ripe barley, becaufe, though in
fuch a cold year it might fuffer as abovefaid in cold
wet lands, yet had it not been for the rain that fell,
and the winds that beat and broke it down at that
nick of time, before it was hardened, it would have
carried a better body than the late-ripe barley, in the
fame cafe, and on the fame fort of land, would have
done. ——The ufe to be made of all this is, that tho'
there is no preventing this evil, yet knowing beforehand

*Cold and wet years occaſion coarfe weak ſtraw*

hand that in such a year your fodder-straw will be coarse, you must therefore apply it to proper uses, else it will deceive you.

§. 12. The colour of corn, viz. of wheat and barley, gives a great preference with the husbandman in a market, which does not a little puzzle the inquisitive gentleman, a stranger to husbandry, who hears it ; but the reason for it is this ; there is an uniformity between the colour of corn and it's weight, and the latter never fails to be accompanied with the former quality ; —— which therefore denotes its goodness. Wheat weighs light, because it has not come to it's full maturity, and so has not sufficiently discharged the watery parts, which proceed chiefly from the coldness of the ground, that wanted spirit to carry the grain to a full perfection of ripeness ; and the defect of colour may be occasioned by too much rain, which sogged the grain in harvest, whilst standing, or in gripp ; for being often wet and dried again, every time it was dried, after being wet and full ripe, the moisture exhaled by the sun's drying it carried also away a tincture of, or the particles of it's colour along with the exhalation of the watery parts, and so consequently the grain must be more porous, less solid, and of course lighter : the same argument will hold for barley.

*The colour of corn denotes it's quality, and why.*

All corn is apt to grow brighter as it grows towards earing, but that, which then most holds the deep green colour, is likeliest afterwards to have the largest and boldest ears, and to bring the grain best to perfection.

*Damage to green corn by dry weather near earing time.*

§. 13. It was a very dry burning time (anno 1702) from the first sowing of lenten corn to the 3d of June, at which time some of my neighbouring farmers were praying for rain : why, said I, you must be in a better condition than I am ; I have not seen your corn, but I know your's was sown ten days before

fore mine, and consequently must better cover the ground, and keep it cool. That might be, said they, but in another respect, because our's was sowed earliest; it may be the worse; in about a fortnight our's will be at the time for getting out of the hood, which it will not be able to do except rain come.

§. 14. I observe the white straw-wheat brings white blossoms, as the red straw-wheat does red ones, and I suppose it is the same with the white oat. *Of the blossom.*

§. 15. The latin writers De re agraria observe, that rainy weather prejudices all sorts of corn at the blooming-time, except the leguminous sort; the reason of which, as I suppose, is, because the wet falls into the husk of wheat, barley, and oats, which at that time opens, and so is corrupted by the wet standing on it, whereas in the leguminous grain the pod lies within the leafy flower, into which the wet cannot enter. *Prejudice from rain at blooming time, and why.*

§. 16. The whiter wheat, barley, and white oats, or the hoods of black oats look as they ripen, and when they are ripe, the better the corn; and the contrary, the coarser, or more blighted. *Sign of good corn when growing.*

§. 17. The disadvantage that late ripe corn lies under in point of coarseness may be collected from the late ripe nuts hanging on the trees, in the beginning of September, or at least at Michaelmass, especially, if rain should fall about that time, for notwithstanding the kirnel of the nut is secured by a shell, yet, at that season of the year, the cold damp air, the dews, and rain penetrate the shells of nuts, whereby the kirnels change their colour, become waterish, and in a manner tasteless; and doubtless the same evil falls on the late ripe corn. *The disadvantage that late ripe corn lies under.*

§. 18. When September is come, say our hill-country farmers, there are frosty nights, and then the corn ripens as fast by night as by day; they always found it so at Easton. *Of frost's ripening corn.*

But,

But, notwithstanding this observation, with which our farmers comfort themselves, that in the frosty nights, at the beginning of September, the corn ripens as fast by night as by day, yet willingly I would not have corn to be so ripened, for in truth such ripening may be more properly called blighting; inasmuch as ripening implies filling the grain, and somewhat leading to it's perfection; but these frosty nights rather shrink, and dry up the grain, and stop it's filling and plimming: in like manner all sorts of fruit may be said to be ripened by the frosts, inasmuch as they precipitate to a rottenness, &c. And my opinion is, that such blighted or frost-bitten barley, not arrived to it's natural ripeness, can never have a goodness in it's flour like other corn that is ripened thoroughly, nor be so profitable for malting; it may possibly be as big as kindly ripened corn.

§. 19. If harvest proves late, as in the latter end of August, wheat and barley, that is then to fill, must run thin, and the same is true of all sorts of grain, and in a wet summer the vale-corn, which usually runs to halm, will keep the ground cold, and prevent the filling of the grains.

*Wheat and barley thin in a late harvest.*

§. 20. A late harvest is seldom, as I believe, a hurrying harvest; because, though in such case there is reason to make all haste possible, yet the coolness of the days, and the long dewy nights, will not let the corn ripen altogether, nor make it shed or britt, as the early harvests cause it to do, all which I have experienced this year 1703.

*A late harvest no hurrying harvest.*

§. 21. Barley, in carrying to market say our farmers, need not be covered, rain it never so hard, but wheat is thought the worse for rain.

*Of covering corn in carrying to market.*

§. 22. Mr. Ray conjectures, that the reason why the grain is generally thin, when corn grows very rank and thick in straw, is, not only because it's strength is exhausted in the grossness of the blade,

*Why rank corn brings a thin grain.*

but

but, says he, that grossness of the blade may hinder it from the cherishing rays of the sun, which are necessary to concoct the nutritious juices, and to convey them into the seed, and he gives an instance of our sowing English corn in America. Hist. of Plants, vol. 2. fo. 1238.

§. 23. Since (as by former remarks does appear) the wheat-ear is worse for it's straw being broken, and for the sun's not coming to it's root, it follows that, where vetches run so rank as to finnow in their halm, the straw and the juices conveyed through it must be so prejudiced as to carry a thin grain. *Thin-grained vetches from finnowy halm.*

§. 24. Anno 1707 the winter proved exceeding wet, and the spring and summer were the same, insomuch that the harvest was very backward, and it was the middle of August before we began to cut wheat : the consequence of these wet seasons, as I conceive, was, that the wheat in cold clay-lands blighted, of which I made a general observation : the reason I take to be, because, these three seasons proving wet, the harvest was backward and late ; and the rain being frequent till harvest, the vegetable juices, especially in clay-lands, were heavy and chilled, and could not rise to nourish the grain and the straw ; for which reason, both being starved, the straw turned white and speckled, and the grain shrank, and, as I observed, in such lands the straw of red-straw wheat did not that year look red, but from it's green colour turned to white ; but in white or warm land the wheat escaped blighting, because there the vegetable particles were attenuated enough to ascend. *Why wet seasons bring blighted corn.*

Tho' the wheat was so much blighted in the year 1707, yet barley and oats this year did not blight, but were full-grained, whether, because they had not been pinched by the winter, not being then sown, or from their lying on a mellower mold and hollower from being later ploughed, whereby the sun might inject his comfortable rays the better, I know not.—We find no summer too hot for wheat, tho' it may for barley, and oats.

§. 25. Of the cause of uftilago or the burnt-ear in corn Mr. Ray gives his conjecture, fol. 1241 and 1242 ;—But my opinion is that it proceeds from a defect in the root, but then that defect muft be attributed to ill feed, with a diftinction that makes no difference in the effect : the feed might be damaged before it was fown, or the nature of the ground might occafion the defect ; for what difference is there between corn originally bad and that damaged by keeping, or taking damage in the field, before it could come up, by being almoft malted, or otherwife injured in the ground by it's ill temper or unfeafonable feed-time ? What happened very obfervable to clear this matter was, in the fpring-feed-time 1704 I fowed very good feed-barley in all my grounds ; therefore no fault in my feed ; fo did many other farmers ; I could find little uftilago in my oats ; they being fowed early their feed came up, and lay not in the ground to take the damage abovementioned, and the oats which were fowed early, on which rain came, had not the uftilago, nor the barley fowed early, except fome little matter occafioned by their being fowed in white lands, but the middle fowing, when the ground had not moifture enough to bring up the corn, nor had had any rain fall on it for a long time, was injured in it's feed, and turned mightily to the uftilago all over the country, but the latter fowing, after which rain came, had little of it : hence may appear the great benefit of rolling. The uftilago is common to the ears of grafs as well as of corn, in which I have frequently obferved it, efpecially in the gramen caninum nodofum avenaceà paniculâ, or knotty-rooted dog's-grafs.

In

In June however (1705) I gathered diverſe ears of black-burnt wheat, all burnt to a black powder; I alſo gathered ſeveral of the ſtrong and good ears; I found the ſtraw of the burnt ears drew with as much difficulty out of the ground as the beſt, and had, to my eye, as good mores; I cut every joint of the reeds in many places, both of the ſound and burnt-eared ſtraw, and found them to my eye, equally ſound, and as much verdure and firmneſs in the ſtems that bore the burnt grains as in the others, and many of the ears I found ſo burnt before they came out of the hoods; ſo that I am again at a loſs to conjecture what the cauſe ſhould be. By the bigneſs of burnt grains it ſhould ſeem, that this misfortune fell on the ear, when it was of pretty tolerable length, and yet before it was half grown in the huſk; for it is moſt certain that theſe grains could not grow after they were burnt. See farther of the cauſes of ſmut and blight under the article Wheat, §. 10. See alſo Barley, §. 24.

# W H E A T.

§. 1. A Wheaten crop is the moſt unprofitable of any to a farmer by reaſon of the charges,—and becauſe a farmer ſees not a return that uſually under a year and an half. A wheaten crop leaſt profitable.

§. 2. It is commonly ſaid, that ground, which has got a ſword, is beſt for wheat, —— and therefore farmers are apt to ſay, that land, which is not inclinable to graſs, is not fit to be ſowed with wheat, till it has got a ſword, —— whereas the leſs ſword any ground has the fitter it is for any ſort of corn, except it be white ground that wants a ſword to hold it together.—But a ſword on ground is an argument that it has lain lay the longer, and lying out of tillage makes all ground the better: I know no other way of ſolving the aboveſaid obſervation of the farmers. Why land with a ſword beſt for wheat.

§. 3. This year, 1717, we had no rain from about the middle of March to the 22d of May, (unless a moderate shower on the 7th of May, and some small thunder-showers, of which last our neighbourhood had no share) and yet my twenty acres of wheat on a side-long white-earth-ground of about six-pence per acre, and six acres more of wheat on the like sort of ground, did thrive something all the while, and lost not much of it's colour, which shews how hardy a grain wheat is : during the aforesaid time we had also for the most part very dry husky winds, hot sun by day, and frost by night : it is true we had an exceeding wet winter, which might beat the white ground the closer.

In cold dry springs and hot dry summers there is a great difference between the wheat and barley harvests ripening; for this year 1714, was such as abovementioned, when I began wheat-harvest July the 20th, and ended August the 5th, — but did not begin to cut barley till August the 16th, and in a lingering manner ended the 30th. The reason was because wheat, being a hardier grain, was not checked by cold, nor heat, nor drought, it's roots being well established and the ground well settled to them; but barley, being a tender grain, was pinched and retarded by the cold ; the ground being late ploughed in the spring lay hollower and lighter, and consequently more susceptible of heat and cold.

§. 4. It is not easy to be convinced, if ground be in good heart, though wheat may look very thin all the winter, and till May, how strangely it will tillow and fill up, if not hindered by weeds : this I have often observed in my wheat.

§. 5. [a] The Bluebury wheat is the red straw-lammas, not the white straw-lammas : there is another

---

[a] Mr. Miller reckons up thirteen characters of wheat, viz. 1. White or red wheat without awns.— 2. Red wheat, in some places

ther sort of wheat they call the white white, becaufe the ear and grain is still whiter than the white-lammas. ——Then there is the bearded or Poland-wheat, which has a stiffer and stronger stalk, and is therefore often sown in wet cold clay-lands about Wiltshire, because the stalk bears the wet better without rotting or lodging. These are the chief sorts I have any experience in.

§. 6. Mr Raymond assures me that he finds red-straw wheat, if sown at the same time with any other wheat, will be ripe a fortnight sooner. Note —— All precociousness in the same species implies a looseness of texture, and weakness in parts : I noted before that the red-straw wheat and rath-ripe barley were apt to fall and be knee-bent, and therefore the one was often sowed, in deep lands that were apt to run rank, with great wheat, the other with battle-door barley to support them, these being stronger in stalk. *Of red-straw wheat.*

§. 7. Mr. Ray tells us of a certain Thracian wheat, which they sow there in the summer, to avoid the cold ; this wheat, says he, is sowed on light ground, and never has but one culm or stalk ; it ripens in three months. What is more remarkable of it is, that it does not yield to any other wheat in weight, and has no bran He thinks however, that this wheat is not of a different sort from the common wheat there, but that it alters it's nature, and grows tenderer by being sown in the spring, which is a property worth noting. *Of Thracian wheat.*

places called Kentish wheat.——3. White wheat.—— 4 Red-eared bearded wheat.——5. Cone wheat.——6. Grey wheat, and in some places duckbill wheat, and grey pollard. —— 7. Polonian wheat.——8: Many-eared-wheat.—— 9. Summer wheat.—— 10. Naked barley, or triticum spicâ hordei.—— 11. Six-rowed wheat. ——12. Long-grained wheat.—— 13 White-eared wheat. But some of these, he says, he takes to be only seminal variations, and not distinct species.

Branch-
wheat.

§. 8. I saw some branch-wheat, so called, be
cause the ear is branched into smaller ears issuing
out of the main ear : of this I have no experience ;
and can only say that a gentleman, who is well acquainted with it's properties, tells me it makes the
best frumenty that is, and the best pudding, and
casts as yellow a colour without eggs as other wheat
does with eggs.

Of smut.
Smut pro-
duced from
poor
ground
sowed with
large-
grained
wheat.

§. 9. Discoursing with farmer Bachelour of
Litchfield about the best choice of seed-wheat ; he
said, he loved generally to choose a middle brownish sort of grain, not the largest bright and smooth
fat corn.—I asked him why he was against a large
fair grain ; he said, because he observed such grain
was apt to carry a smut.—If this be true, as probably it may, I know of no reason to be given for
it, except that Litchfield farm being generally a
poor soil, and lying pretty cold, cannot maintain
and feed the root, stalk, and ear of such fat seed, so
well as it can those of the small grain, and so the ear
of the large-grained wheat mortifies and corrupts in
the sap, for want of nourishment, before it comes to
be flour, which is the time for wheat to take smut.

—— It is manifest from many experiments I have
made, that the number of the roots, the breadth of
the leaves, and the length of the ears, carry a proportion to the size of the grain, but poor ground cannot
maintain it, and so produces a smaller root, leaf, and
ear than such seed would naturally put forth, all
which impairs the stamina of the increase, whereby
the ear is depraved, and liable to smut ; but where
(as at Crux-Easton) ground is strong clay, tho' very
cold, this objection may not hold good.

Another farmer told me, he looked on the small-
grained wheat to be better seed-wheat than the great
yellow wheat ; for, said he, the latter sort is apter
to smut ; besides a bushel of the smaller grain contains so many grains the more, which is a great matter :

ter : he added however, that the smaller the grain the earlier it ought to be sowed ; because, if winter came on upon it, that might prevent it's shooting so many blades, as otherwise it might have done. I soon after consulted two other very knowing farmers about this matter : they were of a different opinion, and said, the bigger the seed was, of either wheat or barley, it would give the greater root more, and have more blades.

§. 10. I looked into Mr. Wilson's smutty and blighted wheat, in order to discover what might be the cause of smut and blight. The smutty ears are perfect in the chests, and almost so in the fulness of the grain, even so far that the chests of many ears did strut ; so that the smut must fall on the grain late, and when it is towards a fulness, for it cannot grow after it has taken smut. I could very rarely find a smutty ear but all it's tillows were so too ; so that from thence I conclude the smut arises from the root, and not from any poison in the air, which would not distinguish between the tap-root and the tillow. I also observed in the fibres of the roots of the smutty wheat, a general brittleness, and the earth more starky and dry about them, and I perceived, for the most part, a stream or streak of a brown stain, the breadth of a pin, in the first joint above the root. So that I am apt to believe that a smut arises from a total defect of sap at the root, and a blight from a partial one, when some of the fibres may still live ; so the grain, being feebly supported, does only shrink or wither.—As for the early smut that falls on the ear, even before it is out of it's hose, wherein the covering or chaff is also smutty, and all in a light powder, this sort of smut seems to arise from the same cause as the former, only the ear having not as then obtained a firmness, it's rottenness becomes more hollow and powdery, and of less consistency than the smutty ears that have obtained

*Of the cause of smut.*

Q 4         a firmness,

a firmnefs. On the whole therefore, notwithstanding the latter part of my remark, §. 25, under the
article Corn in general, where I fay I could not difcover any difference between the roots, ftems, or
joints of the ftems of the burnt-eared wheat and the
found, I am ftill of opinion that both the uftilago
and fmut proceed-from a defect in the root.

Some farmers were faying, that dunged land, as
had been always obferved, was more fubject to
fmutty wheat than folded land. If fo, the reafon
muft be, becaufe the dung hollowed the ground, and
therefore the longer the dung the greater the danger.

I have in another place obferved, that fmutty duft
on feed-wheat may produce fmutty wheat, and no
wonder, feeing the feed immediately after fown fwells
and imbibes the fmut with the moifture, and the nib
or chiffum of the feed is corrupted and poifoned
thereby. The nib of the feed is not one fourth part
fo big as a pin's head.---Seed blacked with uftilago
does not hurt like fmut, becaufe the hot burning quality of the uftilago is wafhed out of it by the rain, and
purified from it by the air, to both which it is expofed.

**Of fowing thinblight-ed wheat.**    §. 11. I fowed new wheat, but obferving much
of it to be withered, and blighted, I fhewed it to fome
of the farmers, and they, but particularly farmer
Biggs[b], faid, it was never the worfe for that, and it
would grow as well as if it were otherwife, and bid me
put fome into the ground to try whether his words
were true or not.——I afked Thomas Elton about it,
and he faid, if it were not blighted and withered to a
fkin, but only fo as to have very little flour, he alfo
thought it would grow ; but then, faid he, I have
known it to die away afterwards.—I afked him, how
he knew it was that wheat, and how he knew it was
for that caufe it died ; he replied, becaufe he had in
fuch cafe fcratched up the root, and found that there
was not flour or milk fufficient to maintain the blade
till it could take root.

[b] Mr. Tull is of the fame opinion with farmer Biggs.

I met

I met farmer White and farmer Bachelour of Litchfield in the market; I told farmer White how thin his feed-wheat proved that he fent me, and that it was exceedingly blighted; and that I was fatisfied, let the farmers pretend what they will, that blighted wheat, if I fowed late in the year, tho' it might come to a blade, yet the flour or milk that ought to maintain it would be fpent before it could * more; and then, if frofts came, it would be in danger of dying.—They agreed with me, that, in cafe it was lrte fowed, it was their opinion alfo, but it would do well if fowed early;—but, faid farmer Lake an hour afterwards, when I was fpeaking to him of it, le tit be fowed early or late, give me a full-bodied wheat.

<sup>*</sup> root.

§. 12. Many farmers, and indeed all I have talked with on the fubject, agree that mufty wheat, though not grown out, will not grow.--I fuppofe it is be-caufe the feminal part is malted, tho' it does not out-wardly fhew itfelf, as it does when it is grown out.

Mufty wheat will not grow, and why.

§. 13. Farmer Biggs fays, he always fows the Bluebury wheat, that is the rath-ripe wheat. The meal-men do not like the white-lammas wheat; they fay, it does not caft fo fine a flour. ——Thomas Elton alfo fays, they feldom fow of the white-lam-mas wheat, —— and both he, and farmer Biggs fay, the mealmen know it from the other better than they do who fow it.---Thomas Elton fays, he has been at Reading with it, and could not have fo much by twelve fhillings in a load as for the Bluebury wheat, tho' of the fame goodnefs.---I afked him, if they did not obferve to fow the white-lammas wheat earlieft, becaufe of it's being laft ripe;---he replied, he found no difference in that, but that it was ripe as foon as the other to the full.

Rath-ripe wheat pre-fered to white lam-mas wheat by the meal men.

§. 14. ᶜ The original of brining and liming feed-wheat

Brining and liming wheat.

ᶜ Mr. Tull obferves, that brining, and changing the feed, are the general remedies for fmut; the former of thefe he has heard

was

wheat seems to be purely an Englifh practice; for which there is a ftory.—Neither the Rei rufticæ fcriptores, nor Pliny, take any notice of it.

Sharrock fays, brining and liming wheat may defend it againft grubs, infects, and worms, and fortify the grain, but he cannot think it any fecurity againft blights, &c. See fo. 99.

I had wheat brined and limed for fowing, but much rain coming, and the ground being wet, I could not fow it for a fortnight; at the fortnight's end I had fundry people with me about meafuring harveft-work, fo I afked their opinion whether fuch wheat would grow or not;—one faid, he had known wheat that had not been brined and limed above a week, and a great deal of it did not grow.—Another faid, it depended on the high degree to which it was limed, for, if it was fo high limed that it fhrunk and fhriveled, it would not grow, but, in cafe the rind looked plump and fmooth, then there was no danger. A third was of opinion, that there was a great difference in the manner of brining it, for, if the wheat had been fteeped in brine, it would be much apter to burn by lying in lime than it would having been only fprinkled with brine in the morning it was limed.——Note, this brined wheat was

was difcovered about feventy years before he wrote, by fome wheat being fown, that had been funk in the fea, and which produced clean corn, when it was a remarkable year for fmut all over England; but he afterwards doubts whether this might not happen by it's being foreign feed, and therefore a proper change for our land. He tells us of two farmers, whofe lands lay intermixed, who ufed the fame feed between them, and from a good change of land, and afferts, that the one, who brined his feed, had no fmut, but the other, who neglected it, had a very fmutty crop; but again he doubts whether this feed might have been changed the precedent year, and fo might not be greatly infect-ed, no more than what the brine and lime might cure. He adds alfo, that fmutty feed-wheat, tho' brined, will produce a fmutty crop, unlefs the year prove very favourable; for favourable years will cure the fmut, as unkind ones will caufe it.

not

not fowed till November 7th, which was feven weeks after it was limed, and yet it grew, and came up fo thick that it feemed to have received no prejudice.

§. 15. It was univerfally obferved this laft winter, (anno 1708) that the wheat which was killed was not killed by frofts, tho' they were very intenfe, but by the winds, which drove the frofty particles in fuch a manner as to penetrate into the roots of the corn; this may be fuppofed to be effected with their angles, which lanced the fibres and cut them in pieces, like as fire by it's fubtle corpufcles in it's rapid motion may be fuppofed to penetrate and divide bodies.——It was plain the wheat on our hills in Hampfhire and our high grounds, was cannonaded, for the driven fnow, as it was carried to the hedges by the wind, battered the wheat and cut off the blade, and the wounds it made opened portals for the fiercenefs of the weather to enter the roots.——Wherever the wheat lay out of or fheltered from the wind, in thofe places it was faved; and the furrows of grounds, where by lying wet (and this was a wet winter) the wheat is always worft, were, if the ridges croft the wind, the beft, becaufe the ridges fheltered the furrows, but, if the ridges and furrows lay parallel to the north, or north-eafterly wind, then the wheat in the furrows was alfo deftroyed, but wheat lying under the fhelter of hedges was faved.——From the fad experience of this year we may in our hill-countries conclude it to be good hufbandry, to have a fpecial regard, in the fowing of wheat-lands that lie expofed to the north or eafterly winds (for it cannot be fuppofed any danger can come from the fouth or weft quarter) firft, to fow under furrow, or at leaft a caft over and a caft under, that thereby the wheat may lie the deeper both from the penetrating power of the winds and from their power of uncovering the earth, and laying the roots of the corn naked;

*Caution— to fow wheat under furrow in the hill-country; not to harrow too fine; nor to cut hedges too early for fear of the cold winds.*

naked; secondly, to leave our grounds a little rough and not harrow them too fine, it being observed that the wheat saved itself much better when the knobby clods sheltered it;---thirdly, to have a regard, where grounds lie bleakly exposed to those winds, not to cut down the high hedges, which may be a fence to it, before February.

Oservation on the growth of wheat.

§. 16. The 20th of November, (anno 1704) I observed the wheat on the ground, and that the first, or capital branch, consisted of an upright spire, between two leaves falling on the ground; but the issues or tillows, be they never so many, had but one leaf on one side of the spire, by which the issues are to be discerned from the main branch; and in both good and poor wheat the difference was the same. ―― I know not therefore what the Latins meant, when they said, wheat must not be raked till it has four leaves, nor barley till it has five.----The same day I observed the tillows of rye-grass, and found that both the capital germen and the tillows do consist of but one spire issuing from the middle of two grass leaves, and therefore different from that of wheat.

Observation on the ears and roots of wheat, and inference to sow little land and good.

§. 17. It was the 23d and the 24th of June (anno 1703) I made the following observations with relation to the ears of wheat: in one field there were, for two acres together, generally in an ear ten chests on a side; about four of the middle chests on each side contained five grains, viz. two on each side the middle grain; but the uppermost and lowermost chests fell off gradually to four, three, and two grains in a chest. ――I went into another field, and could not find above eight or nine chests in any ear there, nor in any of the middle chests above three grains, viz. one on each side the upright middle one; and so again the uppermost and lowermost chests fell away gradually into two, and but one grain in a chest; yet this land had been well dunged.---In

another

another field it was manifest, that part that was
dunged carried not so long an ear, nor so many
grains in a chest, as that part of it that was folded,
and sowed on one earth; but there were many of
the ears of the folded wheat that held out ten chests,
and had five grains on each side in the two middle
chests: how these ears might prove I knew not,
very little of the wheat being blown.——I also observed the partitions of the chests to open, in order
to let out the blossoms; which when shot out, they
closed again, and the blossom hung dangling on the
outside by a hair as fine as a cobweb: till I made this
discovery of the chests opening, I used to wonder
how so fine a thread could thrust out the blossom.---
Then in another field I observed the limed wheat to
be of a most vivid scarlet in the colour of it's blossom, more lively than the flower of that in the first
mentioned field, which was a more dusky scarlet;
yet it exceeded the flower of my other pieces of
wheat, which generally did not come up to the colour of that, having a more wan and sickly scarlet
coloured blossom. ——I also pulled up several roots
of wheat, some of which had ten tillows; for I washed their roots, and found them all joined in one.

Now, if some roots of wheat have ten tillows,
others but two or three; if some ears of wheat have
ten chests of a side, others but six or seven;—— and
some ears have five grains in the best chest, others
but three, and two, I leave it to be considered what
encouragement there is to sow little land and good.
——The ten-chested ears at four middle-chests each
side, with five grains a piece, make forty grains;
the twelve other chests, at three grains in a chest,
make thirty-six. ——— The weak wheat has but
twenty-six grains in an ear, and six tillows less, and
it's two tillows must also hold but in proportion to
the top ears.

§. 21. April

Of the
ears of
wheat on
land shad·
ed from
the sun.

§. 18. I went under a hedge, where my wheat was almoſt as high as my head in the head-land, the reeds very ſtrong, the cheſts ten or eleven on a ſide; yet I obſerved the bloſſoms generally to be very pale and ſickly, of the colour of aſhes on a dying coal, and I ſeldom found above three grains in a middle-cheſt: theſe defects I impute to the head-land being ſhaded from the ſun; for by the length of the reed, the many cheſts, and by my own know-ledge of the ground, it was very ſtrong; but doubt-leſs thoſe grains muſt run very thin at harveſt.

Farther
obſervation
on the ears
of wheat,
and why
nature fur-
niſhes more
cheſts than
ſhe can fill.

§. 19. July 6th (anno 1703) I viewed a field of wheat, the bloſſom being juſt over; I plucked ſome of the cheſts, and found, tho' proviſion had been made for three or four grains in a cheſt, yet in many of them there were not like to be above two or three grains, and I found in thoſe failing grains their bloſſoms pent up and withered, the grains not hav-ing ſtrength to emit: —— and in thoſe ears, that had the withered grains, I found the outmoſt grains in the cheſt on each ſide to be beſt maintained, nature having deſerted the others, not being able to maintain them.

Whereas I had obſerved in the flowering of the wheat, that, the ears being large and the cheſts broad, there were in the middle cheſt of the ear five grains that had flowered, which I apprehend to be the full complement in the middle cheſt of an ear; examining theſe ears and cheſts about a fortnight or three weeks after, I could in none of the middle-cheſts find above three grains of wheat, in many but two. ———— If you aſk, where was the advantage of theſe ears producing ſo many cells, when but two or three grains, or cells in a cheſt came to maturity? I anſwer, the advantage was very great; for in the firſt place they are a ſign of the fruitfulneſs of the root, and, if two cells do decay, the other three will be the better maintained, and have the fuller grain.

Secondly,

——Secondly, where in the wheat flowering-time there are the more cells in a chest that blossom, they can the better maintain the loss by all accidents that may happen; for instance; if one or two grains in a chest fail at flowering-time by a flyblow (it being often the case) there are blossoms enough in the chest to make good that loss by maintaining three good grains in a chest; whereas in ears that are weak, and produce but two or three blossoms in a chest, if those blossoms should be blown, all must miscarry.——I was apt to think however, that of the five blossoms produced in a chest there could but three prove good, nature not being able to maintain more; and this I concluded, because it could do no more by my wheat, which grew in general on exceeding good ground; and the chests were so constructed, that it seemed to me, there could be room for no more grains in a chest; but on coming from Ilsly to Oxford I observed some mighty rich land, that had large-eared wheat, many of the ears containing twelve chests on a side; I am now therefore convinced, nature is not confined, as above hinted, to five blossoms in a chest, for in the middle chest of these ears there had been six, if not seven blossoms, the two middlemost of which nature was not able to maintain, and so they withered, but I told in those chests five compleat grains full-kerned.

§. 20. In viewing my wheat, when it was near full-kerned, I observed some withered ears, which in all their chests looked dead: the grain was shrunk and withered, tho' in other respects good, for it had a sound flour, but the straw was dead to the root, and that drew up easily, the fibres seeming dead and dry; so that this is a farther, and another sort of defect in wheat than either smut or blight, viz. by worm, or burnt. *A defect in wheat not commonly taken notice of.*

§. 21. April 14th (anno 1705) I first observed the manner of the tillowing of wheat: the spring-tillows, *Of the tillowing of wheat.*

tillows, for the moſt part, do ariſe from the foot of
the root of the winter-ſtems or ſhoots, which may
be two, three, or four, according as the wheat is in
proof; they ariſe from that foot, and, when they
break out at firſt, they may be perceived by the eye
in a bud ſmaller than a pin's head, containing a cry-
ſtaline pellucid juice ; which bud is ſecured by the
coat of the outward leaf of the mother or winter-
ſhoot, between which coat and the inſide-coat of the
winter-ſhoot this tender bud paſſes along, as through
a ſheath, whereby it is protected from outward injury, till it is ſo well grown as to break forth with it's
green ſpire ; from the ſide of this winter-ſhoot now
and then only one of the ſaid ſpring-ſoboles does
ariſe, and now and then another on the contrary ſide,
and perhaps a third or fourth on the other ſides, according as theſe winter or mother-ſhoots are in a
flouriſhing condition, till at laſt they, being grown
thick and ſtrong, open the ſocket of the ſaid outward leaf, which girds them cloſe to the mother-
ſtem, and ſo ſtand independent, wide off from it ;
and then that old leaf becomes uſeleſs and dies.——
This day I alſo obſerved a new pearly brood of ſo-
boles at the root of the ſaid winter-ſhoot, in the
manner as the other before deſcribed, no bigger
than a pin's head : but whether it be not now too
late for them to come to maturity is a queſtion : it is
very probable warm and dry weather may very
much conduce thereto.—— The firſt and earlieſt ſo-
boles or tillows above ſaid, being at this time ſhot
up into the open air in a ſpire, ſeem by their growth
to have made a bud very early in the winter, which
another year may perhaps give me opportunity to
enquire into. From many experiments I have
made, by ſowing corn in pots, I find, that, when
a maiden ſpear has been dead, no collateral ſpear has
ſhot from the ſame baſis, but that the tillows are
properly offsets from the maiden ſtem.

§. 22. The

§. 22. The autumn (anno 1714) wanting rain, the ground, at the beginning of wheat feed-time, was but juſt moiſt enough to bring up the corn : the farmers (who kept on ſowing) obſerved that the corn, which came up before any rain had fell, had but a thin blade, and was of a dark colour, wanting the broad leaf and golden colour they expected : it fell out the ſame with me in the ground I ſowed under furrow, tho' the moiſture was ſufficient to bring up the corn thick enough.—Farmer Iſles and farmer Box, my tenants in Wilts, obſerved the ſame thing in wheat they ſowed at the beginning of wheat feed-time.—It's not unlikely but this drought might do no prejudice where the land is very good ; for tho' the thin blade, &c. certainly ſhew the root and ſtalk to be weak, yet in rich land they might ſtrengthen when rain came ; but where ground is poor, when wheat comes up thin in blade, it is a queſtion whether it will ever recover, and get a good root, ſtalk, or blade, tho' rain ſhould come.— This narrow leaf is occaſioned from the earth's not giving up the juices freely at firſt.

When wheat ſprings with a thin blade it ſeldom recovers itſelf in poor land.

§. 23. In turning up wet wheat ſtraw (laid together in a heap the beginning of November 1702) I found in January many looſe grains ſpeared out, but, on account of the thickneſs of the wadd of ſtraw laid on them, they were not able to ſhoot thro' : I meaſured their white ſtiff ſheaths, thro' which their blades paſs, and they were from four inches to five inches and an half long. Now, theſe grains having liberty to ſhoot their ſheaths to their utmoſt extremity, according to the reſpective vigour of each grain, and not being hindered by the ſtraw, I infer that thoſe lengths are the utmoſt lengths their ſheaths will reach to ; ſo that, if the grain is buried below ſuch depth, the ſheath cannot protect the blade, nor give it ſafe convoy farther, but it muſt venture its own ſelf to get thro'. I obſerved however a round wiry ſubſtance the blade

Of the length of the ſheaths of wheat grains.

carried, an inch upwards from the opening of the sheath, and before it opened into the leafy blade, which tho' less in compass, and less stiff than the sheath, yet seemed of a strength better able, than if it had been a leafy blade, to penetrate upwards, if the sheath could not carry it into the air. I infer also from the different lengths of the sheaths, that these lengths depended on the respective powers of the grain, seeing that they had the same bed of straw, and were all buried the same depth : it would be well therefore to try old grains and new, and lay them at different depths, and see what foundation it would give to farther conjectures. I observed the sheaths, which had ran out so far, were much weakened by it, and had not that stiff strength that the sheaths of common sown wheat has, which lies shallow. The grassy blade had shot forth two inches into the dunghill, but looked of a yellow sickly complection.

Of the knots in wheat straw, and the growth of wheat.

§ 24. In cutting many wheat reeds I observed all their lowermest joints were short, of two or three inches in length, and without hollowness, and that they gradually lengthened and hollowed ; which was in reason so ordered by God, for the better strengthening the reed to support the grain. The fourth joint in all the reeds was very hollow and very moist ; several drops of water came from most of them in that joint ; whether it was occasioned by the very wet May and June, or not, I cannot tell. Again, from that joint the next above grew less hollow, and the uppermost, that carried the ear, had no hollowness, but a green strong hood, wonderfully contrived for strength, to support the grain. The hoods of the first joint were dead, (these I take to be the two dying leaves that begin to appear in May) so were the hoods of the second joint, that being of such strength as not to stand in need of them ; but the two last and uppermost hoods seemed carefully to protect those whole joints respectively, and to
strengthen

ſtrengthen them.    I alſo obſerved the tillowing ears
which, tho' they were ſuckers from the trunk of the
tall reeds, that bore the long ears; yet they had two
or three ſmall roots of their own, on which they
ſeemed to depend.    Quinteny obſerves, the ſap
ſhoots to the topmoſt branch moſt vigorouſly : ſo it
certainly is in the wheat-ear; for, if any grains in
the ear are wanting, they are the lowermoſt.

§. 25.  Being at farmer Sartain's at Great Chavel
in Wilts, I ſaid, that one advantage of ſowing wheat
early was, that it might fat ſheep, if it was too rank.
—Sartain replied, he did not approve of that huſbandry; he thought it a preſumption, and ſaid, it
would be very apt to make the wheat fall and lodge,
and carry but a light ear notwithſtanding.— I aſked
him how ſo; he ſaid, it would ſhoot forth a ſmall
weak ſpindle after feeding it, and if the ſtraw was
ſmall the corn muſt be ſo too.— I ſpoke to farmer
Miles on this ſubject; he ſaid, he looked on feeding
not to hurt the wheat in the leaſt, if it were not fed
late : it is true, ſaid he, if it be fed after the ſpindle
begins to ſhoot, it would be the ſame as feeding
French-graſs, for then, as Sartain ſays, the firſt
ſpindle being taken off, there would come up a weak
iſſue or ſpindle by it.—- Sartain gave me three or
four inſtances on his ſide the queſtion, and Miles the
like on his; and the latter carried me to view a
part of Mr. Brewer's farm, which was anno 1699
eat up bare, and had as good a burden of wheat as
any in the country.—— He looks on the difference
therefore to be as above.

Major Liver and I diſcourſing of the miſchief
wheat might receive by being fed down with ſheep,
——— eſpecially, ſaid the major, to feed it as many
farmers do, who ſeem to be cautious, and think to
be ſure to do no harm, and ſo they only put in a few;
whereas, were I to feed wheat, I would put in as
many as ſhould eat it down directly ; for, when there

*Of feeding wheat with ſheep.*

are

there are but a few, they only crop what they should not, viz. the youngest spindles.

I cannot imagine why wheat should be fed at any time, unless it be by one evil to remedy a greater: if the wheat be not so forward as to have tillowed into small stiff spindles, long enough for the sheep to eat it, they can only eat the leafy blade; but I cannot see how that puts the spindle the backwarder; it rather seems to forward it, and strengthen it, forasmuch as the sap, which had the leaf to nourish before, has now only the spindle, which consequently must grow the faster and stronger.—— But if the wheat be so spindled, that the sheep can bite the spindle off, then it will put it backward to a great mischief, inasmuch as so strong a spindle will never grow up again from that more or root, nor carry so good an ear as that would have done: indeed if a favourable spring comes, especially if the ground be good, the country-man may think he can be no sufferer, because he may, notwithstanding this, have a good crop.--Yet it must be confest, that one must resort to the evil of feeding, if the wheat be so exceedingly forward as to shoot into ear too early in the spring.

When I shewed farmer Crap and farmer Ginnoway some young green wheat, and let them see there was a young ear above ground no bigger than a pin's head, they both confest, it was madness to feed wheat with sheep, especially in our hill-country, where the land is not rich; for in such land, if the maiden-ear be eat off, it must be a weak brother that puts forth in it's room, whatever better may happen in rich land.

Mr. Eyre tells me, that farmer Lake of Faccomb is very much against feeding burn-beaked wheat, and says it will occasion it to blight.—— I asked Mr. Eyre why the farmer thought so. He said, he could learn no other reason for it, but that it would be the later ripe, and the backwarder corn is in ripening the more subject it is to blight.——Note, this

this obſervation, however he, or any other notable
farmer came to make it, pretty generally holds true,
though the true reaſon, why feeding wheat ſhould
make it later ripe, the farmers are at a loſs to diſcern.
—— The true reaſon hereof I have before proved,
viz. that the ears of wheat in February and March
are an inch or two above ground, which maiden-ears
the ſheep eat off, and then nature is put back to
form other ears, which muſt neceſſarily put the
harveſt backward, it may be a fortnight, and alſo
produce a weaker ſtraw, more ſubject to lodge
and fall, in the room of the maiden-ſtems bit off,
and probably with a ſhorter and weaker ear,
unleſs the ground be very good. —— This is
like to be the natural conſequence of feeding wheat
with ſheep in the hill-country, where, by reaſon of
the cold, the harveſts at beſt are backward; but
theſe ill effects may not happen where the ground
is warm and good, and the country lies low. — If
proud wheat were mowed two inches above the
ground, this would prevent the miſchiefs of feeding; but then I do not ſee how it would prevent
the rankneſs and lodging of the wheat, ſince, the ear
not being cut off, nature would not be put backward; for the cutting off the leafy-part ſignifies neither one way nor other; for that makes no advances after the end of May, but then rots.

§. 26. Whereas the Rei ruſticæ ſcriptores direct *Of the ſar-*
the ſarrition of wheat when it comes to have four *rition or*
leaves, as taken notice of before, — I have been at a *raking*
loſs to diſcover the four leaves of wheat, becauſe it *wheat a-*
puts forth only three leaves, nor could I ever ob- *mong the*
ſerve more. —— But note, the two collateral leaves *antients.*
die in about two or three months time, and then
more leaves put forth; ſo that in England four leaves
never appear at one time, but in a warmer clime,
as Italy, the latter leaves may put out before the
former are dead, and ſo four green leaves may be
ſeen at the ſame time.

§. 27. When

Sign of
good
wheat.
Sign of
wheat's be-
ing at a
stand in
growth.

§. 27. When the ears strut, and the chests stand open, it is a sign the grain plims well, and is full.

§. 28. In the beginning of May (anno 1707) my servant said, my wheat, for want of rain, was at a stand in it's growth.— I asked him, how he knew it ; he said, by the spikiness and speariness of the tops ; for, when it does not thrive, it runs to a sharpness at top, and does not hold broad as when it thrives.

Time
when the
grain is
first form-
ed, April
15.

§. 29. It was the 15th of April (anno 1702) I first observed, that the ear was so early formed ; for in pulling away the valves, which were five, at last I found the ear in it's cradle, or inmost valve, which valve was of the length of three pins-heads ; the ear itself not above two pins-heads in length : I could not discover it's parts with the naked eye, but with the microscope I could distinguish it's parts plain as in a full-grown ear, and distinguish every seed to be of a watery pellucid substance ; the grain being formed by the middle of April, the weather following seems to be of great consequence.

It was observed this year, 1700, that wheat carried a very short ear ; for it had been a very wet cold May, and in that month, or near it, it was that the ear was formed, and, if the root be chilled in that month, it will not recover it.

The proverbial rhime holds not good on cold hill-country lands, tho' consisting of strong clays, which yet is very true, when applied to Leicestershire, and other deep lands warmly situated ;

" I came to my wheat in May,

" And went sorrowful away ;

" I came to my wheat at ᵃ woodsheer,

" And went from thence with a good cheer.—
For, in cold hill-countries, whoever sees not the ground well stocked with green wheat by the beginning of May, will never see a good crop.

---

ᵃ The word woodsheer is understood for the froth, which, about the latter end of May begins to appear on the joints of plants, and is more commonly called cuckow-spit.

§. 30. There

§. 30. There is a fort of land the country people call * woodſeer ground; in this fort of land, fow early or late, the corn will be edge-grown, that is, much of the blade, after it is come up, will die away and then ſpindle up again; this muſt be occaſioned by the root's being affected, and not only by the blade's receiving an injury, for then the blades of corn in the neighbouring grounds would be the ſame, as being expoſed to the ſame air; ſuch ground therefore muſt be ſuppoſed to be of a hollow ſpungy nature, very ſuſceptible of the air; and tho' it may ſeem to be cloſer and more compact than chalky land, yet really it is not ſo, elſe the chalky land would ſuffer the ſame fate. In theſe woodſeer grounds the roots of the corn are injured by the cold winds coming to them in March, April, and May, whereby they ſicken, and the blade preſently diſcovers it by dying away.

Edge-grown corn on woodſeer ground.
* Spungy, ferny, poor.

§. 31. The lodging of wheat is often occaſioned by a weakneſs in the ſtraw proceeding from the poverty of the land, it not being able to give nouriſhment, and ſo the ſtraw grows limber.—— And in very ſtrong land the ſtraw of red-ſtraw-wheat will run to a greater luxuriancy in height than the ſtrength of the ſtraw will bear, and then it will lodge.

Of wheat's lodging, and the cauſe.

§. 32. This spring (anno 1720) being very cold and wet, and the ſummer by intervals rainy till harveſt, and oftentimes the rain falling with that weight as to beat down the beſt of the wheat in moſt parts, a month at leaſt, if not five weeks before harveſt, yet it did not, as uſual in ſuch caſe, blight, which was wondered at.—— The reaſon ſeems to be, becauſe the ground by cloudy dark weather, and many repeated and frequent rains, was kept cool, and thereby it fed the corn, ſo that it did not ſcorch and burn as in other ſuch years, whereby the green corn that lodged, was not parched up; for it is obvious, it muſt burn and dry up more in hot ſcorching weather,

Of blights on wheat.

weather, when it lies flat on the ground, than standing upright it would do; because by standing upright it shades the ground from the sun.

The country-man observes the blight to appear on his wheat quickly after it's blossoming-time, and so concludes the blossoming-time dangerous for blighting; and in all probability it may be so; for the blight perhaps arises from the cold winds condensing the sap and choaking up the pores of the straw, whereby all nourishment that should pass to the ear is intercepted: but if this blight proceeds from a mildew falling from the air, as many people imagine, it cannot be so; for at the blossoming-time the straw is not dry enough to receive and suck in such mildew; it abounds with moisture at that time, like green hay in swarth, and cannot be prejudiced by rain, as it may be after it is become hay, for then it imbibes the rain; ——but, as I conceive, the blight appears not on the wheat till after the straw becomes somewhat dry; tho' true it is, the mildew's lodging on the wheat at flowering-time, if not washed off by rain, may continue till the straw be dry enough to imbibe it.——The poorer the land is, or the lighter it lies, tho' rich, the less able will it be to feed the roots of the corn so as to overcome the blight.—Now the reason why wheat or barley is supposed to be past blighting when the grain comes to some hardened pith, is, because the mildew coming on the straw then, it cannot affect the corn so as to blight it, it having by that time got such a substance, as to be maintained by very little communication of sap from the root, according to the degree of which the wheat will shrink more or less.——Perhaps the smut may be nothing else but the highest degree of blight, when the mildew comes so plentifully on the straw as totally to interrupt and stop the rising moisture,——or when the particular bit of dung, or such moisture as lies to the root of the corn

is,

is, by that time the corn comes to kern, wholly consumed by the heat of the sun.

Observing the wheat-ears at blossoming-time, I found, that, at shooting forth the blossom, each cell or chest opens more than ordinary, and, when the flower is come forth, it closes again. This observation seems to account for the blight wheat is said to take at blossoming-time, inasmuch as at that time blighting winds and mildews are let into the cell where the grain is; these mildews whether they proceed from the air, and falling on the plant enter into it's pores, and prevent the sap from filling it, or whether they are nothing more than the sap itself, which, in it's passage thro' the pores of the plant, is checked and thickened by the cold winds, and being unable to fly off, settles on the surface, however this be, they are of that gummy nature, that they may easily be supposed to choak the grain.

## Of BLIGHTING AIR.

[e] Country people look on hot glooms and a warm vapoury air to be blighting and to bring caterpillars and green locusts; if so, this seems to be an argument for mildews falling from the air, and not proceeding merely from cold, for the reason thereof may

[e] Mr. Miller gives the following account of blights from the learned Dr. Hales, which in a great measure is agreeable to our author's sentiments.———Blights are often caused by a continued dry easterly wind, for several days together, without intervention of showers, or any morning-dew, by which the perspiration in the tender blossoms is stopped: so that, in a short time their colour is changed, and they wither and decay: and, if it so happens that there is a long continuance of the same weather, it equally affects the tender leaves; for their perspiring matter is hereby thickened, and rendered glutinous, closely adhering to the surfaces of the leaves, and becomes a proper nutriment to those small insects, which are always found preying upon the leaves and tender branches of fruit-trees, whenever
this

may be this; those insects eggs being laid on the leaves of trees and corn, the weather aforesaid coming, which contains glutinous and unctious particles, may fasten those eggs to the leaves and secure them from being blown away, till the sun can bring them to perfection, whereas, if winds had come, or rains, instead of the aforesaid blighting air, most of them might have been destroyed; so that such glooms may well be supposed pernicious; and such air may penetrate into the cells of the chests of wheat, and choak all circulation.———— But on the other hand the mildew may proceed from the cold nights that give a sudden check to the sap, which had before been attenuated by these glooms.

If strong winds come when the straw of the wheat is grown a little stiff, i. e. about three weeks or a month before the corn be ripe, a blight often happens; for the straw, being then stiffened, does not ply with the wind as when full of grassy sap, but by making resistance it loosens the mores or fibres of the roots, which give way or break, as may be seen by the wheat's reclining at the root from the side the wind set till harvest; whereby nourishment is not so well conveyed, and so the corn shrinks or blights, especially in loose ground, as it happened this year

this blight happens; but it is not these insects which are the first cause of blights, as hath been imagined by some; tho' it must be allowed, that, whenever these insects meet with such a proper food, they multiply exceedingly.

The wheat least liable to be hurt by these insects, says Mr. Tull, is the white-cone (or bearded) wheat, which has it's straw like a rush, not hollow, but full of pith, except near the lower part, and there it is very thick and strong. It is probable it has sap vessels that lie deeper, so as the young insects cannot totally destroy them, as they do in other wheat; for when the straw has the black spots (which he calls the excrements of these young insects) which shew that the insects have been there bred, yet the grain is plump, when the grey-cone and lammas-wheat mixed with it are blighted.

(1712)

(1712) but, where wheat lay in a shelving ground, quite under the wind, no damage happened.

This year (1712) about the time the wheat was kerned, and just got into milk, or passing out of it into soft flour, there happened strong westerly winds, which strained the roots of the corn, and made it recline; soon after which it was observed by the country-man, that the corn was generally struck with a blight, especially where the land was weak and light: for some of the fibres of the roots gave way, others broke, and the corn continued to lean from that point, from whence the wind came, till harvest, but in very good land the corn suffered little by the blight. On my clay-lands, tho' the fibres of the roots were strained, yet such of them as were not prejudiced were able tolerably well, from the moisture of the land, to feed the corn beyond what dry and light land could do: ——However the straw of all the wheat in the country looked white, and not stained with black spots.—The reason was, because this blight proceeded not from the fat gummy juices of the air, nor indeed from the coldness of the wind, (either of which may choak the vegetable juices and hinder them from ascending through the straw to the ear, whereby the corn may be starved for want of nourishment), but from the strength of the wind damaging and weakening the roots, which are the feeders of the grain, and preventing them from doing their office.—— I had such ground, which lay under a hill sheltered from the wind, that was not hurt. All corn, on light and dry ground, ought to be cut sooner than corn lying on a flat clay-ground, because from the cold ground a damp steam will arise, and in some measure feed the corn that leans down more than it can be supposed to do from a poor dry ground, when the corn has lost it's support from the root.

Farmer

Farmer Elton told me, that he had the straw of his wheat grievously blighted, when the ears were not touched. —— I told him, I thought that must be, because the wheat was so near ripe that it no longer depended either on the root or the straw for it's nourishment, and consequently any defect in either of them could not affect the ear. —— To which he assented, and said, he believed it was the truth of the case.

§. 33. The worse wheat is, tho' it be never so dry, it will handle the rougher; because thin and coarse wheat is not so plump and globular as fine wheat, and is often so coarse as to be pitted, and wrinkled, which must needs make it less slippery.

*Of wheat's handling rough.*

§. 34. Wheat will handle colder out of a reek that is two years old than it will out of a reek of one year old; —— for in that time, the mists and rimes, especially in the hill-country, will be drove into a reek.

*Of wheat's handling cold.*

§. 35. January (anno 1705) we had a month's season of very wet and rimy weather, in which time my bread proved very white, insomuch as I was uneasy about it: the miller said, he ground the wheat as fine as usual; the cook-maid said, she used the coarse sieve, as she used to do: at last the miller said, the reason must be the dampness of the weather, which made the wheat grind heavy, and not so fine, whereby the bran was the larger, and the flour the less. —— From hence it appears, that wheat, which is heavy and cold, will not yield that flour that dry wheat will, nor consequently that price, which is another disadvantage besides that of not keeping.

*Heavy, cold wheat bad for grinding.*

§. 36. Anno 1715, I observed in other persons wheat as well as my own, it having been a wet harvest, that most farmers had some wheat-corn grown, and that such wheat would not yield so much by three-pence per bushel as other corn that was not grown, and yet in such grown-wheat it may be there

*Of wheat that is grown.*

wa

was not to be found above a grain of grown-corn in two or three handfuls. —— I thought it proper to demand the reason of the farmers, why so few grains of grown-corn in a large quantity of wheat should make so great a difference in the price; at length farmer Isles, of Holt in Wiltshire, gave me the best reason :—he said, where there is but a little grown-corn in wheat it makes a very sensible difference in the bread or pudding made of it; not that the grown-corn only, which is apparent to us, when so little, can make so great a difference, but wherever, said he, so much corn is apparently grown to our eyes, a great deal more is damaged than appears to our eyes ; for the flour of corn will be damaged and clammy, tho' it has not gone so far as to shoot either root or spear : it is enough to vitiate the flour if the nib or punctum saliens has swelled so as to crack or burst the skin.——I told Mr. Raymond farmer Isles's judgment of this matter, and he said, it was a notable observation.

Rain coming before I could thatch a wheat-reek, one fourth part of the round being unthatched, the wheat there took damage by growing; and it is to be noted, that a little grown-corn will do a great deal of damage ; 'tis not only the loss of those grains that ac-tually grow, but a foulness and fustiness also, and a smut that they beget in the germen, that rots the corn, so that such ears will fly into dust, like a puff, when they are struck with the flail, and discolour the whole quantity of wheat threshed with them, tho 'it had otherwise taken no harm.— It is farmer Biggs's opinion, that it is the best to mingle all together, for the buyers will give nothing for the bad. — All my wheat of that reek also felt heavy and cold, tho' not one fourth part had taken damage ; for the unthatch-ed part taking damage, the damp that was thereby re-ceived, and pent in when it came to be thatched, did, it is probable, strike a chill to the whole reek.

§. 37. In

§. 37. In case the spring be far spent, and the summer so advanced, that an early and forward harvest may be expected, and the last year's wheat run coarse, by reason of a cold spring and summer with a backward harvest, it will be best to thresh out such wheat, and sell it before new wheat comes into the market; for the new wheat will carry so much better a body and colour, that the old wheat, when it stands in the market along with the new, will sell to a much greater disadvantage than it would have done, had it appeared by itself.

*Caution to sell off old wheat that is coarse before next harvest.*

§. 38. In Moses's song on the overthrow of the Ægyptians, Exod. ch. xv. ver. 7. it is said,——" Thou sentest forth thy wrath, which consumed " them as stubble,"——whereby it appeareth how ancient a custom it was to burn the stubble. —— ᶠ Pliny takes notice that Virgil gives great commendation to the custom of burning the stubble, but he himself thinks it of no other use but that of destroying the seeds of weeds.

*Antiquity of burning stubble.*

# R Y E.

§. 1. **R**YE is a grain seldom sown in the counties I have been most conversant, and, as for my own experience, it has been very little in it.

Farmer Morrant of Essex assured me, that in their common-field one of the tenants one year sowed rye in but two acres, and there was not that year one piece of wheat in the whole field clear from rye. —It was conjectured it must be the common-field sheep crossing over the two acres of rye, after it was sowed, that carried it about in their claws.

*Rye carried by the sheep from one land to another.*

§. 2. Mr. Putching of Leicestershire informs me, that they sow two bushels of rye on an acre, which

*Of sowing rye in Leicestershire.*

ᶠ Sunt qui accendant in arvo et stipulas, magno Virgilii præconio; summa autem ejus ratio ut herbarum semen exurant. Plin.

is as much as they sow of wheat, because, he says, tho' it is a thinner grain, and so more of it goes to a bushel, yet it is also a tenderer grain, and therefore they give that allowance.———He says, in the common-fields in Leicestershire they winter-feed their wheat by consent, but they do not feed their rye, *They ne-* because it is too tender to bear it, and the sheep *ver feed* would make little holes with their feet in open wea- *rye.* ther, wherein the water would stand to the injury of the rye.

# BARLEY.

§. 1. FARMER Biggs of Hampshire tells me, *Of rath-* he sows much of the rath-ripe barley, that *ripe barley.* he sows it on clay-ground, because the fault of that land is that it's corn will be late ripe, which is mended by that barley: rath-ripe barley, he says, ought to be sown early, or the corn will be thin; he sows it in March. But farmer Elton, his neighbour, says, some sow it first, and some the last of barley: he also says, it ought to be sowed in good strong ground, else it's straw being very hollow will be weak, and so be beaten down and lodge.

It seems that rath-ripe barley should be sown on better ground than other barley, because, ripening the sooner, it may be supposed to exhaust the goodness of the land, and to draw it's moisture from it faster than it can well give it, the corn coming to it's perfection in so much the less time.——— But Mr. Raymond assures me, that with them, near Patney in Wiltshire, they sow it in the poorest sandy ground.

Conformable to what Mr. Raymond had told me, a good farmer, and neighbour to both Biggs and Elton, is positive that on his poor gravelly ground it is much the best to sow rath-ripe barley; for such land will not hold out in feeding the late-ripe corn long enough, but will give off before it is ripe;

therefore

therefore the rath-ripe barley does better, to ripen which there is not so much patience required ; but quære how far this may hold also with white earth, which is the sort of soil Biggs's and Elton's poorer land consists of.

I sowed this year (1707) rath-ripe barley in very poor white ground ; I also sowed the same in very good strong clay-land : no rain fell to bring it up till June, and after that we had frequent showers, and plenty of rain till harvest, and yet I observed my rath-ripe barley in the poor light land miserably bent, broken in the straw, and harled or fallen down : in the strong clay-land it did the same, but not so much, tho' the straw, and the leaf of the straw was blighted, and full of black specks, the ear thin, and it's colour lost in all the rath-ripe barley, whereas the straw of the late-ripe barley was both free from these spots, and stood upright with good strength.——— I do infer from hence, that, seeing the clay-land in our hill-country, tho' in good heart, and the moistest ground we have, and in a moist year too, cannot sufficiently feed the straw of the rath-ripe barley, so as to enable it to stand upright, but suffers it to be languid and withering ; I say, from hence I infer, that rath-ripe barley cannot be a proper sort of barley for us to sow ; because in our hill-country, where the straw breaks or starves three or four weeks before harvest, it must needs be a thin coarse grain ; therefore in our hill-country it is best to sow late-ripe barley, tho' we should provide three or four horses extraordinary against sowing-time, in order to get the corn into the ground a week before May begins.

This year (1707) rain not falling to bring up the spring-corn till June, one half of the seed, that which fell deep, came up without rain, but the rest not till rain came.——— This gave me the opportunity of making the following obvious observation

tion on the misfortune that rath-ripe barley is fubject to in fuch years, viz. that half that came up
firft, by reafon of the weaknefs of the ftraw of fuch
barley (as above fet forth) could not wait for the ripening of the latter edge-grown corn in the fame
field; but it's ftraw bent, broke, and harled, and
the ears buried themfelves among the broad-clover
fown with the barley, fo that I was forced to cut it,
not being able to ftay a week or ten days fonger for
the edge-grown corn to ripen; whereas, the late-
ripe barley ftood fo upright in it's ftraw, that the
corn, which firft came up, would ftay ten days for
the edge-grown corn.

In May, (anno 1702) I afked Mr. Raymond
whether he was not of opinion that rath-ripe barley,
by reafon of the weaknefs of it's ftraw, was often
apt to fall down to the ground, juft when ready to
mow. He replied, with them they had no ftones,
fo that was no hindrance, unlefs by the bending
down of the ears the fcythe might cut off fome of
the ends of them, which mifchief he had not obferved to be more in that fort of barley than any other ;
——but that in rath-ripe barley there is this mifchief, faid he, we hold, viz. if the ground be good,
and the year a feeding year, rath-ripe barley is apt
to run rank, and to fall whilft very green in ear,
which occafions the grain not to fill, and is the
greater mifchief; therefore, faid he, this year I fowed common barley ; but fuch a hot dry fpring as
this there can be no danger.

It was very manifeft to me, this year (1706), that
the ftraw of the early-ripe barley is thinner and
weaker than that of the late ripe barley ; for all my
rath-ripe barley (of which I fowed fifty acres in different forts of ground, and fome of it fide by fide
with the late-ripe barley) did crumple down in the
ftraw, when the late-ripe barley of the fame for-

wardness and growth stood upright; and this year I also observed in all my rath-ripe barley, that the grain was thinner than that of the late-ripe, which I impute to the dry scorching summer; the straw, being thinner and weaker, was less juicy (as we find by giving it to cattle) and sooner dryed up, and the want of nourishment sooner appeared in that sort of barley;—but farmer Biggs says, that in wet summers he usually observes the rath-ripe barley to be the fullest bodied corn.

It seems plain to me, that rath-ripe barley, as it should be sown early, for reasons before set forth, so it ought not to be exposed to the north, but ought likewise to be sown in pretty good ground, either by nature, or made so by art; for we know, the poorer the ground is the weaker and poorer the straw will be in all sorts of corn; and if the rath-ripe barley has by nature a weaker and thinner straw than the late-ripe barley has, and on that account is apter to crumple, to bend down, and to break in the straw before it is ripe, much more will it be apt to do so, when the straw is made much thinner and weaker than naturally it would be, by the poverty of the ground it is sown in.

It is very evident to me this year (1720), that rath-ripe barley ought not to be sown on poor ground, and much less so, in case it lie declivous from the sun towards the north.

**Of middle-ripe barley.** §. 2. An experienced farmer of Somersetshire very much persuades me, that the middle-ripe barley would be the best I could sow at Crux-Easton, and that I should thereby avoid the inconveniencies incident to rath-ripe barley; viz. that of crumpling and falling down, or being knee bent, and that of the thinness of the grain, from thence arising; for if by much wet it falls down too long before it be ripe, the barley will thereby be stunted, and will
shrivel

shrivel and shrink; for no nourishment passes after the breaking or bending of the straw; but this middle-ripe barley, said he, will stand upright till harvest, and then the straw makes better fodder than the other. —— I replied, I had tried it, having bought it for seed, in our neighbourhood, but found no success. —— He said, he did not wonder at that, for he had done the same; but, said he, you must buy it from about Bemerton, near Salisbury; in that case I found it quite another thing: buy a load yearly to keep up change.

It was very evident to me, after I had sowed middle-ripe barley, that the corn which grew on that part of the ground declivous from the sun did not ripen so soon, nor stand so long upright as the rest, but in many places fell down flat into the grass; so that middle-ripe barley, tho' it better bears late sowing, even on a ground declivous from the sun, than rath-ripe barley, yet it will neither bear the one nor the other so well as late-ripe barley will do, nor will it's stalk stand so long.

It is observable that the middle-ripe barley above-said, which was sown at the bottom of the field, lying on a flat, ripened altogether, and looked white and very * suant, being forwarder than that part of the ground which lay on the side of a hill declivous to the sun; but again, four or five luggs wide, in the bottom between the hills, it ripened as soon, and looked as white and suant as in the abovemention-ed bottom that lay open to the sun and air; but on the side of that hill that sloped from the sun the corn was more edge-grown, and lay backward, and nei-ther looked so white, nor was so ripe. This shews that a bottom ground, or a vale pent in between two hills, tho' shaded by one from the sun; yet, by means of the warmth and closeness of the air, will many times ripen as fast as a ground lying declivous to the sun.

* kindly, flourish-ing.

§. 3. It

§. 3. It does not seem very easy to make a conjecture of the nature of late-ripe and rath-ripe barley,
and to give reasons why the late-ripe agrees best
with cold, and the early-ripe with hot grounds, and
with a hotter climate ; but I shall venture however
to deliver my notion of the matter.   I conceive the
reason why one sort of grain is late-ripe, another rath
or early-ripe, is from the stamina and constituent
parts of each grain, which in the rath-ripe sort are
of a looser and opener texture in the fistular parts
and glands.   The rath-ripe barley having finished
it's course, and come to a maturity in less time by
being committed to a warm bed, shews the vessels of
the seed to be less compact, and the fibres and ligatures not so well strung, and their tones looser than
those of the late-ripe ; for the quicker the growth
of the solids are, in animals as well as plants, the
parts which contribute towards such growth and increase are less solid and compact, as carrying with
them a greater mixture of fluids, which are the necessary medium for consolidating the harder or drier
particles, which united make the solids, and therefore, the cement being of a looser substance, no
wonder if the fibres of such seeds are so too : thus
the parts of the rath-ripe seeds are not corded, brac-
ed, or faggotted together with so strong an union
or texture as the late-ripe seeds, which last being
sowed in cold ground, and in a cold clime, the vegetable juices are sent up in less plenty, and the particles that contribute to the solids are not over-flow-
ed with so liberal a quantity of fluids, which are
therefore the firmer maturated and digested ; from
hence it must follow, that the passages of the fibres
and glands in such seeds are streighter, and the juices
are longer in filtrating through them ; from whence
it must appear (which is the question in hand) how
the late-ripe seeds agree best with a cold clime, and
cold

cold ground, and the rath-ripe feeds with a warm
clime, and warm ground ; for the stamina of the
late-ripe feeds are closer, harder, and more compact,
and there is a stated time for every distinct progression in vegetation.  The Rei rusticæ scriptores tell
us,—that after so many days each sort of corn puts
forth so many leaves, then has such a stated time for
flowering, and such from thence for finishing the feed,
and such for ripening it : so, agreeable to the constituent parts of the feed, through which the vegetable juices are to pass, there is such a stated time to
be completed in each station and progression, before nature can rightly finish one work, in order to
another, till the end of her intention is answered,
viz. that feeds of increase are produced from a feed.
——From hence it follows, that colder earth, and a
colder air, answer the nature of late-ripe feed better,
because the vegetable juices are not forced up the
plant in a more furious manner than the vessels can
receive them, or go hand in hand with them in
growth ; for the fibres and fistular parts of a plant,
or a fruit, are to proceed gradually in extension of
parts, as well as in fulness of juices, and there ought
to be such an increase of juices as is proportionably
adapted to the extension of the fibres, that one work
of nature may not outrun the other ; for if the heat
of the ground, or the air, hastens the juices of the
ears of late-ripe barley to maturity faster than the
fibres of the grain (being of a harder texture) will
be extended, or admit of extension, it follows that
such grain will not arrive to it's perfection, or full
growth, but must dry and harden before it is come
to it's full body. - - So, on the contrary, in rath-ripe
barley (in which the fibres are loose, and consequently by nature disposed to a speedier extension) in case
the ground it is sowed in be cold, the fibres of the

feed

feed of increafe will run on fafter in extenfion, and fo to maturity or hardnefs, than the cold juices of cold land, in a cold air, will afcend to plim and plump up the feed, and from this ill match or marriage muft arife a leannefs of feed in the increafe.

By what has been faid of the properties of late-ripe barley, it is evident, that, if it be edge-grown, the ears that are firft ripe will better wait for thofe which lye behind, or are greenifh, than the forward-eft ears of rath-ripe barley can do ; for that will fall down, and be * more loofe, if you delay the cutting of it when ripe.

* loofe at root.

It feemeth to me from the experiments I have made, that late-ripe barley will better endure to be fowed when the ground is wet than rath-ripe barley will do ; the reafon of which I take to be, becaufe the late-ripe barley is (as all other late-ripe feeds of the fame kind are) clofer in it's texture, and more compact in it's parts, and confequently more refifts moifture than the rath-ripe barley does, which is opener and loofer in it's parts, and confequently drinks in moifture more freely, and is fooner chilled thereby, or made drunk therewith, and fo it burfts.

*Of fprat or ttle-door rley.* §. 4. Mr. Clerk of Leicefterfhire informed me, that fprat or battle-door barley required a ftrong good land, that it's peculiar property was, that it would not run up to a length of ftraw, tho' in good land, fo as to lodge, as other barley would, and that it had a ftronger and more pithy ftraw, but not fo good for fodder.

Mr. Ray, fo. 1243, fpeaking of battle-door or fprat-barley, fays, it is thought to be more fafe than other barley from the depredations of birds, becaufe it's grains are more difficult to be torn from the ear than the grains of other barley.

J. Mor-

J. Mortimer, Efq; F. R. S. fo. 100, — the fprat, or Fulham-barley is the beft for rank land, becaufe it doth not run fo much to ftraw as the common fort, and yields much better.

Mr. Johnfon of Bedfordfhire, of whofe judgment I have a great opinion, after he had fown great-wheat in a new broken up very rich pafture-ground (which fort of wheat he chofe, becaufe it was the leaft fubject of any to lodge) and the next year had fown beans, the year following, being the third year of fowing the ground, took me with him to view it, in order to advife with me what grain he fhould fow: he thought it would be too rank for barley, becaufe that is more apt to lodge than oats, and alfo too rank for oats, and was therefore inclinable either to fow great-wheat and red-ftraw wheat mixed, that the former might help to fupport the latter from lodging and falling, it being a rank ground, or elfe to fow red-ftraw-wheat alone, becaufe, next to great-wheat, that fupported itfelf the beft.—I have known great-wheat and red-ftraw-wheat often fowed in the north, in good land, for the fame reafon.—I agreed with his reafons, as being good, but told him, I fhould rather recommend battle-door or fprat-barley, if he would fend for it from beyond London, it being not only a fhorter, but alfo a ftronger ftrawed barley than any in the north, and therefore fitter to fow on rich land, in order to prevent lodging, and was alfo good to mix with other barley, to help to fupport it.

§. 5. Mr. Ray, fpeaking of the fquare-barley, or winter-barley, called alfo big, fays, it is commonly fown in the mountainous parts of northern countries, where other kinds of barley will not bear the winter; but this fort is not hurt by the froft.

The fix-fquare barley, vulgarly called barley-big, is fowed in Leicefterfhire in fmall quantities, but, tho' *Of fquare barley or barley big.*

tho' it is a great increaser, they told me they did not like it, because it was not good for malting, it had so thick a rind. ——— Mr. Glen of Hawthorne said, to sow a little of it for poultry did very well; but, said he, for the most part they sow it in Northumberland, and so far northward, because it will endure the winter, whereas the lenten-barley will hardly ripen with them.

Rich land makes barley thin.

§. 6. Farmer Elton having been at Major Liver's to buy barley for malting, I asked him if he could deal, he said, the major had good barley, but having rented the parsonage of Husborne for six or seven years, he had so much bettered his own ground, that his barley was apt to run out too far in length and be thin. I asked whether the richer the land the thinner the barley. He said, yes, if the ground be not thick and full seeded.

The thinrinded barley not owing to the richness of the land.

§. 7. Mr. Smith of Stanton assured me, that eminent malsters, whom he named, had told him, that the boldest barley and the best bodied for malting came off of the strongest land. —— I suppose their meaning was, where the land lay both very dry and healthy; not land of a cold clayey nature, but such that had mellowness and lightness with it's strength, such as the Leicestershire and Northampshire-lands are, and such as the lands are about Bishop-cannons in Wilts: what Mr. Smith said was on account of the preference generally given to hill-country-barley, which, as I take it, depends on this distinction, viz. the hill-country-barley is generally better esteemed by the malsters than the vale-barley; because the hill-lands are often dry and mellow, as well as of good strength, but the vale-lands are generally too wet, cold, and clayey; instead of which, did the vale-lands exceed the hill-lands in strength, and yet were of a mellow and dry mold, no doubt such vale-land would bring the best bodied barley.

— I speak

——I speak this to shew, that poverty is no ingredient requisite in land, for carrying a plump and fine-rinded barley; yet it is true, that poor land, lying dry and warm, must be allowed to bear better barley than rich land that lies wet and cold; for barley does not stand so much in need of strength in land as of the healthiness and warmness of the soil, tho' both are best, where they can be had.

§. 8. [g] Upon observations made on my barley this year (1711) after I had threshed some of different sorts, viz. that which was earliest, middlemost, and last sown, all of my own seed, as also barley from seed bought of Mr. Cox of Westover, I plainly see the reason why barley sown on our hills, from year to year, of our own seed, without changing, must in time so degenerate, as not only to produce a very thick-rinded, and cold glewish-floured barley, but as small also as a black oat: wherefore Crux-Easton being cold both in it's lands and it's situation, is necessitated to be sown later, and the ground not forwarding the corn in growth, as warmer lands do, the harvest must be later, all which contribute to the producing a thick rinded, and cold floured barley: barley, being tender in nature, requires a warm soil and clime.——Now if you will sow the seed-barley produced from such a place, being

*Of barley's degenerating.*

[g] Mr. Tull, in his chapter of the Change of individuals, says, —— Seeds in their natural climate do not degenerate, unless culture has improved them, and then, upon omission of that culture, they return to their first natural state. He argues in this chapter, that the reason why individuals of all kinds of grain, as wheat, barley, and vegetables in general, degenerate, is owing to the effects of different climates, as heat, moisture, &c. and instances, that flax-seed brought from Holland, and sown here, will bring as fine flax as there, but the very next generation of it coarser, and so, degenerating gradually, after two or three descents becomes no better than the common ordinary sort; —— that common barley, sown once in the burning sand, at Putney in

being coarse, thick-rinded, and cold in flour, it will require more days to root and spear in than the bought seed it proceeded from, which came from a warm land, and will also strike less bold roots to forward the grain towards maturity in the course of vegetation; from whence it is manifest it will still come to a later harvest, and consequently be every year coarser, and every year proportionably degenerate.— As for wheat and oats, they are hardier grains, and will bear sowing early in cold land, and so come to maturity in good time, and therefore will not so soon degenerate, tho' the seed should not be so often changed.

As I have taken notice of barley's degenerating, and becoming coarser and coarser every year, by reason of it's being longer in coming up, so without doubt in such coarse barley the nib or germen, and all it's parts, even the seed of the seed is coarser in it's texture.

**Caution—to sow good seed.** §. 9. Anno 1699, after barley-seed-time there was for about a month a very dry season, so that but very little barley came up, and, except rain came, it was very likely the whole crop might be lost, and, in case a very wet season had come, it had been the same; from whence I observe of what great consequence it is to put very good seed into the

in Wiltshire, will, for many years after, if sown on different warm ground, be ripe two or three weeks sooner than any other, and is called rath-ripe barley; but if sown a degree farther north, on cold clayey land, will in two or three years lose this quality, and become as late ripe as any other. Note, he has no great opinion of this barley, as being of a more tender sort, and thinner bodied than the late-ripe, and not recovering a check from cold or drought so soon as the other. —— Weeds, acorns, hips, haws, &c. says he, are thought to have been originally the only natural product of our climate: therefore other plants, being exotics, many of them, as to their individuals, require culture and change of soil, without which they are liable, more or less, to degenerate.

ground;

ground; for without doubt such seed will better endure all sorts of extremities of weather than bad seed can do.

§. 10. About the middle of April (anno 1705) I sowed twenty-six acres of barley with seed that came out of an unhealthy cold ground, that usually run very thin; so that, however suitable the change of the ground might be, I doubted whether so thin a grain as most of this was could be so profitable as a fuller bodied grain.—To try the experiment, I took sixty grains of this corn, of three different sizes, viz. twenty grains of the biggest, twenty of the middle size, and twenty of the smallest corns: I put the twenty of each sort in three several pots, with rich mold of the same sort in each pot: in eight or nine days time I found thirteen of the fuller bodied corns were come up, nine of the middle-sized, and but five of the smallest; but the fullest bodied corn, both in colour and breadth of blade, exceeded either, and both the other sorts.—In three days after I found nineteen blades of the biggest sort come up, seventeen of the middle size, and thirteen of the least: in three days after the twenty blades of the best and the middle sort were all come up, but of the worst only seventeen blades; but as these blades of the worst sort carried a manifest disadvantage in colour and breadth, and doubtless many of them would never have come up at all in poor ground, tho' the better sort might all have grown, so I question not but I shall find the same disproportion in all the tillows, ears, and body of the grain.

*Experiment to shew the advantage of sowing full-bodied good seed.*

§. 11. If you sow rye-grass, or French-grass with barley, it is to less purpose to be curious in your barley-seed: when you sow grass-seed with barley, it matters not if there be any trumpery of oats, &c. in it.

*Of sowing grass-seed with barley.*

§. 12. At

Caution—
not to buy
barley-
feed till
near fow-
ing-time.

§. 12. At Chriſtmaſs-time (anno 1700) ſeveral good farmers being with me, I was enquiring for peas and barley for feed.---They replied, that the houſing of corn had been ſo good this year, the buying of feed might be ventured on the earlier, elſe they uſed not generally to buy their ſeed-barley, nor ſeed-oats, but juſt before ſowing-time, leſt they ſhould ſmell by heating, and ſo not grow.

§. 13. Mr. Thomſon, malſter, aſſured me, that after barley is malted, and the coome and duſt taken away by ſcreening it, and ſome time after paſt, the malt will grow ; for, ſaid he, I have ſowed it in my garden ; but it will come to nothing ; from which I conclude, firſt, the great conſequence of the flour in corn, to ſtrengthen the root, and to nouriſh the grain in flinging out good roots, which in the malt is ſpent and waſted before it is laid in the ground ; ſecondly, I infer from hence, that the ſeeds of many weeds, after they have lain ſome time in the dunghill, may grow, tho' thereby malted.

Farmer Bond aſſures me, that Mr. Edmunds, the receiver of my Hampſhire-rents (being a malſter) having taken lands in the beginning of May, and no barley being to be had, he, by the perſuaſion of his malting-ſervant, made uſe of barley he had wetted, and was juſt well chitted or ſprouted ; he ſays, he ſaw the crop, and it came up very well, and was as good corn as any he ſaw that year (1703).—So that it ſeems to me, barley a little forwarded by the malſter may be good to ſow, though malt thoroughly made is ſtark naught.

Cook, the gardener, fo. 9. —— I do adviſe my countrymen, if late in ſowing any of their grains, eſpecially barley and wheat, to ſteep them ; if your grain be ſpeared, it is never the worſe, provided you ſow it before the ſpear be chilled or dried.

§. 14. It

§. 14. It is agreed, that is the beſt ſort of barley, that is not blackiſh at the tail, nor has a deep redneſs, but is of a pale lively yellow colour, with a bright whitiſhneſs in it, and if the rind is a little curdled, ſo much the better.

The marks of good barley.

§. 15. It is ſaid, that the curdled-rinded barley is the finer ſort, and has the thinner coat. ——Being in the barn, and handling both the ſmooth-coated barley and the curdled-coated, I perceived the reaſon thereof; for if barley comes to ſweat in the mow, and to dry, if it be thin-coated, it will curdle, but the rind of thick-coated barley, being ſtiff, will not ſhrink, but will lie ſmooth and hollow, tho' the inſide flour ſhrinks from it.

Cauſe of curdled-rinded barley.

§. 16. The 2d of May (anno 1720) farmer Sartain went out into the fields with me, and on viewing three or four fields of barley, which had been come up about a fortnight, he obſerved, that the barley of their country, i. e. North Wiltſhire, came up with a ſtronger green colour, and did not look ſo pale or yellow as in our country, of which I am alſo very ſenſible, and do judge it proceeds more from the coldneſs of the land and country, in the firſt ſown barley, than from the poverty of the ground; becauſe ſuch manifeſt difference will not be at the firſt coming up of the latter ſown corn of our hill-country, nor will ſo great a difference appear between our barley and their's by that time June comes.

Barley at firſt coming up, of a paler colour on cold land.

§. 17. When barley is ripe, it will double and bend down it's head; at the ſame time you'll find ſome ears to ſtand upright, tho' the grain may ſeem full hard and dry, but the ſtraw of ſuch ears, eſpecially at the knots, will be greeniſh, and will therefore be apt to heat in the mow.

To know when barley is ripe for cutting.

§. 18. Mr. Ray, fo. 1243, ſpeaking of barley-ears, ſays, they ſometimes contain twenty grains in each

Of the number of grains in an ear.

each row.——Note,— I never yet saw above seventeen or eighteen.

§. 19. This year (1706) not only in Hampſhire and Wiltſhire (where I ſaw abundance of corn, and had good intelligence from others) but alſo in Banbury-market (where I ſaw the ſacks of corn) as well as in Leiceſterſhire, and by account from Mr. Clerk, in all the counties northward, the barley carried a coarſe and thick rind.— For three months before harveſt no rain fell ; ſo it ſeems, that ſome ſhowers before harveſt are uſeful to make the rind fine.

§. 20. The barley this year (1702) was knee-bent, and would not therefore mow well ; for in ſuch caſe, it being looſe in the ground, the ſcythe, inſtead of cutting, carries the ſtraw away with it root and all, which deadens the ſcythe's cutting what is farther on before it.—— This proceeded from the dry ſummer, whereby the earth being looſe, it looſened the roots of the barley, and conſequently the grain could not fill. —— I obſerved what they call knee-bent, and that the ſtalk was bent from the root in the manner of a bow or hollow for two or three joints, like leaning on the ground, which muſt ariſe from the corn's falling by being looſe, and then it riſes upwards again from upwards of half the ſtraw, toward heaven, as all trees and plants do that fall along ; their ſhoots will ſtill ariſe perpendicularly, and this occaſions the bow in the ſtraw, which is called knee-bent.

When the barley, (as above deſcribed) is knee-bent, in ſuch years, by the breaking and bending of the ſtraw, not only the grain is much thinner and coarſer, by having it's nouriſhment intercepted, but the ſtraw alſo is, for the ſame reaſon, much poorer, becauſe by thoſe breakings and bendings the juices are ſtopt from riſing : ſuch years you muſt expect great waſte to be made in the ſtraw ; the cattle by

refuſing

refuling much of it will make oughts ; and in such cold wet years, in the cold clay-hill country, the barley is apt to look reddish and stained at the germinating or sprouting end.—I would advise all husbandmen to avoid sowing such barley, especially in cold land, for tho' it be not dead, 'tis too much like it, and will come away very untowardly in malting, much of it lying behind on the malting-floor, and, should it come away no better when sown, it would be edge-grown, and as very many grains of such barley will never make malt, so neither can they be fit for seed.

§. 21. July 20th (1704) I observed many full-grown ears of barley lying along in a tract in the field, and withered, which seemed to be a great spoil ; I took them up, and found the hares had bit off the straws at the ground, to make a more convenient track. *Of hares biting off barley.*

§. 22. The same day I observed several grains of barley, almost ripe in the ears, to have wormholes in the outside, like those in nut-shells ; the flour of these grains was eaten up. *Of worms eating barley.*

I have observed that a worm is blown by some fly in the spring underneath the barley-ear, when young in grass ; I do not suppose however the same happens to wheat, that having endured the winter, and being coarser to their tooth ; but I suppose the same thing may happen in black oats.

§. 23. Edge-grown barley, (i. e. such as is not full ripe with the rest, tho' all cut together) is very discernable, tho' it should dry in the swarth never so well ; for such edge-grown barley, when threshed, will look of a horn colour, and have a sleek smooth white coat like good wheat, but it will stand hollow from the flour, because that, being pulpy, is shrunk away from the coat. *Of edge-grown barley.*

§. 24. August

§. 24. August the 15th (anno 1703) I observed much burnt barley, and opening the black grains I found a maggot in many of the wholest of them, where the grain seemed to be preserved somewhat intire ; the maggot lay towards the top of the corn, was of a bluish colour, and had little legs to crawl with.—I suppose the other grains in the burnt ear might have had maggots too, but they being moldered away, the maggots were gone.—And yet it is strange that burnt corn should proceed from this maggot blown by a fly, seeing in burnt corn of all sorts every grain in the ear is burnt, and so is the ear of every spindle from the same root, and the ear is burnt before it gets out of the hose ;—and yet it is strange a fly should choose a sooty burnt place as a fit matrix to lay her flie-blow in.——Quære of this earlier in the year.

§. 25. If corn come into the barn greenish, and is trod in the mow, it will be mow-burnt; for which reason it should be laid light and easy.— The inconveniency of mow-burnt barley is very great, for it will neither make malt, nor will the hogs eat it freely. ——It is as bitter as soot, and when the malsters bite it, it is as red as a fox within-side, and if you sell a parcel of it to a malster, tho' at a low price, he will never come again.

Airiness therefore is convenient to a barn, to keep the corn from heating, for, if it be hastily brought in, as it often must be, and before it is fully dry, it will through heat be parched, and sometimes set on fire : this heat will make the barley red at one end, so that it will never come in malting, and a reek in the barn will often be so hot that there is no enduring to be upon it.—— Farmer Elton once thought that he should have had a reek of barley fired in the barn by heat, and he was forced to cut a great hole down to the bottom of it, but could never stay at it

above

above a quarter of an hour at a time for fear of being overcome by the heat.—— It is barley and oats that are chiefly subject to heat, because the undried weeds are brought in with them, whereas there are not so many weeds among wheat.

# O A T S.

§. 1.[a] A Farmer dining with me, I was giving the reason why oats impoverished the ground beyond other grain, and said, that it was not only because the farmer generally sowed oats, when the land would bear nothing else, and so it being

*Why oats impoverish land.*

[a] Mr. Miller, in his Gardener's Dictionary, reckons four species of oats, viz. common or white oats,—— black oats,—naked oats,—and red or brown oats.——— The first sort here mentioned, says he, is the most common about London: the second sort is more cultivated in the northern parts of England, and is esteemed a very hearty food for horses: but the first makes the whitest meal, and is chiefly cultivated where the inhabitants live much upon oat-cakes.—The third sort is less common than either of the other, especially in the southern parts of England; but in the north of England, Scotland, and Wales, it is cultivated in plenty. This sort is esteemed, because the grain threshes clean out of the husk, and need not be carried to the mill, to be made into oat-meal or grist. An acre of ground does not yield so many bushels of these as of the common oats, by reason the grain is small and naked, and goes near in measure; but what is wanting in the measure is supplied in value. — The red oats are much cultivated in Derbyshire, Staffordshire, and Cheshire, but are never seen in any of the counties near London; tho', as they are a very hardy sort, and give a good increase, they would be well worth propagating, especially in all strong lands.—The straw of these oats is of a brownish red colour, as is also the green, which is very full and heavy, and esteemed better food for horses than either of the former sorts. — Our author speaks nothing of the naked, or of the red oats, but only of white and black, excepting that he mentions the Poland sort, which is also a white oat, and of a shorter grain than the common.

the laſt grain ſowed, he was apt to impute the following poverty of the ground to that only, but that grain is commonly ſown on one earth, and conſequently does not fall ſo deep into the ground as corn ſown on two or three earths, and therefore oats prey more upon the goodneſs of the land, than any other corn ; for they eat up all the fatneſs that the ſun, dew, or rain give to the ſurface of the ground, they lying ſo ſhallow, and for the ſame reaſon ground will bear oats that can bear nothing elſe ; that grain lying ſo ſhallow lives on the nouriſhment the ſun, rain, and dews daily adminiſter.--- And the farmer added, that a load of oats in the ſtraw was heavier than a load of any other corn in the ſtraw, and may therefore exhauſt the ground more,---and note further, the increaſe of oats is greater than of any other grain.

**Of the burning quality of oats.**    Virgil, and the Romans who wrote of agriculture, often uſe *uro* for *emacio* ; (as, *urit avena*) yet we find fire in all caſes enriches the earth : but the old ſignification of *uro* was alſo *to chill*. And cold is analogous to burning, as having the ſame effect, which we ſee by it's withering up leaves.

**Of the roots of oats.**    §. 2. April 30th (anno 1705) I firſt obſerved, that from the oat many rooted-fibres ſhoot forth, and the ſtalk that riſes upward takes new root again on the ſurface of the ground, at a certain diſtance from the firſt root, according to the depth the oat lies in the ground, ſo that the oat has two ranges or tires of roots : no wonder then that oats ſhould draw off the nouriſhment of the earth more than barley.

**White oats require fat ground.**    §. 3. According to the beſt obſervations I can make, white oats require a fat and feeding ground ; for the halm, or ſtraw running to a great largeneſs cannot be ſupported without good juices and moiſture ; I have alſo obſerved, that white chalky ground, tho' in never ſo good heart, will be unfruitful with

white-

white oats; nor will a mixed mold, between white earth and red clay, of which we have a great deal in our hill-country, be feeding enough for them: our red clays, and white clays, when in good heart, carry moisture enough, and are very fit for that grain. ——It seems to me, that white oats may be sowed when the ground is moister than barley will endure it to be, because barley, having a thinner coat, is sooner chilled by quick imbibing the wet, and many of it's vessels may perhaps burst, whereas white oats resist the entering of the moisture; they, having a double hull, are protected, and cannot so soon be drowned.

§. 4. I took in a reek of black oats of thirty-eight loads, and a reek of white oats of twenty-eight loads, and when they were threshed, I found the reek of white oats yielded more than the reek of black oats, of which I spoke to some farmers; they all agreed, that white oats always yielded better than black oats, and said, that an ordinary crop of white oats was accounted as good as a good middling crop of black oats.

*White oats yield better than black oats.*

§. 5. Anno 1703, having sowed white oats they proved blighted, but, as I thought, none had britted; yet in November I saw a multitude of oats springing up very thick; I seemed concerned, as thinking I had had a great loss by the shattering,—but an old husbandman said, it was the nature of white oats, when cut, to spring up again from the old root, but they would die away when the frosts came, but that black oats would not shoot forth blades from the old root.—— Some time after I dug up many of them, and found no such matter, but there was an oat-hull at the root of all of them.

*White oats said to spring again from the old roots.*

Farmer Wey, and farmer Farthing of the Isle of Wight told me, that they, and several other farmers in the Island had cut oats this summer (anno 1707)

which

which came from the roots of the laſt year's oats, and had ſhot roots, and tillowed from thence notably, and yielded very good crops; but, that I might not be miſtaken, I aſked them over again, if it was not from the brittings of the laſt year's oats; but I found they were well acquainted with a baſtard-crop of oats; and they both ſaid, that they had pulled up the ſtubble, and it appeared plain that they were iſſues from the roots of the laſt year's ſtubble.

§. 6. In dry cold ſprings, and hot ſummers following, black oats ſowed on lay-ground, tho' clay-land and rotten, will be as ſubject to blight as winter-vetches ſowed in ſuch lay-ground, as it happened to both anno 1714.

§. 7. Anno 1709; in ſome of my wheaten-ground ploughed up this year, becauſe the wheat was killed by the hard winter, I ſowed, in the beginning of May, in part of it rath-ripe barley, and in part of it a white Poland-oat: both grains were put into a ground of equal fertility and moiſture, and on the ſame day.—I doubted not but the Poland-oat would be firſt ripe, and was therefore ſurprized to ſee the rath-ripe barley come up four or five days before the oats; I obſerved alſo in other grounds ſowed the ſame day the barley to do the ſame.—I ſoon concluded the reaſon to be, that the oat having a double hull, and ſo better guarded from moiſture, could not ſo ſoon imbibe the vegetable water as the thin-rinded barley could, though doubtleſs, the texture of the flour of the oat, and the infolded fibres of the incloſed plant being ſofter, would conſequently grow faſter — The corollary from hence is, that if you would be ſecure of the growing of Poland-oats without the help of rain, they muſt be committed to the earth with more moiſture in it, or before it is ſo dry as it ought to be for barley to be ſown in it; not only becauſe the oats require more moiſture to make

them

Black oats liable to blight ſowed on lay-ground in dry cold ſprings.
Of the Po-land-oat— loves moiſt ground.

them grow, but also because they lie so many days longer in the ground before they come up than the barley does. The drying ground by the heat of the sun may be greatly exhausted of the moisture in a few days, which otherwise had been sufficient to have set the Poland-oat a growing.

§. 8. One of my neighbours was telling of me, he thought oats would be cheapest at Christmass, and he would buy them then against seed-time. — I answered they would never keep, for oats of all grain keep the worst, and they would not grow if fusty, for I knew a great many farmers would lay up barley about Christmass for seed, in order to kill the oats that might be in it, presuming the oats by seed-time would be spoiled for growing. It is manifest that oats take heat in a heap, and by the great wet which comes from them, when heated over the kiln for oat-meal, it is plain they have great moisture in them ; otherwise one would think their hulls would preserve them better than any corn.—From hence it appears why oats are generally dearest at seed-time.

*Oats will not keep well—therefore dearest at seed-time.*

§. 9. I was speaking to another farmer about pined or musty wheat, and saying that it would not grow. He said, it was true ; but added, that pined or musty oats were more difficult to grow than any other sort of corn, and yet, said he, I have known musty corn grow well enough. — I replied, it was because it was sown on it's first growing musty, before it had received any check by growing cold again, it being then taken in it's growing condition. —— He was of my opinion for the reason I gave.

*Musty oats will not grow.*

I had an oat-reek, which, taking wet before it was thatched, when it was brought into the barn seemed to be in an ill condition, and three weeks threshing lying on the floor in the chaff, the heap grew very hot, which I had observed for two or three days, and before I winnowed them I thought they had been spoiled.

*And to know them by their colour.*

spoiled.——Yet my bailiff would persuade me to sow them, assuring me, that he had known heated oats grow very well, though heated much longer after winnowed than these had been.----I got Mr. Bachelour of Ashmonsworth to look at them; he said immediately, when he saw them, they would grow very well; for, said he, they have not lost their colour, whereas oats, that have taken heat so much as not to grow, will look as red as a fox in their hulls. —All who were in the barn said so also, and that they had seen vetches that had been heated look so too.

Of white<br>oats and<br>their til-<br>lows.

§. 10. Being in company with two farmers, we were talking of white oats: they both assured me, they had often heard it said, that white oats came up single from their roots, and did not tillow as the black oats did, but——

I could not find by Mr. Raymond (though I had noted an opinion to the contrary in Hampshire) but that white oats would tillow as much as black, and he sows as many on an acre as he does of black oats;

—— but of all oats whatever, if a ground works rough, so that many grains are like to be buried, they sow the more, viz. instead of a sack, five or six bushels.

Of burnt<br>oat-ears.

§. 11. July 17th (anno 1703) I observed to-day, that the burnt oat-ears have the straw perfect, and of a good green colour, and their pedestal also, on which the grain hangs, the same, and the grain seems to have arrived to a good bigness, as in wheat and barley, before that blight fell on it; for certainly the grain could not grow after.

Of oats<br>shedding.

§. 12. White oats are most apt to shed as they lie; and black oats as they stand.   J. Mortimer, Esq; F. R. S. fo. 104.

Oats will<br>not ripen<br>if cut<br>green.

§. 13. It is commonly said, that oats cut green will ripen lying in swarth.   If by ripening be meant
shrinking,

shrinking, drying, or withering, I muſt allow the poſition ; but if the country-man will have it that the greeniſh oat, cut a fortnight or ten days, or be it but a week, before it is ripe, will proceed in it's vegetable increaſe, and ſwell as well as harden by lying in ſwarth, I muſt deny it. —— This year (1707) I made a full experiment of this matter ; for when the ſpring-corn was ſown, the ground being generally dry, half the oats and barley came not up till the latter end of May, when rain came, whereby in moſt places half the crop was edge-grown. —— So, the forward oats being in danger in britting, we were forced to cut down the greeniſh corn with the ripe, when otherwiſe we ſhould have waited ten days longer : I let them lie in ſwarth above a week, and, when I carted them, I found the hull of the greeniſh oat had got a riper colour, and the pith was well hardened, but pitifully lean and ſhrunk : ſo that, though this is to be done on neceſſity, yet it ought not to be practiſed with ſuch indifferency as is uſual among the farmers.—— Note, the pith of theſe green oats was well paſt the milk, and come to a floury ſubſtance.

# B U C K - W H E A T.

§. 1. [a] MR Ray ſpeaking of buck-wheat ſays, there is no ſoil but what agrees with it ; it loves moiſture, comes up ſoon, and ripens in a ſhort time. The graſs of it, when green, ſerves to feed black cattle, and the ſeed itſelf when ripe is excellent for fattening poultry.

Of it's nature and uſe.

[a] Nullum fere ſo'um refugit : gaudet imbribus, cito provenit, celeriter matureſcit : herbam viridem, priuſquam ſemen matururerit, boves, jumentaque paſcuntur : ſeminë gallinaceum genus paſtum citiſſime pinguaſcit. fo. 182.

T 4    B E A N S.

# BEANS.

§. 1. [b] COlumella thinks that land is not much fructified by leguminous corn, but that they do not much damage the ground. lib. 8. fol. 103. And Palladius has a quotation from him, in which he says a lay-ground is better to sow corn on than a bean-stubble.

§. 2. I find it is an observation with Somerset-shire-men, that when (as it proved this year, 1709) their beans are very good, they are with them very dear, and then wheat also is dear, because the wet springs, which make their beans good, hurt their wheat, and they find by experience that wet and cold springs in poorer and lighter lands runs the beans out into stalk beyond the staple, and then they never kid well, whereas, their deep rich grounds will support the bean under it's freest growth.

§. 3. I very much doubt whether horse-beans will ever ripen kindly in our hill-country of Hamp-shire ; their pod is so very moist and thick, that, before it can be well dried by the sun, the cold days and dewy nights so increase the moisture, that the bean will rot before it can grow dry.——— I the rather believe this, because I sowed garden-beans in February, but could never get those that I designed for seed to ripen.

§. 4. About Bishop's-cannons, All-cannons, and Stanton they sow horse-beans in their common-fields without any laying the ground down to a sword, but about Holt they do not venture to sow ground

---

[b] Palladius, fo. 114. De faba, dicit, satione ejus generis, sicut opinio habet, non fæcundatur terra, sed minus læditur. Nam Columella dicit, agrum frumentis utiliorem præberi, qui anno superiore vacuus fuerit, quam qui calamos fabaceæ messis eduxit.

to

to beans, unleſs it has lain down two or thee years
to graſs, and has got a ſword : the reaſon the farmer
there gives is, becauſe the land about Holt is not ſo
ſtrong as about All-cannons, &c.

§. 5. After the fertility of wheat mentioned by
Pliny, he ſays of the bean ſtalk, that one has been
known to produce a hundred beans. Inventus eſt
jam et ſcapus unus centum fabis onuſtus.   Plin. lib.
18. fo. 277.

*Quantity of beans on a ſtalk.*

§. 6. ' Mr Smith of Stanton ſays, horſe-beans are
abundantly a more certain grain than peas ; that
there

*Of the different kind of horſe-beans, and their management.*

' As Mr. Liſle has but few obſervations on the culture of
horſe-beans, and as Mr. Miller is more particular on that ſubject, I judge the following note, taken from that author, may be
acceptable and uſeful to thoſe, who are deſirous of information
in this part of huſbandry.— " The horſe-bean delights in a
ſtrong moiſt ſoil, and an open expoſure ; for they never thrive
well on dry warm land, or in ſmall incloſures, where they are
very ſubject to blight, and are frequently attacked by a black
inſect, which the farmers call the black dolphin : theſe inſects
are often in ſuch quantities as to cover the ſtems of the beans intirely, eſpecially all the upper part of them ; and whenever this
happens the beans ſeldom come to good ; but in the open fields
where the ſoil is ſtrong, this rarely happens.——Theſe beans are
uſually ſown on land, which is freſh broken up, becauſe they are
of uſe to break and pulverize the ground, as alſo to deſtroy
weeds, ſo that the land is rendered much better for corn, after
a crop of beans, than it would have been before, eſpecially if
they are ſown and managed according to the new huſbandry,
with a drill-plough and a horſe-plough.—— The ſeaſon for
ſowing beans is from the middle of February to the end of
March, according to the nature of the ſoil ; the ſtrongeſt and wet
land ſhould always be laſt ſown : the uſual quantity of beans
ſown on an acre of land is about three buſhels ; but this is
double the quantity that need be ſown, eſpecially according to
the new huſbandry : but I ſhall firſt ſet down the practice according to the old huſbandry, and then give directions for their management according to the new.
The method of ſowing is after the plough, in the bottom of the
furrows, but then the furrows ſhould not be more than five, or at
moſt ſix inches deep.  If the land is new broken up, it is uſual to
plough

there are three ſorts, viz. the Somerſetſhire horſe-
beans, which are the largeſt, and a middle ſort, and
the leaſt or ſmalleſt ſort. —— He ſays the largeſt
ſort are too big for his land, and that he chooſes to
ſow the middle ſort. —— They never ſow them,
he ſays, till the middle of February, or the latter
end ; they ſow five buſhels on an acre, and are not
in danger of rooks after they are come up ; he cuts
them a little before they are full ripe, otherwiſe in
moving the ripeſt are apt to ſhed ; that, take one
time

plough it early in autumn, and let it lie in ridges till after Chriſt-
maſs; then plough it in ſmall furrows, and lay the ground ſmooth:
theſe two ploughings will break the ground fine enough for beans;
and the third ploughing is to ſow the beans, when the furrows
ſhould be made ſhallow as was before mentioned. Moſt people
ſet their beans too cloſe; for, as ſome lay the beans in the furrows
after the plough, and others lay them before the plough, and
plough them in, ſo, by both methods, the beans are ſet as cloſe as
the furrows are made, which is much too near ; for, when they
are on ſtrong good land, they are generally drawn up to a very
great height, and are not ſo apt to pod as when they have more
room, and are of a lower growth ; therefore I am convinced by
ſome late trials, that the beſt way is to make the furrows two
feet aſunder or more, which will cauſe them to branch out into
many ſtalks, and bear in greater plenty than when they are
cloſer : by this method half the quantity of beans will be ſufficient for an acre of land ; and, by the ſun and air being admitted between the rows, the beans will ripen much earlier,
and more equally than in the common way.——What has been
mentioned muſt be underſtood as relating to the old huſbandry :
but where beans are planted according to the new, the ground
ſhould be four times ploughed before the beans are ſet ; which
which will break the clods, and render it much better for plant-
ing : then with a drill-plough, to which an hopper is fixed for
ſetting the beans, the drills ſhould be made at three feet aſunder,
and the ſpring of the hopper ſet ſo as to ſcatter the beans at
three inches diſtance in the drills. By this method leſs than
one buſhel of ſeed will plant an acre of land. When the beans
are up, if the ground is ſtirred between the rows with a horſe-
plough, it will deſtroy all the young weeds ; and when the
beans are advanced about three or four inches high, the ground
ſhould

time with another, he has double the crop of beans to what he has of peas ; and that he never plants them, becaufe planted beans muft be houghed, and where ground is apt to bind, and bake, the hough cannot eafily enter to raife a grete, efpecially where the land is ftony. —— He affures me, that broad-clover will grow very well with beans ; and that he has often feen the experiment of it.

§. 7. When Pliny and the Rei rufticæ fcriptores Of beans fay, that the bean delights in much wet weather,--- loving it muft be confidered that they lived in Italy, a moist land. much hotter country than ours; for in England we

fhould be again ploughed between the rows, and the earth laid up to the beans ; and if a third ploughing, at about five or fix weeks after, is given, the ground will be kept clean from the weeds, and the beans will ftalk out, and produce a much great-er crop than in the common way.—When the beans are ripe, they are reaped with a hook, as is ufually practifed for peas ; and, after having lain a few days on the ground, they are turn-ed ; and this muft be repeated feveral times, until they are dry enough to ftack : but the beft method is to tie them up in fmall bundles, and fet them upright ; for then they will not be in fo much danger to fuffer by wet, as when they lie on the ground ; and they will be more handy to carry to ftack, than if they were loofe. The common produce is from twenty to twenty-five bufhels on an acre of land.—The beans fhould lie in the mow to fweat before they are threfhed out ; for, as the halm is very large and fucculent, fo it is very apt to give, and grow moift ; but there is no danger of the beans receiving da-mage, if they are ftacked tolerably dry, becaufe the pods will preferve the beans from injury ; and they will be much eafier to threfh after they have fweat in the mow than before ; and after they have once fweated, and are dry again, they never after give. By the new hufbandry the produce has exceeded the old by more than ten bufhels on an acre ; and, if the beans, which are cultivated in the common method, are obferved, it will be found, that more than half their ftems have no beans on them ; for, by ftanding clofe, they are drawn up very tall, fo the tops of the ftalks only produce, and all the lower part is naked ; whereas, in the new method, they bear almoft to the ground ; and, as the joints of the ftems are fhorter, fo the beans grow clofer together on the ftalks.

know

know that beans defire a moderate feafon : in hot fummers, like this, anno 1707, their lower bloffoms only kid, and in wet fummers they do not blossom well.

## P E A S.

§. 1. ANNO 1708 ;—when the field and garden-peas this year were near a foot high, I obferved on the very top of them a purfe or neft of buds of bloffoms, lying in a bag toge-ther; and obferving farther that there was no fhow of bloffoms putting forth at the lower joints, I con-cluded our crops of peas would this year mifcarry, and that we fhould only have fome top-kids, all ex-pectation of the lower kids being vain, becaufe the kids on the lower joints are always forwarder in bloffoming and kidding than the upper, or top joints, and, as I faid before, there was no appear-ance of bloffoms in any of the lower gradus of joints: this afforded me fome amufements in reafoning, but, not being fatisfied, in a day or two after I looked into thefe upper pods or bags of bloffoms again, and diffected them ; wherein I found fometimes near thirty bloffom-buds, two or three of which ufually feemed to have got the ftart of the reft, and to be bigger in bulk, and higher in ftature ; moft of the reft feemed to lie in a huddle, without making any gradations ; but as I never had feen, unlefs in the crown-pea, (which carries all it's bloffoms in a tuft at top, like a nofegay) other peas put forth above two bloffoms and kids at top, which feldom come to good, fo I fufpected in this pod, there being fo many bloffoms in it, that they muft form the fucceffive gradations of bloffoming-joints, which did arife from that ftock as from a common root, and fo

that

that every blossom in order, as it grew forwarder than the rest, did shoot forth, above which the main stem still advancing made the blossom left behind the subaltern blossom of a lower joint; to try which I tied scarlet threads just under so many of the said pods, that I might know them again, and according to expectation, I found in four or five days time that I had several gradus of blossoms, arising from joints with lobous leaves above my scarlet threads, and the pod of blossoms still advanced on to the end, leaving behind farther joints of blossoms till the whole stock was spent.

This observation was very pleasing to me, as being obviously fruitful of many corollaries, which I shall set down in order.

Inferences from the foregoing observation.

(1.) By looking into this pod, or purse of buds, while as yet it is so in it's infancy as only to be viewed by a magnifying glass, we may judge what hopes there are of a future crop, provided the succeeding months prove seasonable.

(2.) We may learn from hence what sort of peas to adapt to every sort of ground;—but, before I enter on that part and use of the abovementioned observation, I must, for the better understanding thereof, premise, that the farmers vary in their judgment in no one point so much as in the nature of the pea : it is a common thing in the same parish to have many sorts of peas sown ; and the persons respectively shall every one have a great prejudice to any other sort of pea, but what they sow, having, it is likely, been disappointed of the return other peas made, when they sowed them, and it is likely may soon grow out of opinion of the pea they have made choice of, from the great uncertainty of the produce of a pea-crop ; so that the pea, in the countryman's understanding, has got the character of a very * kittle grain.

* subject to accidents--uncertain.

But

But if the farmer would confider, from the foregoing obfervation, how early or rath-ripe a pea is,
or how late in ripening in it's nature; and that
(feeing all it's ftock or poffe to put forth bloffoms
lies within the foliage of one pod) the art muft re-
fult from thence, fo to fow the peas, in fuch ground,
and at fuch time, that each fort of pea, according
to it's nature, may have time before autumn and
cold weather come to check them, to fend forth all
the gradations of joints or bloffoms, that none may
become abortive, for want of fummer enough for
nature to bring forth her embrio's to maturity,
and finifh the bud-bloffoms into kids.—If fo, then
it is apparent (as all great peas are late ripe, and run
to a great halm or ftalk, and the fmaller the pea is,
the earlier ripe, and of fmaller halm) that the great or
late-ripe peas fhould be fowed as early as the clime
you live in will permit; for thereby fuch pea will
get fo forward as to have time to exert all it's gradations of kids and bloffoms, and to have them perfected before rainy autumn comes, and puts a ftop
to farther vegetation.—Again, fuch great pea ought
to be fowed on a white, or fome mixt land, not too
grofs of juice, but not on a cold clay; for fuch
moifture will keep feeding the halm, and be incon-
fiftent with the firft defign of fowing them early,
that you might have all the bloffoms ripen, feeing
fuch land will retard it's progreffion to fuch maturity; but the faid white, or mixt mold muft be in
good heart, otherwife it cannot maintain a great
pea; fo, vice verfa, it is from hence apparent that
a rath-ripe pea fhould be fowed in a ftrong feeding
land, becaufe fuch land will maintain the pea more
vigoroufly, and that there is no fear of it's halm
growing too grofs, it being naturally fhort, and,
notwithftanding the coldnefs of the foil, there will
be no doubt but the kids will all ripen.

§. 2. There

§. 2. There are a great many sorts of field-peas, whereby the country people are puzzled, and are governed by humour in their choice for sowing, and make great distinctions between the sorts to be ranged under the same class, from their good or bad luck, or good or bad judgment in managing their ground ; insomuch that a neighbouring farmer on the same situation of soil with another, shall be out of patience to hear such sorts of peas commended by his neighbour, with which he has had ill success. ——The sorts of field-peas then I take to be ranged under two heads, viz. the tender and the hardy small sort, and the tender and the hardy great sort, not doubting but all sorts of peas, to be ranged under either of these classes, will equally agree or disagree with the same soil : the tender pea is improper for a cold country, or for cold ground in a warm country, which amounts to the same thing ; the great pea, by reason of it's great halm, is not proper for a strong and fat ground, for the halm will increase to so great a length as not to bear kids. I am satisfied from my peas this year (1704) sown on strong cold ground and peas-stubble, and others sown on barley-stubble, that to lay peas on a mellow light mold, made so by ploughing, is much the best way to bring along, and make a full-kidded pea ; for the latter, tho' not on so good ground, had both those advantages of the former.

*What sorts of ground suit different sorts of peas.*

§. 3. Mr. Raymond, who lives near Patney in Wiltshire, says, in those parts they had used to sow hotspur-peas in their fields, but that now (anno 1708) they grew weary of it. ——— I asked him the reason ; he said, those peas did not run out to so long and leafy a halm, nor lie long enough on the ground to improve and mellow it, but the other peas did much better.

*Of the hotspur pea.*

§. 4. Farmer

# P E A S.

§. 4. Farmer Elton, Mr. Edwards, and I fell into diſcourſe about peas ; it was anno 1700.——They
agreed that Cotſhill-peas were about twenty years
ago the only peas ſowed in this country, i. e. in
Hampſhire ; they are a very large pea, near as big
as a horſe-bean ; they grow exceeding rank, and
kid wonderfully in a year that they take in, but are
a more * kittle grain than the partridge-peas : they
muſt be ſowed early, and run out ſo rank that they
are late ripe, and therefore ſubject to blights : the
farmer uſed to ſow them in the middle or latter end
of February, and to take a very dry time for it ; no
matter if ſnow ſhould fall afterward, he has had three
quarters on an acre ; but they both agreed, that of
late years the partridge-pea has been more in eſteem ;
it is ſo called from it's reddiſh ſpeckles ; it is a more
certain grain, and earlier ripe, and ſo leſs ſubject to
blights than the Cotſhill-pea, which is nevertheleſs
the better pea to fat hogs with, becauſe they will not
be ſo apt to ſwallow them whole.

Farmer Crapp, and farmer Biggs ſay, the Cotſhill-pea does not well in the hill-country of Hampſhire, becauſe the country is cold, and the halm of
that pea runs ſo large, and to ſuch exuberancy of
juice, eſpecially if the field lies to the north, that
the ſun cannot ripen it, nor dry it, and check it ;
ſo that, eſpecially in a moiſt ſummer, it will keep on
blowing, but not kid well.—— I take this to be true,
and yet very reconcileable with what is ſaid in another place of the great increaſe of the Cotſhill-pea in
a certain field, for that is not a feeding cold clay-
ground, but lies warm : on the other hand, why the
farmers ſhould ſay, that the ſmall partridge-pea required the beſt land and the Cotſhill-pea the pooreſt,
is eaſily reconcileable ; — for the good land in the
hill-country is generally the ſtrong clay, but the
halm of that partridge-pea will not run out ſo rank
that

that the fun cannot check and dry it. Again; the mixt fort of earth, running to a whitenefs, is generally poorer than the ftrong clay, yet is not in truth poor, for where the Cotfhill-pea thrives there muft be good ftrength in the ground, to maintain fuch a halm.

§. 5. Mr. Randolph of Woolly, who has been a great fower of all forts of peas, gives it me for a certain rule, that all white-bloffomed peas, whilft green in the kid, will boil green, and all blue or red-bloffomed peas, whilft green in the kid, will boil ruffet-coloured. *Of white and blue and red bloffomed peas in boiling.*

§. 6. Regard is to be had in fowing great partridge-peas under furrow (where the ground is fubject to run to grafs, or is knotted with grafs that is pretty thick fet on the ground) to what may happen to them in cafe of a wet fummer ; as for inftance, if in ground that has born broad-clover for one fummer you fow peas under furrow the following February ; for though perhaps fuch ground may break pretty well in ploughing, fo as for the peas to come through, yet in cafe there fhould come a cold and wet fpring, and a wet fummer, the grafs will, long before harveft, fo grow through the peas, after they begin firft to fall, and at laft fo to over-top them, that you will be amazed, when you come to ftack them at harveft, to fee perhaps what was a very promifing crop of peas in May and June fo devoured by grafs, that the very halm as well as the kids fhall feem withered away, and almoft blighted to nothing. *Of partridge-peas.*

If ground be apt to run to grafs, or be knotted with grafs before it is ploughed, and be fowed to peas on one earth, if a very wet fummer fhould come the peas will be over-run, and eat up with grafs ; to prevent which, and to fence againft this inconveniency in wet fummers, if the peas are fowed on one earth, the ground muft either be knot-fine, or elfe be fallowed to kill the grafs, and fowed on the fecond earth.

§. 7. The blue peas, with us, run much larger than the small partridge-peas, and consequently fill the bushel better : they kid, as I have observed, better than the other, and are a * rather sort, and will therefore bear sowing the later, as about the beginning of April, when the inclemency of the air is over ; and being to be cut greenish, they may be stacked the earlier, which are good properties in our cold hill-country.

§. 8. The Burbage-grey or popling-pea is much sowed in the deep lands of Somersetshire, and called there, the clay-pea.

§. 9. I find by all the judicious farmers I can converse with, that, though peas will not grow on poor light land, but require some depth of soil and strength, yet at the same time peas will not thrive well in a cold wet clay-land, but love a dry healthy soil.

I observe about Holt in Wiltshire, where the land is generally wetter than at Crux-Easton, that they lay up the pea-lands in small round furrows, and they sow the great partridge-pea under furrow, if they can have a season as early as Paul's-tide, i. e. the 25th of January ; and the reason they give for it is, because being sown so early they would lie too cold, if they laid the lands flat.—Though I lie not so wet, yet, my clay-lands being cold, I am of opinion that I ought to imitate this husbandry, when I sow peas early.— The coldness of the situation of Crux-Easton is also a farther reason for so doing, because the cold air will not have so much power of chilling the earth, when laid in this manner dry, as it will have when lands hold wet by lying flat ; for earth will not freeze, nor receive any impression from cold, but on account of it's moisture, in which the more it abounds the colder it will be, according to the degree of the coldness of the air——In Wiltshire, if the land breaks tolerably rotten or mellow, they omit a tining

with

with the harrows, which would also be the best way in our cold country.

§. 10. A farmer in my neighbourhood having most excellent boiling-peas, which they call green-peas, I proposed to sow of them on a lay-ground I had grubbed ; but the farmer forbad it, and said, if they were sown on lay-land, they would run to halm, and not kid : light barley-ersh, he said, was best for them, and that, if they hit, they were mighty increasers ; that they must be sown about the beginning of April, and they yielded as good money, and as certain as any corn, but they were a ticklish grain. *Of green peas.*

§. 11. The country-people say, peas do best on a barley-ersh ; the reason of which must be, because how much finer the ground works so much the more does the earth, every part of it being opened, communicate of it's goodness to the peas-halm, which being gross requires good nutriment to feed it ; and where the ground lies lightest, provided it be not thereby liable to the evil on the other hand of burning, there the rain will wash the goodness of the land to the roots of the corn, and feed it ; and I do believe the sun in summer prepares the thin topmost crust of the earth with rich spirits, which, when washed into the earth, must fructify plants. *Peas do best on a barley-ersh, and why.*

The only reason I can give why peas should thrive so well on barley-ersh, (tho' possibly the land may be much poorer than lay-ground) is, because barley-land has for the most part been mellowed by a wheat-crop the year before, and also fallowed, if not thwarted the barley-year : the ground for these reasons is very mellow and light, and easily admits the rays of the sun, the rain, and the dew, to penetrate to the roots of the peas ; whereas the grossness of the peas-halm so over-shadows the ground from

those

those three powers, that, where the ground lies more close and hard, those powers are not so accessible to the roots of the peas ; for this reason it follows, that land, if not of a very light nature, is to be fallowed and thwarted for peas : peas ought also to be sowed early in the year, that they may ripen between sun and sun ; the grosness of the halm so much resisting the powers of the sun, and obscuring him when he grows weak, that the peas cannot ripen in good time, and, if the ground lies not mellow and warm, they run out to halm and do not kid well ; for the juices of the ground ought to be well digested also, to be fit to make flowers come in the joints of the peas-halm, in order for blossoms : besides, the earlier you sow your peas, the more hopes you have of the blossoms in the upper joints coming to perfection, which by their backwardness are generally lost ; and if these upper kids can get forwarder than the coming of the locusts or green louse, so as to be too hard for their teeth, they will (by being earlier sowed) escape all that damage ; and note, as it is in the green herb, so the early coming of all insects depends on the clime, and the nature of the soil, be it cold or hot, if the insects are such whose seeds are laid in the earth.

[a] Pliny, speaking of the bean, says, in some of the northern islands and in Mauritania it comes up of it's own accord, and without tillage, but that it is of a wild sort, very hard, and unfit for boiling.—I note this, because it's seed sowing itself falls on un-tilled ground, and therefore boils hard ; for we observe in peas, that the more mellow the ground is,

---

[a] Nascitur et suâ sponte plerisque in locis, sicut septentrionalis oceani insulis, quas ob id nostri fabarias appellant, item in Mauritaniâ, silvestris passim, sed prædura, et quæ percoqui non possit. Plin. lib. 18. fo. 283.

the

the better they boil, therefore boil well from barley-erſhes.

Farmer Biggs obſerved to me, that laſt year (1702) he had the experience of ſowing peas after barley, in a ground where peas had been ſown the year before the barley, and that, though it was in a bottom, yet he had poor halm, and poor kids, whereas on two or three lands adjoining, and much poorer land, where peas had not been ſown ſome years before, he had a very good crop of peas.

§. 12. Mr. Raymond ſays, he has always ob-ſerved, that land, which has carried peas one year, will not be fit for them again in ſix years time: if you ſow them ſooner, they may poſſibly run to halm, but will not kid ſo well, and ſo, ſaid he, our neigh-bouring farmers have obſerved.——I ſuppoſe white or light land, being much the ſooner robbed of all the ſpecifick nutriment of the grain by the crop of the ſame grain it carried laſt, cannot be ſo often re-newed to peas as clay-land may, and the oftener the land is dunged the ſooner it will recover, I judge, that ſpecifick nutriment adapted to each grain. *Land ſow-ed to peas will not bear peas well again for ſix years.*

§. 13. Peas, of all ſorts of grain, degenerate ſooneſt, at leaſt in two or three years, be the land ever ſo good. Evelyn, fo. 324. *Peas dege-nerate.*

§. 14. The honey-comb or pitted-pea ought not to be ſown on the hills in Hampſhire, for ſuch a pea is a cold pea, as not being fully ripened, but ſhrunk, and will not grow well in cold ground. *The honey-comb or pitted pea.*

§. 15. It is ſaid hop-clover ought never to be ſowed with peas; they'll cover the clover ſo as to kill it; peas will kill the very weeds, and that is one of the reaſons why peas prepare the ground for barley. *Hop-clover not to be ſowed with peas.*

But farmer Biggs aſked me why I had not ſowed a certain field, ſown to peas, to hop, or broad-clo-ver; and on my anſwering that I doubted whether

U 3                                                        the

the peas might not have killed it;—he replied, there was no fear of peas hurting it, where the ground was not rank,—and so I found; for at the lower end of the field, where the farmer sowed his goar-vetches, I sowed hop-clover, and it came up as well as any where.

§. 16. I observed the green halm and leaf of my peas sown on a summer-fallow carried a strong deep green, and had a blue vapour on the halm and leaf, like the blue steam on plumbs, which accompanied them to their flowering; but on peas less in proof, the leaf is of a paler green, and has less of that blue vapour.—I take this blue vapour to be an exsudation from the plant, and is the effect of a good insensible perspiration, and denotes health in the plant, and such plumbs and corn as have least of it are less in proof.——This blue exsudation goes off the leaves and stalk a little before blossoming-time, and then they grow paler.——We had a cold cloudy dripping season during the blossoming-time of these peas (anno 1715) and it was very observable to me, that both my sorts of peas (of which I had an hundred acres, great grey partridge-peas, and blue popling-peas) blossomed very blindish, as peas will do in hot scorching dry weather at the blossoming-season; so that I fully concluded that neither of the extremes, either of wet or drought, were so agreeable to peas as moderate rain with heat at their blossoming-season; but the continuance of many days cold rain must be prejudicial;——yet whether the hot burning dry weather be not worse than the other is a question.

§. 17. If it be a dripping and rainy harvest, in the pea-season, between the showers, when the upper part is dry, tho' the rain may have wet the ground through the wadds, to turn the wadds of peas will save the kids from britting and shedding;

for

for nothing makes peas more subject to open the kids than lying fogging in the wet; therefore, in hacking them, to make the wadds small, is a preservative, if the weather be showery, against their britting, because the smaller the wadds are the sooner they dry.——Of this I was very sensible this harvest (anno 1707) it being very showery; for the Newbury-men's wadds being hacked large, britted much, when our people's lesser wadds suffered no damage: add to this, that the smaller the wadds the sooner will the peas be fit for carting, whereby a day gained often saves a whole crop from damage.

§. 18. When peas are well blossomed, there are two blossoms that divide themselves in forked-foot stalks on every stem; whereas many years there is but one blossom on each stem.

*Mark of peas being well blossomed.*

§. 19. Monsieur de Quinteny says, fo. 156. —— That the blossoms of peas commonly spring out from the middle of the fifth or sixth leaf, from whence there springs an arm or branch, that grows exceeding long, and produces at each leaf a couple of blossoms like the first.——On reading this I went and viewed my peas, in a field where they were extraordinary good;——I found for the most part that no blossoms appeared till, reckoning upwards, you came to the sixth or seventh leaf, but where the pea-halm seemed not to be in good heart, no blossom appeared till you came to the eighth or ninth leaf, nor could I in any of the field-peas find any collateral bearing branch to issue out, as described by Monsieur Quinteny, but I did observe such a branch to issue out in my hotspur garden-peas.

*Mr. Quinteny's observation on peas blossoming not true in field-peas.*

§. 20. The top-blossoms of peas bring forth but a small blighted kid, and hang late on the halm before they kid at all, so that they seldom come to good;——but in my vetches I observed many collateral tillows on the stalks, even from the root upwards. so that there were commonly five or six

*Vetches greater increasers than peas, and, of the fly that breeds in them.*

U 4 collateral

collateral branches arifing, one above another, in two or three joints on a ftalk. ———— I alfo obferved a downy cotton bud to arife from the fecond and third joint, juft above the leaf, and fo for the moft part all along, where there were no kids: this bud, though but fmall, feemed to me to be a bud defigned for a flower, but mifcarried by the unhappy feafon of the year. So I infer from hence, that vetches, where they hit, are much greater increafers than peas.—Whereas I was of opinion, that the mifcarriage both of peas and vetches happened from the eggs of flies laid in the upper pod of each, I am now of the contrary way of thinking, viz. that the mifcarriage of the crop, both in peas and vetches, is in their lower bloffoms, which ought therefore to be earlier looked into, it being of no great confequence how the upper pods are deftroyed, becaufe the kids never come to perfection: neverthelefs it is not unlikely but the maggot bred in the upper pods, whether by flies or eggs, or not, may travel downwards, and eat up the lower kids and leaves.

More on Mr. Quinteny's obfervation.

§. 21. It is faid by Quinteny, (as before cited) that peas commonly bloffom at the fifth or fixth leaf; which is, as I fuppofe, in dry and hot fummers, when the halm is checked from running too grofs, and to fo many joints; but when in a wet year the halm runs out to a great length, the ftalk at the fifth, fixth, or feventh leaf, is fo grofs and overfhadowed by the other leaves, that the juice is not concocted enough till it has advanced more into the fun, fo as to emit the bloffoms.——And it ftands to reafon, that peas fet on fticks fhould kid better than thofe that lie all along,—and the well bloffoming of beans feem to depend on the fame reafon, therefore field-peas when fowed thick do the better uphold themfelves by their ftrings, to let in the fun and air, till they fall by the weight of their kids.

§. 22. It

# PEAS.

§. 22. It is obſerved both in Hampſhire and Wiltſhire, that peas never kid well that year, in which they blow blind, that is, when their bloſſoms open not full, as it happened anno 1705 — a wonderful dry ſummer.

If the bloſſoms open not full, it is a bad ſign.

§. 23. When I was at Holt anno 1712 — I obſerved in the peas, while bloſſoming, that where there was but one ſingle bloſſom on a foot-ſtalk, there generally grew up a little ſpur, near an inch behind the bloſſom, on the ſame ſtalk, in height about the length of a barley-corn. I ſuſpected that another bloſſom had grown thereon, and that the claſpers of the peas had taken hold of it, and pulled it off by the power of the wind, or that ſome other accident had deſtroyed the bloſſom; but at this time looking a little nicer into the matter, I laid open ſome caſes, wherein the bloſſoms unblown lay in a cluſter, as in a purſe, and there I obſerved, that generally to the foot-ſtalks of the ſingle bloſſoms there alſo grew a ſpur; only here the ſpur was very ſmall and ſhort, not of half a barley-corn's length, and very tender; theſe ſpurs advance in ſtature and ſubſtance as the contiguous bloſſom grows, and by that time the kid grows full, it will be as long as two or three barley-corns, and of ſtrength proportionable, like a pea's-ſtalk: ſo that one might well ſuppoſe a pod had grown on it, and been pulled off by ſome violence, but doubtleſs it is an effort in nature towards producing a bloſſom, ſince it is ſeated in the very place where a bloſſom grows, whenever the foot-ſtalk carries a double bloſſom; and I preſume in rich land, and a hotter country, there rarely fails being two bloſſoms on every foot-ſtalk.

Of the ſpur at the end of one of the ſtalks of the pea.

§. 24. I have obſerved, when ground is in good heart, and rain falls ſeaſonably to feed the peas, that their bloſſoms blow ſtrong (as before taken notice of); and further here I add, that the two outermoſt and

The leaves of the bloſſoms turning back a good ſign.

larger

larger leaves of the blossoms, which look like hoods, expand themselves in so strutting a manner as to bend backwards ; when they do so, it is a sure sign of vigour ; from such blossoms there will certainly come a noble kid ; whereas, when the blossoms blow blind or faint, some of them fall off, or tho' they should be strong enough to produce a kid, 'tis commonly but a poor one, and often of a ram's-horn figure ;— and it may often be seen, that, when the first blossoms blow vigorously, in a hot dry summer, (but to effect this, there must be good heart in the ground too) if the dry weather continues, the latter blossoms shall blow very sickly, and make but starved kids, and many of the buds will want strength to put forth a blossom, and wither ; yet if a lucky rain comes in time, it will save them, and so strengthen them, that they'll go on blowing with a lively colour.

*Sensation of plants, particularly peas.*

§. 25. By the expansion or contraction of the leaves of peas the degrees of the cold nights may be seen ; their flowers also, if put into warm water, will in an instant open ; which shews the wonderful consent of parts, and communication of particles in some plants, analogous to the spirits of men, by which there is such a quick sensation through the nerves.

*Peas not so well ripened nor so hard in the hill-country as in vale.*

§. 26. This year (1716) I housed my peas, as I thought, in excellent order, they having taken no rain, and being thoroughly ripe ; yet, when carried to market, they were softer than other peas, nor would they rattle when handled in the sacks like some others.——The reason of which must be, that in our hill-country the weather towards autumn is not hot enough to push them on to that thorough ripeness as in the vale, and as they must lie some few days in the field, after they are cut, to be thorough dry and hardened, so our days are cooler, and our nights both cooler and more dewy than in the vale, and therefore our peas are not dried to so great a degree

gree of hardneſs as theirs; and this difference (cæteris partibus) holds good in other corn between the hill-country and the vale.

§. 27. In Leiceſterſhire they ſet all their peas abroad in ſtacks, and houſe none, becauſe (as they ſay) ſetting them abroad gives them a good colour, whereas laying them up in a barn makes them look dark.

*Cuſtom in Leiceſterſhire.*

# VETCHES.

§. 1.[a] ACcording to Columella, if, when you cut up vetches and lupines green for food, you leave the roots to grow dry in the ground, they will impoveriſh, and take away all it's ſtrength; and he ſays, it is the ſame of beans.

*Opinion of the antients concerning vetches.*

§. 2. Farmer Biggs ſaid, vetches were the moſt profitable grain that could be ſowed; that a load of them would go farther than two load of hay; he ſaid farther, if they were ſowed on land ſomewhat light, where they would not run up very rank, they were excellent for ſheep, being reaped a little earlier than they are for the horſes, and when dried the ſheep would eat up every little bit of ſtalk.——Thomas Elton ſaid, vetches were the moſt profitable grain that could be ſowed, but he held that goar-vetches were apt to ſcour too much, eſpecially if the weather was wet and cold.—— Farmer Lake and farmer Bond agreed, that goar-vetches were beſt for horſes when they were juſt in kid, but earlier than that, eſpecially in cold and wet weather, they were too groſs, and not ſo hearty.

*Opinion of various farmers of the profit from vetches.*

§. 3. I was telling the abovementioned farmers, that ſome of my vetches ſeemed to be uncovered,

*Vetches will grow even without harrowing.*

---

[a] Si lupini et viciæ radices defecto pabulo relictæ inaruerint, ſuccum omnem ſolo auferunt, vimque terræ abſumunt, quod etiam in faba accidit. Columella, lib. 2. cap. 14. Pallad. ad idem, lib. 1. ſect. 6.

and

and not to have been harrowed enough. —They said, if vermin did not meet with them, vetches would work themselves into the ground, and that they had sown them when so much rain followed that they could not harrow, and yet had as good a crop of vetches as at other times.

Vetches improve ſtrong red clay-land. §. 4. I had a very fine crop of vetches in a falling white land, of about three loads upon an acre, yet the ſucceeding crop of barley was but ordinary; and indeed it ſeems to ſtand to reaſon, that a good crop of vetches is only a conſiderable improver of ſtrong, or red clay-land; for in ſuch land they do not only run ranker, whereby the halm betters it, but it alſo mellows ſuch land, which is very material towards a barley crop; whereas in poor white land, tho' the vetches may kid well, yet they ſeldom run to a good halm; nor is it material for white land to be hollowed and made light by the vetches, it's heavineſs being no defect before; therefore I hold, that, tho' a good crop of vetches be on a white and poor land, yet it is not a ſoil to be depended on, without folding, toward a barley-crop.

White land bad for vetches. §. 5. .I ſowed winter-vetches (anno 1703) on poor white land, and had but eleven load of vetches off ſeventeen acres, beſide the tythe, and yet it was a very wet dripping ſummer, which favoured their growth extreamly; otherwiſe there might not have been two load on the ſeventeen acres: this ought to be a caution not to ſow vetches on poor white land.

Not to crop vetches. §. 6. Wheat will endure the winter better than winter-vetches; for, if wheat loſes it's top by the cold, it will grow again, but if vetches are cropt, though they come to halm, they'll neither bloſſom nor kid. —— It is the ſame with peas as with vetches, if they are bit; — and if they kid not tolerably, the beſt way is to give them to the horſes.

§. 7. By

§. 7. By sowing a good quantity of winter-vet- ches there are several advantages, the least of which, and the most obvious, is to render the ground fit for a barley-tilt, and so knot-fine as to be capable (after it has been, if you please, winter-folded, as an addi-tional richness) of being ploughed up and sown on one earth.——And if the summer be wet, so as the meadows afford grass enough for hay, and the year is not encouraging, thro' frequent rains, to cut the vetches for dry fodder, and make them into hay, the seed however (preserved for sowing) is profitable. ——But the greatest benefit arising from vetches (in case the summer be burning-hot, so as the meadows afford little hay) is that in such time the vetches cut, when the flowering is just over, or when the pods are half full with seed, are of great use to supply the defect of hay, and make the nobler fodder for the year's being scorching ; for at such times the vetches are not apt to run to such lengths as to rot on the ground, and you have commonly a good season for making them into hay, and by cutting them thus early for fodder, viz. by about the 20th of June, you may hope to have ploughed up the ground again by the beginning of July, and sown thereon a crop of turnips.

§. 8. It is admitted by all knowing persons in husbandry, that a good crop of winter-vetches en-riches land more, and prepares it better for a crop of barley than a crop of peas does.———— One reason of this may be, because a crop of winter-vetches co-vers the ground longer than peas do.——But another reason seems probable to me, because honey-dews are bred and generated in great quantities in the joints of the stalks of winter-vetches, and in the fold-ings of their leaves (which increase the bud of the blos-soms) partly by the exterior dews, partly by the ex-sudations therewith mixing, being condensed by the heat of the sun, and boiled into a syrup, which con-

tains

tains fixed falts, and are afterwards by great rains washed off the vetches, and carried into the earth, to it's great enrichment.

§. 9. It is the general opinion of farmers I have talked with on this fubject, that winter-vetches always do beft after a barley-crop : I have tried them after oats with good fuccefs.

*Good after a barley-crop.*

§. 10. I have found by experience, that if winter-vetches are fowed on one earth, and on lay-ground, though clay-ground that turns up pretty mellow and rotten, yet they will, if a hot fummer comes, be more apt to blight than winter-vetches fowed on a clay-ground, which breaks fmall, after two or three former crops have been taken from it : fuch ground clofes better to the roots.

*Better after other corn than on a lay ground if fowed to one earth.*

§. 11. Farmer William Sartain of Broughton in Wilts fays, the rule in the vale for fpring-vetches being dear is, when there is a wet fpring, when, if the barley-land does not work well for a barley-crop, they like to fling in a crop of fpring-vetches in order for a winter-crop of wheat at Michaelmafs ; and from this principle a wet fpring has occafioned fuch a demand for fpring-vetches that he has, in fuch cafe, fold them for feven fhillings a bufhel.

*A wet fpring makes vetches dear.*

§. 12. As the drieft fummers make feed-vetches dear at Michaelmafs, fo they are more fo in cafe of a bad fummer for fown graffes, that is, in cafe the fpring of the foregoing year was fo dry that the fown grafs-feeds did not come up well ; for then, in the hill-country, the fcarcity of grafs, made more fcarce by a hot fummer, muft occafion the fcarcity of vetches.

*Dry fummers the fame.*

§. 13. If a hufbandman finds by the courfe of the winter that oats are dear, and like to be dearer in fummer, he is not wife, who takes not care to fow a good quantity of goar-vetches in the fpring, efpecially if they are cheap.

*Caution—to fow them if oats be dear.*

§. 14. Vicia

# VETCHES.

§. 14. Vicia multiflora, apud Ray, vol. 1. fol.
903.——Anglice tufted-vetches. —— Mr. Bobart of
Oxford assures me, that wheresoever this vetch
grows in the meadows, it is a sign of the land being
very rich.

*Tufted-vetches a sign of rich land.*

§. 15. I have sometimes known many quarters of
goar-vetches sowed only to the intent of ploughing
them in : the best way is first to roll them, before
you plough them, or else you could not make good
work, that is to say, the way is to roll one land upwards, and the other land downwards, that so the
plough need never to go against the grain, the vetches being first laid flat before the plough in the
rolling.

*Of plough-ing in vet-ches. Vid. sow-ing vet-ches.*

I spoke to Mr. Bishop of Dorsetshire of the husbandry of sowing goar or summer-vetches, and
ploughing them in instead of dunging. — He commended the way very much, and said, in many countries, where they had more arable than they could
dung, they had no way better than so to manage it ;
but doubtless the winter-vetches are more advantageous for that purpose, because the summer-vetches
would come up so late, that they could not plough
it up again early enough to summer-fallow it, whereas the winter-vetches would come up so early, that
the cattle might feed them down, and they would
afterwards be got up high enough to be ploughed in,
— but this husbandry is for deep land ; for in light
land upon a rock, where the rock is but four inches
beneath the surface of the land, the vetches so sown
would never come up.

If any think fit to sow vetches for ploughing in
under the furrow, in order to improve the land, I
think it easy to prove, that winter-vetches are pro-
perer for that purpose than goar or summer-vetches
are ; for though goar-vetches run much grosser, and
in that respect would be better ; yet, in regard they

**are**

are tender, and will not endure being sowed till spring, they cannot get to a sufficient growth for ploughing in till towards August, by which time the vigour of the sun, which should precipitate their putrifaction by raising noble salts from them; will be so much abated that little can be effected that way; whereas winter-vetches being sowed before winter, and having a root confirmed before spring to proceed on, will be forward enough to be ploughed in by a week or a fortnight in June, and the quantity of their salts, lying so much more under the power of the sun to extract them, will amply compensate the ground for want of the larger halm.

ᵇ The antients practised this husbandry of ploughing in winter-vetches, esteeming it equal to a coat of dung, as we learn from Columella.

Observation on the growth and blossoming of vetches.

§. 16. I took a view of my vetches in blossom to see in what different manner they blossomed from my peas (taken notice of before); and I found, that whereas good peas, that blow well, have two blossoms on the same stalk, on divided pedestals; so, good vetches have two blossoms growing close to the stalk at every joint.— I observed under the uppermost tuft of blossoms in some of the vetch-halm two blossoms at every joint of the four upper joints, and at some of the five upper joints; then three or

ᵇ Vice fimi lupinum certe præsidium expeditissimum est, quod cum exili loco circa idus Septembris sparserit, et inaraverit, (which is sowing under furrow) idque tempestive vomere vel ligone succiderit, vim optime stercorationis exhibebit; succidi autem lupinum sabulosis locis oportet cum secundum florem, rubricosis cum tertiam egerit: illic, dum tenerum est, convertitur, ut celeriter ipsum putrescat, permisceaturque gracili solo; hic jam robustius, quod solidiores glebas diutius sustineat, et suspendat, ut eæ solibus æstivis vaporatæ resolvantur. Columella, fol. 109 —But it seems that advantage cannot be made of the lupine-vetch in England; because it will die if sowed before winter; and if sowed in the spring, it will not be forward enough to answer these ends.

four

four lower joints had but one a-piece, and the halm
carried four or five joints lower, on each of which
there were very small woolly buds, but such as might
blow afterwards, if the weather proved favourable.
——From whence I infer, that, if vetches have their
complement of joints, they amount to fifteen, and,
if they carry their complement of blossoms, there are
two at each joint ; I observed no more on any joint,
and much of the halm had two blossoms only on the
two upper joints, and but one on the joints beneath,
and possibly left off blossoming at the fifth joint :
again I observed, that many seventh and eighth joints
carried two blossoms, when the uppermost had but
one blossom on each, and I found many of the fallen
or falling-off blossoms of the lower joints blighted.
Note, this was but in white land. ——— In another
field of vetches I afterwards observed but four or
five joints in a halm, and but one or two of the uppermost joints to have two blossoms.

It was this year (1712) observed by many farmers
that the vetches kidded at the top and not at the
bottom, that is, they run on, and spent many more
joints than usual without putting forth either blossom or kid : ——I thought the peas also did the same.
——— I am at a loss how to assign the reason why vetches and peas should some years run out into kid at
the lower joints first, and other years leave many
lower joints unfruitful ; unless it be, that the blossoms being all formed in a cluster, as before described, the clusters in wet years run on so fast and furi-
ously into joints, that they pass on too quick to make
a due formation of the lowermost blossoms ; by
which means the unformed bud of the blossom,
which nature designed for fruit, is converted into a
false birth, and an imperfect essay ; and so the same
evil happens from blossom to blossom, and makes
it late before this fury of the sap is spent, and fruit-

ful bloffoms perfected.———Again,—when a very
dry fpring happens, as this year it did during the
three latter weeks of April, and the whole month of
May ; it feems to me, that the buds of the lower-
moft bloffoms of the cluster, which doubtlefs are
firft formed in embrio, are ftarved through drought;
and fo the joints, on which they fhould have grown,
are left naked ; but by the coming of more favourable weather the upper joints prove fruitful ; fo that
a due medium in the temperature of the year between drought and wet feems to me to be the moft
fruitful feafon.——— Again, — I have obferved,
when two or three joints have bloffomed and kidded,
and more bloffoms, perhaps two or three gradations,
remained unkidded, the feafon of the year being early enough, and the weather at that time being warm
enough to finifh them into kids ; yet, if a feafon of
cold rain then came, thofe bloffoms would not produce kids, becaufe as it feems to me, a good medium or temperature of the air is neceffary for that
purpofe, in order to digeft the juices, which are chilled by cold rain, and dried up by hot burning weather.

**Of froft ripening goar-vet-ches.** §. 17. Walking with a farmer in fome goar-vetches in September (1700) they feemed very back-
ward, whereupon I afked him if he thought they
would ever ripen for feed ; he replied, when the
frofts came they would ripen ; — by which he meant,
that till then (the fun now declining in it's ftrength,
and there being great dews and long nights) the
halm would keep feeding on ; but when the frofts
came and checked the grofs nourifhing of it, then
the kids would fill better.

**Vetches, when blighted, not fo apt to open and fhed.** §. 18. I was queftioning whether fome winter-
vetches cut for feed fhould not be brought in, left
rain fhould fall and make the kids open, many of
them being dead-ripe ;—but the farmers faid, no
fear

fear of that, for tho' they might feem to be dead-ripe, yet they were alfo blighted, which is apparent by the fmallnefs of the grain (and fuch I obferved them to be) and therefore their kids will be tough, and not fo apt to open as at another time, when of the fame ripenefs.

§. 19. After all that has been faid of the great profit arifing from vetches, yet, if we compare it with that arifing from broad-clover, we fhall find the advantage on the fide of the latter, viz.

*Profit of vetches and broad-clover compared.*

| | | £ | s | d |
|---|---|---|---|---|
| Vetches | Sowing an acre of vetches at two bufhels per acre, and two fhillings and fixpence per bufhel ——— | 0 | 5 | 0 |
| | Ploughing and harrowing an acre | 0 | 6 | 0 |
| | Hacking or mowing ——— | 0 | 2 | 6 |
| | Total ——— ——— | 0 | 13 | 6 |

| | | £ | s | d |
|---|---|---|---|---|
| Broad-clover | Sowing twelve pound on an acre, at 3 d. per pound ——— | 0 | 3 | 0 |
| | Mowing an acre ——— | 0 | 1 | 0 |
| | Total ——— | 0 | 4 | 0 |

The difference in favour of broad-clover is —— —— 0 9 6

The labour of carting, reeking, thatching, and fowing are the fame ; but, if you buy the feed of each at market, the vetches are in carriage vaftly greater than the clover ; for a load of vetches, reckoning five quarters to a load, will fow but twenty acres, whereas a fack of clover will hold two hundred and fifty pounds, which will fow more than twenty acres. Again, the fecond year's crop of clover, (if you let it grow the fecond year) is a very great profit beyond the rent of the ground ; — fo that there is no reafon to fow winter-vetches in any ground that will well

X 2

bear

bear broad-clover; for it is certain, every thing considered, there is near twenty shillings disadvantage, communibus annis, by sowing vetches in land that will bear clover.


## REAPING and MOWING.

Of the time of cutting corn.

To be cut before it is full-ripe.

§. 1. [a] THE antients reaped their corn before it was full-ripe, as Pliny informs us.

It is certain there are very great disadvantages in letting some sorts of corn stand till it is full-ripe before it be cut.——First, both the chaff and the fodder are worse,—and, if such ripe corn takes wet, the increase in malt is lost, if barley, it having already spent itself,—— and if it be wheat, the flour is much the worse, and the wheat diminished,— but if corn be cut greenish, it will bear a pretty deal of wet without damage, for it will not drink up the wet like corn full-ripe; but rather only take in so much as to be kindly fed by it;—— but if any sort of corn be blighted, the sooner it is cut down, tho' but half ripe, the better, for nourishment can no more be conveyed to it by the straw, whereas by lying in gripp it will be fed: —— it is like feeding sick persons with clysters, when they can take no nourishment at their stomachs, or turning a child to weaning, when it will thrive no longer with the nurse's milk.

Especially weedy corn.

Corn that is full of weeds ought to be cut three or four days sooner than ordinary, that the weeds may have time to wither, and yet the corn not suffer by being over-ripe; whereas, if the corn in such case be full-ripe, it will be liable to take damage by brit-

[a] Secandi tempus cum spica deflorescere cœpit, atque roborari: secandum antequam inarescat. Plin. fol. 314.

ting

ting as well as loss of colour, or by rain, if it be kept out till the weeds are withered.

§. 2. If corn, or grass is so long as to lie down, they observe to cut with the corn, not against the head of it that is falling ;——but if it stand upright, they observe as much as possible always to cut cross the furrows, and the same in meadows, if there be any furrows, that they may cut the bottoms ; for, if they cut along the furrows, the rising lands will carry the scythe over the bottoms, so that it will leave the grass uncut. *Manner of cutting corn or grass that is lodged.*

§. 3. If corn comes in wet, or not well dried, though it will not take much harm in the mow, yet as soon as threshed, and laid together on an heap, it will in a week's time sweat and cling together ; and be as white with moldiness as if flour had been strewed on it ;—such corn therefore ought, as soon as threshed, to be sent to market, and sold. *Wet corn to be sold as soon as threshed.*

§. 4. It is said, for corn to lie in swarth a day is very good though a shower of rain should come ; for it makes it feel dry and slippery, and thresh the better :—and Mr. Edwards blamed a neighbouring farmer much for hurrying in his corn so fast, if there was but any likelihood of a shower ; whereas, said he, a day's rain never did it harm, but rather good, and wheat after cut was the better for a wet day. But, said farmer Biggs, there is nothing lost by carrying it in before such shower of rain may fall ; for, tho' it will feel cold, yet, not having laid abroad to take the sun and rain, it will not be shrunk so much as if it had done so, and the fewer grains will go to fill the bushel, and that will make amends. *Corn is better for lying a day in swarth after it is cut.*

§. 5. Mr. Edwards cautions me not to make great barley-cocks, nor great oat-cocks, but middling ones : if the corn be thick, said he, the task-workers will be for making great cocks, which the men cannot pitch into the cart, when they take off *Not to make great barley or oat-cocks, and why.*

X 3 the

the tops, unless they trample on the cocks, which makes the corn brit, especially when dead-ripe.

In hot summers to employ the more reapers to make expedition.

§. 6. In hot summers you are to consider, that wheat is plump, and full in berry, and the plumes or chaff starky, and not tough, as in cold wet summers, whereby it holds the corn the closer, and you ought to man your harvest accordingly by setting on in hot summers the more reapers ; for such corn, when scorched up by the sun, and full in grain, will soon take a stain, and damage by wet, and brit, and be blown out by the wind : when you have it dead-ripe, and of a good colour, it is all you can desire : therefore in such case the less it lies abroad in gripp or shock the better ; to which end the higher they cut the wheat, so as to cut the less grass, the better ; that it may be the sooner in order for carting.

Why they leave a high stubble in Leicestershire and Northamptonshire.

§. 7. The chief reason, as it seems to me, why in Leicestershire, Northamptonshire, and such deep lands, the farmer cuts the wheat high from the ground and leaves a high stubble, is because in low vale countries, where the land is rich and deep, and inclosed countries, the wheat, after it is cut, and lies in gripp, does not lie so exposed for the sun and wind to dry the gripps after being sogged with wet, as it does in the hill-country ; therefore the higher the stubble is left the gripps are thereby born up the higher, and lie the hollower from the ground, and consequently are the easier dried by the sun and wind.—It is also to be remembered, that the fatter and richer the land is the sooner the gripps will grow after they have taken wet, in case they lie on the naked ground, and sooner than they would in such case do in the hill-country, where the land is poor ; ——therefore it is very proper to leave the wheat-stubble the higher, that the gripps may thereby be born up from the ground ; besides, the shorter the sheaves are made the more the barns will hold,

hold, and the use of the after-stubble, which makes excellent * elm, will compensate the loss of the straw. * thatch. In some places they mow it for drying malt.

§. 8. The forwarder any countries are in their harvest, whether by the forwardness of the year, or the natural heat and warmth of the soil, so much the bolder may the husbandman be in leaving his wheat the longer abroad in the field, to take it's airings, and grow mellow, which makes it thresh better and look finer : for example, when the wheat-harvest falls out in the middle of July, or at least before the latter end of it, as it did anno 1714, there can be little danger in letting the wheat lie abroad four or five days, or a week, in case it be cut not over-ripe, even tho' a rainy day or two should come ; for at that time of the year the sun is so hot, the days so long, and the grass so short, and the dews for the most part so little, that the corn, tho' it has a good rain, soon grows dry ; whereas in the middle, or the latter end of August, the rainy season generally comes in, the dewy nights grow long, the grass rough, and the sun's drying power much abated, so that, if rainy weather should come, the wheat will be much more apt to grow.

*The forwarder and warmer any country is, the longer the corn may lay in gripp.*

§. 9. Red-straw wheat ought not to stand till it is so ripe as white-straw may do, because the red-straw wheat is much apter to brit, if wind should come ; therefore the common saying is, that red-straw wheat must be gathered knot-green, that is, whilst the knots in the straw are green.

*Red-straw wheat to be cut greener than white-straw.*

Beyond Winchester they cut red-straw wheat greenish to amazement, a fortnight earlier than we should do, and let it lie in gripp a fortnight, often turning it ; and for reaping, turning, and binding into sheaves, they pay six shillings per acre, whereas at Crux-Easton we pay four shillings, ——but they think theirs the best husbandry.

# REAPING and MOWING.

**Blighted wheat fhould be the fooner cut.**

§. 10. It is agreed, that wheat fhould be cut fooner for being blighted ; becaufe the ftraw of blighted wheat, by ftanding till the corn is full-ripe, will become fo brittle there would be no handling it. And it is farther agreed, that blighted wheat fhould be longer in gripp than other wheat that it may plim, which it requires more time to do : it will make it threfh better, and come the clearer from the hull.

**Blighted corn known by the mowers.**

§. 11. In mowing, a blighted patch of corn is known as foon as the mowers put the fcythes into it ; for it is foft and tough, and they had as good cut againft wool ; befides it is more-loofe, that is, loofe at root.

**Wheat for feed fhould be cut riper.**

§. 12. Wheat defigned for feed ought to be cut riper, or at leaft to lie a longer time abroad in gripp or fheaf than otherwife it need to do, or elfe, being for prefent threfhing, it will not come clean out of the ftraw, and the fofteft grains will beat flat ; but, if it be defigned for a reek-ftaffold, and for keeping, it will, by lying and fweating in the mow, tho' carried in fomewhat greenifh, and without lying in gripp or fheaf, come out of the ftraw, and threfh very well.

It is certain, that the gripps of wheat, tho' laid as light and hollow as poffible, will by the weight of the ears fall to the ground, and take harm, if fuffered to lie long out in wet weather ; though the ear of the gripp be fet hollow, yet it will fall lower than the root-end of the ftraw.

**Straw worfe for lying out.**

§. 13. Though moft corn is the better for lying in fwarth or gripps to take the dews, yet the ftraw is the worfe for it for fodder, except it was cut before it was ripe, and only lie till fufficiently ripened to be carried in.

**In hot dry fummers wheat need not lie long in gripp, and why.**

§. 14. Take notice,—in hot dry fummers, when corn ripens fully, and it's own virtue gives it a colour, and plumps up the berry ; there is no need

to

to let wheat lie out in gripp before it is sheaved, nor in sheaf, as you would do in a cold summer, unless it be very grassy or weedy; but in cold summers the wheat is horny, and wants a colour; and the berry is thin and wants to be plumped; and the chaff of the chesses is clung, and wants to be mellowed in order to make it thresh the better: whereas in good and fruitful years the grain is full and swells the chaff, even till it opens, and so the wet will soak in the sooner, and stain the colour of the wheat; and in such good years it ought to be considered, that the ears are heavy, and, when they are in shock, they spread and hang over, being lopheavy, whereby the sheaf opens wider, and lets the rain into the bonds sooner than in cold summers, when, the wheat being light, the ears in the shock stand more upright and closer together.

§. 15. It is most adviseable to turn gripps of wheat lying out very early after being cut down, in order to get them dry as soon as possible; by this means you keep them the longer from growing, in case of rain; for when gripps have lain some time sogged with wet, if dripping weather, or only driving mists should continue, all the art imaginable cannot prevent their growing. *Caution to turn the gripps.*

§. 16. In a hill-country, especially where there is cold clay-land, singular regard ought to be had in harvest-time, not to gripp up the wheat into sheaves too early in the day; for in such a country the gripps take so great a damp by having laid on the ground, that, tho' the straw, and chaffy ears may seem to be dry, when the dew is first gone off, and after the sun may have shined an hour or two on the gripps, yet there will remain an inward dampness in the corn, and in the inside of the straw, which being so reeked up will come damp from the reek at threshing time. ——— Therefore the after-noon *Not to gripp up the wheat too early in the day, in a hill country.*

noon is certainly beſt for gripping and binding into
ſheaves, but ſo that they may be finiſhed before the
heat of the day is over ; yet the bonds ought to be

laid in the morning, that they may not crack.—My
opinion farther is, that in ſuch a country corn can never be better houſed, if thorough ripe, and hard,
and not weedy, than by gripping and carting as faſt
as it is cut down ; for the dampneſs it takes by lying on the ground in the cold nights is not ſo eaſily
recovered.

§. 17. The farmers do not always look well after the
binding up of their ſheaves, but ſuffer the reapers,
for diſpatch, to bind the bonds juſt underneath the
ears, inſtead of binding them at the other end : the
conſequence of which is, that they will hardly hold
together to be ſlung into the cart at harveſt, and will
certainly be in great danger of falling to pieces before threſhing-time,

I was telling one of my harveſt women, that ſhe
muſt rake oats for me on the morrow morning ; ſhe
replied, it muſt be after the dew was off the ground,
for till that time ſhe ſhould be making bonds for
the ſheaves ſhe had gripped for the farmer ; for after
the dew was off they could not be made.——I aſked
her why ; ſhe ſaid, the ſtraw would not twiſt after
the ſun was up, but would be brittle, and break off
below the ears.

It rained in the morning while my wheat lay in
gripp, but ſeeming to hold up a little, I told one
of my reapers, he might make bonds. He replied,
unleſs it was like to be dry it was to no purpoſe to
make bonds ; for, when the bonds are made, they
muſt lay a gripp or two on them to keep them in
their places, otherwiſe the heat of the ſun will make
them untwiſt ; and therefore, unleſs it was likely to
to be fair, it is improper to lay the gripps upon the
bonds, for the bonds being preſſed down will grow

ſooner

sooner than any other corn, if rain should come, because they lying undermost cannot dry.

Sheaves ought not to be bound up wet ; if they be, they will be moldy : tho' the bonds must be made in the morning-dew, yet the sheaves ought not to be bound up till perfectly dry.

The reapers were complaining, the weather was so hot, that their bonds laid in the morning would not hold at noon, when they came to bind ; but, said they, old Cole's held ; for he turned three or four stubble or bottom-ends of the straw to the ears of the bond, which made them hold, they being thereby tougher, greener, and stronger.

If in harvest-time you foresee a little rain, it is best to gripp, and bind up into sheaves, because a little rain will so wet the grippings, that they cannot be bound up, and it may hold so, on and off, till greater rains come, but the sheaves being bound will soon be dry ; but if you foresee a hard rain, it is better not to bind up into sheaves, for the sheaves will then be wet to the bonds, and must all be opened again.

§. 18. If rain comes in harvest-time, with a driving wind, it is the most dangerous of any weather for sheaves of wheat, and for sheaves that are wet to the bonds it is worse, as all farmers do agree, than downright soaking rain. *Driving wind with rain the worst of weather for the wheat-sheaves.*

§. 19. In a wet harvest there is this benefit in making small sheaves, that being thinner at the top, and falling closer, the rain does not fall down into the middle of them, and so go through them into the bonds, as it is apt to do in great sheaves, which lie broader, and take a larger compass. *Of making small sheaves in a wet harvest.*

Care ought to be taken that the sheaves are made small, in case you are obliged to gripp and bind up wheat that is weedy, or thistly, into sheaves, as for particular reasons you may be, viz. for fear of rain, *For weedy corn.*

or

or on a Saturday-night, because you fear the weather on Sunday, that so the air, wind, and sun may have the greater power to dry them, which they could not do, if they were made large.

**To lay the sheaves flat the first night.** §. 20. Mr. Whistler and Mr. Edwards, men of very good judgment in farming matters, were of opinion that it was best the night after the wheat was bound, if the weather was not catching, to lay the sheaves, one by one, flat on the ground, whereby the straw would close together, and stand with the ears stiff and upright, and not be apt to lay open, and then five or six sheaves being put into the shock would abundantly better keep out the rain.

**Not to lay the ears in the furrows.** §. 21. Some of the reapers had laid the ears of the grippings in the furrows of the lands, and the halm-end out, whereas they ought to have laid the straw-end in the furrows, and the ears out, and then the ears would have stood sloping-up, and have lain dry, though rain had come, but the other way it would quickly have grown,—and so I found it to do.

**Of cocking wheat in Wilts.** §. 22 In Hampshire they never cock the wheat in the field, as they do in Wiltshire, whereby they may leave it out a month longer without damage : and, if they did so, the wheat would thresh much the better, for the air dries it ; whereas when carried forthwith into the barn, it is tough, and sticks to the chaff.

In making the wheat pooks in Wiltshire, the sheaves are set with the ears uppermost in the circle, and so on in every rundle, till at length it draws into a point ; and then the sheaf is opened and turned with the ears downward, like a shackle for a hive ; for an ear turned downwards will not grow, nor take wet by half a year's wet weather, and the bottom of the sheaf being broader than the top, every uppermost circle hangs over the sheaves of the undermost circle, like the eaves of an house. — In a pook may be

be put a load or two; it is a very good way to fecure corn againſt rain, and to give the weeds that
may be amongſt it a drying-time.—In my opinion
however this method is not to be uſed where the
wheat is deſigned for a ſtaffold, becauſe, if the
weather prove wet, mice will run thither for ſhelter,
and be carried in with the pooks.——Farmer Miles
ſays, in that faſhion, without thatching, they make
wheat-reeks in the Iſle of Wight.

§. 23. In wet harveſts, I adviſe, when the wea- <sup>Caution</sup>
ther clears up, to ſend ſome of the moſt diligent and <sup>regarding</sup>
ſkilful perſons into the field to ſearch the tythings of <sup>the ma-</sup><sup>nagement</sup>
ſheaves, and to obſerve well which lie moſt on the <sup>of the</sup>
weather-ſide, and ſtand moſt hollow, and open at <sup>ſhocks in</sup><sup>wet wea-</sup>
top, and to remove all ſuch together by themſelves, <sup>ther.</sup>
and place them to ſuch advantage, that the ſun and
wind may beſt go through them, moving them off
from the ſides of hedges, &c. and taking up ſuch
ſheaves as may be blown down.

After rainy weather, tho' the wet ſhould not have
gone to the bonds of the ſheaves, yet it is good,
when dry weather comes, to ſet the ſheaves of
every tything apart, ſo that the air may come to
every ſheaf, and particularly to take care to turn
the weather-ſide of each ſheaf to the wind to dry the
ſooner; for tho' the wet may not have gone to the
bonds, yet the ſheaves are inwardly cold and damp,
but will by this method be much ſooner fit to be
carted.

§. 24. My next neighbour, anno 1696, unſheaf- <sup>Damage</sup>
ed ſome of his wheat to dry it, and opened it, and <sup>from open-</sup><sup>ing the</sup>
turned it ſo often, that the ears broke off, whereby <sup>ſheaves to</sup>
he loſt half his corn; caution therefore ought to be <sup>dry them.</sup>
uſed in this caſe, leſt by curing one evil we create
a worſe.

§. 25. A ſmart ſhower of rain fell on my wheat- <sup>Wheat, if</sup>
ſheaves, and it was thought it went down to the <sup>wet at bond</sup><sup>only will be</sup>
bonds; whereupon, the next day being fair, the <sup>damaged</sup>
men <sup>in the reek.</sup>

men took apart each tything, and set the shocks upright at some distance asunder, spreading open the
ears of the shock to let in the sun and air ; —— but
afterwards my bailiff found that the rain had gone
through the bonds, so that he was for unbinding
them, and opening them to the sun ; — for he argued, that if the inside of the sheaves were but wettish
only, and from the ear to the bond were dry, such
sheaves would grow moldy in the reek, and strike
such a damp, that would cause many ears to grow,
and therefore he advised to open them.— I did open
them, and found them to be dampish, and some of
them wet beyond the bonds. This was done to six
load of wheat, and the sheaves were bound up again
without much loss of time.

§. 26. One of my reapers, when he had made up
some wheat into sheaves, the wheat being long-eared and lop-heavy, said, rain had not need meet with
those sheaves before they were carried home. —— I
asked him why so ; he said, because the ears being
long and heavy were bussle-headed, ——— that is,
did hang their heads downward into the sheaf, so
that (in case a rain should run down to the bonds)
neither sun nor wind could enter in to dry them,
whereas, said he, when the ears are short, and not
heavy, they stand upright and hollow, so that the
sun and the air may easily dry them.

*Wheat long-eared and lop-heavy should be carted soon for fear of wet.*

§. 27. I ordered my mowers to set their cradles
down as close to their scythes as they could, for the
benefit of the swarths, the barley being very short :
if they had not done so, they had lost half the corn ;
but their cradles carried the short barley together in
a swarth abundantly the better, by which means it
might be raked with less loss —— N. B. To see that
other mowers do the same in such case.

*Caution in mowing corn.*

§. 28. If one cuts grass, where stones are, with a
new scythe, and it should strike against a stone, the
scythe will break out into flakes, but an old scythe
that

*Cut grass in stony ground with an old scythe.*

that has been feafoned will only be blunted, and may eafily be ground out again.

§. 29. If corn harles or lodges, a fcythe cannot carry a cradle, becaufe the fingers of it will be pulled to pieces by the harled corn in drawing the fcythe back; but in that cafe, a bow on the fcythe is moft proper, which will carry the fwarth away before it altogether.

*A fcythe for cutting lodged corn.*

§. 30. The thinner and poorer barley and oats are, and the weaker in ftraw, they ought to be cut a little the fooner, and lie in fwarth; for otherwife the ftraw, if they are full-ripe, will not ftand againft the fcythe.

*Thin and weak barley and oats fhould be cut the fooner.*

§ 31. I fowed broad-clover with barley, and, by all the country-men's judgment, it was deemed proper to mow this barley a week fooner than otherwife it need to have been, becaufe the clover grew up rank, and it was agreed, that, if the barley ftood till it was full-ripe, or but near it, as the clover would require four or five hot days to dry it before it could be houfed with the barley, it would in that time, in cafe two or three days rain fhould fall, be turned black, whereas, being cut thus early, it would take no damage by fuch weather, but require to ftay abroad as long as the clover.

*If clover be rank in barley, the barley fhould be fooner cut.*

§. 32. I had barley this year (1702) knee-bent in a very extraordinary manner, and, being dead-ripe, it was crumpled down, and harled by contrary winds; I added my own men to the mowers for difpatch: but my men having only grafs-fcythes, which are not fo long as the others, could not difpatch like them; —— but farmer Biggs and farmer Knapp faid, that in this cafe the fhorter fcythes were more profitable to mow with than the others, and miffed lefs of the corn.

*Knee-bent barley to be mowed with a fhort fcythe.*

§. 33. Barley has been fo rank in fome places in a wet fpring that it has been thought fit to mow it, and

*Better mow than feed rank barley.*

and in such case it may be better to mow it than to feed it, because the scythe only takes off the rankest, but the sheep feed upon all indifferently.

**Of letting barley lie out in swarth.**

§. 34. This year (1702) the weather being encouraging, I left out barley five or six days in swarth, which, though both blighted and edge-grown, plimmed, and gained very near as good a colour as the best.

**Benefit of turning the barley swarths in wet weather.**

§. 35. The 30th of August (anno 1708) I cut barley from day to day, and continued to do so for a week; from the 30th of August, for three weeks together, we had every day rain, more or less, but most of the time rain fell plentifully every day.——— I ordered my barley in swarth to be turned every other day during these three weeks, to keep it from growing; and though the swarths during this time, that lay uppermost to the air, were hardly dry for any six hours together, ——— and the undermost barley of the swarths, which lay next the earth, was generally fogged every day, and dungish till turned, as abovesaid, yet I had none of my barley grew.——— This was chiefly owing to the late season of the year before our barley ripened, and the continued cold rains, which did not much forward the growing of the barley, as they would have done, had the harvest been forwarder; for, had the rain been accompanied with hot sun and glooms between, it would in half the time have made it grow. ——— I mention this, that in such case, when such a year may happen again, I need not to be frightened, as we all were this year: in our hill-country the winds also contributed much to save us.

**Oats on a side-land to be mowed earlier than on a flat.**

§. 36. The first year that I took one hundred and forty acres into my own hands, I had the side-lands sowed to oats. ——— It was agreed by every body, that those oats ought to be mowed two or three days sooner than if they were on a plain, because, say they,

if

if you let them be as ripe there as in a plain one should do, the straws will be so hard and dry that the scythe will skim over them.— The reason of this is, because in such ground a man has not so good a stand, nor can put that strength to the scythe, his swing being weaker, as he might do in a plain, and so the straw yields and bends. — Two acres of oats mowed per day in such land is accounted as good a day's work as three acres in plain land.

§. 37. My labourers came from mowing vetches to mow peas, not having their hackers with them, and they were loth to go home for them for a piece of a day: I soon came to them, and found that the scythe made great waste, and cut off abundance of the kids in the middle,—and they themselves could not but be ashamed of their work. I mention this, because I am told it is the custom in some parts of England to mow peas. *Peas hurt by mowing.*

§. 38. I am told, that between Caln and Chippenham the land is almost as light as ashes, and of about six shillings per acre, and that there they neither mow nor hack their peas, but pluck them up.— Quære, whether this was not, for the most part, the condition of the east-country-land, and whether their wool will not pull off better than with us. *Peas plucked up in light land.*

§. 39 The blue pea, or green pea, which is for boiling, is to be cut green, when the peas are thoroughly full-kidded, before the upper side of the kids toward the sun be turned, as they will turn white; for then that whitish half will not boil well, nor the peas sell in the market for boiling.——An old experienced farmer told me this, whereupon I went and gathered some of my own peas, which I thought not ripe enough to cut by ten days, according as the partridge-peas are cut, and when I shewed the kids, he said, by all means, it was fit they should be cut. I wondered at it, and asked if they *The blue or green pea for boiling should be cut early.*

would not turn black; he said, no, they would keep their green colour, though wet weather should come upon the halm, and turn it as black as a hat.—But they ought not to be threshed any time before they are boiled, or sowed; for in four or five weeks they will finnow.

**Partridge-peas, if cut green, turn black.**

§. 40. Mr. Jackson of Tackham assured me, that he sowed partridge-peas, which by having been cut green were turned as black as a hat, and yet he had as good a crop as he ever had: this crop I saw, and they were very good peas.

**If vetches do not kid well they should be sooner cut.**

§. 41. The different opinions of my two ox-hinds divided me much about the season of cutting my winter-vetches.——The one was for having me cut them when near full-kidded, and seemed most to regard the kids. ———— The other regarded the halm more than the kids, and said, the horses were as fond of the halm, if taken in season, as of the kids, therefore the halm ought not to be suffered, if one can help it, to rot on the ground—Farmers Elton and Oliver agreed, that if the vetches fell out of the kids into the manger, the horses would not eat them, and said, if vetches in the grain were set before horses, they would not care for them, so said Mr. Edwards's servant;—— but Elton added, there was moderation on both sides to be regarded, and extreams to be avoided, but, if the vetches did not kid well, he thought the best way was, especially if the season was like to be dry, to cut them the sooner, for so they would make the best fodder.

**Vetches should lay out before given to horses.**

§. 42. My winter-vetches were very well kidded, and almost fit to be cut, and housed for winter-fodder. ———— Several farmers were of opinion, they were then in very good order for horses; but if, whilst I gave them green to my horses, they were cut and laid on the ground two or three days to wither a little, they assured me
they

they would be more hearty; for it would take somewhat from their grossness.

§. 43. When you cut winter-vetches for winter-fodder, in the timing it you ought to consider, that when they are cut green, they require a long time to dry in, during which, especially if the weather be wet, the vetches will continue growing, and the kids, tho' lean when you cut them, and but two rinds, yet will fill out, and almost perfect their seed in the fortnight's time that they must, for the most part, lie abroad; therefore of whatever size you would have the berry of, you must cut the vetches at least a week before they come to that growth. —— You ought always to cut them so early that there may be no danger of their kids splitting, and shedding in the foddering with them, which they will do, in case you suffer them to be near ripe; besides, the riper you suffer the seed to be, the coarser will the straw or halm be at the bottom, especially if the vetches through a wet summer are grown gross.

*Time of cutting vetches.*

§. 44. If vetches are short, as being blighted, or otherwise, and dead-ripe, it will be difficult to hack them, but impossible to mow them, because their halm, which will be hard and dry, having no weight to bear against the scythe, will yield, and the scythe will slip over them.

*Vetches short and dead ripe cannot be mowed.*

§. 45. When I was mowing my meadows at Eatton (anno 1701,) about nine in the morning, one of my mowers began to complain, that about this hour, when the dew went off the grass, was the worst time of all the day for mowing grass: and so it is, said he, for corn too.——How, said I, worse than at noon, and after? he said, yes.——Then I went to the other mowers, who were mowing in another part of the meads, and asked them at what time of the day the grass mowed best; they all said at noon. Why, said I, your fellow says—, &c. (as above)

*Grass mows best at noon.*

Y 2

above) and therefore before the dew is gone off, I thought had been the best time.——They said, no; a hard scythe will cut the grass best at noon, but a soft scythe while the dew is on the grass.—— Why then, said I, do they say (if noon, which is in the heat of the day, be best) that the grass cuts best after rain? for in this dry time we have at present, I hear you complain of the ill mowing of the grass.—— They said, that is, because the drought has lain so long upon the ground as to make it hard, so that when the scythe cuts close, it dances upon every little roughness, whereas, was the ground a little moistened with rain, the scythe would cut it, and every little excrescence would be pared off; and then the scythe would not scratch so often, nor so often be blunted.——— I went to the first, and asked him of the truth of what they said, and he said it was so.—— So that it seems they were both in the right; and though grass mows best at noon, yet it mows worst, when the dew is just going off: the reason they could not give me, but I suppose, that on the first going off of the dew the grass is not stiff enough to stand so strong against the scythe, nor so heavy, nor weighty as when it was loaded with dew, which made it lie close; yet at noon, when the grass was become dry and stiff, it stood closer than when the dew was on it.

§. 46. In our hill-country, where grass is short, I hold it best to give one shilling and six-pence per day for mowing; I rather choose to do so than to agree by the acre, that the work may be more carefully done.

§. 47. As one of my labourers, an old experienced hind, was mowing, he complained of the old rowet, that hindered him, and deadened his scythe.—— It was some time before I knew what he meant; at length he pulled up some spiry tough capillary grass,

about

*Better to mow by the day than the acre in the hill-country.*

*If grass be not fed clean against spring, the old rowet damages the grass and blunts the scythe.*

about three inches long, which was the old winter-grass : It seems I had not fed the grass down so low as I should have done against spring, which did harm to the young grass that was to be cut ; for, if that had been fed better, the young grass would have come away thicker, and not have choaked up the scythe. He compared it to the young wool, which (when sheep have been pretty well kept in winter, and then checked in the spring) comes up under the first wool, and deadens the shears, so as to make it troublesome to cut with them.

§. 48. I was mowing broad-clover, where some *Grass, tho' thin, should* of it in gully-places was short, and I proposed to *be cut.* miss those pieces, and not mow them, but the mowers were against it, and said, the shortest, when mowed, would come away much better for mowing, and fill towards the next crop.—Mr. Edwards being present said, that farmer Elton had once some poor patches in his mead, which, being short, he would not be at the charge of mowing, but those patches were thinner for it afterwards in future crops.

# RAKING.

§. 1. THOUGH mowing and raking of *Two rak-* corn are the same price per acre, yet *ers to one* you must have double the number of rakers that *mower.* you have of mowers, in order to make equal dispatch, because the mowers have not the lets and hindrances that the rakers have : the mowers can continue mowing in moderate rain, as well as begin early in the morning, whereas the rakers are stopped with every shower, and commonly lose two or three hours in the morning in staying till the dew is off the ground.

§ 2. If the land be stony, and the straw of the *Rake the* barley short, it will do well to rake up the barley *barley and cock it soon* and cock it soon, lest rain should come ; for rain will *in stony* 

*10 land.*

so beat the barley into the ground, that there will be no raking up half of it.

**To employ men rather than women at raking barley.**

§. 3. Anno 1701, my broad-clover came up with my barley so high, that they were forced to cut the barley under the ear : I thought the barley would rake much the better for the broad-clover, inasmuch as it would be kept up from sinking into the ground.

—— But the mowers said, no; that the broad-clover was so long and thick, and the stubble left so high, that it would be hard work to run the fork along under the swarths, as also to draw the teeth of the rake through the mattings of the grass.—— I believe therefore it would be more for the farmer's interest to employ men at this task than women.

**One to rake oats after the cart——two to rake barley.**

§. 4. One person is counted sufficient to rake oats after the cart ; unless in a very high wind, but to rake after the barley-cart, be the wind never so still, two persons are always reckoned necessary.——

## CARRYING of CORN.

**When barley is short two, pitchers to one loader**

§. 1. WHEN the barley-straw runs very short, it is good husbandry to have two pitchers to one loader in the field ; otherwise time will be lost.

**Wet corn to be put round the sides of the barn.**
**Blighted wheat to be carried as soon as can be.**

§. 2. If a load or two of corn comes in wet, in case your barns are boarded, it will do well to scatter it round about the sides of the barn.

§. 3. If wheat be struck with the blight, the straw in such case is hollow and spungy, and easily drinks in wet ; therefore, if the corn be tolerably dry, and in order, and the weather be anywise suspicious, it is adviseable to get it into the barn as fast as possible ; for if such loose straw should once soak in wet, and showery weather should follow, it will be much longer before it can be got dry, and fit to be carted, than other corn.

§. 4. A

§. 4. A rimy day is better to carry home oats in <sup></sup> than a hot day; for in hot dry weather the oat-straw will be so sleek, that it will be troublesome loading and tying it together, so as not to slide off from the cart, or not to swag to the side the cart may lean on, and so over-turn it.—Again, oats will be tougher, and less apt to brit in carrying on a rimy day than on a hot burning day.

To carry oats in rimy wea-ther.

§. 5. Mr. Hillman, and another experienced farmer, said, it was most profitable at harvest to carry light loads near home, and bigger loads farther off, not only because, in case it be near home, the larger loads take up more time in binding them, but also because one man can pitch down at the barn faster than two men in the field can pitch up, especially after the load rises to a height.

Carry ligh loads near home, and larger far-ther off.

## T H R E S H I N G.

§. 1. IT appears from Hammond, on Matt. iii. 12.—the Jews threshing-floors were on the mountains, and open fields, where the wind could have free access, and so it is, he says, in some parts of Spain.—By Varro it appears the threshing-floors were generally uncovered, yet some were otherwise, but the uncovered threshing-floors were laid round that the water might run off. Lib. 1. c. 55.

Thresh-ing-floors of the anti-ents, and in hot coun-tries.

ª In some places they threshed out their corn with flails on a floor, in others they trod it out with mares, and in others beat it out with poles.

§. 2. It seems the antients had some use for chaff, viz. in making of floors, though palea signifies indeed straw as well as chaff. Cato, fo. 18.

Used chaff or straw in their floors.

ª Messis ipsa alibi tribulis in area, alibi equarum gressibus exteritur, alibi perticis flagellatur. Plin. lib. 18. c. 30.

§. 3.[b] In countries subject to rain they had their barns contiguous to their threshing floors, and their floors also were covered, of which see Varro, fo. 34. —— Some, he says, fortified the sides of their floors with stone, others made an entire stone pavement; he agrees with Cato, that rubbing the floors with the lees of oil was necessary to prevent the growth of weeds in them, and a protection against vermin, particularly ants and moles, to which oil is poison.

*Earthen floors in Leicestershire.*

§. 4. Mr. Tate was finding fault with the stone and earthen floors of Leicestershire, and said the farmers were wedded to them, notwithstanding one Sturt (as I think he named him) who lived at Wickham, and had been the greatest commissioner in England for buying up corn, had assured him, that those floors communicated such dampness to the wheat, that it was the worse, either for keeping or exporting, by six-pence in the bushel.

*Threshing in hot countries.*

§. 5. In Italy, and other hot countries, they usually thresh and winnow their corn as soon as they have cut it down, or at least a great part of it, and this is done, before they bring it into the house, on a floor made in the open air. —— Being kept poor they have but very small farms; —— and I am apt to believe that in Judea they did thus, because their possessions were cantoned into so small divisions. See Ray, fo. 402.

[b] Amurca perfundere solent areas, ea enim herbarum est inimica, et formicarum, et talparum venenum; quidam aream ut habeant solidam, muniunt lapide, aut etiam faciunt pavimentum: nonnulli etiam tegunt areas ut in Bagiennis, quod ibi sæpe id temporis anni oriuntur nimbi. Varro, fo. 46.

Arcas amurcâ conspergito, sic herbæ non nascentur. Cato, fo. 14.

Quatenus ad aream; huic autem nubilarium applicari debet, maximeque in Italia. propter inconstantiam cœli, quo collata semitrita frumenta protegantur, si subitaneus imber incesserit: nam in transmarinis quibusdam regionibus, ubi æstas pluviâ caret, supervacuum est. Columella, lib. 1. fo. 93.

§. 6. Iron-

§. 6. Iron-clayted shoes do not well to thresh wheat in, especially if it be new corn ; for such shoes squat and bruise it much : a thresher's shoes should by right be soled with an old hat.

§. 7. One of my servants being threshing peas, I asked him whether the floor was not too small for two men to thresh in together ; he said, no, not to thresh peas in, but it was too small for two men to thresh barley, or other corn in, because the flail makes the straw of light corn fly away, and the threshers must keep moving to follow it, and so would be streightened for room ; but a wad of peas, when laid down on the floor, not only lies heavy, but harles together also, and lies for the most part in the same place it was at first laid down in, and so the threshers need not keep moving, but stand in one station, by which means they will not stand in each other's way.

§. 8. A good thresher assured me, that twelve bushels of oats were counted a good day's threshing, but he had lately for several days together threshed fourteen bushels, and winnowed them ; but those oats yielded extraordinary well. He said likewise, that twelve bushels of barley was a good day's threshing, and in the country the common price was eight-pence per quarter ; but five or six bushels of wheat was a very good day's threshing, and, in case the corn was clung, and yielded ill, sometimes three bushels was as much as could be threshed in a day.

I have for some time been uneasy about the small quantity of wheat my threshers used to thresh in a day : my best thresher seldom in any year exceeded a sack in a day : I had this day (November 5th anno 1714) a serious argument with him about it, another good thresher being present.—The first persisted, that it was well known to the threshers of the country that they could as easily thresh six bushels

of

of wheat in a day at Netherton-farm, it being a warm gravelly bottom, as they could thresh four bushels in a day at Ashmonsworth, or Crux-Easton, for on such cold lands the corn threshed tough.——— The other said, he had threshed at Netherton-farm for two or three years, and that they commonly reckoned the same difference in threshing, as above-said, between the wheat of that farm and the wheat of the cold hill-land of Faccomb, where the village stands. ——— So that the difference between the cold hill-lands, and the warm vale-lands, with regard to threshing, I now look on as a settled point.——— And note,—in such a cold hill-country as our's at Crux-Easton is, men thresh harder to perform their day's-work than in the vale, where the corn threshes easi-er, because the stroke of the flail must in such cold countries be forced down stronger, to beat out the corn, than in the vales, where a lighter stroke does more work.

It is to be considered, that Faccomb, and my neighbours wheat yields more in a day's threshing than in the clay-lands, because their lands being lighter, the straw runs shorter, and consequently more sheaves are laid on the floor, and the more ears of corn must therefore be laid there; whereas on my clay-land the straw runs longer, and con-sequently the fewer sheaves and ears of corn are laid on the floor to fill it.

§. 9. One week in particular our wheat yielded very little flour in grinding, and had abundance of bran, of which the miller also complained.——— My thresher assured me, the reason was, because I had threshed that wheat whilst the weather was damp; for, said he, then the wheat will be cold, and will not grind well, notwithstanding the weather be ever so dry afterwards: but if threshed dry, and put into sacks, it will not afterwards grow heavy, and

*yet*

Wheat to be threshed in dry wea-ther.

yet if threſhed in open weather, and then put into ſacks, it will be muſty in leſs than three weeks time.

§. 10. The beards of the barley will come off much better in threſhing for the ſwarth taking the dew. Of threſh-<br>ing barley.

§. 11. I had a mind to threſh out ſome vetches in the field; they were ripe, but a little ſoft, on which, intending immediately to ſow them, I aſked the farmer, (ſhewing him them) if they were not too ſoft to threſh; he ſaid, all the danger was that, if threſhed on a floor, the flail and the man's feet would bruiſe and break them, but to threſh them on a hurdle, with a cloth, would do well. Of threſh-<br>ing vetches<br>when ſoft<br>with damp.

§. 12. I was aſking a good farmer in my neigh-bourhood, whether it was beſt to carry rye-graſs, or clover-hay for ſeed, to the barn, or the reek, and threſh it out afterwards, or to threſh it out in the field at hay-making; the farmer ſaid, they did it both ways, but, ſaid he, I think the beſt way is to threſh it out in the field; for, if the ſun be hot, it will brit very much, and there will be great loſs in carrying it home, eſpecially if you go through nar-row lanes, and then it will ſlack and give in the mow ſo that it will threſh but ordinarily, whereas, if threſhed in the field about noon, when the hay is dry, one man will threſh as much as three men can do the other way. Rye or<br>clover-hay<br>beſt threſh-<br>ed in the<br>field.

§. 13. ᶜ As my bailiff was winnowing peas for ſeed, I obſerved a vaſt quantity of charlock among them; he ſaid, it could not be helped; for charlock Caution—<br>to ſcreen all<br>ſeed corn.

---

ᶜ Mr. Duhamel tells us, it is a cuſtom in that part of France he writes of —— to half threſh the ſheaves without untying them, when there is a great deal of weed among the wheat. By this means, ſays he, they get the ripeſt and beſt grain, and few ſeeds of weeds; for the weeds being ſhorter than the wheat, are generally at the bottom of the ſheaves. Pag. 188.

was

was a feed that the fan would not feparate from any
fort of corn, but it might be done with the fcreen.
—— So I ordered them to be fcreened before they
were fowed, and I advife the fame to be done with
all forts of corn defigned for feed.

Moft chaff
produced
by wet
harvefts.

§. 14. Farmer Riggs, and farmer Briftow were
faying, that all forts of corn yielded but few hulls this
year (1702.) (Note, it was a very dry fummer and
harveft). I afked them, what might be the reafon
of it; they faid, that wet harvefts made the hulls
come off the wheat-ears much more than dry ones,

* beards.

and likewife the * oyls from the barley, but efpecially the fmall feathery hulls that are at the bottom
of the barley-ears ; and in fuch years the ftraw
threfhes very brittle, and breaks into little pieces,
which adds much to the heap of hulls : it is alfo poffible the oyls may grow longer in wet fummers.

Of a ftraw-
houfe.

§. 15. Allow, if you can, an empty fpace of barn-
room in harveft-time, to receive the litter, and fod-
dering-ftraw, that you threfh out before cattle may
come to fodder ; otherwife fuch ftraw will be fpoiled by throwing it into your back-fide.

# R E E K S.

Houfing
fummer-
corn pre-
ferred to
reeking.

§. 1. I A M upon experience an enemy to reeking
corn abroad that you have barn-room for,
except it be wheat : if you propofe to threfh out
your corn within the compafs of a year, the damage
it may take by mice in fo fhort a fpace is inconfiderable, efpecially if by harveft-time you have got
the dominion over the mice by ftore of cats, which
a gentleman delighting in hufbandry ought to value as much as many do their hounds : the damage
fuftained by mice will, I fay, be inconfiderable in
comparifon of the charge of reeking corn abroad.
The computation of which laft will run thus, viz.
fuppofing

suppofing it to be an oat, or a barley-reek of thirty
two load, fuch a reek cannot well be fuppofed to be
finifhed in lefs than two days; in loading and
pitching to reek muft be employed,————

|  | l. | s. | d. |
|---|---|---|---|
| Seven men at harveft-wages —— | 1 | 8 | 0 |
| Two teams of horfes, two days | 0 | 14 | 0 |
| Thatching ———— | 0 | 3 | 0 |
| Two load of ftraw —— —— | 0 | 15 | 0 |
| Elming —— —— | 0 | 2 | 0 |
| Stowing it in the barn afterwards feven men, a day ———— | 0 | 7 | 0 |
| A team of horfes, a day —— | 0 | 3 | 6 |
|  | 3 | 12 | 6 |

Befides damages by birds devouring the fides, and
in hard weather pulling off the thatch, accidents by
wet, charges and wafte in taking in, and hindrance
from taking it in, it may be a month, by hazy weather, or by not being able to fpare people to do it,
whereby many inconveniencies may be fuftained,
and the mice to be maintained are near the fame.

§. 2. It is a common folly of the bailiff or other
fervants in hufbandry to act without apprehenfions
of rain, when there is no appearance of it : if reeks
are making in hay-time, or harveft, tho' the mafter
has provided ftraw in abundance to fecure them,
yet, becaufe the day's-bufinefs begins early in a
morning, the fervant is loth to beftow the time in
carrying fo much ftraw to the reeks as would fecure
them in cafe of bad weather, and, becaufe the bufinefs of carting holds out late in an evening, the fervants

*Negligence of fervants in not fecuring reeks againft wet weather.*

vants are loth to leave a half-made reek secure against all weather by pitching up straw enough upon it. —— It is the master's business therefore to consider the temper of servants, and, if such works may be termed works of supererogation, to gratify with good ale rather than let them be undone.

*Barley-straw not equal to wheat for thatching reeks.*

§ 3. I laid abundance of barley-straw on the ridge of a long vetch-reek, and brought it up sharp; I believe when the reek was cut the straw was three foot thick, and yet the wet had run through this covering, and done considerable damage to the vetches :——— the reasons of it were two; first, barley-straw is more woolly and spungy than wheat-straw, which is close and hard ; secondly, the reek sweated and heated pretty much, and it is observed in such case the covering of straw is hollowed, and softened, and the reek thereby the apter to drink in the wet.

*Of making a wheat-reek.*

§. 4. I made my wheat-reeks on staffolds, and, when I came to thatch them, I made a question whether the perpendicular-side to the weather should not be thatched as well as the eaves ;—— my thatcher said, it was needless;—— I replied, that farmer Crapp had told me, though he had housed wheat in a reek-house, yet for want of having the sides boarded, the wind had blown the rain against the sides of the reek, so that it had received great damage.—— The thatcher replied, he knew of that very well ;—— for they had not minded to lay the ear-ends of the sheaves uppermost and upon a rise, all along as they made the reek, and to lay the straw-ends of the sheaves downwards ; which if they had done, it had been impossible for the rain to have drove upwards to the ears ; but on the contrary, in making the reek they laid the straw-ends of the sheaves higher than the ear-ends : consequently the rain that was blowed into the straw-ends must necessarily run downwards to the ears.

Harry

Harry Miles of Wiltshire was saying, that people in our country have not the way of making a reek well ; for as they work it up, they should still keep the middle full, and then, when the reek sinks, that will throw the sinking of the reek to the outsid , and so make the outside lie the closer ;—whereas, if the middle be left hollow, the reek will fail-in in the middle, and the outside will be hollow.

It is proper in topping a wheat-reek to use a load or more of small sheaves, according to the size of the reek, because a reek cannot be so conveniently drawn-in and narrowed at top with great long sheaves as with slender short ones ; therefore your husband-man ought to take care to order such to be provided, and out of the same ground from whence he makes his reek, in case he means to lay only the corn of a particular ground in the same reek.

Though a wheat-reek be well made, yet the bonds of the outer sheaves will be apt to grow, if long unthatched.

§. 5. We were setting up an oat-reek designed to contain twenty load, but by the foundation of faggots I rather judged it fit to hold forty load ;— but the work-men said, the case was different between oats and barley ; for barley-straw, being rough-er in it's oyls, would not slip and slide as oat-straw would, it being sleek and slippery ; therefore barley might be over-laid the foundation on all sides as much as you pleased, but an oat-reek, which way so-ever it inclined, would be apt to slip away and tumble down ; therefore an oat-reek must not be widened beyond the foundation ; especially if the corn is carri-ed in dry, as this was, and so the more likely to slip. *Of making an oat and barley-reek.*

§. 6. Farmer Wey of the Isle of Wight, ob-serving sparrow-holes under the eaves of a reek, said, if the birds roosted in those holes o'nights, it *Of mice in a reek.*

was

was a certain sign there were neither mice nor rats in the reek, for if there were, they would by their squeaking and running about at night so disquiet the birds, that they would not endure it : he had, he said, heard many ancient husbandmen make that observation.

Peas and wheat keep damp in reeks in the hill-country.

§. 7. I took-in a load of great partridge-peas out of a reek that was well thatched, and had stood a year and an half : to my great surprize the peas were as soft as when the reek was made, but they were sweet and sound ; I kept the reek for my horses.——The reason of their softness doubtless was the damp winter-air, and Crux-Easton mists, which the strong winds had forced into the very middle of the reek :——I made the same observation a little before of a wheat-reek I kept over the year, and threshed the latter end of the second winter.

Of a hay-reek.

§. 8. A great matter depends on the well reeking of hay, for hay will often swag and pitch in the reek after making, and must then be filled out with thatch to make it shoot off the rain as well as the rest of the reek.

Of the form of a reek, and it's heating.

§. 9. If a reek of hay be not well brought in, it will be apt to heat, and in that case a long reek is best, because it may be made as long, and as narrow as you please, and therefore will not be so apt to heat ;—but there is the most loss in such a reek, because more of it, in proportion to what it contains, lies exposed to the weather ;—— therefore, if it be well dried, and well brought in, a round reek is the most profitable ; nevertheless, if it be water-meadow-hay, let it seem never so dry, I hold a long reek to be best, for such hay will, notwithstanding it's dryness, be apt to heat. —— That indeed might be prevented by keeping the middle of the reek hollow from the bottom to the top ; but, when that is done,

all

all the sides of that hollow will be very finnowy, and a pretty deal of waste will be made that way too.

§. 10. Farmer Biggs, as we were speaking of the diverse ways of securing a reek of ill-got hay from heating, said, after I had told him of other ways, that they had of late years (before anno 1700) found by experience, that to cut a side-hole through the middle of the reek, of about four foot, or four foot and an half diameter, and to secure it by under-propping it with wood, was the best way, and the same method was used to prevent corn from mow-burning, either in a barn or in a reek. *Of secureing hay from heating.*

I observed at farmer Pain's at Gausuks in the Isle of Wight, in a hay-reek cut into the middle some faggot-ends appear; I asked him the meaning of it; he said, it was an excellent way to preserve and secure a hay-reek from heating, which was done in this manner; —— within about a yard of the bottom of the reek they fixed the first faggot end-wise, and then filled up the hay round it, and then placed another, and so on till within two or three foot of the top, and then they covered it, so that no wet could fall down to hurt the reek, and let it sweat for three weeks, during which time it would smoke like a chimney, and after that you might take out the uppermost faggot, and fill up the vacancy with hay, and then top-up the reek and thatch it for the winter.

§. 11. Last summer (anno 1701) I made a hay-reek, and a hard rain came upon it before it was thatched; but the mishap was, I thatched too soon after the rain was over, that is, before the outer-coat was well dry: in opening it for winter-spending I found, that as deep as the wet and the damp of it had struck-in so far the hay was finnowy, and dead, whereby I might lose a load of hay; but in case I *Not to thatch a hay-reek after rain till it is quite dry.*

had not thatched it till the outſide had beenfully dry, the hay had recovered it's old ſweetneſs, and ſuffered no damage.

§. 12. Being informed that a vetch-reek I had ſet up had heated, I went to obſerve it, and, thruſting my hand into it, all along the ſide againſt which the wind ſet I felt no heat, nor in that end that took the wind oblique, but at the farther end from the wind, eſpecially towards the farther corner of that end, it was conſiderably hot within ſix inches of the outſide; ſo that it is the wind that drives the heat to and fro in a reek, and cauſes the pitching and yielding of it to that ſide it drives the heat to, and that vetch-reek, the wind being changeable, did for a week after it was made accordingly pitch from ſide to ſide.

*Of heating.*

# G R A N A R I E S.

*Of keeping wheat.*

§. 1. [a] SOME, ſays Varro, have their granaries raiſed high above the ground, and ſome make them under ground, but in either ſort they take care to keep out air and moiſture, for if they get in, they will breed the weevil. Wheat ſo laid up has kept good for fifty years.

§. 2. Brown quotes authorities, that in Ægypt wheat laid up in the ears in granaries has laſted one hundred and twenty years, and ſays, more ſtrange it may ſeem, how after ſeven years the grains conſerved ſhould be fruitful for a new production; for Joſeph delivered ſeed to the Ægyptains to ſow their

---

[a] Aliqui ponunt triticum in granaria ſublimia, &c.——Aliqui ſub terris, &c.——Et curant ne humor, aut aer tangere poſſit, quo enim ſpiritus non pervenit, ibi non oritur curculio; ſic conditum triticum manet vel annos quinquaginta, &c. Varro, fol. 47.

land

land for the eighth year; and Theophraftus fays, feed of a year old is the beft for fowing, that of two years old is not fo good, but, when more than three years old it is quite barren, but proper however for bread-corn.—Yet feeing corn may be made to laft fo long, the fructifying power well may be conceived to laft in fome good proportion, according to the reafon and place of it's confervation. Theophraftus fays in another place,—In a certain part of Cappadocia called Petræ wheat has preferved it's fructifying power even to forty years, and has been good for fowing.[b]

§. 3. In

[b] Mr. Tull fays, the moft fecure way he knows of preferving wheat is by drying it, and relates a ftory of a neighbour of his in Oxfordfhire, who acquired a large fortune by this practice. His method was to dry it on a hair-cloth, in a malt-kiln, with no other fuel than clean wheat-ftraw; never fuffering it to have any ftronger heat than that of the fun. The longeft time he let it remain in this heat was twelve hours, and the fhorteft time about four hours; the damper the wheat was, and the longer intended to be kept, the more drying it required; but how to diftinguifh the degree of dampnefs, and the number of hours proper for it's continuance on the kiln, he faid, was an art impoffible to be learnt by any other means than by practice. His fpeculation, that put him on this project, was, that it was only the fuperfluous moifture of the grain that caufed it's corruption, and made it liable to be eaten by the weevil. When dried, the bakers allowed it to work better than new wheat, and every grain would grow after it had been kept feven years.

As the method propofed by Mr. Duhamel for the prefervation of corn, by ventilation and kiln-drying, not only appears reafonable and practicable, but has, according to him, been confirmed by experiments, I have here given an extract from his book, as a hint to the reader, referring him, for farther fatisfaction, to the original, where he will find draughts of the buildings, and inftruments made ufe of for this purpofe.

## Mr. D U H A M E L on the Prefervation of Corn.

After having expatiated on the neceffity and ufe of preferving corn in granaries, efpecially in France, where they are frequently in danger of famine, he proceeds as follows.

Confideration des grains 1753. To Page 12.

Z 2

§. 3. In difcourfe with feveral notable farmers on country affairs, they feemed to agree, that a brick granary, except lined within-fide with boards, would damp

To preferve corn according to the common method requires immenfe granaries which muft be very dry, and built very ftrong, and, in thofe who have the care of them, great affiduity, fkill, and probity are requifite ; and we may conclude that the want of fuch edifices, and the difficulty of procuring proper perfons to have the care of them, is the reafon that magazines are not fo much multiplied as could be wifhed.

I hope, fays he, by the method I fhall propofe, to obviate all thofe inconveniencies. By thefe means a large quantity of corn will be preferved in a fmall compafs, without danger of heating or fermenting ; it will be fecured from the depredations of animals and infects ; and you need not fear even the incapacity or infidelity of thofe that are employed to take care of it ; and all this without trouble, and at a very fmall expence. But before I propofe my method, I fhall defcribe the common practice of the provinces about Paris. The inconveniencies will be eafily perceived, and you will be better enabled to judge of the great advantages arifing from the method I propofe.

Page 14. When corn is laid up in a granary with intent to be kept a great while, the cuftom is to fpread it only eighteen inches thick ; 'tis true that, when it is old and very dry, the granary perfectly free from moifture, and the joifts ftrong enough to fupport the weight, they may lay it fomewhat thicker ; but as we muft fix on fome determinate height, I chofe this as the moft common in large granaries. That the corn may not lie againft the wall, they generally have a paffage of about two foot all round. By this means they prevent the corn from being loft by running down the chinks that neceffarily happen at the edges of the floor ; they remove it from the holes made by rats and mice ; they take care to prevent the dirt, which falls chiefly from fuch places, from mixing with the corn ; they remove it from all moifture that may come from the fweating of the walls, or from any defect in the roof : laftly, the grain is more expofed to the air, and they contrive to leave a paffage for it's reception. This is the cuftom generally obferved, and probably has been found neceffary.

Page 15. The corn being thus removed from the walls, the fides of the heap make a declivity, which as far as it reaches, contains but half as much as if the fides of the heap were perpendicular, and this makes a lofs of near a foot all round the granary ; laftly, they leave a fpace at one end, fufficient for turning the corn ; all this greatly

damp and moldy the corn that lay next the sides, especially on the weather-side, which they called the south-west side ;——they gave instances of some farmers who had suffered by it ;——and a
carpenter

greatly reduces the contents of the granary, and, to make it more clear, I shall give an example.

Suppose a granary eighty foot long and twenty-one broad, which makes one thousand six hundred and eighty foot superficies : you must take off for the passage and the slopeing of the corn, at least three foot on each side, which makes six foot for the whole length, or four hundred and eighty square feet, which being taken from one thousand six hundred and eighty there remains but one thousand two hundred, from which you must take at least fifty foot for the space necessary for turning the corn and the passage at the other end : so that you can reckon only on one thousand one hundred and fifty foot square of room, which at eighteen inches deep will contain one thousand seven hundred and twenty-five cubic feet of corn, which will weigh about ninety-two thousand pound.

It appears from the foregoing example what immense build- Page 17. ings are necessary for a large magazine, and the vast expence that must attend the building and maintaining them. The buildings at Lyons called les graniers de l'abundance, of which we shall speak hereafter, will furnish a further proof of it.

It follows then that it will be of great advantage to lay up a great quantity of corn in a smaller compass, and we shall make it appear in the following discourse that it may very easily be done.

Corn, tho' dry to appearance, contains a great deal of moisture. I have put new corn in glass bottles well stopped : the moisture that came out of it appeared on the inside of the bottle, and the grain grew mouldy. At certain intervals, in the year 1745, I weighed a quantity of wheat of the last harvest, I exposed it for twelve hours to the heat of a stove or kiln, which raised Mr. Reaumur's thermometer to fifty degrees : it lost an eighth of it's weight, and yet was only dried ; for being sowed it came up.

In 1744 I put some wheat, and other grain, of the harvest Page 18. of 1742, into a stove heated so as to raise Reaumur's thermometer to 38° which is 8° higher than our hottest summers ; both the sorts of corn, that were used for the experiment, in twenty-four hours were found to be diminished $\frac{1}{32}$ ; they were put again into the stove, which was heated to 51°, and in twenty four hours after were diminished nearly $\frac{1}{8}$ ; besides that which was weighed, there were some separate parcels

Z 3

both

carpenter being there did attest it.— They said that mice would neither meddle with barley nor peas, if they could get any thing else.— They said, it had been

both of new and old corn set apart, to try what degree of heat it would bear without destroying it's vegetation. I sowed some that had suffered $12\frac{1}{2}°$, some 38, and some 51 : and in all these cases, the new came up, but the old did not.

It is remarkable that, be it never so hot during harvest, the sheafs that lie at top of the heap are harder to thresh than those that lie at bottom, which is the consequence of moist vapours that rise from the corn.

Page 20.  If you put a large heap of corn in a granary, and do not stir it for a considerable time, or if you only fill a barrel, after some time, upon running your hand into it, you will find a sensible heat in it and a small moisture ; some time after it acquires a vinous smell, then turns sour, and at last moldy; in a word it ferments, and is no longer fit to make bread, and sometimes even the fowls will not eat it.

It is to prevent fermentation that they lay it so thin, as eighteen inches, in the granaries, and turn it so often.

If it has been a wet season, and much rain fallen during harvest, they are obliged to turn the corn every three or four days ; but when corn is well conditioned, and the first year is passed, it may be sufficient to turn it once a month ; some turn but once a fortnight in the months of May, June, July, and August.

These are the expences, and the care that attends it is not inconsiderable, especially in summer, when the farmer has so many calls and occupations in the field ; nevertheless the proprietor must keep a strict eye upon his workmen; for, besides the frauds they will commit, especially when corn is dear, they frequently stir only the top of the heap, so that the bulk of the corn which you think has been turned was never stirred at all.

Page 22.  Whoever can save these expences and cares, will render the preservation of grain much more easy ; and that is what we hope to shew in the following work.

Wheat is not only the nourishment of men, but many other animals are particularly fond of it. Nobody can be ignorant of the great waste that is made in granaries by rats, mice, and birds : it seems possible to defend it from these depredations by carefully stopping all passages, laying snares, poison, &c. but all these precautions will not suffice to prevent the pillage of these animals, who, besides what they eat, waste a great deal by means of the holes they make, through which the corn runs down, and it is lost.

been commonly afferted that mice would not touch wheat, where they could have oats; that many therefore would lay oats in one half of one fide of their

loft. If the farmer makes holes for cats to go in at, the birds will take the advantage of them, and the cats themfelves contribute to the wafte by their excrements, which form heaps of infected corn.

Our labour, therefore, will not be loft, if we can arrive at a method by which we may have nothing to fear from thefe animals, and that without the ufe of cats, fnares, poifon, &c.

One of the greateft obftacles to the keeping of wheat, is the infects that breed in it: the chief are the weevil and moth. How often have the naturalift, the philofopher, the lovers of the publick good, endeavoured to fearch out means of exterminating thefe infects, which increafe fometimes to fuch a number as to devour a great part of the grain? All the methods that have been propofed have either proved ineffectual, or impracticable; the only one ufed in our province is the paffing all the corn over a wire fcreen; part of the weevils, and the corn they have damaged, falls through into a copper veffel, which they fet under the fcreen; but this tedious and expenfive operation, only diminifhes the evil without curing it; inftead of which we hope to propofe a method, by means of which you will have nothing to fear from any fort of infects, and that without charge or trouble.

The bufinefs is, in order to render the prefervation of corn Page 25. eafy, firft, to keep a great quantity in a fmall compafs; fecondly, to prevent it's fermenting, heating, or contracting any ill tafte; thirdly, to guard againft the rapine of rats, mice and birds, without expofing it to the damage occafioned by cats; fourthly, to preferve it from mites, moths, weevils, or any other infect, and all this without charge or trouble. Let us fee if all this may be brought about, and give an account of the experiments we have made on the fubject.

We caufed a cafe or little granary to be made, of oak plank two inches thick, forming a cube of five foot every way; at fix inches from the bottom we made a flooring, or fecond bottom of lattice work, placed upon joifts of five inches thick; covering it with a ftrong canvas; and this little granary was filled quite full of good wheat; it contained ninety-four cubic feet, weighing five thoufand and forty pounds.

Before we proceed any farther, it is proper to obferve, that fuch a granary of twelve foot cube will contain one thoufand feven hundred and twenty-eight cubic feet of corn, whereas the

granary

their barn, and wheat in the other half of the same side, but they themselves never found but that the mice would eat heartily of both.

## THATCHING.

granary we instanced in the beginning of this work, which had one thousand six hundred and eight square feet of superficies, could contain, in the common method, no more than one thousand seven hundred and twenty-five cubic feet of corn.

Page 27. This is an immense saving both of room and expence, since for about sixty pounds you may build such a granary of brick or stone fifteen foot square and twelve foot deep, which will contain two thousand seven hundred cubic feet of corn; whereas a granary, in the common form, to contain that quantity, would cost eight or nine hundred pounds.

The little granary being filled quite full of corn, is to be covered with good oak planks, so closely joined, that neither rats, mice, or even the smallest insect can get in, leaving only some vent-holes, with trap-doors, or covers fitted very exactly to them, of which we shall speak hereafter.

Thus is our corn deposited in a small compass, and perfectly secured from rats, mice, birds, and even insects, provided there were none before in the granary, or among the corn; but if there should, we shall hereafter prescribe a method of destroying them.

Page 29. It is notorious in this climate, that corn laid up in great heaps will soon ferment and spoil, to prevent which it is necessary to force out the tainted air, and supply it's place, from time to time, with fresh, in short to establish a current of air, which shall pass through the corn, and carry off the dampness.——For this purpose we proposed to make a false bottom of lattice work covered with coarse canvas (but if it were for a large granary, wire in the manner of a sieve might be better) through which the air might pass, and be forced out at the vent-holes at top.

Page 31. This purpose is answered by bellows, and the most proper for the purpose are those contrived by doctor Hales (as described in his book called a Description of Ventilators) being constructed without leather, or any other matter that is liable to be destroyed by vermin.

Page 35. A large pair of these bellows being so fixed as to receive the air from without, and convey it between the bottom and false bottom of the granary, when you would ventilate the corn, open the vent-holes at top, and work the bellows, which will drive the air through the whole body of the corn with such force as to make the dust fly out of the vent-holes, and when confined to one small opening will blow up some grains of corn a foot high.

Every

# THATCHING.

§. 1. **I** Was telling a Dorsetshire farmer how useful Of reeking ftraw. it was to have wheat-ftraw faved againſt an unforeſeen occaſion, and for which it was often wanted.

Every ftroke of the bellows conveys two foot cube of air into Page 36. the granary, which, at the rate of four hundred and twenty ftrokes in five minutes, will fupply eighty thoufand fix hundred and forty cubic feet in a day, that is to fay in eight hours working.

The proportion of air in a heap of corn is found by calculation to be about $\frac{1}{11}$, but fuppofing it even a third part, it will be changed two thoufand fix hundred times in a day, with one pair of bellows; but my granary has two pair.

The corn I chofe for this experiment was of good quality: I Page 39. ventilated it, not more than fix days in a year, without the help of fire, which was fufficient to keep it fo well that the beft judges allowed it to be as good as could be.

When the bellows had not been worked for feveral months, the corn was allowed, by good judges, to look and fmell perfectly well, but they objected that it did not handle well, that is, that it had fome little dampneſs in it. The bellows were worked for half a day, and that objection was entirely removed.

In hot countries corn may be preferved for a long time by be- Page 49. ing depofited in a vault or ciftern, fo clofely ftopped that the air can have no accefs; but experience fhews, that this method will not fucceed in our climate, the fun not having power to exhale moifture from the corn fufficient to prevent it's fermenting, when laid in a large heap; and this is further proved by feveral experiments of corn dried in a kiln, which, tho' it's weight was very confiderably diminifhed, did not lofe the vegetative quality, but grew very well.

It follows from thefe obfervations that it is neceffary to take Page 51. away the fuperfluous moifture, and reduce our corn to the fame degree of dryneſs as that of the hotteft countries, in order to preferve it in great bodies.

EXPERIMENT on ninety-four cubic feet of wheat (not dri- Page 55. ed) which was preferved by ventilation only, above fix years.

In the month of May, 1743, ninety-four foot of wheat was put in one of the little granaries beforementioned; it was of the harveſt

wanted.——He allowed, it was very good huſbandry, and added that he commonly uſed to reek
his wheat-ſtraw, which would take no damage for
a year

harveſt 1742 and of an excellent quality, perfectly clean, and ſo
dry, that it loſt only $\frac{1}{18}$ of it's weight by a ſmall quantity of it
for a trial being dried on a kiln with the heat at fifty degrees of
Reaumur's thermometer. This wheat was well cleaned from
duſt, and depoſited in the granary without being dried by fire.

The firſt three months it was ventilated for eight hours once a
fortnight, the reſt of the year 1743 and all 1744 it was ventilated once a month, all the year 1745 and part of 1746 but
half a day once a month, and after that but once in two or three
months.

In the month of June 1750 the granary was emptied, and the
wheat was found to look and ſmell very well, but felt a little
rough in the hand, becauſe not having been moved for ſix years,
the little hairs that are at the extremity of the grains, and the
particles of the bran were roughed up; but after paſſing twice
through the wind-ſcreen that objection was entirely removed,
and it was found by the bakers, paſtry-cooks, &c. to be perfectly good.

This was corn of eight years old, ſeven of which it was pre-
ſerved in the granary without any ſenſible diminution, and without any damage from rats or other animals; it cannot be ſaid
without expence, becauſe there was a man employed from time
to time in the ventilating, but it is very eaſy to reduce that expence almoſt to nothing, as will be ſhewn hereafter.

Page 62. EXPERIMENT on ſeventy-five foot of new wheat extreamly
moiſt, grown, and that had already contracted a bad ſmell.

The harveſt 1745 was very rainy, and all the corn grown in
the ear; in the common granaries it was always in a ſtate of fermentation, tho' laid but a foot deep, and turned every four or
five days.

Seventy-five foot of this grown corn, which ſmelled very ill,
and was ſo moiſt as to wet the floor of the granary where it lay
a few days, was put, in this condition, and without being dried,
into one of our little granaries with ſmall hopes of ſucceſs.

As the corn was very hot when put into the granary it was
ventilated three or four times the firſt week, once in eight days
during December and January, and, as it had then loſt great part
of it's bad ſmell, from that time till June once a fortnight.

Then

a year or two ; and, if there was no occasion for it, it would make litter and dung at last ; therefore, as wheat-straw in some years proves very short, or blighted,

Then perceiving, by running one's hand into the top of the heap, that it heated, we concluded it was going to be entirely corrupted, which determined us to empty the granary ; but, when we had taken out about a foot of the top, we were greatly surprized to find the rest fresh, having very little bad smell, and drier than that preserved in the common granaries. So that we regretted having emptied it.

The reason why the top was the worst was, the moist vapours being always forced upwards in ventilation ; and we apprehend if instead of emptying the granary it had been ventilated oftener, the moisture that was at top might have been dried away.

This experiment teaches us one thing of importance, which is, that in this sort of granary the top of the heap is most subject to heat, so that if the grain taken out of the vent-holes is in good condition, you may conclude the rest to be still better.

EXPERIMENT on five hundred and fifty-five foot of wheat Page 69. of the year 1750 (which was very damp and difficult to preserve) put into one of our granaries without being dried on a kiln.

It must be allowed that in this method it is very material to clean the corn well before it is put in the granary, because it is impossible to do any thing more to it till it is taken out for sale, but above all you must be careful to clear it from smut or blighted grains ; for we find, by experience, that they will communicate a bad smell to the whole.

This five hundred and fifty-five feet of wheat was so well cleaned, that, tho' at first it had $\frac{1}{6}$ part of smut or blighted grains, there remained scarce any appearance of either when it was put into the granary, only a light dust that it was impossible to get rid of, on account of the moisture of the grain, which made it adhere too fast to be removed by screening.

This wheat so well cleaned was put in one of our granaries, which had the bellows moved by a wind-mill.

There was no want of wind during the years 1751 and 1752, and, as it required neither expence nor trouble, it was often ventilated, which preserved it very well, and not only dried it, but also cleaned it, in a great measure, of the bad smell it had when it was put in.

When

blighted, in neither of which cafes it will be fit for thatching, fo it is prudent to fave and reek what one can fpare, when it proves long and good.

§. 2. It

When it was taken out it was very full of a fine duft, which feparated from the grain in proportion as it dried, but, after having paft the wind-fcreen, it was found to be very good, and was bought by the bakers at the top price of the market.

Page 72.

By this experiment it appears, that very moift corn, which has a great difpofition to ferment, may be preferved in thefe granaries by ventilation only; but he thinks it not fafe to truft to this fole precaution ; becaufe, if a calm fhould happen about the month of June, fo as to rob us of the ufe of our ventilating-mill, at a time when all nature is difpofed for fermentation, the whole might be fpoiled.

To prevent which, he propofes two methods.

Page 72.

## The FIRST METHOD

Is to keep corn near a twelvemonth in a common granary, during which time you will have opportunity to ufe all means of cleaning it, by which operations it will lofe fo much of it's moifture, as to be perfectly fit for the granary of prefervation.

This method will anfwer for fuch as defire to preferve the produce of their own lands only, and are already provided with a common granary : but thofe that would buy a large quantity of corn, when the price is very low, for the chance of felling at a better market, muft follow the

Page 75.

## SECOND METHOD.

You muft have a common granary fufficient for cleaning the corn before you put it in the granary of prefervation ; but as foon as it is well cleaned you muft dry it in a kiln (which is here-after defcribed) for by this operation, which is neither troublefome nor expenfive, you will in a very little time dry it, more than if it had lain in a common granary for a year. After which operation you may put it in the granary of prefervation without any fear, having only once paffed it through the wind-fcreen to cool it, and clean it from duft ; as will appear by the following experiments.

EXPERIMENT

Oat straw of no great use.

§. 2. It is of great use to have a reserve of barley-straw, or wheat-straw, to fling some loads of
either on the peas, and barley-reeks, to secure them
when they are obliged to lie a long time unthatch-
ed;

Page 76.

EXPERIMENT on ninety foot cube of fine wheat, which was
preserved without ventilation, after having been dried in a
kiln.

This wheat, tho' very full of smut and dust, was so well
cleaned as to have no fault remaining but dampness; it was
dried in a kiln, by which it lost a little disagreeable smell which
it had before; when it was thought to be sufficiently dried, it
was deposited in one of our granaries of preservation, which had
bellows adapted to it, but there was no occasion to make use of
them.

It appears by the foregoing experiment, that wheat well
cleaned and dried need not be ventilated.

Page 78.

EXPERIMENT on seventy-five foot cube of small wheat,
mixed with smut, which had been dried in a kiln.

Our different screens cleaned the large wheat perfectly, but
with all our care we could not free this small wheat from smut,
dust, &c, of which much remained, and the kiln did not clear it
from the bad smell it had contracted.

Frequent ventilation would undoubtedly have taken away
that bad smell, but this experiment being to try the effect of the
kiln only, we determined not to ventilate, unless there was great
danger of it's corrupting, which did not happen; but yet the
bad smell increased so much that we were obliged to kiln-dry it
again after it was taken out of the granary, and to screen it several times, by which means it made tolerable good bread.

This experiment shews, first, how necessary it is to clean the
corn well before you put it in the granary of preservation, and
that, in some cases, both ventilation and kiln-drying are necessary; secondly, that corn, which has contracted a bad smell,
may be cleared of it by the kiln and wind-screen.

Page 80.

Having found by the foregoing experiments that good corn,
well cleaned, and properly kiln-dried, may be preserved without
ventilation, and that good corn tolerably dry may be preserved
by ventilation only, we conclude it must be most advantageous
to join both methods, especially for large magazines.

EXPERIMENT

as for oat-ftraw, it is of no great ufe, unlefs to cover an oat-reek, or peas for fatting hogs, or corn for fowls.

§. 3. When

Page 80. EXPERIMENT on eight hundred twenty-five foot cube of fine wheat lightly kiln-dried and ventilated.

This wheat was of the year 1750, and confequently but of a middling quality; after being well cleaned, and lightly kiln-dried, it was put in the granary of prefervation about feven foot deep, which granary had bellows worked by a wind-mill.

This corn had a bad fmell, which was not entirely diffipated by the kiln, but was entirely cleared of it by ventilation; it was not only well preferved, but fo meliorated, and became of fo good a quality, that the bakers preferred it to all other, and bought it two-pence per fack dearer than the fame wheat preferved in the common method.

Page 82. It is certainly moft advantageous to unite both methods, not only becaufe it is the moft effectual in preferving the corn, but it is alfo the leaft trouble and expence: for to kiln-dry it fufficiently to keep without ventilation requires a large fire and long attendance, and to preferve it without kiln drying will require very frequent ventilation, whereas by joining the two methods you render both very eafy, lefs expenfive, and the fuccefs more certain.

In all thefe experiments we have never fuffered any thing by moth, or weevil, tho' the common granaries were greatly infefted with them at the fame time; this is a good prognoftic, but we muft not conclude from hence that this method will abfolutely prevent the mifchief: it may be fuppofed, that the care we had taken, in thefe experiments, to clean the corn, had entirely freed it from them, and may be objected that this great care cannot be taken in large provifions, and that, fhould any get into the heap, they would be more dangerous, inafmuch as they would not be difturbed for fo long a time; thefe reflections determined us to make the following experiment.

## Of the M O T H or W O R M.

Page 84. The moth lays it's eggs on the corn, the eggs produce a worm or caterpillar, which feeds on the corn, and fpins a filky web all over the furface, fo as to make a cruft fometimes of three or four inches thick, which is entirely fpoiled, befide the bad fmell it communicates to the whole.

In

# THATCHING. 367

§. 3. When straw is heaped up together in order Of helming to be helmed, it is fit at the time of wetting straw for thatch- for helming that there should be two persons to keep ing. the heap close together by beating it, whilst one flings water on it; otherwise, if the straw lies hollow, the water will run so fast through it that it will not take wet.

§. 4. It is found by experience, that in thatching Of binding barns, &c. it is more profitable to bind on the on the thatch with pitched ship-cordage untwisted (which thatch. is sold at market-towns) than to bind it on with withs, not only because the cords bind faster, which

In winter 1746 we collected all the wormy crust (from our or- Page 87. dinary granaries) which was very thick, the moths having been very numerous the preceding summer : these crusts were broke and screened, and what grain could be got from it (which undoubtedly was impregnated with the eggs of the moth) was put in one of our granaries which contained seventy-five foot cube, and ventilated from time to time all winter,

About the end of May if you opened the vent-holes at top, a vast number of moths flew out, which shewed they did not like their situation.

In the month of June 1747, the granary was emptied ; the moths and worms were all perished, and there was found only a thin crust on the top, of about $\frac{1}{8}$ of a inch thick, and the corn had lost part of the bad smell it had when put into the granary, insomuch that it sold for the current market price.

## Of the WEEVIL.

The weevil is of the beetle kind, it devours a great quantity Page 89. of corn, old as well as new, but does not communicate any bad smell to it, as the moth does ; it will endure the heat necessary for kiln-drying, and is numbed but not destroyed by intense cold, they are generally found collected in heaps, which feel very warm, which warmth probably is necessary for hatching their eggs, and if so, they will not be in a condition to propagate their species in our granaries. No smoke will destroy them but that of sulphur, and that gives a bad smell to the corn.

In the month of May 1751, we put some weevils into our gra- Page 95. naries, and when it was emptied in August 1752, we found none.

is

is much to be regarded in places expofed to the wind, but becaufe they alfo endure longer : this method likewife faves the time of twifting the withs, as well as prevents the damage done to the young coppices in cutting them, and often unfeafonably too : if you pleafe, the fame perfon who thatches may alfo bind on the cords, which faves one labourer's hire, but it is thought to be better that a labourer fhould be withinfide to bind, becaufe he can do it ftronger, which is of great confequence.

**Of helming long before thatching.**  §. 5. I told Mr. Hillman near Andover that the mice got into my wheat-ftaffold, tho' it was impof-fible for them to come up by the ftaffold.—He afk-ed me whether I did not make up the helm fome time before I thatched with it, for, if I did, the mice might very likely be carried into the reek.

**Of wetting the helm to top reeks.**  §. 6. It is very good hufbandry to top hay or corn-reeks with well wetted helms, that they may be well fparred down, and the fpars will then ftick well in them ; whereas, if you top with dry ftraw, the top will be liable to be blown off, becaufe it lies loofe and hollow, nor will the fparrs ftick faft in dry ftraw.

**Of thatch-ing with oat-ftraw.**  §. 7. I was thatching my cart-houfe with oat-ftraw ; it was March the 14th (anno 1703) — my oats not having lain long enough in fwarth did not threfh clean : the thatcher told me, he feared abun-dance of them would grow in the thatch, and would damage it by rotting after they had grown, and ftop the rain from running off, efpecially if a wet feafon, which would make the oats grow, fhould enfue, but, if it fhould prove a dry fpring, they might be malt-ed ; faid he, had this ftraw been laid on in winter, the cold would have killed the oats in chitting, and fo the damage had been prevented.

MALT

# MALT and MALTING.

§. 1. FARMER Sartain and others skilled in malting do allow, that barley, as soon as it is housed will work very well, and make very good malt, provided it took no wet in the field, after it was cut, but if it did, they say, it will not work well.

§. 2. Mr. Slocock of Newbury, a maltster of long experience, informs me (it having been a dry season for a good while) that the forward barley, which was already cut, and carried into the barn, was dried up with the drought, and would not therefore make so good malt as that which should be housed after rain : it is true, said he, such dry barley will raise an increase and smell well, and will put forth a beard, i. e. a root, but it will not put forth a spear to run half the length of the barley-corn, and so cannot make good malt, because the hardness of the rind binds up the spear from shooting. —— So, it seems, a rain on dry shrunk-barley not only thins the rind, but loosens it also from the flour, that the spear may the better shoot up between. Mixt barley, that is, such, of which some was brought in drier than the other, will never make good malt ; it will not come all together ; it is the same with old and new corn.

§. 3. Barley, when first cut, before it has sweated in the mow, will come as well as afterwards, but whilst it is in it's sweating it will not come at all.

§. 4. Discoursing with Sampson Cress of Holt in Wiltshire, an observing malster, about the art of making malt, I told him among other things, that I found the lighter the kiln was loaded in drying off a kiln of malt the sweeter the malt would be ; for should the kiln be loaded some six inches deep, nei-

*Marginal notes:*

Barley as soon as housed will malt well.

Barley very dry when housed will not malt well.

When sweating in the mow it will not malt.

Of the malt-kiln and of changing the water.

ther the flame nor the smoke would pass off well,
but the malt would be suffocated with smoke.——
He replied, that he believed, if my kiln was choaked with such a thickness, it could not have a good
draught, but must be a faulty kiln ; for, said he, a
good kiln ought to have such a draught as to roar
like wires on a river, or like a furnace under a
brewing copper. —— Again,—I told him the opinion of several judicious maltsters about changing the
water in the cistern while the barley is wetting, especially if it be coarse or cold, because a slimy water
would run from it.—He agreed, that in the fore-
end of the year, before the barley had taken it's due
sweating, be the barley never so good, it must be
very proper, because the water such barley is steeped in will be foul, and the giving it a second wetting or running of water must needs cleanse it, and
tend to the making sweet malt. —— In the same
manner, said he, it is likewise proper to do by barley wetted at the latter end of the year, towards
spring, because, when the weather grows warm, water soaking barley forty-eight hours will grow sour,
and begin to corrupt. —— The next day I talked
with William Sartain of Broughton, and Mr. Whatly of Bradford, Wilts, who are both of them maltsters ; they admitted it to be advantageous for the
corn in the cistern to change the water at any time,
except in the middle of winter, when the weather
was too cold. —— As to the quick draught of the
kiln, and it's roaring (as above hinted) that, they
said, in many malt-houses depended on the corner
the wind sat in, and on the opening of doors or
windows ; that though such fierce fires were best for
high-dried malt, yet a gentler fire was best for the
pale-dried malt.

Of drying the malt on the floor.    § 5. The two maltsters mentioned in the last observation agreed, that you cannot keep barley too

backward

backward on the floor, nor give it too much time, in case it neither harles at root nor spear, and that, receiving it's drying on the floor, it would require the less fire and wood.

§. 6. The hill-country barley has a much finer coat, and consequently more flour than the barley of the vale : the hill-country barley will be watered or wetted in four tides, whereas the vale-barley requires five, and the hill-barley, when it is watered, will in it's coat look as clear as the horn of a lanthorn.—— Note, every day is a tide, and every night is a tide.

*Hill-country barley preferable to the vale for malt.*

§. 7. On observing that the straw-dried malt I made at Crux-Easton wanted the fine elegant flavour that was common to such malt made at Holt, &c. ——I discoursed Sampson Cress about it,—and he suspected two errors in my method of wetting ; first, that the water I both wetted my barley and brewed my malt with was not agreeable, for, if that was wanting in either case, though I might brew very sound drink, yet it would want that fine flavour I complained to be deficient : though, said he, I have a well, yet I fetch my water both for wetting my barley, and brewing my malt, from Staverton-river ; for pond, or well-water, that is either foul or unpleasant tasted, will want the spirit when made drink of, and he wished me to use chalky water out of my well for both uses, for that is the water, said he, I would use if I had it. —— Secondly, it is possible you do not change your water often enough at wetting ; for it is common for the first water, to come away slimy, like ox-drivel, as you may find by taking up some of the barley out of the cistern, and the water will taint and grow sour, if not changed during the five tides ; which will give an odd taste to the malt, or at least rob it of it's flavour ; you should at least change the water once, especially in the two warm seasons of making malt, viz. in the spring, and at

*Of changing the water, and of the choice of it.*

autumn,

autumn, for then the weather is warmer than in winter, and will fooner taint; but if you fhould change the water three times in warm weather, you will find it the better, and you will do well to have a hogfhead of water ready to run into the ciftern as foon as the former water is let out, becaufe the barley by lying clofe may be apt to heat. —— He faid, he finds with him a hogfhead of water will wet a quarter of malt.

In the fpring, and at autumn, when the weather is warm, he thinks four tides enough, becaufe the water being then warmer than in winter, four tides will penetrate more than five tides in winter.

He faid, in cafe barley would not work well, becaufe it was coarfe and cold, he gave it fix tides, and changed the water after the third tide; otherwife it would be flimy before it could be flung on the floor, nor would it without fo many tides take water enough to come * fuant;——therefore, it is a great error in my maltfter in fuch cafe to give barley only four tides, as I have found he does.

* kindly, well.

Of the quantity to be wetted in proportion to your floor.

§. 8. I propofed to my maltfter, to wet but three quarters of barley at a time, that it might have longer time on the floor, left, by wetting more, which would require more room, one heap fhould prefs too faft on the other;—but he was againft it, and faid, it was beft to wet as much as the floor would carry, which was four quarters at a wetting; for, faid he, the more outfides you make the worfe the barley will work; (as it ftands to reafon it fhould) for the outfides which lie to the air, never work fo well as the infide, and the more heaps you divide your quantity of barley into the more outfides you make.

Not to heap up the malt, that it may heat before drying.

§. 9. I afked William Sartain, whether he approved of the cuftom of flinging up the malt from the floor into an heap before the kiln, and letting it heat before they dry it; he faid, by no means; but,

faid

he, it is an old way, and they did it becaufe it's being heated by fo doing would forward it in the drying, and fave fuel, but it makes it high coloured.
Whatly fays, it will both give it a higher colour,
and make it bite freer, i. e fhorter, but he does not,
he fays, ufe it. Sampfon Crefs fays the fame, but
condemns the practice. It was an old way among
maltfters, but they have found it to be wrong.
Whatly fays,—fome ufed to let it take heat till one
might almoft roaft an egg in it, but furely, fays he,
that muft make the drink apt to turn four.

§. 10. In the fpring, and at autumn, the barley
will be apt to come rugged, i. e. put forth a fingle
root at a time, inftead of pufhing forth all it's roots,
in a manner at once : this is a fault :— in fuch cafe
the forwardeft root will be apt to draw all the fubftance of the flour away, and rob the reft, and prevent them from fhooting forth, and fo you can never have good malt.——To prevent this inconveniency, you muft turn the heap often, and give it air,
and fpread it thinner, in order to keep it cool ; which
will check the tap root from running out fo haftily,
and give the other roots time to come on ; without
which you cannot make good malt.

*Of turning the malt often at fpring and autumn.*

§. 11. If you are defirous of having your drink in
the greateft perfection, I would recommend it to
you to have regard to the following obfervations ;—
Firft, to take great care that your malt be well fcreened, that being never thoroughly done by the maltfter ; and therefore ought to be done over again by
you ; for if you keep it, not being exceeding clean
from duft, and all manner of foulnefs, it will in a
little time decay and corrupt, and will give an ill
tafte to your drink, nor will that fine well, but be
muddy.—Secondly, to let your malt fettle five or
fix days in the fack after you have ground it ; for
it will then much better fall to flour, and grow dry,

*Rules for managing malt in or-der for brewing.*

whereas

whereas otherwise it will be clammy, and the water will not dilute it [a].——Thirdly, the older your malt (but exceeding twelve months at least) the better; the time therefore for buying of malt is before any new barley can be threshed out; for after new barley comes to market the maltster will be mixing the new malt with the old, but old malt will go much farther than new.——Fourthly and lastly, let your malt be well dried; for slack-dried malt will not keep; for keeping it ought to be well dried.

**Close pressing the malt a prejudice to it.** §. 12. October the 4th (anno 1712) Mr. Hillman, maltster, of Andover, visiting me, we discoursed about making malt: Mr. Hillman said, the act of parliament that laid the duty on malt was a general prejudice to it's being well made; for before the act the maltsters used to fling the barley out of the cistern or stone into the floor, and then cast it forward again, that the sour water might run off, and then fling it back into an heap, or a couch of only ten or twelve inches thick, that it might lie easy;—— but now the maltsters, out of lucre of having the couch measure the less, thereby to lessen the duty, fling the corn out of the cistern as wet as possibly they can, that the weight of it may press it the closer together, and to that end they lay it in a heap or a couch of twenty-four inches high, without flinging it off for the water to drain away, whereby the undermost corn is pressed so dry that it is killed, and **molds.** never works into malt, but [*] finnows; and by this means the sour water not running off gives the malt a sour and churlish taste, which never wears off.—— The damage the undermost barley receives (as above described) from the close pressure of it puts me in mind of the common expression of the country-man who says, that when barley is first sowed it ought to

[*] This rule contradicted §. 19. —— at least in pale-dried malt.

lie

lie eafy, the reafon of which he knows not, but obfervation and experience confirms him in it.--From
hence, it may not be improper to borrow a hint
how to account for the reafon of it:--it feems to me,
as fome creatures, for example amongft fifhes the
eel, or the miller's-thumb, will live with lefs air
than other fifhes, fo alfo it is with corn, amongft
which fome forts of grain are eafily fuffocated and
choaked, and the vegetable punctum faliens (or
heart) ftifled for want of a fufficient pabulum of air
in it's tender infancy, when oppreffed with heavy
wet clay ; whereas in more porous earth, which
lies light, and whereby there comes a freer accefs
of air to the feed, the vegetable progreffion is fupported and carried on in the feed. ——— I think it may
well be made a quære whether barley fowed in a pot
of mold, and put into an air-pump, where the air is
drawn out, would not rot and finnow, inftead of
growing,-- and whether, if the fame experiment was
to be made on barley and wheat put into an air-pump,
the wheat would not fpear out with the help of a lefs
quantity of air than the barley, becaufe we fee
wheat will grow under a clofer, heavier, wetter, and-
colder earth, from whence the air is more excluded,
than barley will do. ——— Thomas Beckley of Bourn,
maltfter, fays much to the fame purpofe with Mr.
Hillman, and that fometimes the keeping the barley
longer in couch than ordinary for the excifeman's
coming contributes to the fouring the malt ; and
the clofe preffing it in the ciftern, by the deepnefs
of it, whereby it lies the harder, hinders it alfo
from coming.

§. 13. An old and an experienced honeft malt- *To know when bar-ley is fully malted.*
fter did affure me,—that if the germen, or the
fpire-end of the barley, which runs between the flour
and the rind, was not as high afcended between the
rind as the root-end was put forth. fuch barley-corn
was not fully malted, and that no more of the grain

would be converted to flour than as far upwards as the point of the germen ran, and that by biting the grain one might find the difference; for that part of the grain not malted would be hard and tough, and being ground would be fat, dauby, and clammy in the liquor, and would not drink it up.

My maltster sent me malt, which my butler was not pleased with; he said, there were many grains in every handful of it, which were not malted at all, and many grains that were but half malted, of which I might be satisfied, if I made trial in water; for the corn, which was not malted at all, would sink to the bottom, and the half-malted grains would swim an-end, like a fishing-quill.—I called for a bason of water to make the experiment, and found it to be true.

§. 14. The maltsters have frequently a bushel and an half increase in the quarter, when they do not screen the coomb well, but in the London-trade there is not above a bushel increase to be had, because for that market the malt must be made very * knot: if malt be sent to London, and be not made knot, it will heat, and the coomb fall off in sifting, and tumbling it out at the wharf, and then it will not hold out the measure it was sent for, which will occasion dissatisfaction between the factor and the maltster.

*Of the increase in malting.*

*\* fine, clean.*

§. 15. I find they agree, that pale-dried malt, if care be taken to give it it's gentle heat with a soft fire, may be dried as hard as the highest-dried malt, though generally speaking the pale-dried malt is slacker dried; but in case time be taken in drying it well, they know not why it should not make as strong drink as the high-dried malt, and both the malt and the drink keep as long.

*Of pale-dried malt.*

§. 16. Mr. Edwards says, that he has used, and brewed with a bushel of wheat-malt, and twelve bushels of barley-malt to the hogshead to his very

*Of wheat and oat-malt.*

good

good fatisfaction. ——He alfo fays, that Sir Robert
Sawyer ufed always to put wheat, beans, and oats
to his malt.——He likewife fays, that a bufhel or
two of oat-malt to twelve bufhels of barley-malt
will ripen the drink much fooner ;—and further,
that oat-malt and barley-malt equally mixed, as
many of the country people here ufe it, makes very
pretty, pert, fmooth drink, and many in this country (in Hants) fow half barley, half oats, for that
purpofe, and call it Dredge.

§. 17. 1696. Fern-dried malt is not of late years Of fern-
looked on to be fo good as malt dried with other dried malt.
fuel, though fome years ago it was in vogue, but
people foon found their error : it ufed formerly to
yield 2d. in the bufhel extraordinary, but now it
yields 2d in the bufhel lefs.—— It makes the ale
tafte maukifh.

§. 18. If malt be burnt, the longer it lies by the Of burnt
better it will recover itfelf, lofe it's heat and look malt's reco-
paler : I had fome drink made of malt, that being keeping.
rafhed would have been quite fpoiled, had it been
ufed directly, but by keeping it a year and half by
me it was fo well recovered, that there was no lofs
in it.——Pale malt is beft to be brewed as foon as
it is ground, but the high-coloured malt is better
for being kept a while after it is ground before it
be brewed, becaufe it is too hard to break to pieces,
and molder in it's flour, till the air by being imbibed has loofened it's parts.

§. 19. I find by my own, and the experience of Of new and
other obferving maltfters, that for brewing drink old malt.
malt is in perfection about three weeks or a month
after it is made ; for by that time the fire will be
out of it, and it will then be fulleft of fpirit; whereas the more it flackens afterwards the more the fpirits
go off, and with them the ftrength of the fmell abates,
as may eafily be perceived. —— Therefore, though

malt

malt takes leaft damage kept in a great heap, yet I find they all agree, that one had better make October drink with new malt than with old, becaufe if both years barley be equally good, the new malt will brew ftronger drink than the old, but this more especially holds in pale-dried malt, becaufe it may fo happen that high-dried malt may be fo fcorched as not to be mollified, or have the fire enough out of it for brewing till many months after it's being made, and by long keeping that fuffers leaft.

They hold that it is more profitable for the malt-fter to fell old malt than new, becaufe, before it is flacked, and while but newly come from the kiln, much more goes to the bufhel.

# H O P S.

Of fetting the hop-hil-locks at a diftance.

§. I. [a] MR. Perdue, the greateft hop-mer-chant in Winchefter, fays, he fets his hop-hillocks at double the diftance others gene-rally do, and that he is fure he is a gainer by it ; for thereby in poles, and otherwife, he is but at half charges, and has as good a burden of hops as other people ; for the fun having power to fhine through the poles, and to ftrike it's heat to the bottom, brings bloffoms from the very bottom, the fap being checked and dried up by the fun, whereas, when the poles are fet thick, the hops carry bloffoms only at the top.— Quære whether the fame reafon holds not, for fetting beans thinner.

[a] Our author having but few remarks on hops, they, who defire information in this particular, may confult Mr. Miller's Dictionary, under the article Lupulus, where they will find a full account of this plant, with feveral curious experiments made by the Reverend Doctor Hales.

§. 2. Hops

§. 2. Hops that feel clammy are the best; there- Of choos-
fore may be chose in the dark.      ing hops.

§. 3. The true virtue of the hop lies chiefly in Of the hop-
the feed, and not in the leaf, which but few under- feed.
stand; they choose the hop by the colour of the leaf,
whereas the brightest leaved hops are the worst sort,
because they are not full ripe, and consequently were
gathered when the feed was in the milk, whereby it
shrinks to nothing; but the hop in perfection has a
nut-brown leaf, and it's feed being full ripe has a
good pith; which is what gives the grateful bitter, though the generality of people are ignorant
of this.

§. 4. Hop-poles for the second year ought to be Of hop-
sixteen foot long, the first year wanting none; poles.
the third year they ought to be twenty foot long;
after that twenty-five foot, and never longer.——If
the girt of a twenty-five foot pole be eight inches at
the butt-end, it is reckoned a compleat pole: ash is
better for poles than withy by five shillings in the
hundred, in the twenty-five foot poles.

# GRAZING.

§. 1. I T seems to me (as before hinted) that the Jews skil-
Grecians, Romans, Phœnicians, &c. de- led, in the
rived their husbandry from the Jews; for it is not ment of
to be supposed, but that Abraham, Isaac, and Ja- cattle.
cob, and his sons, who were such wise persons as
they are recorded to have been, and so conversant
in cattle, must be excellently skilled in that branch
of husbandry. See Gen. xxxiv. 5.——- And that
Jacob's sons were wise persons may be seen by their
conduct before Joseph their brother.—— That Moses,
who was excellently skilled in all the learning of the
Ægyptians, and afterwards kept his father Jethro's
flock forty years, must by means of his advantages
in

in education have made vaſt diſcoveries in the nature of cattle is moſt certain, and what converſe the
patriarchs had with all the eaſtern nations, whereby
thoſe nations might be informed, is well known.

Antiquity<br>of this<br>branch of<br>huſbandry. §. 2. Doctor Patrick in his comment on Gen.
xxix. obſerves that Rachel's name in Hebrew ſigni-
fies a ſheep. —— And Varro derives many ancient
families from the names of cattle. Lib. 2. c. 1.
De ruſtica. —— And lib. 1. fo. 29. he ſays, the
paſtoral care was the firſt employment in the world,
and that agriculture came in of later years. — It ſeems
indeed that thoſe names, that honourable families
anciently aſſumed to themſelves, were borrowed
from the names of cattle, as thinking the paſturage
of them more profitable than tilling the ground; —
and we find of Jacob, notwithſtanding his flocks
were ſo large, that yet his proviſion of corn was but
from year to year; for in the ſecond year of the famine in Ægypt he wanted corn, ſo that it ſeems he
thought it more profitable to trade in cattle, and
their fleeces, than to go to markets with corn.
It is to be obſerved that Rachel kept the ſheep, as
being an honourable employment, not but ſhe had
others under her as aſſiſtants and ſervants.—G O D
himſelf is named the ſhepherd of Iſrael: ſheep-ſhear-
ing, not reaping of corn, was their greateſt feſtival.
See Patrick, fo. 506. —— In the hot countries it
appears, that their cuſtom was to bring their flocks
to the wells, and into ſhades, to drink in the heat
of the day, and, when that was abated, to drive
them to feed again, as appears from Geneſis xxxix.
7. —— It is yet high day, &c. See Doctor Patrick's
Comment; and Cant. i. 7. —— and Palladius in his
Calendar ſays, that the cattle uſed to be drove out
to feed in the ſummer evenings, when the dew firſt
began to fall, ſo that then they uſed to tend their
cattle late, and the morning dew was alſo taken by
　　　　　　　　　　　　　　　　　　　them,

them, which, and Virgil's faying, Et ros in tenerâ
pecori gratiffimus herbâ, is contrary to our practice;
and fee Varro, l. 2. c. 15.—Notwithstanding however what may have been conjectured by various
writers, and the preference given by them to the
pastoral charge, in regard to it's antiquity, it is plain
from Genesis iv. 2. that and agriculture were near
of the fame date, for Abel was a keeper of sheep,
and Cain, the elder brother, a tiller of the ground.

§. 3. Mr. Brown, in his Vulgar errors, fo. 41. Of the co-
observes, that if sheep have any black, or deep ruffet lours of
in their faces, they want not the fame about their cattle.
legs and feet;——that black hounds have mealy
mouths and feet;—that black cows, which have any
white in their tails, do not mifs of fome in their
bellies, and if all white in their bodies, yet, if black
mouthed, their ears and feet maintain the fame
colour.

§. 4. That Jacob's sheep brought forth speckled Of party-
lambs, on viewing the rods at the time of concep- coloured
tion, is imputed by Patrick to the divine will rather cattle.
than to the force of imagination; yet he owns, that St.
Austin, and fome others, imputed it to the operation
of natural caufes, and alledges the like thing done in
Spain between horfes and mares.—Lord Pembroke
told me, it was common in Spain to cover a mare
with a Turkifh carpet, and to lay another before
her, when they brought the stallion to cover her.
——I have always obferved, that it is a common
expreffion, on feeing a party-coloured horfe, to fay,
" He was begot on a common :" it being fuppofed,
that there the mare might, at the time of conception,
have feveral different coloured horfes in view.——
But no wonder that thefe arts are not mentioned in
the Rei ruftic scriptores, they not being practifed
by the Romans; for their endeavours were to avoid
party-coloured breed, either in sheep, horfes, or
horned

horned cattle ; for which reason they would not
keep such cattle of any sort, of either sex ; and it
seems to me, that Jacob proposed to Laban the
ring-streaked, spotted, and speckled cattle for his
hire, not only as unlikely to proceed from the white
cattle, but also as the cattle of less value than the
white cattle ; for in these countries, as has been before remarked, they did not affect cattle of medly
colours, and, as it is likely, because they thought
those cattle of the worse natures, as not having been
created so from the beginning; all cattle at first
being of one colour in the same individual, as
black, white, red, &c. and the mixture of colours
whereby their natures are weakened, arising from
the copulation of males and females of different
colours.

Cattle in<br>low case<br>not to be<br>put into<br>rich land.

§. 5. The stronger and richer the land is, the
more must cattle be kept up to a good pitch ; for,
if on such land cattle are in the winter suffered to
run to poverty, or are brought into it poor, they'll
be liable to the yellows, and the blain, and most sort
of distempers ; for it is the same as if you should
offer strong meats to weak stomachs, or to persons
in a low state of health.—It was agreed by farmer
Chivers, farmer Harding, farmer Earle, and farmer
Stevens of Pomeroy (notable Wiltshire dairy-men)
that cattle in good case, and in heart, would for a
little while feed on the coarsest fodder, be it straw or
hay, which cattle low in case, would starve before
they would touch, and therefore such cattle have the
weaker stomachs.

Observa-<br>tion on<br>Virgil—Et<br>ros in tene-<br>ra, &c.

§. 6. Great cattle choose to feed with their heads
from the sun both morning and afternoon, feeding a
different way in the afternoon from what they did in
the morning.—Our cattle in England, seem not to
care to feed among the dew in the morning before
sun-rise ; but like to stay till the sun has began to

warm

warm it; so that it seems the saying of Virgil, ——
" Et ros in tenerâ pecori gratiffimus herbâ," ——
should be underftood in England of the dew after
sun-rife; perhaps in Italy, where the days are so hot
and the grafs in the day-time roafted with the fun,
the cattle may like to lick up the dew early in the
morning, and doubtlefs in England our cattle vary.
much in their hours of feeding between summer and
winter.

§. 7. I obferve in the hill-country, that in sum- Cattle<br>choofe the<br>higheft
mer-time cattle covet to pafture on the higheft part
of the field, for fake of air, and go not down to the ground in<br>hot wea-<br>ther.
low part of the ground to feed, it lying clofe from
the aïr, till towards the evening, when the bottom
of the field is alfo cool; the oxen likewife, which
come from the plough, and are hungry, will go up
to the height till towards fun-fet, though that part
be very bare of grafs.———My shepherd said, on a
certain day, that he would drive my sheep into the
road on the wafte to feed, becaufe the day was cool
and airy; for, said he, if I drive them thither in a
hot fultry day, they will not feed, but will lie in the
rutts.—The reafon for their doing fo, as I conceive,
is, becaufe they find great relief by the ftream of air
which runs along the rutts, as in a channel, when
perhaps no motion of air is fenfibly to be perceived
elfewhere.

§. 8. When cattle in fummer-time go late to Sign from<br>their going<br>to feed.
shade, and come out from shade earlier than ordina-
ry, to go to feed, it is a shrewd sign their commons
grow short.

§. 9. Large cattle will taint poor ground with Of cattle<br>tainting<br>ground.
pafturing on it, and will make mamocks, that they
will leave and not eat; when at the fame time, in
rich land, and a good pafture, they would eat up all
the grafs clean; and that this should be fo ftands to
reafon, becaufe, at beft the poor ground not being
very

very toothsome, a little addition to it of unfavouri-
ness, by pissing or dunging, will occasion the cattle
to forsake that part, especially about June, when
poor ground begins to fall off from growing;
whereas in good sweet ground the taint does not near
so much overcome the sweetness of the grass, and for
variety's sake it may be pleasant and grateful to the
cattle, there being still a considerable degree of natural sweetness left to recommend it. —— In poor
grounds, such as hill-country-downs, the sheep will
feed them down close, notwithstanding the ill favour
of their tails: the reason for the sheep feeding them
so bare and close is apparent; for, wherever they
lay their tails, there is time for such part to out-
grow the taint, the grass being always kept young,
and tender, and in a springing and growing condition, which is not the case in poor hill-country ground
set apart for pasture for great cattle, which must
therefore be hained, so as to be raised to a good bite,
for the grass that may be tainted in such pastures, is
of a good length, and the greatest part that is above
ground is tainted; when great cattle therefore are
forced to eat it, they may be observed to walk along
biting the tops of it; that is, such part as has grown
up since the taint.

§. 10. In case you design the feed of the second
year's broad-clover for your cows and horses, as not
having provided new broad-clover for them, of one
year's growth; such second year's broad-clover,
designed for the support of your cows and horses,
ought not, in our hill-country, to have been fed the
first year, but with cows, and a few horses; for if
such ground be fed with sheep the first summer, it
will much damage the produce of the second year;
because they will wound, and bite into the roots of
the clover.

*Of feeding clover.*

§. 11. It

§. 11. It had been a very dry and burning hot season for six weeks, during the latter part of April,
and all May, (anno 1702) and I had an hundred
sheep and three beasts fatting in broad-clover : I often thought my servants had neglected to drive them
to water : for they had no water in the pasture : so,
not trusting to my servants, I drove my fatting-cows
myself, in the evening, to water, but could not persuade them to taste it, neither that day, nor the
next : I also drove my sheep to water, and waited
patiently on them half an hour, but could not persuade them to touch it. — I observed the dung of the
sheep to be very moist ; and fat, and pappy like
cow's-dung ; whereas, when sheep feed in other
grass, they are naturally very dry, and costive :
from whence I infer, that the leaves and stalks of
the broad-clover being so juicy, no cattle need so
much water with it as with other grass, if they may
not even do without any at all.

*Cattle fed in broad-clover need little or no water.*

§. 12. Farmer Miles of Holt assured me, that
about them, in Wilts, oxen and cows were in great
danger of being swelled by being put into broad-
clover, whenever any rain came, though it was dry
when they were put in : they had also, he said, in
those parts, lost sheep by putting them into broad-
clover, and into green wheat likewise, in the spring.
—I said, I had this spring (anno 1720) fed my wheat
down with my flock, by putting them in for two
hours in a morning, after they came from fold ; and
I had found no hurt by it. — He replied, he supposed that would do them no harm, but what harmed
them was keeping them in longer, and letting them
lie down.

*Of cattle swelling in broad-clover.*

§. 13. A farmer in my neighbourhood had like
to have lost several oxen this year. (1720) by putting them into broad-clover, though he watched
them : one of them being so much blown, that he
thought

*Of letting out the wind from a beast swelled by broad-clover.*

thought he could not be faved, the farmer ignorant-
ly ftruck the bullock with his pen-knife into the
hollow place under the free-bone, under the loin,
which was wrong, and the bullock died; whereas,
he fhould have taken a pair of ftrong pinchers, and
in that hollow place have taken hold with them on
the bullock's hide, and have pulled it from the flefh
with all his ftrength, and then have ftruck his pen-
knife into the hide only that he had loofened, and
not into the bullock's flefh, whereby his guts were
hurt, but, inftead of that, fhould have run in between the hide and the flefh, and a wind would have
iffued out ftrong enough to have put out a candle.
—In cafe a bullock, not thus blafted, has a blain, do
the fame thing, by lifting up the hide in the fame
place, and then make but a fmall orifice, fo as to
thruft in a pen-knife only, and a great deal of wind
will iffue out.

I was fpeaking afterwards to an old experienced
farmer on this fubject, and he faid, he had not in
thirty years time loft a cow by broad-clover, nor did
he think it more dangerous than other grafs, unlefs
cattle came hungry to it out of the ftraw-barton, or
were very poor in cafe; for then they would knaw
it unreafonably, and it was very grofs and windy;
but cows that had the fame fpring been firft in other
grafs, would not be very greedy of it, nor would, in
that cafe, over-fill themfelves; for they will eat any
grafs of the field before broad-clover.

I believe broad-clover is not fo apt to hurt cattle
on our dry hills as on the deep lands.—I alfo believe, the thicker it is fowed it is the lefs apt to hurt
becaufe it runs the finer.

The reafon, as I conceive, why broad-clover is
apter to blow a cow than a horfe, is, becaufe a cow
licks it in with her tongue, at a greater length, and
fwallows it larger than a horfe does; for he chews it
more,

more, as not chewing it over again as the cow does in the cud, and so it goes first down into the cow's stomach more gross, and with less of the salival juice to correct it than that which the horse swallows down has.

Another farmer of my acquaintance in Wiltshire had two beasts died with the rise of grass, by putting them into the aftermass of his mead, which was very luscious, it having had a mighty quick growth occasioned by warm rain; and his cattle having for some time fared hard, they eat so greedily on their being first put into the aftermass, that they quite choaked up their first stomach, called the farding-bag; for, upon opening the cows, that stomach was found full of raw indigested grass.

Mr Bachelour of Ashmonsworth, and farmer Crapp, and farmer Biggs, discoursing upon broad-clover, farmer Biggs said, by mixing it with hop-clover, he had never lost a cow in his life; and so said farmer Crapp.

§. 14. The summer, anno 1717, being showery, the hop-clover came up thicker than ever I knew it, and grew to that height among the barley, as, at harvest, to flower; and we were forced to turn the barley-swarths, on account of the great quantity of hop-clover that we unavoidably cut off by the scythe with the barley.—I hoped therefore, that so great a bite of hop-clover, as my fatting-oxen might have after harvest, would bring them forward, they being well advanced in flesh before; and the hop-clover being sweet, I had great expectations from it; but for a fortnight I could only keep my oxen to hold their flesh, and then for another fortnight I found they lost flesh, though the bite of the clover did not so abate, but that it seemed thick enough to support them: my working oxen also filled themselves very well for near a fortnight; but when the head of the

*On feeding oxen with hop-clover.*

hop-

hop-clover was taken off, they fell off their flesh.
——My ox-hind said, the cattle were forced to pull
up so much of the barley-stubble with the grass,
that it greatly abated the goodness of it. From
hence for the future I may learn experience, and
know how far I may depend on such hop-clover for
fatting my working oxen.

Cows, sheep, and all sorts of cattle, will choose
rather to feed on broad-clover, if it be kept down
pretty close, than on hop-clover, when it has once
run into flower; for of the two the hop-clover is the
bitterer.

What<br>grass best<br>to fat cat-<br>tle in Sep-<br>tember and<br>October. § 15. My ground will almost fat cattle in spring,
when the sap is flush; but it must be the aftermass
of good ground only, when September and October comes, that will support a bullock, and carry
him on when near fat: the poverty of grass at that
time may be seen by it's dying away, or losing it's
colour: then such grass is lost on a bullock.

Of winter-<br>rowet, &c. §. 16. Mr. Bissy (my tenant in Wilts) a very experienced grazier, was telling me, how much a beast
would thrive with his winter-straw, in case he had
the liberty of going abroad, and, besides his straw,
picking up some winter-rowet, which would give
him a better stomach to his straw.——I replied,——I
found that by experience; but our hill-country-
meads contained so few acres, they would not afford
much winter-rowet; but, said I, though rowet,
which is of a deadish nature, and afforded the cattle
little better than a change only, made the straw
more grateful, yet I observed, by giving them with
their fodder a taste of the first spring-grass, which
was luscious and gnash, nothing would sooner wean
them from, and take them more off their stomachs,
not only to straw, but to the best hay also; and
therefore I carefully kept them from such grass.——
He replied, it was, generally speaking, very true;
but

but yet that their spring-grass beasts would (before the quantity of grass was sufficient for a maintenance wholly thereon) eat heartily of straw or hay, early in the morning, and whilst the dew was on the grass; for in the spring the cattle do not care for such grass early in the morning, nor till it has been warmed by the sun, and the dew taken off it; because such grass is very cold by the wet lying on it, and the juices are then as yet unconcocted, and you may see the bullocks, at such time, stand under the hedges, forbearing to feed till the dew is off. — All this seems very reasonable, whereas on the contrary, in the summer-time, when the crudities of the grass are taken off, all cattle are more desirous of feeding in the mornings and evenings, while the dew is on the grass; in which sense only Virgil is to be understood, when he says, —— " Et ros in tenerâ pecori gratissimus herbâ."

§. 17. I lopt several pollard-oaks this spring (anno 1705) whilst in bud, and let the loppings lie, in order to be faggotted : the beasts of the common came and browsed on them, and the oak-buds killed five of the udder-cattle; see therefore, and prevent such evil for the future.

*Oak-buds, poison to cows.*

§. 18. I was telling my ox-hind, I doubted some weanling-calves I had wanted water.—He said, that was easy to be seen; for, if they suffered for want of water, they would not fill themselves, though there was never so much grass, but would look mighty hollow and thin, and go about bleating.

*Calves will not eat if they want water.*

ᵃ Varro advises to water cattle twice a day in the summer and once in the winter.

This winter (anno 1718) I was fully convinced of the great advantage it was to cattle to have water at command in their toddering-yards, so as to have re-

a Boves æstate ad aquam apellendos bis, hyeme semel. Var. fol. 56.

course

courfe to it when they pleafed ; for the cattle in my cow-yard where they have no water, (but when they are drove to it, and that but once, or at moft twice a day, and fometimes are neglected, or drove unfeafonably) were in general much more out of countenance, and leaner than four or five cows that the parfon joifted for me, and which fed on the fame ftraw, it being the tythe of my farm. — The difference lay only in this, that his cows went when they would to the pond in his yard.—Gentlemen-farmers, having fo many irons in the fire, ought to depend as little as may be on fervants, but fhould provide fuch conveniencies as may, as much as poffible, anfwer the fame ends, without the care and trouble of fervants.

I wintered this year (1719) twenty two-years yearlings in the French-grafs, where they had alfo the running in the woods, and were foddered in the ftraw-houfe, and thus they lived very lufty till March, when, the rowet being gone in the field, and the bud beginning to fwell in the coppice, I was forced to remove them, and bring them wholly to ftraw ; I was afraid they would have been much pinched, their rowet being gone, and lofing their range, and being confined to the backfide ; and for three or four days they feemed to look hollow ; but then they filled again, and did very well, and I do not a little impute their doing fo well to their having plenty of water at command, and to the warmth of the yard : I note this, that I may not fear the confequence in fuch another year.

**Stalled-oxen not to be kept too close.** §. 19. Stalled-oxen, if tied up to the houfe, which is clofe, have been found of late years (fince 1705) not to hold to their ftomachs fo well as when one fide of the houfe is open, like a penthoufe ; becaufe, when an ox grows fat, he is naturally very hot ; therefore it is beft to have the fides of the fatting-ting-houses open.——— In yoking-time, whilst they plough them, if they·slip a cord, they never fight, but when fatting, it is likely they may.

§. 20. Farmer Elford of Dorsetshire says, that cattle, which are used to be housed on nights in winter, will be tender, and expect it, and will in winter fall away in their flesh if they have it not; therefore he, not having the conveniency of housing them, takes care not to buy a cow, if he perceives she has been used to be housed.——— I asked him how he could perceive that by a cow in a fair; he said, very easily; for such a cow would have the hair of her sides towards her tail clung with dung; which they, who bring her to market, cannot get off without great difficulty; the hair will sooner come away than they can separate the dung from it. *Of housing cattle.*

§. 21. Poor cattle may.be kept to their good behaviour by slight inclosures; but by experience I find, that cattle well kept, and high in proof, must have very strong bounds, else, when they rise in case, they will soon break through, especially if they want water, or take a dislike to their pasture. *Cattle in proof require strong bounds.*

§. 22. The annexed figure represents a clog to hang at the bottom of a yoke, or shackle, to prevent a beast from leaping; it may be increased according to the bigness of the beast. *A clog for cattle.*

c, the hole through which the shackle comes.———
    b, eighteen inches.——— a a, three foot long.

§. 23. Being to send five yearlings to the coppices, that I might hear whereabouts they were, I was to put on bells; so I bid my wood-man get withs for the *Of bells to hang on cattle when turned into the woods.*

the bells. He said, by no means; for a with would be apt to gall their necks, and the flies would blow the sore places, and, besides that, withs would be apt to hang in the bushes; but a good strong whitleather collar would do very well; but, said he, an iron collar, made of a smooth plate, is better, and will not gall, and the bell will sound much better than either with a with, or a whitleather collar; because the iron collar holds the bell off from resting on their breasts; whereas, with the other collars, the bell lies on their breasts, whereby the sound will be deadened.

# FODDERING.

**Of convenient partitions in a foddering-yard.** §. 1. IN the foddering-yards of backsides, or other out-houses, to have several divisions, over and above what is constantly used, has great conveniencies in it; one of which is, that in them you may dispose of a two-yearling cow, or another cow, at the time of bulling; not only to keep them from a bull, but from the other beasts also, that would be leaping such a cow, whereby they may hurt each other, &c. —— Especially cows forward with calf will be apt to warp by leaping a bulling-cow.

**Cattle, if once foddered, will not do without it.** §. 2. The open winters make hay the dearest, if a hard frost and snow come at the forehand of them; for if cattle once come to fodder, they must be held to it, or they will receive great damage. — In washy weather all the hay one can give to cattle will not make them thrive, but in dry frosty weather they'll thrive with their meat.

**Cattle grow lousy on bad hay.** §. 3. I am assured by a farmer of Woodhay, in my neighbourhood, in the vale, that there is abundance of hay there so sour and rushy, that it is not so good for cattle as straw in a good year, and he has known cattle to grow lousy on such hay.

I was

I was telling this to another farmer, and he said, it was true, and that such fodder ought to be given to cattle but a little at a time, so as not to cloy them; for, if they should be once cloyed with it, they would starve rather than feed on it.

§. 4. Anno 1704, I let my cows go at large from their foddering-yard, during the winter, and so on till April, when they picked up some grass; and those that had calved I baited with hay: the consequence of which was plainly this, that by Mid-April my cows would not stand to eat any straw at all, but were, during the months of March and April, so weaned from straw, by baits of grass and hay, that they fell off from their straw quite, and grew much leaner, and worse in flesh than they had been, and apparently worse than the farmer's cows, which were, after the winter months, wholly pent up to their straw, and to the pond.

*Cows used to hay will not eat straw.*

§. 5. All sorts of cattle that chew the cud, as sheep, cows, &c. care not to graze after each other, nor to eat one another's leavings in the foddering-yards; but cattle that do not chew the cud will eat after those that do, and vice versa.

*Cattle that chew the cud like not to eat after one another.*

§. 6. ª Pliny tells us, where hay was scarce it was usual to feed their cattle with chaff and barley-straw. Of chaff, says he, that is the best sort, which is the thinnest and smallest, and nearest to dust; the best therefore is from millet, the next from barley, and the worst from wheat, except it be for hard-labouring beasts.

*Of chaff.*

§. 7. On sound experience I am convinced, that in our hill-country we ought not to have any depen-

*Cattle must not be sent from the foddering-yard, in the hill-country, till the middle of May.*

---

ª Ubi fœni inopia est, stramento paleam quærunt, hordei stipulam bubus gratissimam servant:——Paleâ (chaff) plures gentium pro fœno utuntur; melior ea quæ tenuior, minutiorque et pulveri propior, ideo optima e milio, proxima ex hordeo, pessima ex tritico, præterquam jumentis opere laborantibus. Plin. lib. 18. c. 30.

dence

dence on sending our cattle out of the foddering-yard to grass before the middle of May, and therefore we ought to be provided with winter-fodder for cows accordingly ; for this year (1720) there was a very wet spring, and it continued so throughout March, April, and May, and yet the natural pasture-grounds did not afford a bite for the great cattle till the middle of May; indeed the hop-clover might be fit to support them a fortnight sooner ; but it is a hard matter, tho' one should have a good stock of that grass, to get the shepherd's leave to hayn it from the sheep for that end, he stands so much in need of the hop-clover grass for his sheep from the middle of March to the beginning of May.

**To fodder early in winter mornings.** §. 8. At the beginning of winter, suppose the latter end of October, and a good part of November, while cattle still continue out in the field at grass, it is very necessary to fodder them early in the morning, while the hoar-frost hangs on the grass, which they will not eat kindly of till the sun has warmed it.

**Of racks.** §. 9. The stradling racks are best for foddering, if made strong enough, i. e. so as not to be overturned ; for these racks may be lifted up as the dung mixen rises, which those fixed in the ground cannot be.

**Cribs better than racks in the hill-country.** §. 10. It is a practice in many places, especially in the vale, to tie their cow-beasts up to a rack to fodder ; but if one rightly reflects on the places where it is done, we shall find it only used where the fodder is good, being either hay, or very good straw; but in the hill-country of Hampshire, where the cattle have straw-fodder only, and that not so good as the straw in the vale, the custom is to fodder their cows in racks, or cribs, in the open yard, which they think better than tying their cattle up to racks in houses ; for tho' in cold and rainy weather

the

the houses may keep their loins dry, yet in countries where the fodder is coarfe, efpecially after wet and backward harvefts, when the fpirit of the ftraw is wafhed out by the rain, the giving cattle ftraw from racks, from whence they cannot pick and choofe, as from cribs they may, is judged to tend to the impoverifhing the cattle, whereas in cribs they can pick the fweet from the coarfe.

Afking a great grazier in Somerfetfhire, in what method he fed his fatting-beafts, he told me, he thought it was beft for them to reach up to a rack. — I faid, I thought not, becaufe reaching and hawling might give frequent qualms to the ftomach of a fatting-beaft, efpecially when near fat.— He replied, he did not know but it might; yet if you give them their meat from under them, they will blow upon it, and fpoil half of it; fo that, if their meat be given them from under them, it ought to be given to them fo little at a time, that their breath may not taint it.

§. 11. My fhepherd affures me, that my fheep, and other cattle will not eat my fpring-vetches made into winter-fodder fo well as they will the winter-vetches, the halm of the latter having, he fays, more ftrength and fpirit in it than that of the former, the halm of which is loofe and woolly. — This feems very reafonable to me, for the fpring-vetches, and the ftraw of rath-ripe corn of all kinds run in a pa-rallel, as white, and black oat-ftraw, rath-ripe, and late-ripe barley-ftraw, and I believe the fame may be faid of rath-ripe peas-ftraw, and great partridge peas-ftraw.

*Rath-ripe ftraw not fo good fodder as late-ripe.*

Several farmers in my neighbourhood have af-firmed to me, that the ftraw of the Patney barley, otherwife the rath-ripe barley, was hollower, and not fo good fodder as the other; but farmer Farthing of the Ifle of Wight affures me, that his cattle eat his

white

# FODDERING.

white oat-ſtraw better than his black; and Mr. Smith of Biſhop-Canons tells me, that his cattle eat rath-ripe barley-ſtraw better than late-ripe; ſo that it ſeems, the ſtraw of thoſe countries runs finer than ours, their land better agreeing with the grain.

*Cattle pre-*
*fer ſtraw*
*that is juſt*
*threſhed.*

§. 12. There is a manifeſt difference in cattle's eating their fodder, when freſh threſhed, and when it has been threſhed two or three days, eſpecially if the ſtraw be but indifferent, and coarſe fodder.——I have been often ſenſible of this, but more particularly this year (1719) in foddering with peas-halm, when the cattle eat it very well all the week-days, while it was given to them as faſt as it was threſhed, but ſome, that had lain all Sunday on the floor, they eat but indifferently on Monday; and the more ſo, becauſe a dry cold wind had blown on it through the crevices of the barn-door.——This alſo the man, who threſhed the peas and gave the ſtraw to the cattle, ſaid was manifeſt to him.

*Short*
*ſtraw pre-*
*ferred to*
*long.*

§. 13. It is ſaid, the longer the halm of the corn is the worſe it is for fodder; the ſhorteſt ſtraw makes always the beſt fodder.

*Oat-ſtraw*
*bad fodder,*
*and why.*

§. 14. I aſked farmer William Sartain of Broughton, Wilts, his opinion of oat-ſtraw to fodder cattle with. His opinion was, that it ought not to be given frequently to cattle for fodder, but only a little now and then, by way of change; for, he apprehended, there was a roughneſs or harſhneſs in that ſtraw, which made the gums of beaſts, or the roofs of their mouths ſore, and ſaid it was the opinion of many that it ſet their teeth on-edge.——But whatever was the cauſe, or howſoever they were affected, certain it was, that after the cattle had been held to oat-ſtraw awhile they went off their ſtomachs, nor would they heartily fall to other ſtraw, nor even to hay, after it.——Another farmer afterwards in
discourſe

difcourfe affirmed it was difagreeable to cattle, and ought not to be given them too often, nor too much at a time, and he thought that it's toughnefs might loofen their teeth by the ftrength they were forced to ufe to chew it, aud fo it made them unfit to mafticate other meat for fome time afterwards.

§. 15. Farmer Biggs and farmer Crapp vifiting me, the former faid, he doubted his fodder would fall fhort, becaufe he had fowed fo much of his barley on one earth, and his ftraw was much the worfe for it.——Neither farmer Crapp nor I could well apprehend that : but faid he, the man who threfhed for me, told me, that he had obferved it to be fo. —I afterwards afked feveral farmers and threfhers concerning it, each apart : they feemed to be at a lofs how it fhould be,—but at laft I found one, who readily replied, he had often heard it accounted fo, and that the ftraw of fuch barley was much deader than that of barley fowed on two earths, and that it would ftarve cattle, if held long to it.——I can conceive no reafon for it, except it is becaufe barley fowed on one earth is generally fowed on poor, light, or white land, —— and fo the ftraw cannot be fed with fo much fap and juice as otherwife it might be, and therefore may be drier at harveft than the ftraw of corn fown on richer land, and which in it's own nature may require two earths.——An old labourer of mine agreed with Biggs's threfher, and faid he could tell one-earth barley from that fowed on two earths by mowing it; but I could not learn how.

*Barley-ftraw of feed fowed on one earth bad fodder.*

§. 16. Mr. Smith of Wilts affures me, that, amongft them, they give not barley-ftraw to their horfes, but peas-ftraw, if it be anywife well houfed, and that they always look on the great partridge peasftraw to be better fodder (cæteris paribus) than the fmall partridge peas-ftraw. This I mention here, becaufe

*Peas-halm for fodder.*

cause I have above noted, that rath-ripe straw of all kinds is worse fodder than late-ripe straw is.—— Mr. Smith also says, if their beans are well housed, they give their horses bean-straw, and they eat it very well.

When peas-halm has fallen all along on the ground, and laid for some time, as it may sometimes do, till the grass shall grow through it, such peas-halm is not fit for fodder, the leaves being in a manner rotted off, and the halm is only fit for dung.

**Thistles used for fodder.** §. 17. If thistles are cut young, when they are withered the cattle will lick them up, though, whilst they are green and growing, they will not touch them.

**Elm-leaves good fodder.** §. 18. Elm-leaves gathered green, and suffered to dry in the sun upon the branches, the spray being stripped off in August, will prove a great relief to cattle in winter, or in scorching summers, when hay and fodder is dear; the cattle will eat it before oats, and thrive exceedingly with it; but you ought to lay these boughs in some dry place, to prevent their musting.—— In some parts of Herefordshire they gather elm-leaves in sacks for their swine and other cattle : but some say, they are ill for bees, in that they surfeit of the blooming seeds, which make them obnoxious to the lark, and that therefore they do not thrive in elm-countries. J. Mortimer, Esq; F. R. S. fo. 333.

**More profitable to winter oxen than heifers.** §. 19. In winter an ox will pay better for his hay, and thrive faster than a heifer, though her calf should be young within her ;—— therefore 'tis more profitable to winter oxen than heifers.

# CONTENTS

## Of the First Volume.

# CONTENTS.

*End of the* FIRST VOLUME.